Daybreak

Writings on Faiz

Daybreak

Writings on Faiz

Compiled and Edited by
YASMEEN HAMEED

OXFORD
UNIVERSITY PRESS

OXFORD
UNIVERSITY PRESS

Oxford University Press is a department of the University of Oxford.
It furthers the University's objective of excellence in research, scholarship,
and education by publishing worldwide in

Oxford New York

Auckland Cape Town Dar es Salaam Hong Kong Karachi
Kuala Lumpur Madrid Melbourne Mexico City Nairobi
New Delhi Shanghai Taipei Toronto

With offices in

Argentina Austria Brazil Chile Czech Republic France Greece
Guatemala Hungary Italy Japan Poland Portugal Singapore
South Korea Switzerland Turkey Ukraine Vietnam

Oxford is a registered trademark of Oxford University Press
in the UK and in certain other countries

Published in Pakistan by Oxford University Press

© Oxford University Press 2013

ISBN 978-0-19-906589-9

Typeset in Gentium Book Basic
Printed in Pakistan by
Kagzi Printers, Karachi.
Published by
Ameena Saiyid, Oxford University Press
No. 38, Sector 15, Korangi Industrial Area, PO Box 8214,
Karachi-74900, Pakistan.

For my brothers
Azhar and Asad

Contents

Publisher's Acknowledgements

Grateful acknowledgement is made to the following for permission to reprint copyright material:

Oxford University Press for 'Introduction to Poems by Faiz', 'Poetry's Theme', 'Two Loves', and 'To the Rival', *Poems by Faiz*, translated by Victor G. Kiernan, reproduced by permission of Oxford University Press, India, New Delhi, 1971.

Carlo Coppola, 'Another Adolescence: The Prison Poetry of Faiz Ahmed Faiz', *Journal of South Asian Literature* 27.2 (Spring-Summer 1992): 'Faiz in English: How Five Translators Worked their Art'; 'We who were Killed in Half-lit Streets', 'Eleven Poems and an Introduction by Faiz Ahmed Faiz,' and 'We', translated by C.M. Naim and Carlo Coppola, taken from: C.M. Naim and Carlo Coppola, eds., *Dialogue Calcutta* 19 n.d. [Some of these translations have appeared in *Mahfil*. Copyright 1971].

'Translating Faiz', first published in *Columbia: The Magazine of Columbia University*, June 1985, reproduced by permission of Naomi Lazard; and 'Prison Daybreak', 'If you look at the City from Here', and 'Any Lover to Any Beloved', *The True Subject: Selected Poems by Faiz Ahmed Faiz*, trans. Naomi Lazard, Oxford University Press, Karachi: 2012.

University of Massachusetts Press for 'Introduction—The Rebel's Silhouette: Translating Faiz Ahmed Faiz' and Oxford University Press, India for 'Evening'; 'Ghazal'; and 'On my Return from Dhaka' trans. Agha Shahid Ali, *The Rebel's Silhouette* Copyright © 1991 by Agha Shahid Ali and published by the University of Massachusetts Press; and *The Rebel's Silhouette* South Asian Edition, reproduced by permission of Oxford University Press, India, New Delhi, 1991.

Fathima Kamal, 'A Few Days More' and 'Visitors', *The Unicorn and the Dancing Girl*, trans: Daud Kamal, ed. Khalid Hasan, Lahore: Student Services, 1988, Print.

Salima Hashmi, 'Gently' and 'And then Spring Came', trans. Shoaib Hashmi, *A Song for This Day*, Lahore: Sang-e-Meel Publications, 2009.

Waqas Khwaja, 'Go forth into the Streets Today in your Fetters' and 'My Heart, Fellow Traveller', ed. and trans. Waqas Khwaja, *Modern Poetry of Pakistan*, Iftikhar Arif, ed., 1st edn., Champaign, University of Illinois: Dalkey Archive, 2010.

Mahmood Jamal 'Palestinians Martyred in Foreign Lands' and 'Last Night your Lost Memory', trans. Mahmood Jamal, *Modern Urdu Poetry*, Penguin, 1995.

Riz Raheem 'Dedication', trans. Riz Rahim, *In English: Faiz Ahmed Faiz*, Bloomington, IN: Xilbris, 2008.

Baidar Bakht and Kathleen Jaeger, 'Freedom's Dawn', trans. and eds. Baidar Bakht and Kathleen Grant Jaeger, *An Anthology of Modern Urdu Poetry*, Vol. 1, Karachi: Al-Muslim, 1984.

Shiv Kumar, 'In your Ocean Eyes', trans. Shiv Kumar, *Selected Poems of Faiz Ahmed Faiz*, New Delhi: Viking, 1995.

Shamsur Rahman Faruqi, 'Faiz and the Classical Ghazal', Shamsur Rahman Faruqi, *The Flower-Lit Road: Essays in Urdu Literary Theory and Criticism*, Allahabad: Laburnum, 2005.

Zed Books, 'Poetry, Politics and Pakistan', Ralph Russel, *The Pursuit of Urdu Literature—A Select History*, London: Zed, 1992.

Gopi Chand Narang, 'Tradition and Innovation in Faiz Ahmed Faiz', Gopi Chand Narang, *Urdu Language and Literature*, Vanguard, n.d.

Jugnu Mohsin and Vanguard Books, 'Faiz's Legacy—Love and Revolution', by Safdar Mir, *An Introduction to Poetry of Faiz Ahmed Faiz*, ed. Imdad Husain, Lahore: Vanguard, 1989.

Tauseef Hayat for:

'An Interview with Faiz' by Tahir Mirza, *Viewpoint*, Feb. 1976;

'Faiz in London' by Khalid Hasan, *Viewpoint*, 11 June and 18 June 1981;

'Faiz gave us the Living Word' by Karrar Husain, *Viewpoint*, 14 Feb. 1985;

'A Life Devoted to Peace' by Mirza Hasan Askari, *Viewpoint*, 12 Feb. 1987;

'Faiz and His Poetry Today' by Maryam Salganik, *Viewpoint*, 19 Feb. 1987;

'Poet and the Modern Age' by Rimma Kazakova, *Viewpoint*, 19 Feb. 1987.

Frances Pritchett, 'The Sky, the Road, The Glass of Wine: On Translating Faiz' taken from <http://http://www.urdustudies.com/pdf/15/07pritchett.pdf>.

Ludmila Vassilyeva, 'Faiz and the Soviet Union', translated from Urdu, *Parvarish-e Lauh-o-Qalam*, Karachi: Oxford University Press, 2007.

Salima Hashmi and Ayesha Jalal 'Freedom Unbound: Faiz's Prison Call', *Two Loves-Faiz's Letters from Jail*, ed. Kyla Pasha and Salima Hashmi, Lahore: Sang-e-Meel Publications, 2011.

Aamir R. Mufti for 'Faiz Ahmed Faiz: Towards a Lyric History of India', Aamir R. Mufti, *Enlightenment in the Colony: The Jewish Question and the Crisis of Postcolonial Culture*, Princeton: Princeton University Press, 2007.

Sean Pue for 'Faiz Ahmed Faiz and N.M. Rashed—A Comparative Analysis', paper read at the Faiz Colloquium organized as a centennial event, Lahore University of Management Sciences on 12/13 February 2011.

Muhammad Umar Memon, editor *Annual of Urdu Studies* for ' "Let them Snuff out the Moon": Faiz Ahmed Faiz's Prison Lyrics in *Dast-e Saba*', Ted Genoways, *The Annual of Urdu Studies* 19 (2004).

Royal Book Company for 'Poets (Socialists)'—excerpt taken from *Twentieth Century Urdu Literature*, M. Sadiq, Karachi: Royal Book Company, 1983.

Moneeza Hashmi and Salima Hashmi, 'Faiz' by Alys Faiz, *A Black Rainbow Over My Homeland: A Commemorative Volume on Faiz Ahmed Faiz, Mouin Beseisso, Alex La Guma*, edited by Kalpana Sahni, New Delhi: Afro Asian Writers' Association, n.d.

Pakistan Academy of Letters, Islamabad for 'A Conversation with Faiz', by Muzaffar Iqbal, *Pakistani Literature* (vol. 1 no. 1) (1992).

Acknowledgements

I am deeply indebted to all the authors who consented to have their work included in this book.

I am also grateful for the support provided by the Gurmani Centre for Languages and Literature at the Lahore University of Management Sciences (LUMS) to carry this work to completion.

INTRODUCTION

In the process of compiling this book, as I read through *The Times and Trial of the Rawalpindi Conspiracy* by Hasan Zaheer, what struck me hard were two simple words that repeatedly appeared in the biographical notes of the accused. Thirteen of the fifteen ended with the words 'has died.' Has died. Has died. Has died. . . . The words kept reverberating.

Does anything matter when people are gone? When real actors in the play of life no longer exist? The Progressive Writers' Movement, the Communist Party, The 'conspiracy' are all part of history, to be stowed away in yellowed pages, in recorded documents.

So what is relevant? What is it that continues to rush forth the blood, that sparks warmth, that brings back to life, dead moments? What is it that is possessed with the power to go on living, long after what created it has faded into oblivion?

For a poet to remain relevant, when poetry itself is changing its orbit of relevance, there must be an explanation. Faiz's popularity is not entirely dependent on the unchanging state of affairs around us, as may generally be believed. This may only be partly true. There must always be some intrinsic quality in a piece of art to keep it relevant and contemporary. Being alive and relevant does not necessarily mean being the most approved or the most appreciated, although a piece of art or writing is usually expected to be noticed, discussed, mentioned or quoted. Among his contemporaries, who were significant, outstanding poets, with substantial creative output to their merit, Faiz's popularity is unrivalled. He is one of the few and fortunate, who live on in the hearts of admirers, whose lines are committed to memories and who are remembered with reverence and affection. Popularity however, may not be the best criterion for assessing the literary quality of any piece of work. But Faiz's case is an exception. Faiz may have shared some not-so-perfect creative experiences with his readers but at its best, his poetry performs to near perfection, the true function of art. His best works, even within a limited range of thematic choices, offer in a single piece, all the essentials of pure art. This is a quality that even the harshest of critics may find hard to overlook. The Progressives may have been averse to the idea of pure art, but Faiz did use it as a weapon—more than a tool—to deliver his message. He sometimes went to the extent of even concealing his voice entirely, in the magnificent, mesmerizing, classical beauty of art itself.

What is pure art, may be a question with countless answers but Faiz's poetry does validate the notion that commitment to pure art can also warrant for ideological beliefs, a longer lease of life.

Also, Faiz almost always, narrates his very own experiences. His verse reflects, not just the exterior influences of life or his beliefs, but a deeper sense of loyalty as to how these beliefs must be interpreted and transformed into poetry. In his own words:

> The writer's prime duty is his duty to himself. The writer is capable of describing only what he has emotionally and intellectually experienced. This is an essential condition for the creation of real literature; all the rest is juggling with words, thoughts and images. Or with slogans . . .[1]

Born in 1911 in Kala Qadir (Near Sialkot in Pakistan) Faiz Ahmed Faiz grew up in an age that was not only turbulent for the region where he lived, but for the entire world. The First World War raged while he was still a little boy, ideas sparked by the Russian Revolution simmered through a land which was itself rife with conflict—the Hindu-Muslim gulf and the struggle for freedom.

On the larger sphere, the troubled times of the nineteen thirties and the rise of Fascist powers in Europe urged the world towards another great war. Literary trends in the West were changing, influenced by movements that had already taken root. Surrealistic tendencies charged through times of high modernism. Works like Eliot's 'Wasteland', James Joyce's 'Ulysses' and Virginia Woolf's 'Jacob's Room' were creating commotion, and ripples touched the shores of the East as well.

Here in the subcontinent, a shift towards didactic realism towards the end of the nineteenth century was already initiated by Muhammad Husain Azad and Altaf Husain Hali. By the early twentieth century, Iqbal's more creative and motivating voice had taken over the literary world by storm. Futuristic ideas swept through younger minds. Two intellectually driven waves emerged, one propelled by the Marxist vision, the other by the thrust of modernism. In this state of affairs was born the Progressive Writers' Movement. In 1936, when the movement was launched in Lucknow, Faiz as a young man of twenty five was already committed to it and remained so ideologically, to the last day of his life.

More has been written on Faiz than any other Urdu poet of the subcontinent after Ghalib and Iqbal, and compilations and selections from this kind of work have also been published. Such compilations not only bring to light some long forgotten pieces but also put together diverse views on a single subject. Interested readers find them quite useful.

This book was initiated as a project of the Gurmani Centre for Languages and Literature at the Lahore University of Management Sciences (LUMS) to mark Faiz Ahmed Faiz's centennial. In this book I have tried to put together articles and essays that provide a comprehensive overview of the poet's persona, his work and major happenings that influenced his literary career. It is also a pointer towards the kind of interest his poetry has generated beyond the world of Urdu.

Victor Kiernan's 'Introduction to "Poems by Faiz"' was first published in 1971 along with Kiernan's fine translations of Faiz's selected verse. It not only traces Faiz's creative development but also explores the culture of the Urdu poetic idiom that is so essential to understanding Faiz's own use of language in his verse. Kiernan was not only Faiz's translator, he was also a close friend, therefore his account delves more sympathetically into Faiz's literary life and engagements just as his translations remain more close to the spirit of the original than those of most other translators.

'Not seldom his (Faiz's) talent has been thought to be drying up,' writes Kiernan, 'though it has always flowed again; not seldom he himself talks of giving up composition, which with him is not facile improvisation but demands long, arduous effort. It may be a related fact that any sort of communication with other minds has become for him, as he once said to me, more and more difficult.' Such and other insightful observations give the reader a glimpse into the anxieties and subtleties of the creative process.

Naomi Lazard is also a well known translator of Faiz. Her introduction to 'The True Subject' brings forth an entirely different experience of translating Faiz. Lazard has no knowledge of the original language and is dependent on the poet for the first and literal version of the text in English which she uses to transcreate rather than translate the verse.

Agha Shahid Ali writes about his own translation of Faiz and gives an entirely different perspective of a translator who knew well the Urdu language but chose, with the permission of the poet to transcreate his verse.

Frances Pritchett very interestingly compares four translated texts of the same poem and critically analyzes them line by line. One could disagree with some of the comments or suggestions but the essay is an incisive study of the difficulties of translation and how texts and their meaning are perceived and reproduced by different translators. Carlo Coppola, in one of his essays does the same, using five texts of the same poem. These essays could be of particular interest to other translators.

Carlo Coppola's pioneering work in English on the Progressive Writers' Movement as well as on Faiz makes him a very significant contributor. There are two essays in the collection that deal with the prison poetry of Faiz. Carlo Coppola reviews the entire period whereas Ted Genoways limits his analysis to only a single collection of Faiz.

Except one, all articles are original writings in English. 'Faiz and the Soviet Union' by Ludmila Vassilyeva was originally written in Russian as a chapter of a book on Faiz and later reproduced in Urdu by the author herself. This is the only article that was specially translated for this collection. It is an engaging account of Faiz's Soviet experience and presents some rare facts and interpretations. The Rawalpindi Conspiracy, a tragic happening but one that enhanced Faiz's creative dimensions is equally significant. Ayesha Jalal's brief account, which is an introductory piece to 'Two Loves' (a compilation of letters written from Jail to Alys Faiz) informs about this happening that has gained another kind of significance in the world of literature due to Faiz's association with it.

Rimma Kazakova's and Maryam Salganik's brief articles, although not entirely personal are charged with emotion. Both these Russian scholars are Faiz's translators as well.

Karrar Husain's piece does not read evenly as the writing is in the form of notes he had prepared for a lecture. His 'Faiz Memorial Lecture' was delivered about a little above two months after Faiz's death. Karrar Husain's own merit as an intellectual and scholar makes these notes significant. An excerpt from his book published in 1983, M. Sadiq's piece has the same relevance and so does Safdar Mir's 'Faiz's Legacy . . . Love and Revolution.'

Mirza Hasan Askari's close association with Faiz reveals some interesting aspects of Faiz's personality and temperament and Khalid

Hasan's account of the time spent with Faiz in London is a memoir written with great devotion. Alys Faiz's account is of course unique as was the togetherness shared by the two for over forty years.

Aamir Mufti's and Sean Pue's purely critical and literary approach is enriching, introducing an entirely new dimension to Faiz criticism. Mufti argues that the defining theme in Faiz's poetry is derived from the legacy of 'Partition' whereas Sean Pue compares Faiz with one of his highly competent contemporaries, N.M. Rashed. Writings like these would determine the direction that Faiz criticism might move towards in the future. A generation that has not seen Faiz or known him personally could be expected to move away from Faiz's person and explore critically the literary scope of his work.

Narang's essay in this book has also been published in Urdu but this version, a condensed one is the author's own and is an interesting study of Faiz's metaphorical system that he is considered to have designed and carved out of the classical poetic language. Shamsur Rahman Faruqi convincingly debates against this very concept in 'Faiz and the Classical Ghazal'. Ralph Russell's objective criticism of Faiz's work as placed against the political phenomenon of this region is one of the most keen and incisive essays in this collection.

Fourteen of Faiz's translators are also represented in the book. Some translators are undoubtedly better than others, but instead of only the best few, I have included relatively better translated poems of some lesser known translators as well.

Faiz's own views on art and literature, presented in the two interviews, I presume would also be of interest to the readers.

I would sum up by saying that the material available on Faiz in Urdu is not only more in quantity, it is also far more diverse and qualitatively superior. The writings in English however have their own worth. There are very few Urdu writers who have communicated with readers and critics outside the bounds of their own language and these articles by authors from all over the world reflect the interest generated by Faiz's poetry outside his own cultural and literary milieu. I hope more would be added to this body of writing in the future.

I am grateful to Ahmed Bilal, our Research Associate at the Gurmani Centre for helping me collect the material for this collection and to Zulkifil Hyder for assisting me in the final stages of compiling and proof reading. I want to specially thank Professor C.M. Naim for introducing me to Professor Coppola, without whose contribution this book would have remained incomplete. I am also grateful to OUP for accepting to publish this book.

Note

1. Faiz: 'Circles of Being', translated by Alex Miller, published in *Lotus*, vol. 57, 1986.

1

INTRODUCTION TO 'POEMS BY FAIZ'

Poets in this century, like leaders of nations, have emerged from some unexpected nooks and corners. Faiz Ahmed's forbears were Muslim peasants of the Punjab, that green patch between mountain and desert, between middle India and inner Asia. His father, born with the instincts of a wanderer, set off in early life to Afghanistan, where he rose high in the service of the Amir Abd-ul Rahman,[1] and acquired some of the habits of a feudal grandee. Having fallen foul of his royal employer and escaped in disguise, he turned up in England, where his advent aroused curiosity in the highest circles: Afghanistan was always a sensitive spot in the perimeter of the empire. Cambridge and Lincoln's Inn, a bizarre exchange for Kabul and Kandahar, made a lawyer of him, and he returned at length to his birthplace to practice: not with great financial success, for lavish habits were hard to shake off, and an old man's tales of bygone splendour fell on less and less credulous ears.

If his son inherited an adventurous bent, his journeys of discovery were more of the mind, and it was not until long after he had grown up that he roamed far from home. It may have been a good thing for him that he did not go to Europe to study, as a young man of wealthier family would have done. Too many Indians of that day came back from the West full of enthusiasms that failed to survive transplantation, or that they could not spread to others. Faiz Ahmed imbibed the ideas of the 1930s, more gradually but tenaciously, from books or smuggled pamphlets, travellers' tales, and that impalpable genie known as the Spirit of the Age. They rooted themselves in his own soil, he saw them and their shadows by familiar sunlight; they took possession of his imagination, a stronghold from which ideas are less easily dislodged, as well as of his mind.

He studied, chiefly philosophy and English literature, at Lahore, the provincial capital and centre of the network of affiliated colleges making up the University of the Punjab, where a number of gifted young men came by education in the fullest sense of the word. In due course he gained a junior lecturing post in a college at Amritsar, where I first had the good fortune to get to know him, thirty years ago. It was a Muslim college in the city sacred to the Sikhs, where the communal passions already fermenting were strong. But there was no hostile frontier then as now between Amritsar and Lahore, and the Punjab was still in many ways a Sleepy Hollow where life moved at the pace of the feeble cab-horses drawing their two-wheeled *tongās*, where young men could indulge in old carefree idle ways, with long hours of debate in coffee-houses and moonlight picnics by the river Ravi. In this mode of living, verse-making played a part it has long since lost in the busy practical West. It was a polite accomplishment, a hobby cultivated by men, and a few women, in varied walks of life often, to be sure, a racking of brains over elusive rhymes not much more elevating than a Londoner's crossword-puzzle. The *mushāirā* or public recitation by a set of poets in turn, the novice first, the most admired writer last, was a popular social gathering, as it still remains; an audience would often guess a rhyme-word or phrase before it came, and join in like a chorus. Radio, then getting under way, was lending it a new medium, broadening into an entertainment for a whole province what had begun long ago as the recreation of a small court circle. It might be highly artificial, as when participants were supplied beforehand with a rhyme to manipulate; and a scribbler well endowed with voice could make the most hackneyed phrase or threadbare sentiment sound portentous by delivering them in the half-singing or chanting (*tarannum*) fashion, or the declamatory style of recitation, that many affected. Still, the institution has helped to keep poetry before the public, and, along with floods of commonplace, to make known an occasional new talent.

Faiz Ahmed rhymed with the rest, and unlike some innovators complied with usage by adopting a pen-name or *takhallus*—that of *Faiz*, meaning 'bounty' or 'liberality'[2]: looking back one may be tempted to read into it a meaning not yet in his mind, dedication to the service of his fellow-men. He emerged quickly from among the poetasters of whom every year engendered a fresh swarm, though not by dint of cultivating an aesthetic deportment, as some did. To outward appearance he was a good-natured, easy-going fellow, fond of cricket and dawdling, those favourite pastimes of Lahore, and readier to let others talk than to talk himself. It was characteristic of him that when reciting his verses, whether among a few friends or in a crowded college gathering, he spoke them quietly and unexcitedly.

Their quality was naturally mixed. The fine quatrain that stands at the beginning of his first book of verse published in 1941 (*Ash'ār. . . .* 'Last night your faded memory filled my heart') was not the first to be written. He began with exercises, conventional enough, on well-worn topics, sighing over the cruelty of a non-existent mistress or extolling the charms of the grape. These also were invested with some fanciful attributes, for beer and whisky, not wine, were the liquors that the British presence had familiarized in India, and for literary purposes a beverage had to be poured not from bottle into glass but from flask into goblet. (*Shīshā*, a classical word, has come to be used for 'tumbler', but there is no term for 'bottle' except the impossible English word, spoken with a long 'o' and rhyming with Indian pronunciation of 'hotel'.)

But if Lahore was still on the surface an uneventful place, the tides of history were washing to and fro in India and the world outside, and their ripples reaching the Mall Road and the Kashmir Gate. Independence was only a decade away, and Faiz's lines were soon being coloured by patriotic feeling: almost as soon, by socialist feeling, for socialism was the new revelation that young idealists could invoke to exorcise communal rancours, by uniting the majority from all communities in a struggle against their common poverty, and to make independence a blessing to the poor as well as to the elite. History was to take a different turning; older forces and allegiances were to prove stronger, for a long time to come at least. But for young poets and story-writers, national and social emancipation seemed to go together, and both to go with their own new-found freedom to try new subjects and methods. They were reading, and sometimes imitating (Faiz seldom, if ever, did this directly) Western writers like T.S. Eliot, Auden, and Day Lewis. Their Progressive Writers' Association was a force in the land, and the Punjab had its own branch. Besides taking part in this, Faiz, with the realistic sense he has always had that the poet is also a citizen, was getting in touch with groups of workingmen, and would spend evenings teaching them reading and writing and the ABC of politics.

Indian marriages were not made in heaven, but arranged, as they still often are, by careful parents, particularly in respectable Muslim families, whose women went out heavily veiled from head to foot. Faiz was once comically indignant at being invited to speak on Shakespeare in a girls' college, and made to address an unseen audience from the other side of a screen. In such an environment there was a double blessing for him in his marriage with an English-woman of remarkable character (whom I have the good fortune to have known even longer than I have known him); she had been ever since his best friend and guardian angel, and, with two daughters he is devoted to, had brought into his life a security that nothing else could have given it.

Before 1939 he had made a name for himself in literature; the war and its aftermath made room for him in political history too. This is not the place for a detailed review of his political or civic activities, but it is proper to emphasize that the ideals inspiring them have had a vital part in his literary development as well. They involved him in dilemmas inescapable in an India verging on revolution or civil war, and then in a raw new Pakistan painfully collecting itself into a nation. No straight road through this chaos was to be found, and every individual had to make decisions of his own. In all that part of the world movements and loyalties have been apt, like its rivers, to come and go suddenly, one day in full spate, the next dried up. Faiz has remained all this time faithful to what might be called an enlightened, humanistic socialism; the kind of activity open to him has fluctuated with circumstances.

After the Nazi invasion of the Soviet Union in 1941, Faiz like many Indians saw the war in a new light, as a contest in which the destinies of mankind were at stake, and with the approval of his associates joined the welfare department of the army; he was to be met with now on the Mall in the uniform of a lieutenant-colonel, solemnly returning salutes from British soldiers. After independence came in 1947, accompanied by partition, he continued to hope, as he has always done, for good relations between the two countries. When Gandhi was murdered by a Hindu fanatic, for trying to protect the Muslim minority in India, Faiz was, as a London newspaper said, 'a brave enough man to fly from Lahore for Gandhi's funeral at the height of Indo-Pakistan hatred'.[3] This hatred had been inflamed by the massacres, most terrible in the Punjab, that raged during the process of partition. To Faiz these horrors could only be expunged by the building of his new nation on principles of social justice and progress. One of his best-known poems, 'Freedom's Dawn' (*Subh-e āzādī*) expressed the tragic disillusionment of finding the promised land Can'ān—or so it seemed to him—only flowing with milk and honey for feudal landowners and self-seeking politicians.

With the removal by death of Pakistan's first and most trusted leaders, and reform and development sluggish, this disillusion soon became widespread. Editor now of the *Pakistan Times* of Lahore, Faiz made use of prose as well as verse to denounce obstruction at home and to champion progressive causes abroad; he made his paper one whose opinions were known and quoted far and wide, with respect if not everywhere with approval. He served as vice president of the Trade Union Congress, and secretary of the Pakistan Peace Committee. This period ended abruptly with his arrest, along with a number of other figures, civil and military, in March 1951. The Rawalpindi Conspiracy trial unfolded its slow and somewhat mysterious length, during which a death-sentence was a lingering possibility, down to 1953, when Faiz was condemned to four years' imprisonment.[4]

His health suffered, but he was able to read, and think his own thoughts, and collect materials for a long-promised (but still, alas, unperformed) history of Urdu literature. To him as a poet, his prison term might be called a well-disguised blessing. His wartime work had been heavy; he lamented that as soon as a new couplet began to stir in his mind he had to get up and go back to his office. After the war his editorial desk was even more enslaving. He might indeed point to the files of his newspaper, as Lamb did to the ledgers of the East India Company, as his real works. Worst of all has been a social environment prodigally wasteful, everywhere south of the Himalayas, of the time of men whose time is of any value. Far more than in the West, a writer's admirers show their appreciation of him by thronging about him and making it impossible for him to write, or to keep to any rational plan of work; custom imposes on all alike the same monstrous proportion of talking to thinking as that of sack to bread in Falstaff's tavern bills. Even Faiz's wife has only been able to rescue him by half or quarter from this asphyxiation. Prison enabled him to write what for him was a considerable number of poems, in which his ideals took on fresh strength by being alloyed with harsh experience, and which were eagerly devoured by the public, in spite of the charges weighing over him.

Released in 1955, Faiz took up journalism again, but this quickly brought another, briefer spell in jail, one incident in a prevailing confusion that political affairs were falling into, and that led to the assumption of power by the army.[5] This did away with political confusion for the next decade, but also with nearly all political life, and it drastically curtailed the freedom of the press. Faiz's health moreover

was no longer good, and a habit of perpetual cigarette smoking, with a
marked prejudice against physical exercise in any form, has not in these
latter years improved it. He had to look for other kinds of work, cultural
rather than political and in a way more congenial. He helped to make a
film, which won international awards, about the lives of the fisherfolk,
whom he visited and greatly liked, among the rivers of East Pakistan
[now Bangladesh]. He had plans for a national theatre, and with his wife
sponsored a variety of local dramatic experiments. Drama is an art that
found no entry into Islamic countries through the ages, and that Faiz
believed might have a serious function in a new nation like Pakistan. In
other elements of culture, Indian Islam was rich, and it was his design to
bring to light all that was capable of healthy growth among them, to help
to form them into a modern national culture. He went back to his first
vocation, teaching, and undertook the reorganization of a Karachi college
founded by charitable endowment for poor students. When politics
began to throw off, early in 1969, a long immobility, his concern for the
country's future showed itself as keen as ever. On 1 March, he made a
long statement, full of practical good sense, to a round-table conference
of progressive groups at Rawalpindi.

He has been living of late years in Karachi, that odd medley of
Victorian facades and modern industry and spreading suburban villas;
always with a hankering for the picturesque dilapidation of the old city
of Lahore, and even, in sentimental moments, for his paternal village,
where it may be conjectured that he would quickly die of boredom. In
these years he has travelled the world a good deal, as his literary fame
spread; it was of course in socialist countries that he came to be known
first. He has been in China, and several times in the USSR, where a
translation of all his poems in Russian verse was published in 1960; the
Muslim areas of Soviet Asia had a special attraction for him, and he for
them. He has been in the USA, and Cuba; and in England, though
regrettably seldom, considering his English wife and friends and literary
connections. Once he was tempted as far north as Edinburgh, where he
found that he had miscalculated the temperature of a Scottish winter.
Most remarkably, he has made frequent short visits to India. Urdu poetry
has been one of the slender bridges left standing between the divided
countries, and Faiz's poems are welcomed on both sides of the border.
Some of his best poems have been in honour of peace.

Amid these gropings and wanderings, Faiz has continued to write the
short poems that made him famous. He has written, altogether, too little;

a small collection of poems now and then, with gaps of years in between, and a number of essays, collected in 1964 into a volume of literary criticism. Not seldom his talent has been thought to be drying up, though it has always flowed again; not seldom he himself talks of giving up composition, which with him is not facile improvisation but demands long, arduous effort. It may be a related fact that any sort of communication with other minds has become for him, as he once said to me, more and more difficult. Through verse, when he is successful with it, he overcomes this difficulty; at a more modest level an evenings' conviviality may transform him from a rather tongue-tied companion (a day with whom once reminded an intelligent young woman, a family friend of ours,[6] of the silences of Colonel Bramble) into a ready and entertaining talker, with a lively sense of humour that finds little or no outlet in his verses.

What he has written, however much less than what he might, has brought him to something like the position of an unofficial poet laureate in West Pakistan, a land where poetry still makes an appeal potent enough to disarm some political and even religious prejudice. Criticism, even abuse, for his opinions have never ceased to come his way, and there are traces of this to be discerned in some of his poems. To be a nationalist writer is easy, to be a national writer hard. As a poet whom his countrymen are proud of, and at the same time a target of frequent attacks, Faiz's situation has been a contradictory one, reflecting the contradictory moods of a nation still—as Iqbal said of all the East—in search of its soul.

Some of Faiz's poetry is simple and direct, but often it is couched in a literary idiom, some knowledge of which is needed for its appreciation, and one more artificial—or artful—than most. Urdu itself as a language might be called a bundle of anomalies, beginning with the fact that this language of many virtues has no true homeland. It originated, from the early stages of the 'Muslim,' or rather Central-Asian, conquest of India, as the lingua franca of the 'camp' (its name derives from the same Turki root as the English word *horde*). It was a mixture of the Arabicized Persian used by the invaders, themselves a miscellany of Turks and others, with some of the still unformed Hindi dialects of the upper Gangetic valley, or 'Hindustan'. In verb structure it was native Indian, a fact which entitles it to be classed as an *Indian* language; in vocabulary largely foreign, much as a simplified Anglo-Saxon base was overlaid after the Norman conquest with French or low-Latin words. Urdu and English both began, therefore, about the same time, as pidgin dialects, or hybrids, and gradually evolved into self-sufficient languages, with special qualities derived from their mixed antecedents, qualities of contrast and modulation of great significance for poetry. Some of Shakespeare's effects could only have been achieved in such a medium, and Urdu can combine the harmony of Persian with the energy of Arabic and the simplicity of rustic Hindi.

During its centuries of growth, Persian served as the administrative and literary language of the Muslim ruling circles, Sanskrit continued to be the learned language of Hindus. But Indian vernaculars, including Hindi, hitherto a group of dialects rather than a language, were also taking shape; and when with the crumbling of Muslim political ascendancy in the eighteenth century, Urdu emerged as successor to Persian, it was bound to have to compete, sooner or later, with some of these others, Hindi in particular. Its original function as a lingua franca now belonged to the colloquial mixture often called 'Hindustani', on the level at which modern Urdu and Hindi are virtually identical. Muslims and Hindus had lived side by side for ages (and most Muslims were descendants of Hindu converts), and in humdrum practical matters understood one another well enough. For more complex ideas—which neither had in fact been cultivating with much freshness for a long time—they had acquired little of shared vocabulary. Hence when modern conditions brought the necessity of thinking on new lines, an elite culture suffused on each side with religious influences drew them in opposite directions. Learned Urdu has a diction heavily Persian and Arabic, learned Hindi heavily Sanskritic; and their scripts, the Persianized form of Arabic on the one hand, the Nāgarī or Sanskrit on the other, complete their mutual unintelligibility. It would be like this in English if half its users formed their technical and philosophical terms from Hebrew instead of Greek, and used Hebrew letters instead of Roman. Thus Urdu, originally a channel between older and newer inhabitants of India, in the past century has come to be one of the stumbling-blocks to fellow feeling.

Urdu had grown not where there were most Muslims, in modern West and East Pakistan [now Pakistan and Bangladesh respectively], but where Muslim political and cultural ascendancy was firmest, which was always in and round the capital cities—Delhi, Agra, Lucknow, Hyderabad. Muslim civilization everywhere in history has been an urban civilization. This means that today Urdu as a mother-tongue finds itself marooned in the heart of Hindu India, chiefly in the UP, the old Hindustan, where some nationalists are disposed to question its title to exist, and some of its lovers—not all of them Muslims— regretfully feel it to be doomed to a slow decline; though on the other hand some new opportunities have come its way, notably in the cinema. In Pakistan it is being brought forward as a national language, as Hindi is in India. But East Pakistan [now Bangladesh] has proved faithful to the Bengali that it shares with West Bengal in India. In the western Punjab, nucleus of—[West] Pakistan, Urdu is the vehicle of literature, of the newspaper press, and of formal or ceremonial speech: it is employed for every-day purposes of writing, and is challenging English as the medium of higher education. But all familiar converse is carried on in Punjabi, a vernacular shred like Bengali with a province of India; a language, or as some would say a group of dialects, standing to Urdu in something like the relationship of the broadest of rural Scots to the most refined of Oxford English.

When the Mughal empire faded, and with it the old cultural links with Persia, it was chiefly the poetical part of the legacy of Persian that Urdu fell heir to. For public business, legal or administrative, and higher education, English was the successor. The Muslim community, socially an unbalanced one of feudal cast, with only an embryonic middle class, had few professional or commercial men with reason to write prose; and fallen from power, unable for long to adapt itself to new times, it had stronger feelings than thoughts, an impulsion towards emotional verse more than towards rational prose. In Ghalib the language found the poet still regarded as its greatest. He belonged, until the Mutiny swept it away, to the shadowy Mughal court at Delhi, with its poignant contrast between present and past to kindle his imagination. Urdu prose on the contrary was virtually making its first start with Sir Syed Ahmad,[7] who likewise began in Delhi but shook its ancient dust off his feet and entered English service before the Mutiny; his mental life was one of wrestling with the problem, for Muslim India, of its present and its future. Subsequent progress has been uneven, and since the birth of Pakistan it has been a disputed issue there whether, or how rapidly, Urdu can be made the medium of higher education, scientific included.[8] Faiz is one of those most firmly convinced that it is capable of meeting every modern requirement. As a poetical medium, Urdu might almost be a language made up by poets for their own benefit; a one-sided benefit no doubt by comparison with Eastern languages like English whose foremost poets, from Shakespeare down, have so often been first-rate prose writers as well. But this double faculty may be a thing of the past. Modern English may be too far secularized, overloaded with utilitarian burdens, to be capable any longer of poetry. A language like Urdu, with a smaller prose content, has so to speak a lower boiling-point, and boils up into poetry—

or vaporizes into verse—more readily. As one consequence of this
freedom from dull workaday business, Urdu may have gone on being tied
more closely than need be to the apron-strings of classical Persian. This
continued to be studied and read after its fall from power in India, and
in West Pakistan still is so quite widely. Almost any Persian noun or
adjective might be brought into an Urdu verse, just as any Greek word
can nowadays be incorporated into English prose. Persian syntax too,
notably the use of the *izāfat* (-e) to join a noun either with its adjective
or with its possessive, is retained to a much greater extent than in prose.
Until a generation ago a whole Persian line or couplet might be inserted
in an Urdu poem.

Between Mutiny and Great War, two shifts, not unrelated, were taking
place in Urdu poetry. It was coming to be less a lament for a lost past, and
more an expression of the sensations of a Muslim community struggling
to find its place in a changed world. Secondly, its main inspiration was
migrating, with the coming of Iqbal, from the old centres, Delhi and
Lucknow, northward to the Punjab; from early in this century to the
partition, the two regions disputed the palm warmly between themselves,
the older one priding itself at least on higher polish and technical
proficiency. Some analogy may be drawn between them and their
counterparts in Ireland. In Hindustan the leading Muslims were gentry
of old family, descendants of conquerors from abroad, but becoming in
course of time more 'Indian' than the solid mass of Muslims in the north-
west; as the Anglo-Irish gentry in southern Ireland were in most ways
except religion, more Irish than the solid mass of Protestant settlers in
Ulster. In Ireland's literary renaissance early in this century, Anglo-Irish
southern Protestants played a large part. Urdu poets in Hindustan had
been playing some such part. The shift northward to the Punjab (which
scarcely had a parallel in Ireland) meant in the long run a turning away
from India, and presaged the birth of Pakistan—or so we may see it in
retrospect—decades before anyone dreamed of such a thing.

On the surface the Punjab might have seemed too dull and torpid to
be a nesting-place for poetry. There were only two big towns, and hardly
any modern industry; big landlords loyal to the British power, the creator
of many of them, held a preponderant influence. Geography has in some
epochs isolated the land of the Five Rivers, at other times filled it with
vibrations from round about, according to the condition in which
neighbouring regions have been. When these have flourished, it has been
a meeting-ground of ideas, as of trade-routes, instead of a backwater. It

merges south-westward into the Indus valley, south-eastward into the Gangetic; north-east it has had historic links with Kashmir, north-west still closer ones with the frontier, Afghanistan, the roads into Persia and middle Asia. Hardly any other corner of Asia occupies such a focal position. Seldom since early Indo-Aryan times an intellectual leader, it has repeatedly been plunged by forces within and pressures from without into emotional and social turmoil. The coming of Islam, which in the end was to split the province in two, affected all of it in some degree, and helped to generate the ferment out of which came Sikhism, the one new religion that India with all its religiousness has given birth to since Buddhism. But this turned into a military domination, without much cultural vitality of its own; and in the nineteenth century Persia and Central Asia, the old neighbours to the north, seemed to be at long last expiring, while British rule concentrated Indian energies in the seaboard provinces, and treated the Punjab mainly as a recruiting-ground for the army.

By the end of the century, however, Persia was rousing itself again, and Islam in Asia stirring in its sleep; while from southward the European ideas that had long been at home in Bombay and Calcutta were now filtering into the Punjab. As in other ages, these new currents were to make for bigger upheavals here than elsewhere among a folk even in their physical proportions larger than life compared with most other Indians. Inevitably old communal jealousies would revive alongside of new things. Altogether it was a land riddled to an exceptional degree with contradictions old and new; one of sturdy peasants as well as landlords, one steeped in rustic humour and realism as well as possessing in Lahore a city which did not forget that it was once the Mughal imperial capital; a province that others seemed to have left far behind, but with lurking energies and untested capabilities waiting to break out, for good or evil, when the sleeping giant should awaken. It might even be said that Urdu poetry was taking wing to the Punjab because here it found most contraries and complexities to stimulate it. All three communities were writing Urdu verse, and in the same idiom; Muslims were easily in the lead, and have provided all the important names. Less at home in the new age than their Hindu neighbours, they struck the visitor as having, by and large, less practical capacity, with far more imagination.

Tagore could address his Bengali compatriots in their own language, which besides a very long poetic tradition had also during the nineteenth century acquired a modern prose. Punjabi was rich in little but folk-poetry, and the other chief purpose it had served was as a vehicle for part of the Sikh scriptures, which invested it as a written language with associations distasteful to Muslims. They relegated it to colloquial purposes for which Urdu was too high-flown—somewhat as Beatrice told Don Pedro he was too fine a husband for her, she would need another for weekdays. For Urdu this was bound to involve a certain removal from actuality, such as Burns's verse underwent when he wrote in English instead of Scots. It brought the countervailing gift of an exotic, romantic vocabulary like a southern breeze laden with tropical scents. Words from far away made a more sensuously thrilling impression on the ear than familiar homespun ones, and through the ear on the fancy. Muslim habits of hearing or reciting Quranic passages in half-understood Arabic must have worked in the same manner. It may be guessed that the Urdu poet does not always have before his mind's eye so lively an image of the things he is speaking of as a European would; his mind is a stir with words which are for him sounds, evocations, ancestral memories, less closely tied to tangible objects; of the 'two worlds' he so often sets against each other, it is the invisible rather than the visible in which he is roaming.

All this harmonized with the situation of the Muslim class literate enough to have a full command of Urdu—though its poetical appeal could be felt more widely. It was a narrow middle class oriented by circumstances more towards fantasy than towards reality, overshadowed economically by Hindu competitors with far more capital, and also far more willingness to scorn delights and live laborious days in the pursuit of money. It was chronically pulled opposite ways: it wanted to grow, learn, move with the times—or, impatiently, leave them behind; both from diffidence about its ability to compete, and an inborn distaste for competitive money-grubbing, it was often apt to shrink into its shell, to retreat along the old caravan trail winding away into the heart of Asia and its luxurious dream world of shining dome and legend and remote superb names. Ultimately the outcome of these contrary impulses, irreconcilable within Indian horizons, would be the demand for a separate State. In the meantime Urdu and Urdu poetry were, next to religion, the Muslims' lifeline, giving them a sense of identity, a collective vision.

So much of the spirit and tone of Urdu poetry derives from Persian tradition that this ancestry must often be kept in mind, even when a poet like Faiz is alluding to quite contemporary matters. Verse forms and metres, besides diction, have helped to preserve continuity; and, still more strikingly, a common stock of imagery, which can be varied and recomposed inexhaustibly in much the same way that Indian (and Pakistani) classical music is founded on a set of standard note-combinations (*rāgās*) on which the performer improvises variations. All this was part of a culture that, like Europe's later, came into India fully-fledged, acquiring there a fresh colouring, new accompaniments—such as the *mushāirā*—yet never becoming altogether Indian.

Persian poetic attitudes were social. Whereas the Chinese poet so often purports to be wandering lonely as a cloud over his mountain, the Persian is to be found reciting in a 'circle', or 'gathering', or 'assembly', or breaking away from it only in a fit of literary frenzy. Behind this fiction lay the reception-room or hall of royal court of feudal mansion, where men of letters competed for the patron's favour and rewards; a rivalry of which today's *mushāirā* is an imitation. Its setting was nocturnal, lamp-lit; a reader may call up in his mind the scene that Faiz evokes in a line of 'Lyre and Flute' (*Shorish-e barbat-o-nai*), a Mughal chamber with walls honeycombed into small niches, each holding its lighted candle. By time-honoured custom, another candle or lamp was placed before each poet in turn as he recited. When we are transported out of doors, it is to a garden, the formal garden or rather park with its water-channels running in straight lines from pool to fountain between flowerbeds and avenues, still to be seen in its perfection at Lahore in the Shalimar Garden and the precincts of Jahangir's mausoleum, or at Agra in those of the Taj Mahal: an exquisite oasis in a thirsty land, a paradise shut off from the sorry scheme of things outside by a rectangle of high wall. Here is the Islamic urban civilization refined to the last degree, a haven within a haven. On the scorched plains of upper India, as in inner Asia, Nature itself is man-made, the marble cascade replaces the waterfall, all the vulgar reality of yokel, spade, manure-heap is forgotten. Readers brought up on English poetry have found it easy to enter into the spirit of Chinese poetry, simple and naturalistic, haunted by the sound of rock-perched trees and winds; no poet from the Islamic realm has captivated them so much, except Omar Khayyam, self-banished into the wilderness that came up as close to the gates of the old cities of middle Asia as night in those latitudes succeeds day.

Faiz observed, when asked about this absence of free Nature, that the poets of former days were courtiers, feudal retainers of uncertain rank, whose duty was to be at hand whenever their patron wanted to be refreshed with wit or fancy, not to disport themselves in the countryside.

He himself has a love of gardens, fostered by early acquaintance with the classic shades of Lahore, and with a later, less formal park there, the Lawrence (now Jinnah) Bagh, one of his youthful haunts, for which he has pined during his sojourn in Karachi.[9] He is no gardener, but in jail did make an attempt at growing flowers from packets of seed requisitioned from distant Scotland, while a fellow-prisoner of more mundane tastes devoted his garden plot to rearing chickens.

Feudal patronage was capricious, and the rhymer often, like Shakespeare, in disgrace with fortune and men's eyes. It went with this, and with things deeper in the fibre of Indo-Muslim society, that though habitually addressing a company, he did so as an individual alone in the group: he assumed frequently a tone of repining, lamenting a hard lot in a bad world, the demeanour of a martyr, despised and rejected by men and mistress. This posture too has descended on much Urdu poetry of our time, producing on occasion a disparity almost ludicrous between a writer's heartbroken accents and his jolly countenance off duty. But the poet composing under the eye of an autocratic patron and of an inflexible religion could not give vent to his gloomier feelings in any open manner, or seem to be finding fault with the order of things as by God and the Sultan established. True, in the fiction of these symposia the patron was not supposed to be present in his own person: art requires some, if only fictitious, equality among its devotees, and the patron might be a poetaster himself, and take his turn to recite his own productions under his own pen name. The last Mughal emperor, who had few cares of State to oppress him, was no mean performer. It was, then, the 'Sāqī' who was supposed to preside, and be the centre of attraction: the wine-pourer, elevated into a mysteriously fascinating woman with whom all present were supposed to be hopelessly in love—an idealized, rarified version of the educated courtesan whose reception-room was the nearest that Muslim India could come to a European salon. It was under colour of bewailing the hard-heartedness of this demi-goddess that the poet could most easily give voice to his grievances against life at large. A true poet would be expressing something deeper than his own private disappointments. Ghalib we may think of as lamenting, in effect, the passing of an empire and a civilization, and generations of Muslim readers must have felt their own nostalgia echoed in his lines.

The oblique allusion, the conventional symbol, could be understood by each hearer in his own fashion, and applied to his own condition; for in that society all, from highest to lowest, were haunted by the same sense of mutability and insecurity, of the need for a protector. Hence evolved a kind of 'metaphysical' style, an elaborate play of fancy and ingenuity; once established, within a pattern of society only very sluggishly changing, this could keep a remarkably tenacious hold. It has kept it even in our changing times: abstracted and generalized in this manner, the perplexities and distresses of man's social being have from age to age a common complexion.

Love might stand for defiance, self-assertion, as well as resigned self-pity. It has played this part in many times and places, under a multitude of guises, always somewhere between life and art; where women went veiled, it was bound to stand closer to art and fancy. The poet's world is an imaginary city, like that of Faiz's poem, 'The Hail of Stones' (*Khatm hu'ī bārish-e sang*); in this city there is always a *kū'e malāmat,* or 'street of reproach': a poetical depiction of the entertainers' quarter where courtesans and ordinary prostitutes and dancing-girls lived. Here a reckless lover will be carrying on a clandestine affair, heedless of the frowns of dull elders or precisians, the *rumores senum severiorum.* Or he may rush out from the town into the wilderness, and roam to and fro endeavouring to cool his distemper in its blank emptiness.[10]

All this lover's fever might represent, or the hearer was free to think of it as representing, the spiritual seeker's thirst for divine truth; and in this signification in turn, literal melted into metaphorical, and God himself might be either reality or symbol. In a society saturated with religious forms and phrases (though, like aristocratic Europe, seldom religious in its conduct) poetic imagery was bound to flow very often into their mould. In Islamic orthodoxy, there was small room for anything artistic, except the sublime simplicity of its best architecture. But side by side with it was the mystical cult of the Sufis, who sought through prayer and spiritual exercises, sometimes music and dance—eschewed by the orthodox—even by means of drugs, to soar from the dull earth into contact with, or absorption into, the divine essence.[11] This cult came from Persia, but helped to make Islam in India more Indian, by its affinity with the *bhaktī* stream in Hinduism. In the Punjab more than elsewhere the two escaped from the cloister and joined and fermented among common people, helping to create a body of folk-poetry where the religious brotherhood of man blended with thoughts of social equality, deliverance from feudal bonds.[12] Much of the mood and phraseology of Sufism, its catalogue of the 'states and stages' (*hāl-o-maqām*) of the pilgrim soul, its vital relationship between the spiritual guide and his disciples, was taken over into poetry, and had a further existence there as part of the counterpoint of mask and symbol. When a poet did not picture himself seated in a court circle, it would often be the circle of disciples round their master that he conjured up. Nor were the two so far apart as might seem; mystics had often clothed their thoughts in verse, courtiers and even rulers might also be disciples; a divine Beloved could melt imperceptibly into an earthly one, an ideal feminine, an unattainable mistress who was also the wine-pourer at the never-ending feast, as uncertain, coy, and hard to please as Fortune, dispenser of life's never-ending deceptions.

Love and religion shared besides a common emblem in wine, another refinement of gross fact into ideal essence. If in the feudal courts liquor forbidden to the faithful ran freely, and a Ghalib might be a serious drinker, poetically wine stood for exaltation, inspiration, and the tavern was the abode of truly heart-felt spiritual experience as opposed to the formal creed of the mosque. Drunkenness and madness are near allied, and the later—junūn, 'rapture' in the literal sense of possession by a spirit (jinn)—retained some of the aura that surrounds it among primitive people; it might be either the passion of the worshipper of beauty throwing the world away for love or the ecstasy of the acolyte despising material success in his heavenly quest.

All this vogue of 'madness' was a recoil from the hard fixity of life, the rigid framework within which man as a social animal imprisons himself, the sordid egotism forced on men who, whether poets or politicians, could only rise at one another's expense. It gave relief to the vague craving that every society generates, if only in its younger or more idealistic members, for something better, higher, freer. Against the omnipotence of Church and State there could be no rebellion; but veiled protest was allowable, under the form of praise of the individual prepared to defy convention, which as a harmless safety-valve became itself a tolerated part of the convention. Wine, love, mystic flights, were all momentary refuges from the bondage of reality. They fostered some poetry, as well as much literary posturing and affectation; the time would come when a poet like Faiz, standing at a new point in history, would be able to give them a fresh meaning, as symbols of a revolutionary challenge to the social order instead of merely token defiance of it or a withdrawal from it into fantasy.

Ambiguity belonged to the essence of this style; in its visionary landscape things melted into one another like dreams, and everything had a diversity of meanings, or rather, any precisely definable 'meaning' was lost in a diffused glow. A poet might really have mystic moods, or might really be in love—with a woman, or, as in Greece or Rome, with a man; but for his poetry, for his hearers, that was not the real point, any more than for us when we listen to a piece of music whose composer may have felt religious, or been in love.[13] The most characteristic verse form was the *ghazal*, a string of any number of couplets in any one metre, rhyming AA BA CA DA. . . .[14] These should not aim at any obvious logical sequence, but owe their coherence to the recurrent rhyme and to a stream of association eddying beneath the surface. Its standard topic is love, its tone one of graceful trifling, and in ordinary hands it is not much more than a metrical exercise; so much so that in modern Urdu it constitutes a poetic hemisphere by itself, and a writer may be classed either as a serious poet or, with a touch of disparagement, as a *ghazal-writer*. The form has nevertheless been used by the foremost poets for the weightiest purposes; and it too has helped to provide a rainbow bridge between the impressionism of the past and the realism of the present.

One who notably turned the *ghazal* to new purposes was Muhammed Iqbal (1877–1938), the greatest Urdu poet to arise since Ghalib.[15] Born like Faiz at Sialkot, close to the mountains and close to the religious and cultural frontier that now divides India from Pakistan, he was a Punjabi of the professional middle class who wrote English prose and Urdu and Persian verse; a Punjabi, that is, whose mental horizons were far more expansive than those of his own province, and who as a result in some ways soared above its realities, in other ways fell short of them. In Urdu he wrote chiefly short poems, lyrical, religious, or satirical; in classical Persian long didactic poems addressed to the whole of Muslim Asia. He went through an early phase of addiction to English models, including description of Nature, and at the same time of attachment to the ideal, of equally Western source, of a free Indian nation with Hindu and Muslim as fellow-citizens. He studied in England and Germany, and was impressed especially by Nietzsche. Later his antipathy to Western imperialism in India and Asia deepened, but there also came disenchantment with the Indian national movement. He found an alternative in the vision, conjured up out of the hopes and doubts of his community, the Muslim middle class of the Punjab, of a grand Islamic revival and renewal, in which all the Muslim peoples should arise from their slumber, at once firm in their ancient faith and strong in modern knowledge. The glorious daybreak he was looking forward to did not dawn; most of the Muslim peoples were not yet finding their way either back to a renewed faith or forward to a modern organization. Even to him it grew clear that Pan-Islamic hopes would not be realized soon, and he turned his attention more to the predicament of his own community, and came to be identified with the programme of a separate Muslim state. He is therefore, though he died a decade before the partition, venerated—often uncritically, as in all such cases—as the moral founder of Pakistan.

Religious enthusiasm led Iqbal regrettably far towards seeing everything as an antithesis between Eastern faith and Western reason, identified with Western materialism and imperialism. Nietzsche too encouraged him to uphold the instinctive against the rational, feeling against thought. It was an antithesis that reflected the historical contradiction of his whole position; the inspiration of Faiz's life had been the hope of overcoming it with the aid of a new synthesis, that of socialism, seen as the reconciler of old culture and modern science in a refashioned society. He too doubtless has found history caught in unexpected crosscurrents, and not always moving as he hoped to see it. And despite the vast distance separating the two men, the prophet and the humanist, Faiz stands recognizably in the same line of succession. Iqbal left no true inheritor either of his philosophy or of his manner. But Faiz, who appeared on the literary scene just when Iqbal was departing from it, is not only the most gifted poetically of those who have come after: he has had all his life the same fundamental sense that poetry ought to be the servant of a cause, a beacon to 'poor humanity's afflicted will', not a mere display of ornamental skill.

Between the two, a curious medley of contrasts and resemblances can be noted. In point of diction they are not very far apart, though Faiz has written verse only in Urdu, being no more drawn to Persian as a medium than, at the other extreme, to Punjabi. At certain moments he has achieved a striking simplification of expression (as in 'Speak' . . . *Bol*, a landmark of its period); more often his pen is dipped as deep as Iqbal's in Persian and Arabic. Even while he, along with most of the Muslim progressive writers of his generation, adhered as Iqbal had done in youth to the ideal of a united India, he was repelled by the prospect held up by Gandhi of a united 'Hindustani' language, a nondescript neither Hindi nor Urdu. There were many different roads by which a Muslim might travel to Pakistan. All the same, a fondness for allusion to things Hindu, even religious, has not left him; and it is worthwhile to observe that whereas

Iqbal's great model and master was Rumi, the Persian mystical poet of mediaeval Asia Minor, Faiz has looked up above all to Ghalib, the arch-poet of modern Muslim India.

In the colouring of their work there is the strongest contrast between Iqbal and Faiz. At his most natural Iqbal is ardent, impetuous, direct; Faiz is more delicately suggestive, and even less easily translated. One paints a picture that seems bathed in sunlight, the other in moonlight. Iqbal's daylight, on the other hand, owes little to our diurnal sun. As Faiz once pointed out in a lecture in London, Iqbal employs surprisingly little imagery of his own, and shows only the scantiest awareness of the physical world about him, no recognition of nature except in some early poems. To the Western reader, brought up on naturalism, Faiz's own external world may appear stylized enough, like the landscape of a Persian miniature. But his imagery has grown increasingly free and profuse, until some of his later poems almost seem to dissolve in it.

Of his human environment, each was keenly aware, each in his own way a 'committed' poet. Both combined older modes, elegiac, romantic, introspective, with a fresh note of criticism of society, and desire to alter it. Because they were animated by faith in something fresh and great, some cause above themselves for which to enlist public support, both were able to make use of the symbols their readers knew by heart, but to lend them fresh significance. Some contemporaries of Faiz, more negative and individualistic in outlook, were inclined to abandon them, in favour of a more direct and 'modern' handling of their subjects. For the poet appealing to collective emotions the symbols could still prove their value, clothing in familiar garb, ideas too new and raw to be transformed immediately into poetry; though both Iqbal and Faiz might resort to them more sparingly as time went on.

Both frequently call up the traditional company of listeners, Iqbal—whose public recitations were confined as a rule to religious or political gatherings—assuming at times the figure of the spiritual leader seated among his disciples: Faiz haunted, in spite of republicanism, by whispers of long-crumbled palace halls. Iqbal was fond of the standard image of moth and candle, though his moth might now be a labouring class foolishly bowing before the idols of the rich.[16] Faiz has been loyal to that of garden and rose-bed, a rose-bed now as likely as not to typify the masses, the poor, buffeted by the rude winds of tyranny. In these literary parks the flowers are always crimson, and their colour carries overtones of passion, suffering, wounds. A comparison would be worth making with the swain and shepherdess and pipe of Europe's pastoral convention. A closer one would be with the use of peacock, deer, red flower, to symbolize longing for the lover in the Punjab hill paintings of the eighteenth century.[17] In poetry the Western reader may be in danger of visualizing symbols too literally, and may do well to make an effort to see them from an indistinct distance, as things transmuted into thoughts, half-way towards the condition of the fossil imagery that all languages are strewn with.

Iqbal moved towards a Love that was a disembodied force, that also meant idealism, or enthusiasm, or *élan vital*. Faiz began with the stereotype of the cruel beauty, but a stable marriage, and domestic life of more modern pattern than Iqbal's, carried him towards an image more human and companionable, though still only elusively suggested by comparison with Western love-poetry, and, like the ghostly Sāqī, interchangeable with other things, not now divine, but Cause, or Country, or People. It has been noted that Faiz has far more than Iqbal of a sort of 'masochism' habitual in Urdu poetry, which seeks the pangs of love rather than its fulfilment.[18] Iqbal's pan-Islamic thinking brought to his mind memories of the Muslim as world-conqueror; Faiz was concerned with the Muslim of his own times, as an underdog, and in some manner was able to fuse sympathy for hard-pressed labourer or peasant with the traditional grief of the lover. In a society long accustomed to frown on free choice both in love and in political allegiance, each of these represented risk and adventure; and in Faiz's prison poems especially, separation from a woman and from a movement, or homeland, merge into one another. A Western reader may feel that this variant of the old symbolism succeeds better in a short piece like 'This Hour of Chain and Gibbet' (*Tauq-o-dār kā mausam*) than when elaborated as in 'Two Loves' (*Do 'ishq*); though this may be found interesting as an illustration, and perhaps as a further warning against figures of speech being taken too concretely. In like fashion, wine may stand now for political truth or insight instead of spiritual, madness for the enthusiast's self-sacrifice in a progressive cause. Amid this readjustment or reshuffling, readers, the best qualified may disagree about precise shades of intended meaning, as happened with some lines in 'Freedom's Dawn' when it came out; or they may discover esoteric messages not intended at all by the author, whose poems are sometimes meant to mean no more than they say. 'Be Near Me' (*Pās raho*), for instance, is a pure lyric.

Iqbal and Faiz both looked abroad for ideas as well as at home. Their Punjab has for ages been receiving from outside, from Persian, Greek, Turk, Briton, and yet has remained itself. Iqbal was only going to one more source when he brought Nietzsche into the Punjab, and Faiz when he helped to introduce Marx. Iqbal wrote of the tribulations of the poor majestically, as if looking down on them from heaven; he preached revolt of downtrodden peoples, relief of downtrodden peoples, relief of downtrodden classes by wealthier men infused with Islamic fraternalism. Faiz belonged to a generation that examined poverty at close range, with its dirt and its sores, and he learned its problems in social, economic detail. Still, Iqbal too had known of Marx, and paid tribute to him in more than one poem, and Faiz on his side has written verses religious in complexion. It was not unfitting that in 1968 he helped to design a documentary film about the life-work of Iqbal, even if this aroused some conservative criticism by its emphasis on the radical notes in the elder poet's writings. Iqbal was an Islamic thinker with a strong dash of what has been coming to be known as 'Islamic socialism'; Faiz might be called a socialist with a groundwork of Muslim culture and feeling. He is indeed one of those many 'cultural Muslims' in many lands today who think of themselves not as religious in a specific sense but as heirs to a long experiment in civilization, and to a great ethical tradition which always did homage to truth and justice and to the upright man prepared to uphold them at all hazards. Pakistan's chance of growing into a nation both truly modern and genuinely founded on an Islamic past will depend, it may appear at least to an observer outside, more on the contribution of such 'cultural Muslims' than on anything else.

Iqbal and Faiz both belong very deeply to the Punjab, and when Faiz goes abroad it does not take long for him to begin to wish himself back in his own country. But both needed a world-vision to sustain them, a hope wider than their native limits, those of a province richer hitherto in promise than in fulfilment. Iqbal after his early travels shut himself up most of the time in a small room whence his thoughts could range abroad unchecked, and draw nourishment from an Orient that he half saw, half imagined. Faiz has had for a second or spiritual home the socialist lands, the socialist world movement, the peace movement. Disappointments with progress abroad as well as at home were bound to befall both. And though both achieved fame in their own country early, each often had occasion to feel misunderstood or isolated. Significantly, more than one poem by each of them has the title 'Solitude', and one of those by Iqbal[19] and one by Faiz (*Tanhā'ī*) are among their very finest. Between these two, the contrast also is revealing. Iqbal's is in Persian. He is alone in a universe that still contains a God, though a distant and silent one; Faiz's knows only human beings, and they too are distant and silent. Iqbal as in many short and some long poems pictures himself as a traveller voyaging across immensities of space, Faiz is shut up in a deserted banqueting-hall, and it is night.

It may be remarked that in all this realm of poetry, *death* is a far less prominent theme than it has always been in Europe. Exile, separation, loneliness, take its place, in a society more closely knit, in spite of wealth and poverty, than any known to the morbidly individualistic Europe of Horace, or Shakespeare, or our own day; a society of which the literary group gathered round patron or Sāqī was the microcosm. Not the disappearance from life, but the banishment of the member from the group, has had, here as in Chinese poetry, the deepest poignancy. In other poems, Faiz calls up imaginary companions to converse with in solitude, even (in 'My Visitor' . . . *Mulāqāt mērī*) a personified loneliness. Two late poems ('Black-out' . . . *Blaik-āūt* and 'Heart Attack' . . . *Hārt ataik*) are concerned with illness, but what is uppermost in them is still not the thought of death in itself, but that of separation. Illness, like prison, divides and isolates. Social bonds so close-knit have made for social inertia, but there may be discerned in them now the possibility of transition to a new social order, of socialist character, and with this a survival of many values, human and cultural, likely to wither in a long interval of competitive industrialism, as the common man's feeling for poetry has withered in the West.

What relation there should be between artists and public movements has been the most crucial art-problem of our century. In Iqbal's case it may be open to conjecture that the short poems, where he was able to fuse intense personal feeling with public themes will outlive his long didactic works. Faiz too at his best, as in 'Freedom's Dawn', has succeeded in fusing them. But he has been taxed with trying at times too deliberately to be progressive, and writing verse more political than poetical. Some of this criticism may have been captious, but the risk is a real one. Even in some poems of high quality may be felt a certain faltering at the close, when he seems to try to resolve his discords without quite finding the right key.

He has been saved from becoming merely, or too facilely, a political writer, like so many others, or as Iqbal was too frequently preacher more

than poet, by a strong inner resistance, a matter of both temperament
and conviction. All imaginative writers are conscious of divided minds,
opposing intuitions, and Faiz more than most. Readers have noticed how
often in his earlier and middle work, his poems turn—like 'Poetry's
Theme' (*Mauzū‘-e sukhan*) or 'Lyre and Flute' (*Shorish-e barbat-o-nai*),
originally entitled 'Two Voices'—on a kind of duality, as if he were
struggling to reconcile two contradictory visions of life. He is himself an
odd mixture, an Oriental mixture, one is tempted to say, of indolence and
energy, an inclination to contemplate existence through a cloud of
cigarette-smoke and a compulsion to act. To get him to answer a missive
is as nearly vain as any human endeavour can be; the 'violent hatred of
letter-writing' that Coleridge found in Wordsworth is at least as strong
in Faiz. Yet the spirit of the age has drawn him along a path necessarily
toilsome, at times perilous.

Artists everywhere in our age, and the age itself in a vaster, more
chaotic way, have faced conflicting claims of old and new, present and
future, each right in its way; of Utopia and possibility, emotion and
reason, worker and intellectual, individual and society. Perhaps by now
we have seen enough to conclude that the artist's true function is not to
identify himself too closely with one demand or the other, but to mediate
or hold the balance between them. And perhaps it is in this direction
that instinct and experience had guided Faiz. Some of his fellow-writers,
in India and Pakistan as elsewhere, have withdrawn into ivory towers,
some have made themselves mouthpieces of political leaders, some
have stopped writing. Faiz's inner divisions, painful as they may have
been, were a symptom rather of health than of weakness, of civic spirit
combined with an artistic sense too strong to let him be swamped by
the tidal force of a movement. Like all great and heroic movements,
the revolution of the twentieth century has been apt, to its own cost
as well as theirs, to reduce individual men and women to units in its
army, ciphers in its great account. The individual is nothing, the cause
everything, proclaimed the Jacobins of 1793, and all world-over-turners
since then have echoed them. Accident has helped to save Faiz from being
submerged; the absence in his own country of any strong organization
with aims akin to his, which has thrown him most of the time on his own
resources.

Two other magnets, literary conservatism and innovation, have
exerted their rival pulls on him. His style has been altering in recent
years, and becoming in some features more experimental. He has

resorted fairly frequently, as he never did in earlier days, to what in Urdu is called 'free verse', which means not prose chopped up into odd lengths, as in English, but lines of varying length in one regular metre, an escape from the end-stopped couplet that has so often shackled invention. This more open manner has been accompanied by a wider choice of subjects, and a more flexible imagery. In other ways—whether or not belief in a planned pattern of society is related to respect for organized patterns of verse—he has remained more conservative, and his influence has been against neglect of the technical side of his art. 'Faiz has brought respectability back to grammatical writing', a friend wrote lately, and has rescued some of his juniors from a morass of incomprehensibility.[20] He himself told me some years ago that he thought the rhyme-schemes in his first volume had been too free and easy, and made young imitators careless; for this reason, and in order to give each poem a more sharply defined form, he had set himself to adhere more closely to fixed sequences. Innovation for its own sake has not attracted him; he has not translated foreign verse into Urdu, as some have done, and has shown no curiosity about possible new metres.

All this may give his mode of writing something of an old-fashioned look, by comparison with the more westernized idiom of so many writers up and down the world who have so obviously read T.S. Eliot and his successors. But such writers are apt to be intellectuals without roots in their native soil, whereas a style like that of Faiz, even though in origin feudal and aristocratic, can awaken a responsive thrill in the common man. No doubt it will be called on to make further changes, in his and other hands, as time goes on. The old symbolism may be approaching the end of its useful life, having performed a final service by helping to launch modern ideas that can now take their own poetic course. Some other time-honoured conventions have more obviously had their day. Complaints have been heard of too much antiquated phraseology, of poets shutting their eyes to the life around them, the changing seasons, the sun and wind and rain of the Punjab. Formerly the old dream-pictures of Persia and Turkestan could serve to express for Indo-Muslims their sense of being a community in but not of, India. Now most of these Muslims have their own sub-Himalayan homeland, they may well want to hear from their poets about their own skies, flowers, lives, instead of those of the half-mythical native land of their half-mythical ancestors. To go on harping on too many old strings will be as fatal to Urdu poetry as to plunge into unintelligible modernism, and leave it to linger as a mere ghost of the past, haunting the hall of Faiz's poem where no one will ever come any more.

Urdu and its poetry have had a strange history; what the future holds for them must be uncertain. It is not out of the question that Faiz may prove to have been the last important figure. Over the language itself a question mark hangs, though the same is true in one sense or another of every language, including the one most used and most misused, English. Urdu began as the speech of the camp, and became that of the city, but it has still to show that it can become that of a nation, or with what functions—for Pakistan like India is, and must remain a multilingual country. In the western Punjab, today its literary stronghold, there are some who are turning their minds to Punjabi as the proper medium for poetry. To hold its ground Urdu will need to show itself able to produce more, and more varied, prose, as well as poetry still able to thrill. So far, in the two decades since independence, its progress has been halting, and poetry—it seems generally agreed among those competent to judge—has not on the whole maintained the standard achieved before 1947. Some gifted writers have flagged, new talents of distinction have been few.

Of the older group, Faiz has gone on writing, and gone on developing, and now links his generation with the younger one where his most responsive hearers are to be found, captivated partly by his romantic note, partly by his idealism. Much remains for him to do; he has done enough to be looked upon as the most significant Urdu poet, in Pakistan or India, of the time since Iqbal, and he and his poems will keep their place as a strand in the history that our epoch has been weaving.

Notes

1. A Scotswoman who knew him in Afghanistan wrote in fictional form an admiring account of his efforts to establish order. See Lilias Hamilton, *A Vizier's Daughter*, London, 1990, Print.
2. He is therefore, in full, Faiz Ahmed 'Faiz'. His own name, religious like nearly all Muslim names, would mean 'Bounty of the highly praised one'—the Prophet. (He writes himself 'Ahmed' not 'Ahmad'.)
3. In an article at the time of Faiz's first arrest. See *The Observer* [London], 11 March 1951, Print.
4. Sajjad Zaheer wrote: 'The writer of these lines was a co-accused with Faiz in this case . . . and he can testify to the high morale, the patriotic fervour, the serenity and the undaunted courage and faith in the high destiny of his beloved people which Faiz exemplified during this whole period'. Sajjad Zaheer, 'Faiz and His Poetry,' *New Age* [Delhi], April 1956, Print.

5. It is due to the late administration of President Ayub Khan to state that Faiz's *Zindāṅ Nāmā* (Prison Thoughts) was written before its term of office and that although he was known to be not in sympathy with this administration, the sponsoring of the present volume by UNESCO was authorized by it, in recognition of his position as one of the country's most eminent writers.

6. Miss Achla Chib (later Mrs Eccles).

7. This is the view of Mr M. Usman, lecturer in Urdu at Government College, Lahore, who gave me much light on this and many other subjects when I was living in the College in 1965.

8. R.K. Yadav discusses the position of Urdu in Pakistan as well as in India. See R.K. Yadav, *The Indian Language Problem*, Delhi, 1967, Print.

9. Faiz expresses a degree of scepticism about the generalization in this paragraph.

10. Faiz points out that the *kū'ē malāmat* might connote the worldling or the pharisee, as well as the seeker of illicit pleasure.

11. See for example A.J. Arberry, *Sufism*, London, 1961, Print; Khaliq Ahmad Nizami, *Some Aspects of Religion and Politics in India during the 13th Century*, Aligarh University, 1961, Print.

12. My friend and former colleague Mr Kishen Singh, of the Punjabi College at Delhi, has given me valuable information about this folk poetry, of which he has been a lifelong student.

13. Much Elizabethan sonneteering has a similar character. Cf. Professor Arberry's remark in his English edition of Iqbal's long poem *Javēd-nāmā* (p. 13) that 'Persian is a language almost ideally suited to deliberate vagueness'.

14. Ralph Russell of the University of London has written a most illuminating essay: Ralph Russell, 'The Pursuit of Urdu Ghazal', *American Journal of Asian Studies* (November 1969), Web. See also by him and Khurshidul Islam, *Three Mughal Poets*, London, 1969, Print; and also *Ghalib: Life and Letters*, Vol. 1, London, 1969, Print.

15. A number of Iqbal's *ghazals* will be found in my *Poems from Iqbal*.

16. See the poem 'Capital and Labour' in my *Poems from Iqbal*, pp. 21–23.

17. W.G. Archer, *Indian Painting in the Punjab Hills*, London, 1952, pp. 5–39, Print.

18. This point of contrast was stressed during a discussion by Mr S.N. Chib.

19. No. 113 in *Poems from Iqbal*.

20. Dr Nazir Ahmad, in a letter of 20 August 1967. The same critic however has found occasional phrases of Faiz to be in very unorthodox Urdu. (Examples, for the student: 'This Harvest of Hope', line 17; Song, line 14.)

[All publication details in notes 13, 14, 15, 16, 18 and 19 are not mentioned. In note 20, 'This Harvest of Hope' and 'Song' are from *Poems by Faiz* by Kiernan—Editor]

POETRY'S THEME

Original: *Mauzū'-ē sukhan* from *Naqsh-e Faryādī* (1941)
TRANSLATOR: VICTOR G. KIERNAN

Twilight is burning out and turning chill,
Night comes fresh-bathed from where the moon's spring flows;
And now—these eager eyes shall have their will,
These avid fingers feel the touch of those!

Is that her fringed veil, is it her face, her dress,
Behind the hanging gauze, that makes it glow—
And in the vague mist of that rippling tress
Does the bright earring twinkle still, or no?

Subtly once more her loveliness will speak,
Those penciled lids, those languorous eyes, again;

Dusted with that faint powder, her pink cheek,
On her pale hand the henna's delicate stain.
Here is the chosen world of rhyme and dream
My muse inhabits, here her darling theme!

—Under the black and blood-red murk of ages
How has it fared with Eve's sons all these years?
How shall we fare, where daily combat rages
Of death with life? how fared our forefathers?

Why must those gay streets' swarming progeny
So draw breath that to die is all they crave?
In those rich fields bursting with bounty, why
Must no ripe harvest except hunger wave?
Walls dark with secrets frown on every side,
That countless lamps of youth have sunk behind;
Everywhere scaffolds on which dreams have died
That lit unnumbered candles in man's mind.

—These too are subjects; more there are;—but oh,
Those limbs that curve so fatally ravishingly!
Oh that sweet wretch, those lips parting so slow—
Tell me where else such witchery could be!
No other theme will ever fit my rhyme;
Nowhere but here is poetry's native clime.

2

FAIZ AND THE CLASSICAL GHAZAL

When Faiz's *ghazal* is discussed, usually the first thing said is that Faiz has given to traditional symbols (*'alāmat*) a new meaning and a new meaningfulness. It is also said that an important reason for Faiz's popularity is the way his feet remained firmly planted in classical soil, while the house he built on this foundation had walls inscribed with the new problems of a new sensibility. For the present, I will not raise the question of whether 'gallows', 'noose', 'murder', 'preacher', 'street of the beloved' and other such words are even 'symbols' at all. Our classical *ghazal* was not familiar with the concept of a symbol, and it's not likely that a thing which did not exist even conceptually in our poetics, should not only be present but should also be something our poets were aware of. The efforts which have been made in our country to understand and appreciate Urdu poetry in the light of half-baked notions founded on Western terms and concepts, have usually been unsuccessful. The attempt to prove the presence of symbols in Urdu *ghazal* has a conspicuous place in the list of these unsuccessful efforts.

Well, not to prolong the discussion of this point, I only want to say that Faiz's *ghazal* is unquestionably adorned with the conventional words and image-clusters (*talāzimāt*) which are a notable feature of our classical poetry. The question is whether in reality Faiz's classicism and originality lie only in the fact that he was not ashamed to try his strength against the 'rival' and the 'shaikh' in the 'beloved's street.' It is necessary to examine the question—in part, because Faiz's poetry is in any case of a markedly limited scope and compass, and because his admirers assert that Faiz's classicism is limited to giving new meanings to these same words and image-clusters. This amounts to detraction in the guise of praise. The question must also be examined because in the process, light can be shed on some fundamental aspects of the classical *ghazal*. And there is one more reason: in Pakistan, since Faiz's death certain people have been trying to prove that he was a faithful Muslim, a lover of the Prophet, and a mystic, a tender-hearted Sufi. Thus it would not be entirely surprising if after some time, Faiz were understood to be a classical Sufi poet as well, so that his real literary achievement would be taken as limited merely to reviving the memory of scaffold and noose, Qais and Farhād.

The first question is, if a poet uses conventional words that have come down from ancient times, while he himself is a poet of the present age, on what basis will we decide that he has given these words new meanings? For example, consider these two *she'rs*:

> No pleas for union, no petitions of grief, no fables, no complaints—
> Under your regime the sad heart has lost all its rights!
> ℬ
> Murdering a lover was never far from any beloved's mind—
> But before your regime, it wasn't the general practice!

Obviously the first *she'r* is Faiz's, and the second is Dard's (1720–1785). On what basis will you decide that the first *she'r* refers to political oppression, and the second to the tyranny of the beloved? If you say that both *she'rs* refer to political oppression, then it can be said that using the traditional themes and words of the *ghazal* with a political meaning is no special characteristic of Faiz. And if you say that Faiz's *she'r* refers to political oppression because we know that he was a progressive, a revolutionary, etc., then the implication is that these conventional words have no status of their own, their meanings keep changing according to the poet. If the poet is a Shia, then his meanings are Shi'ite, if the poet is a Sunni but is *Ahl-e Hadīs* as well, then his meanings are Sunni *Ahl-e Hadīs* etc. It's clear that in this way Faiz's individuality is again endangered. It might be said that since Faiz is a progressive, when he speaks of the sad heart losing all its rights under someone's regime, the force itself is different, the beauty itself is different. But this implies that before deciding about the strength or weakness of any *she'r*, we should ascertain the political beliefs of the poet. Obviously those meanings of a *she'r* that cannot be discovered without obtaining information about the beliefs of the poet, must in the last analysis be held invalid. For first of all we do not have information about the political beliefs of all the poets; in fact we do not always know even the poet's name. And the second point is that if the beauty or meaning of the *she'r* is held to depend and rest on this information which is external to the *she'r*, then we'll be forced to say that the *she'r* itself has no meaning. If we accept this view, all the doors to criticism and analysis will be closed, and Faiz's poetry itself will be in danger, for the necessary consequence will be that Faiz's poetry has no excellence in itself. The real truth therefore seems to be that because Faiz was a revolutionary, a progressive, etc. there's a kind of pleasure in ascribing a political meaning to his poetry. Otherwise, if he had written these very *she'r* in Dard's day, or even Ghalib's day, no one would have paid any special attention to them.

It may be said that Faiz's great achievement really lay in making the classical diction come to life again, and making it popular in the *ghazal*. For by Faiz's day, it may be said, all those beautiful words had either already been abandoned, or had lost their meanings. But these words are in fact part of a whole conventional system; and all the assumptions of the *ghazal* world depend upon them. As long as that conventional system and those assumptions exist, these words cannot lose their meanings. It is impossible that some conventional term—for example, 'tyranny and oppression'—should have meaning in Mir's *she'r* and have no meaning in modern *she'r*. It can indeed be said that conventional words like 'tyranny' and 'oppression' can lose their interest and freshness. Thus what we are really claiming is that these words had lost their interest and freshness, and Faiz endowed them with renewed interest and freshness. Then the question comes up, how did Faiz perform this feat? You will reply that he gave them a political meaning. But this is clearly circular. For again that same problem arises that the quest for political meaning in Faiz's poetry rests on our knowledge that Faiz was a political and revolutionary individual. That is, if we encounter the *she'r* with the line, 'But before your regime, it wasn't the general practice' in Faiz's collected poetry we would discover political and revolutionary meanings in it, and if we found it among Dard's poems we would consider it merely love poetry. Thus the interest and freshness we find in the classical *ghazal* imagery used by Faiz, is due to our awareness that Faiz had certain political views. That is to say, Faiz did not endow such imagery with any special poetic excellence—it was only the magic of his politics.

Of course, I don't accept this conclusion; in fact, I consider it incorrect. I know that in our time, many poets besides Faiz have used the classical *ghazal* imagery, and they have even agreed with Faiz's views and shared his convictions, but in their poetry the classical images do not have the same beauty as they do in Faiz's poetry. Thus Faiz's greatness cannot be founded on the claim that he gave a political meaning to the classical romantic, conventional imagery of the *ghazal*. Many modern poets—Makhdum, Majruh, Sahir, Ghulam Rabbani Taban, and others—have done as much, and not one among them is the equal of Faiz. If it be said that Faiz was the first to achieve the feat of arriving at new meanings, not even that is true. Among the Progressives, Makhdum was the first to make systematic use of the *ghazal*, while Hasrat Mohani, Muhammad Ali Jauhar, and Iqbal had re-established the use of classical imagery in the *ghazal*. In the preface to his collection *Dast-e Tah-e Sang*, Faiz mentioned Hasrat Mohani. In this preface he wrote that he himself began to write poetry around 1928. At that time Muhammad Ali Jauhar was alive, and his political *ghazals* were echoing in the halls of literature. Hasrat's prestige as a *ghazal* poet had already been thoroughly established, and Iqbal had become a kind of ideal for all the new poets (including Josh). Faiz himself wrote an elegy for Iqbal that can be counted among the best poems of the Progressive poets. Thus when Faiz began to write, there were abundant examples before him in which political themes had been used.

In the light of this analysis, we are obliged to say that the classical beauty and excellence of Faiz's *ghazals* cannot be ascribed to his habitually using certain conventional words, and endowing them with political meanings. In the world of criticism we often find ourselves in the difficult situation of being able to perceive beauty, but unable to explain it. Murray Krieger, in his *Theory of Criticism* (Baltimore, 1976) has elucidated this point. He says:

> If we have an experience that we describe as aesthetic, we are likely to seek to find its cause in the stimulating object, to which we then attribute aesthetic value. But the issue for us as critics is whether the cause is in us or in the object. In a literal sense of course, the source of the response must be in us, since there are other people who do not feel it when confronted by the same object and since without us there is no such response, however powerful the object and its stimulating propensities. . . . But I have raised the normative issue that transcends such literalistic reductions: does the object have an aesthetic character that we apprehend or do some of us read such aesthetic character into it, projecting it out of ourselves? If we have discovered that character, so that our experience—to the extent that it is aesthetic—is an appropriate response to that character, then we ought to be able to describe it and expect it to sponsor a similar experience with other readers.

Later, Krieger says that the critic must be able to distinguish between the object in experience and the 'experience of an object'. That is, the critic must be able to say that the beauty he finds in a verse is not the invention of his own mind, and by describing this beauty he must be able to claim that from verses which possess this beauty such and such a type of experience can be obtained. If the experience of a poem is described in such a way that its separate parts retain their own individuality, then the claim of those parts to offer a 'unified' and 'self-enclosing' experience becomes doubtful.

Krieger uses the terms 'unified' and 'self-enclosing' to remind the reader that poems are organic wholes, that no element of a poem can be singled out as greater than the rest, and that poems contain their meanings within themselves. These formulations, which are regarded in the West as faintly Neo-Aristotelian, have parallels in Perso-Arabic poetics too. One might cite the work of classical Arab critics like Qudama ibn Jafar, who denied that the meaning of a poem existed outside its words. In any case, the critics' dilemma that Krieger describes is common enough, and most critics of Faiz do not escape it. By stressing the so called political content of Faiz's poetry, they unwittingly run the risk of devaluing Faiz's real achievement. The admirers of Faiz's classicism say that in Faiz's *ghazals* the words are one thing, and the political meaning which Faiz's beliefs have given them is another. But since those very words have been given political meaning by Majruh and others as well, but have not been given the beauty that they have in Faiz's poetry, Faiz's admirers have not succeeded in explaining how the same words work so effectively for Faiz, and remain ineffective for others.

In order to resolve this question, let us examine certain points illustrated in the following two *she'rs*. The first is Hafiz's, the second is obviously Faiz's:

The eagle of tyranny has spread his wings over the whole city
Is there no bow of a recluse, is there no arrow of a sigh?
৵
This is the city of the unjust ones
where is there any justice or compassion?
You fools, Supplication wanders from door to door,
beating her head in vain.

Leaving aside the fact, that Hafiz's *she'r* is of a very high order and Faiz's *she'r* is not among his good ones, the question to be asked is: in what way can we decide that Hafiz's *she'r* is not political and Faiz's *she'r* is political? Or again, can we say that although much inferior to Hafiz's *she'r* Faiz's *she'r* deserves praise because it has a political dimension, or a political dimension too? (That is, a political dimension in addition to some other dimension). Can we establish criteria for political poetry, in the light of which we can distinguish it from non-political poetry? Is it possible for us to show that non-political poetry, while remaining within the bounds of conventions, can become political poetry, since the conventions are context-neutral? Is it possible for us to stay entirely within some conventional framework, while the meanings that emerge are non-conventional?

To answer all these questions would take whole chapters. For the present I only want to say that Hafiz's *she'r* can sustain a political meaning, but we cannot call it political in itself, because the political meaning that we pull out of it will be related to its signification (*m'ānaviyat*), not to its real meaning. And the power of metaphor is that it opens doors for signification. We have no criterion by which we can declare this *she'r* nonpolitical, but neither do we have any criterion by which we can declare it purely political. The signification of a *she'r* is part of its meaning, but the circle of its meaning can be narrower than its signification. Faiz's *she'r* in comparison to Hafiz's *she'r* is less effective because the meaning on which its signification is based is a lesser meaning than that of Hāfiz's *she'r*. When I speak of a lesser meaning, my point is that in Hafiz's *she'r* there are four metaphors and four images—that the metaphors are also images: the eagle of tyranny, the wings spread over the whole city, the bow of a recluse, the arrow of a sigh. Then, the presence of two things (which are mentioned in the first line) proves the absence of two things (which are mentioned in the second line). Faiz's *she'r* is devoid of these merits.

Where Faiz has used classical imagery successfully, he has always achieved *kaifiyat* or *mazmūn āfarīnī*. *Kaifiyat* can be loosely translated as 'feelingfullness': that is, a direct appeal to emotions without any special depth of meaning or obvious recourse to metaphor or imagery. *Mazmūn āfarīnī* can best be understood as finding a new aspect of a traditional theme, approaching a traditional theme from a new angle, or giving a new direction to a traditional theme. By 'traditional theme' I mean, of course, the set of stock topoi of the *ghazal*, each of which can subsume a large number of subsidiary and related images.

In any case, neither a political dimension, nor a philosophical dimension, nor a romantic dimension, nor any other dimension, contains any merit in its own right that could make it a bearer of poetic excellence. The discussion has focused on Faiz's *ghazals*, but he used *ghazal* images in many of his *nazms* as well. Thus I present the first two lines of Faiz's 'We who were Killed on Dark Roads', then a Persian *she'r* by Hakim Kashi, a sixteenth century Indo-Persian poet:

> *Loving the flowers of your lips, we were sacrificed on the dry branch of the scaffold.*
>
> ༂
>
> *In the course of loving you I too was sacrificed.*
> *What a pity that from the tribe of Majnūn no one now remains!*

The dignity of its *mazmūn āfarīnī* and suggestive implications (*kināyā*) make the Persian *she'r* something monumental. Faiz's *she'r* contains a little wordplay, but the well-worn, threadbare feel of its imagery creates self-pity instead of dignity. Where there is *mazmūn āfarīnī* there is no self pity. Faiz was among those of your modern poets who had a sense of the importance of these classical terms and concepts. He even wrote an essay on some of them. We, under the influence of Western education, have chosen to become strangers to those terms. When our literary intuition causes us to sense a classical tone in Faiz's *ghazals*, we are not able to make use of traditional terms and concepts in our efforts to ascertain the true nature of this tone. Thus we have been content merely to say that Faiz has used 'shaikh', 'brahman', 'holy man', 'street of the beloved', 'rival, 'destination', 'gallows', 'noose', and other classical, conventional terms, with a new meaning. In many of Faiz's best *she'rs*, there are no conventional terms—what can then be the secret of their success? Here are some of Faiz's most famous *she'rs*, taken from different *ghazals*:

> ༂
>
> *The thing that was not mentioned in the whole story,*
> *That was the thing that displeased her very much.*
>
> ༂
>
> *When we were apart how many nearnesses we achieved—*
> *When we were together, what separations came upon us.*
>
> ༂

If we are still strangers after so much friendliness,
How many meetings will it take for us to become friends?
ॐ
What they took for a mirage turned out to be the fountain of eternal life,
The dream, which didn't reach even to the mind, was the only true one.

Note the *mazmūn āfarīnī* of the first and fourth *she'rs*, and the *kaifiyat* of the second and third. The way Faiz brought a classical tone to life in the *ghazal* is a notable chapter in the history of our poetry. In his *ghazals* the classical intellectual world of the Urdu *ghazal* comes alive, a world in which *mazmūn āfarīnī* and *kaifiyat* played an important part. In Faiz, the magic of *kaifiyat* echoes even in the *nazms*. It is thus necessary for Faiz's poetry to be examined afresh, in the traditional context of the *ghazal*.

GHAZAL

Original: *Ghazal: Dil mēṅ ab yūṅ tērē bhūlē hu'ē gham ātē haiṅ from Dast-e Sabā* (1952)

Translator: Agha Shahid Ali

The heart a desecrated temple
    in it all statues of you broken
Those forgotten sorrows
    my memories of you return
    gods abandoned by their worshippers

One by one by one
    the stars light up the sky
In step with them
    you approach me in the dark
    your final destination

Tonight increase the pace
    with which the liquor is poured
    Oh tell the drummer to play a breathless beat
Worshippers have abandoned the mosques
    they're coming here to the wine house

It is the night of waiting
    tell her let no more time elapse
This pain of longing may dull
    already my memory is beginning to blur
    at any moment I may forget her

3

FAIZ AHMED FAIZ
POETRY, POLITICS, AND PAKISTAN

The poetry which the Progressive Writers' Movement produced did not reach the heights which the short story did. But one poet secured for himself an important place in Urdu poetry and upheld some of the major values of the progressives for nearly half a century, from the middle thirties right up to his death in 1984. This was Faiz Ahmed Faiz. By the middle fifties, he was already recognized as the leading Urdu poet of Pakistan, and rapidly became the most popular Urdu poet of the whole subcontinent.

As we shall see, it was not solely the excellence of his poetry that won him this position, but his poetry is nonetheless his most important legacy to us and demands our main attention.[1]

Faiz began his career as a poet at a time when different categories of poets catered for different and often conflicting, tastes. First were those, mainly *ghazal* poets, who were content to continue virtually unchanged, the classical tradition, and regarded any departure from it as a departure from poetry itself. Two other groups wrote in conscious response to what they felt to be the demands of new times and new conditions. One comprised the progressives and their sympathizers, and the other, those equally self-conscious innovators whose major organization was the *Halqa-e Arbab-e Zauq* (Circle of Men of Good Taste, or more literally, Circle of Possessors of Taste). The tone of this somewhat pretentious title captures very well the lofty disdain that they generally felt for their numerous contemporaries who had not been blessed with 'good taste'. Their quarrel with the progressives stemmed from their view that art and propaganda were mutually exclusive, and that art must be for art's sake alone. (It must be said that some of the progressives provided ample fuel for this fire, producing verse, which, if clearly progressive, was equally clearly not poetry. However, it should also be said that some of the 'men of taste' made the opposite mistake and assumed that anything that was presented as a poem and was clearly not propaganda must therefore be art.) The progressive school included some whose hostility to the 'men of taste' was matched by a hostility to the *ghazal*, which they regarded as an outmoded, mediaeval form.

Faiz from the very beginning held himself aloof from all these extreme views. His poetry of all periods shows a certain catholicity of taste and a command of a wide range of skills, which enabled him to win acceptance and esteem from the audiences for all three trends. *Ghazals*, poems on overtly progressive themes, and 'modern' poems, which do not, however, express anything inconsistent with progressive values—all are to be found in his collections of verse. So too are poems in the tradition of the *qavvālī*—popular devotional Muslim verse—and of the *tarānā*— rousing verse embodying the sentiments appropriate to popular political campaigning. Faiz maintained this breadth of range to the last, and it is one of the bases of his exceptional popularity.

Eight collections of his verse were published in his lifetime. The first, *Naqsh-e Faryādī*,[2] was published in 1941 and includes poems dating from 1928–29 onwards. The last dated poem in his last collection, a *ghazal*, was written in November 1984, only a matter of days before his death. *Poems by Faiz*, a good selection of poems with parallel verse translations by V.G. Kiernan, was published under the auspices of UNESCO in 1971. Almost all the poems, Kiernan says, 'were chosen by Faiz himself, and all the translations have been discussed with him,[3] and Kiernan has added an introduction[4] and notes. The selection covers the first four collections, and a few poems from (at that time) uncollected verses. Although these four collections comprise only about half of Faiz's total output. Most of the poems I discuss in this essay are taken from them. There are two main reasons for this. The first is that Faiz's best-known poems (and in my view almost all his best ones) are included in these first four collections, while the last four have relatively few. And a second, rather more mundane one, is that *Poems by Faiz* (which was recently republished[5]) provides the maximum help both to those who are able to study his verse only through the medium of English and to those, whose study of Urdu is still in its relatively early stages. Kiernan's translations are appreciably better, and certainly closer to Faiz's originals, than any of those by subsequent translators, and for students of Urdu, there is the help afforded by the Roman transliterations and the literal translations, which the book provides.

Three of the first four collections include forewords by Faiz himself, and in the forewords to the first and the fourth (*Dast-e Tah-e Saṅg*), he tells us something of their themes and of the varying backgrounds against which they were produced. Almost all the poems of the period 1928–29 to 1934–35 were the product (to use the coy words of his introduction to his first collection) of a *mū'ayyan* ('established') emotion. One guesses that by 'an established emotion' he means one generally recognized as being commonly experienced—that is, love—and this is confirmed by his description of this in the introduction to his fourth collection, where, speaking of these same early poems, he describes them, in words only a trifle less coy, as springing from 'that affliction of the heart which befalls most people in their youth.' Numbers of these, not surprisingly, are in the *ghazal* form.

The earliest of his most famous poems, *Mujh sē pahlī sī mahabbat, mērī mahbūb na māṅg*, 'My beloved, do not ask of me, my former kind of love' ('Love, Do Not Ask' in Kiernan's translation) begins the second part of *Naqsh-e Faryādī* and marks, he tells us, the beginning of a new consciousness, an awareness that a man's love for a woman cannot be the be all and end all of life, and that he must be aware of, and deeply affected by, the suffering of the poor and exploited. A better poem is 'To the Rival' (*Raqīb sē*). In the traditional *ghazal*, the rival is a stock character, the type of the false lover whose professions of love, all too often accepted by the poet's beloved as sincere, are in fact a deception, practiced to achieve his own selfish ends. In Faiz's poem by contrast, he is one whose love is as sincere as the poet's own, and one with whom the poet feels a common bond, and indeed a common bond, stronger than he could feel with any other, since both he and his rival have forged it from identical experience. Faiz goes on rather abruptly to say that from this experience 'I learned to be the friend of suffering creatures', and that now whenever he thinks of the suffering and the exploitation that is their lot, a fire over which he has no control sets his heart aflame. In 'Poetry's Theme' (*Mauzū'-e sukhan*) however, he declares that, aware as he is that the sufferings of the poor afford themes for poetry, the charms of his beloved are such that only they can be the theme of his poetry. But it seems that he did not always feel like this. Only a few poems before 'Poetry's Theme' comes one of his best, directly political poems, 'Speak' (*Bol*). In Kiernan's translation it reads:

Speak, for your two lips are free;
Speak, your tongue is still your own;
This straight body still is yours—
Speak, your life is still your own.

See how in the blacksmith's forge
Flames leap high and steel glows red,
Padlocks opening wide their jaws,
Every chain's embrace outspread!

Time enough is this brief hour
Until body and tongue lie dead;
Speak, for truth is living yet—
Speak whatever must be said.

I shall return to this poem below.

Naqsh-e Faryādī was published in 1941.[6] A second collection, *Dast-e Sabā*,[7] did not appear until eleven years later, in 1952, and presumably includes all the verse he had written over these eleven years. These were years in which he had acted on the conclusions he had reached in the mid-thirties and played an active part in social and political movements. He had been a leading light in the Progressive Writers' Association from the start. In June 1942, convinced now that with the entry of the Soviet Union into the Second World War, it was the duty of progressives everywhere to support the war effort, he joined the army, in which he served until December 1946, leaving with the rank of Lieutenant-Colonel, and (in 1943) having been awarded the MBE. From February 1947 to March 1951, he edited simultaneously two progressive daily papers, the English-language *Pakistan Times* and the Urdu *Imroz*—the duties of an editor in Pakistan being perhaps rather less onerous than Western readers might suppose. He also publicly identified himself with the trade union movement, and in 1951 was Vice-President of the Pakistan Trade Union Federation. In the relatively free political conditions that prevailed up to 1951, he also served in posts to which he was appointed by the Pakistan government, going to San Francisco in 1948 and Geneva in 1949–50, as a member of the Pakistan government delegations to the International Labour Organization (ILO).[8]

But independence had not brought into being the kind of regime that could maintain the unity of all those who had fought for it, and, both in India and Pakistan, the new rulers began to turn with increasing ruthlessness against the mass of the people whose support had brought them to power. The strength and depth of Faiz's feelings on political issues had evidently increased over the years, and in *Dast-e Sabā*, poems on political themes occupy a prominent place. Despite his earlier disclaimer in 'Poetry's Theme', he has now found in these themes the inspiration, which produces true poetry no less effectively than themes of love. In 1952, when this collection appeared, only five years had passed since the political settlement of August 1947, which brought independence to the subcontinent and its simultaneous partition into the two states of India and Pakistan. Two of Faiz's best poems express the widespread disappointment which the aftermath of independence had brought.

'To a Political Leader' (*Siyāsī līḍar kē nām*) reproaches the type of leader at whose call his followers have fought against almost impossible odds to achieve their aims, whose whole political capital consists of this heroic, self-sacrificing support—and who now wants to curb the forces which he himself had mobilized, even if by so doing he jeopardizes all the gains that have been won. 'Freedom's Dawn' (*Subh-e āzādī*) speaks directly of the August 1947 settlement, described in its first line as:

$$\text{یہ داغ داغ اُجالا، یہ شب گزیدہ سحر}$$

'This much stained radiance, this night-bitten morning', and goes on to say that this is not the dawn that those who had fought for freedom had laboured so hard to bring. Our new rulers, says Faiz, tell us to rejoice because the struggle is over now. Not so, he says:

> Night's heaviness is unlessened still, the hour
> Of mind and spirit's ransom has not struck;
> Let us go on, our goal is not reached yet.

These two poems, and the earlier poem 'Speak', exemplify a marked characteristic of Faiz's progressive poetry. He never speaks, as some of his contemporaries do, in the strident tones that raise the hackles of all except the converted, but maintains what I have called the universality of the traditional *ghazal*, which enables it to speak to different people's different conditions (and indeed this is a quality of much of the world's great poetry.) I have read (somewhere that I cannot now recall) that 'Speak' was written soon after the outbreak of the Second World War, and reflects the very widespread indignation of politically articulate Indians at Britain's high-handed declaration of war on India's behalf, and at the restrictions of political liberties imposed in the name of wartime needs. But nothing in what the poem actually says restricts it to that situation (and in the notes, Kiernan, quite properly, does not think it necessary to tell us anything of the circumstances in which it was written). Moreover, the poem tells its audience to speak, but doesn't tell it what to speak. And so it remains a spirited call to all free men, in any country and any age, to speak out boldly what free men have a duty to say, even though they risk imprisonment if they do so. 'To a Political Leader' has the same sort of universality. Readers encountering it for the first time when *Dast-e Saba* came out in 1952, would almost certainly assume that it was addressed to the leaders of the new post-independence states. But Kiernan's note tells us that it was the mass uprisings of August 1942 that had inspired it.[9]

'Freedom's Dawn' has the same universal quality. Some of Faiz's left-wing critics have criticized it for an alleged ambivalence, arguing that *anyone* who is dissatisfied with the post-independence regimes of India and Pakistan can identify with it. But that view is quite untenable. The poem's theme is the disappointment of those who had fought for independence—and not of anyone else; and it captures admirably the sort of helpless restlessness after 1947, of millions of people who had felt that independence would see the birth of a brave new world without quite knowing what that brave new world would be like, and who now felt that whatever independence ought to have brought, it was certainly not this. Faiz's left-wing critics would presumably have wanted him to produce a poem, which would have told its readers why independence had not brought the results they had hoped for and what must now be done to remedy the situation. But I know of no Urdu poem which has done this, and I very much doubt whether this kind of demand is one that poetry can meet. Poetry demands what one may call a certain generality; greater specificity belongs to the domain of prose.

It is about half-way through *Dast-e Saba* that we find the poem in which he, at last, completely harmonizes the love one feels for a lover, with its demand for self-sacrifice, with the wider, more inclusive love that makes similar demands. In 'Two Loves' (*Do 'ishq*), Faiz expresses his equal dedication to his mistress and to his still recently established country, Pakistan, speaks of all that he has suffered in his love for both, and concludes:

Yet my heart feels no regret for either love
My heart bears every scar but that of regret.

This stand is one which thenceforth he never abandoned. And though 'Two Loves' does not explicitly say so, it is clear from other poems that when Faiz speaks of his commitment to his country, he means first and foremost commitment to the cause of the poor and exploited masses of its people.

The poetry of the years to 1952 constantly reflects an awareness of dangers that lie ahead, speaks of the risks of suffering, imprisonment and even execution that those who fight for the cause of the people will be obliged to face, and calls upon them to be steadfast in the fight. By the time it was published, Faiz was himself in jail. In March 1951, he, a number of leading communists, and a group of army officers had been arrested and charged with taking part in a conspiracy to overthrow the Pakistan government. It was not until just over four years later, in April 1955, that he was released on bail. (He was acquitted in September 1955). Most of the poems in *Dast-e Sabā*, and all the poems of Faiz's third collection, *Zindāṅ Nāmā* ('Prison Writings'), published in 1956, were written during his imprisonment. One of Faiz's fellow-'conspirators' in the Rawalpindi Conspiracy Case, as it was called, was Major Muhammad Ishaque, and in a long and valuable introduction to *Zindāṅ Nāmā*, he gives us a fairly detailed account of Faiz's imprisonment. He was arrested on 9 March 1951, and for three months, held in solitary confinement in Sargodha and Lyallpur (now Faisalabad) jails and deprived of writing materials. Then, until July 1953, he was in Hyderabad jail. The 'conspirators' were then split up and sent to different prisons. Faiz and Muhammad Ishaque were among those who were allocated to Montgomery (now Sahiwal) jail, and it was from there that Faiz was released in April 1955.

Faiz, in a short essay prefaced to his fourth collection *Dast-e Tah-e Saṅg*,[10] has described what the experience of imprisonment did for his development as a poet. He says that the verse he wrote in jail continues that strand in his poetry, which began with 'Love, Do Not Ask'.

But the experience of imprisonment, like that of love, is in itself one of fundamental significance, and opens up new windows of thought and vision. Thus, in the first place, all of one's sensations are again heightened, as they had been at the onset of youth, and the sense of wonder at the coming of day, the shades of evening, the deep blue of the sky, and the feel of the passing breeze comes back once more. Another thing that happens is that the time and distance of the world outside become unreal. Things that are near seem far away, and far away things seem near, and the distinction between tomorrow and yesterday vanishes, so that sometimes a moment seems like an eternity and things that happened a century ago seem to have happened only yesterday. And thirdly, in the leisure of isolation from the world outside, one finds time for thought and study, and time to devote more attention to adorning the bride of poetry—in other words, time for polishing one's verse.

Both Faiz and Ishaque speak of different distinctive periods ('moods', as Ishaque calls them) of the verse of these four years of imprisonment. The first, says Ishaque, was that of the three months of solitary confinement, where Faiz composed and memorized the short poem that now stands first in *Dast-e Sabā*. Kiernan's translation of it reads:

> If ink and pen are snatched from me, shall I
> Who have dipped my finger in my heart's blood complain—
> Or if they seal my tongue, when I have made
> A mouth of every round link of my chain?

and his note on it tells us that it is 'one of several poems that Faiz composed in solitary confinement, when deprived of writing materials, and was only able to write down several months later.' Ishaque says 'Faiz Sahib used to say that in those days he felt greatly inspired and all manner of themes would come to mind; some poems he could not remember afterwards, but those he could are included in *Dast-e Sabā*.' He then lists seven of them. Kiernan's selection includes three of these: the one just quoted, 'This Hour of Chain and Gibbet' (*Tauq-o-dār kā mausam*) and the *ghazal*, 'Among Twilight Embers' (*Shafaq kī rākh mēṅ jal bujh gayā sitāra-e shām*). All three express courage in the face of every danger, and confidence in what the future will bring. Thus in 'This Hour of Chain and Gibbet', he calls the time:

> This hour of chain and gibbet and rejoicing
> Hour of necessity and hour of choice.

And tells his captors:

> At your command the cage, but not the garden's
> Red rose-fire, when its radiant hour begins;

No noose can catch the dawn wind's whirling feet,
The spring's bright hour falls prisoner to no net.

Others will see if I do not, that hour
Of singing nightingale and splendid flower.

For some reason, Faiz himself in the essay just quoted is silent about these first three months, and speaks of only two periods—the Hyderabad one (June 1951 to July 1953) and the Montgomery one (July 1953 to April 1955).

He says of the verse of the two-year Hyderabad period, that it is dominated by the—'sense of wonder', and instances one of the last poems in *Dast-e Sabā*, 'A Prison Nightfall', (*Zindāṅ kī ēk shām*) as an example:

Step by step by its twisted stairway
Of constellations, night descends

Graciously on that roof's high crest
The moonlight's exquisite fingers gleam;

ဢ

One thought keeps running in my heart—
Such nectar life is at this instant,
Those who mix the tyrants' poisons
Can never, now or tomorrow, win . . .

Ishaque says of this period that 'all the physical comforts that are possible in jail were provided,' and that although there were a number of charges against them that carried the death penalty, the 'conspirators' were in excellent morale and confident that somehow victory would be theirs. But Faiz, on 14 July 1952, suffered a heavy blow when his brother, who had come to visit him in jail, died of a sudden heart attack.

In July 1953 when Faiz, Ishaque and others were allocated to Montgomery Jail, Faiz was first sent for two months to Karachi to undergo medical treatment, and it was not until September 1953 that he began his almost continuous stay in Montgomery. (For three weeks in March 1954, Ishaque tells us, they were sent to Lahore to have their teeth attended to.) Faiz says that these years were a period of 'boredom and fatigue'. Almost all the poems in Zindāṅ Nāmā were written during these two years.

Ishaque says that Faiz felt the constraints of prison life in Montgomery all the more keenly, because in hospital in Karachi, he had been relatively free. 'His friends had no difficulty in coming to see him and these were reasons why he came to feel intensely the blessings of freedom.' When he came to Montgomery Jail, therefore, he felt the extremity of the contrast. He began, too, to feel more keenly what must be the plight of other political prisoners in other countries. His salute to the freedom fighters of Africa, 'Africa, Come Back', belongs to this collection. Already in Dast-e Sabā, he had written 'To the Students of Iran Who gave their Lives in the Struggle for Peace and Freedom'—expurgated in Kiernan to read, 'To Some Foreign Students' . . . and to omit all references to Iran (and with an anxious note '. . . this poem should be taken in a general sense, not as referring to any particular place or time,'[11]) Ishaque says that in Montgomery Jail, they read in the American periodical Time, an account of the shooting of Iranian students in prison, printed alongside pictures of the place where they had been killed. 'Faiz feels a special love for (Iran), the country of Saadi and Hafiz. He was upset and disturbed for several days,' and eventually gave expression to his feelings in a poem 'The Last Night', in which he portrays the . . . 'thoughts that pass through the mind of a prisoner on the night before his execution next morning.' (This poem, for some reason is, as far as I can ascertain, not included in any of Faiz's collections.)

In Zindāṅ Nāmā too is a poem, 'We Who Were Killed in the Dark Streets', written in May 1954 after reading the letters of Julius and Ethel Rosenberg, the American couple who were executed, despite worldwide protests, after being found guilty (wrongly, as many believed) of betraying atomic secrets to the Soviet Union. Ishaque regards the poem Darīča ('The Window') as the most complete expression of Faiz's mental state at that time. Faiz himself singles out 'O City of Lights' as typical of this period. Both are included in Poems by Faiz by Kiernan.

'The Window' begins:

In my barred window is many a cross

and goes on to list some of the things that are crucified on these crosses:

On one the heaven's spring cloud is crucified
On one the radiant noon is crucified

Yet every day they return, revived to be crucified again.

Zindāṅ Nāmā is only the third of Faiz's eight collections of his poems, but the first three collections provide ample materials for a study of all that is best in his poetry, and I shall make only occasional references to later poems.

I have hitherto spoken mainly of Faiz's political poems, because I believe these to be his best. But as I said at the outset, there are also poems of other kinds. Some of the best are his love poems, often, though not always, in *ghazal* form. The very first poem in *Naqsh-e Faryādī*, comprising only two couplets and headed simply *Ash'ār* (couplets) but in Kiernan's translation entitled *Last Night*, is one such poem. This translation reads:

> Last night your faded memory filled my heart
> Like spring's calm advent in the wilderness,
> Like the soft desert footfalls of the breeze,
> Like peace somehow coming to one in sickness.

Another short poem, also in *Naqsh-e Faryādī*, is in Kiernan's translation, headed 'Her Fingers' and reads:

> The softness of her fingers is in this dawn-wind's hand;
> And as it stirs, the fancy comes today to my mind
> That her soft hands are searching through the ranks of our friends
> To find what are their heartaches, to feel where are their wounds.

A *ghazal* of five couplets in *Zindāṅ Nāmā*, unusually simple in its language and with a long, strongly rhythmic line

$$- - \cup\cup - - \,|\, - \cup\cup - \,|\, - - \cup\cup - - \,|\, - \cup\cup -$$

begins:

> When are you not with me in memory?
> When is your hand not in mine?
> A thousand thanks that as night follows night, no night is a night of separation.

The *ghazal* ends:

> If you gamble in the game of love, stake as much as you like—why be afraid?
> If you win, what happiness! And even if you lose, all is not lost.

Another poem of two couplets in *Dast-e Tah-e Sang* is headed *Tanhā'ī* ('Solitude') and reads:

> Today loneliness like a well-tried friend
> Has come to be my evening wine-pourer.
> We sit together waiting for the moon to rise
> And set your image gleaming in every shadow.

Finally, there are poems, which are neither political nor poems of love. It is a striking feature of his poetry that he is not afraid to portray in a poem, any emotion that he feels deeply. Such poems are clearly not 'propaganda' (and this allows the 'Men of Good Taste' to approve of them) and though most have nothing in them to offend progressives either, some of them do. For progressives—or at any rate, the most puritanical among them—it is a cardinal sin to despair. Well, Faiz sometimes felt a keen sense of despair, and since he felt it, he expressed it. His poem *Yās* ('Despair') is on that theme and nothing else, and contains no sop to the puritan progressives (such as, for example, an expression of regret, confession of weakness and so on); it belongs to the late 1920s, the days of the great world economic crisis, days in which, says Faiz, graduates looked in vain for employment, 'days when suddenly children's laughter died, when ruined peasants left their fields to work as labourers in the cities, and when respectable women took to prostitution.' It was written in the period before Faiz became a revolutionary, but he quotes it in his foreword to his fourth collection, *Dast-e Tah-e Sang*, published in 1965, without any adverse comment, and evidently did not include it in those poems of his youth which (as we shall see) he regarded as not reaching a 'tolerable' standard.

Faiz himself says that 'The period after *Zindān Nāmā* was one of some mental turmoil. I had lost my profession of journalism. I had again to go to jail. The period of martial law arrived. . . .' (In September 1955, Faiz had resumed his post as editor of the *Pakistan Times*, but in December 1958, in the early days of Ayub Khan's martial law regime, he was again imprisoned and the *Pakistan Times* and associated newspapers were in

1959 taken over by the military regime.) Faiz continues, '. . . and in the
mind and atmosphere of that environment alike, conditions gave rise to
a feeling that once again, the road ahead was to some extent blocked and
one must look for other ways forward.' It was a period, he says, of
'stagnation and waiting'. He is writing, presumably somewhere around
1964 or 1965, because although the piece is not dated, it appears as a sort
of foreword to *Dast-e Tah-e Sang* and, one imagines, was written to serve
as such. He continued to live and write for another twenty years, and one
wonders whether he ever really emerged from the mental state he
describes. At all events, 1955 marks the beginning of a new period. To
the best of my knowledge, he never wrote any account of his development
over these years to continue his account of the period 1928 to 1955, so
we do not know what he thought about it.

I have already said that I shall not discuss more than an occasional
example of his verse of this period. I shall, however, say something of his
role both as a poet and as a prominent figure in the public life of Pakistan;
and this requires some further discussion of the 1934 to 1955 period as
well.

At the beginning, I said that it was not solely the excellence of his
poetry that won him the pre-eminent position he came to occupy.
We should note here, some of the other factors that contributed to
his standing. Generalizing them, one might say that Faiz was always,
both in politics and in literature, sufficiently identified and sufficiently
unidentified with a number of different groupings to get the best of a
number of worlds. To say this is not to question his sincerity—a quality
which is not the exclusive property, either of the committed or of the
uncommitted—but simply to state a fact. Let us first take the literary
field.

Faiz was Punjabi, but like most Punjabi Muslim writers, he always
chose to write in Urdu which, since the decline in Persian, has been the
dominant language of culture of the Muslim community throughout the
subcontinent. (The few poems which he wrote in Punjabi towards the
end of his life, do not significantly alter the picture). His attainments in
Urdu were such, as to excite both the pride of his fellow-Punjabis and
the admiration of the *ahl-e zabān*—the people of Urdu mother tongue.
The first were proud that one of them could write Urdu well; the second
admired the exceptional attainments of one who was not one of them;
and no poet of Urdu mother tongue could have won this kind of esteem
from both publics.

Secondly, as we have already seen, he wrote in a way, which enabled him to appeal to each of the (broadly speaking) three different audiences for poetry.

Two factors outside the field of poetry also contributed to his prestige. Firstly, in 1941, he married an English wife; and secondly although his sympathies were with the poor, he was not one of them, and lived a decent, respectable, reasonably comfortable life, which his respectable contemporaries recognized with a feeling of satisfaction as being very much like their own. (In my experience, these essentially snobbish attitudes held by people in South Asia—and, for that matter, elsewhere—are not perceived as being in any way inconsistent with advanced revolutionary views.)

Faiz's imprisonment as one of the accused in the Rawalpindi Conspiracy Case brought, along with the hardships, an enhanced fame; so that when he came out of jail, he had a larger and more appreciative public than when he went in.

Finally, by this time he was the leading progressive poet in Pakistan, a sort of personal embodiment, unique in Pakistan, of the by now, virtually defunct Progressive Writers' Association.

Thus conditions that came into existence independently of his will or his contriving, brought him to the fore. He was a highly intelligent man and, as the words I have quoted above imply, now began to take stock of his new position.

It seems to me that from the time of his release after the Rawalpindi Conspiracy trial, Faiz made up his mind that he was not again going to do anything that could land him in prison, and that he was going to lead as comfortable a life as possible, proclaiming the same message in his poetry as he had always done, remaining in the limelight, but refraining from any dangerous political activity. At all events, he suffered imprisonment only once after that, when Ayub Khan established his martial law regime in 1958. (He was in jail from December 1958 to April 1959.) I am told that far from being imprisoned on Ayub Khan's instructions, he was imprisoned without Ayub Khan's knowledge by an over-zealous subordinate, who thought that Faiz's imprisonment would please the Americans, and that pleasing the Americans was an important part of Ayub's policy. My informant tells me that when the officially approved organization of Pakistani writers protested, Ayub Khan told them that he had given no orders for Faiz's imprisonment and gave immediate instructions for his release. After that, until the end of his life, Faiz lived a life of considerable material comfort, surrounded by rich and influential friends, who would entertain him lavishly and treat him to the whisky of which he was so fond.

His position in the political and social life of Pakistan was somewhat similar to his position in poetry—one of an avoidance of full commitment to any clear cut stand and one which therefore, enabled him to steer clear of anyone's strong disapproval. Always on the left, but never either a Communist Party member or so close a fellow-traveller as to be identified with it, his stand may be fairly described as a blend of Marxism with a kind of secular Pakistani nationalism, a blend of a kind which made him close enough to the communists to win their praise and respect, but not so close as to forfeit the friendship of the more liberal elements of the Pakistani establishment, or indeed of that establishment as a whole, in its more liberal moments. In international politics too, he came to occupy a similar position, especially during the years when Pakistan moved from its one-time stand of clear and uncomplicated alignment with the West in the early days of the Cold War. Thus, Faiz indeed contributed, both as a poet and as a citizen, to the cause of peace and friendship between nations, but one doubts all the same whether he would have been awarded the Lenin Peace Prize in 1962, and whether Pakistani opinion would have been so pleased at his receiving the award, had he been either closer or less close to either of the two positions between which he stood. His standing internationally contributed further, both to his fame and to his comfort. During his sojourns in the Soviet Union, he was provided with all the comforts of the life to which he had accustomed himself—and so also, though less frequently, in China, Cuba, the USA and other countries he visited.

Other features of Faiz's behaviour contributed to this sort of blurring of the lines. Kiernan says that in his personal relationships, he is famous for his silences and one could say the same of him in the political field. Even his friends would, I think, find it hard to tell how far these were the silences of uncertainty and how far the deliberately ambiguous silences of political tactics. His travels abroad had something of the same character, so that one of our mutual acquaintances once said to me in some exasperation, 'When Faiz ought to stay in Pakistan, he comes out, and when he ought to stay out he goes back.'

His acceptance of government posts, in the conditions of relative political liberty, which existed until 1951, is, I think, both understandable and justifiable. His continuing acceptance of them in later years is, to say the least, rather less so. Under the Z.A. Bhutto regime of 1971–77, he was Cultural Adviser to Bhutto and continued to hold this post until Bhutto's overthrow by Ziaul Haq, long after Bhutto's savage and vindictive nature was inflicting imprisonment, torture and humiliation of the most shameful kind upon those who crossed him. In 1977, when General Ziaul Haq again established martial law, Faiz thought it best to leave the country; but nobody forced him to: he went of his own free will to take up a well-paid post of editor of a Soviet-supported literary journal. He remained abroad until returning to settle in Lahore in November 1982, two years before his death.

All this brings one back to his role as a poet, for this sort of ambiguity represents, in a way, a somewhat novel development of an old tradition. In the old quasi-feudal autocratic society, the *ghazal* poet was, amongst other things, the licensed critic of the establishment, and was protected by two generally accepted conventions. The first of these was the nature of the *ghazal* itself, which permitted many of its verses to be interpreted simultaneously on several planes of meaning, some more 'dangerous' than others. The second was the convention that *in his poetry* he had a right to be as unambiguously rebellious as he pleased—but at the price of having his words regarded as 'only poetry', and not to be taken seriously outside the poetic symposium—the *mushāirā*—where they were uttered. Faiz took full advantage of this time-honoured convention. But he did more than that. Whether by conscious design or not, he, in some degree succeeded in extending the range of operation of this convention beyond the bounds of the *mushāirā* into society at large, and brought into being a situation in which his role as a poet enhanced his role as politician, and his role as a politician enhanced his role as a poet—but in politics too, reaping the same advantages and paying the same price for them as the classical poet did, in his more restricted field of operation. (Not that he pushed his luck too far. I was intrigued when a banker, a co-speaker with myself at a condolence meeting for Faiz in London soon after his death, said that he disagreed with Faiz's political views—views which, however, he had never heard him express except in poetry.) Given the present stage of development of Pakistani society, to do what Faiz did was not too difficult a task, but Faiz's success was all the same remarkable. And having said all that, one must add that Faiz's poetry reflects very faithfully the feelings of vast numbers of his radically inclined fellow-countrymen, including most of those whose favourite arena of radicalism is the drawing-room.

This, as it may appear, rather harsh-sounding judgement can be supported both by the similar judgement of his close friend and fellow-'conspirator' Muhammad Ishaque, which I shall quote below, and, more importantly, by reference to his poetry.

There is a lot of Faiz's poetry that does not appeal to me; but I should hasten to add that I can say the same of almost all the poetry I have ever read. I read a poet's work, feeling as I do so that much of it is eminently forgettable, and some is enjoyable—and, occasionally, with a thrill of delight, 'This is real poetry.' I feel this, for instance, in reading Mir, whose *best* poetry I love; and I think that it is a poet's best poetry that he deserves to be judged by. Mir's best poetry puts him in the first rank of poets. I don't think that Faiz's does.

To do him justice, Faiz was of the same opinion, at any rate about his first published collection *Naqsh-e Faryādī*. He begins his foreword:

> The publication of this collection is a sort of admission of defeat. A few of its poems are perhaps tolerable, but a few tolerable poems don't make up a publishable book. In principle, I should have waited until I had accumulated poems of this kind in sufficient number, but it has begun to seem pointless to wait any longer.

Later in the same foreword, he speaks of 'the commercial reason' for not omitting his early verse. He says that the poems in the first part of the collection (occupying 36 pages of its total of 72) are mostly love poems (described, as we have seen, as a *mū'ayyan* ['established'] emotion which made it easy to write in established forms). He says that he experienced it when he was young, and adds that 'the roots of the experiences of youth are not deep'—on which one feels inclined to comment, 'Speak for yourself.' However, the roots of the experiences which these early poems of Faiz express, are indeed not deep, and one feels that when he and Kiernan made a selection for the UNESCO-sponsored translation, they were right to exclude almost all of them. Even the few that they included cannot for the most part be numbered among his best poems.

This seems to be the point at which to say that 'commercial reasons' continued to weigh with Faiz throughout his life. The sort of ambiguity which one encounters in every aspect of his life is in evidence here too. He wrote verse which appealed, and, one feels, was consciously designed to appeal, to each of the three audiences I have described, and perhaps all the more so to the first two—the 'traditional' and the 'modern'—

because in general he took his stand with the progressives, and his 'traditional' and 'modern' poems therefore made a greater impact than would have been the case, if all his verse had been in a single style.

Of poetic tradition, he wrote towards the end of his preface to *Naqsh-e Faryādī*, 'I have not thought it appropriate to depart unnecessarily from traditional styles' adding that he had made only minor departures from the traditional rules of metre and rhyme. 'Quite right!' one thinks. 'He has had the good sense to reject the view that the traditional forms, and above all the *ghazal*, are outmoded, 'feudal' forms that no progressive poet should employ.' But when one looks at his *ghazals*, one cannot help feeling that along with good and effective ones in which the best *ghazal* traditions are used to express age-old but still powerfully relevant feeling, or are without violence, adapted to wholly contemporary themes, there are others of the kind that any competent versifier could have written at any period of the *ghazal's* history. One such *ghazal* is that in *Zindāṅ Nāmā* which begins:

گلوں میں رنگ بھرے بادِ نو بہار چلے

Let colour fill the flowers, let the breeze of early spring blow

It is one in the repertoire of one of South Asia's most popular *ghazal* singers, Mehdi Hasan, and, one feels, finds a place in it because it expresses in easily intelligible language, well-worn and wholly unremarkable themes to which any popular audience can at once respond. Any *ghazal* which a singer as popular as Mehdi Hasan sings, gains a currency which contributes substantially to the fame of its author, and one feels of not a few of Faiz's *ghazals* that he wrote them for him, and a number of other famous singers, with that sole aim in view and not because he had anything much to say in them.

One has much the same mixed feelings about poems on which Faiz's appeal to the moderns must have been based. Faiz knew very well that a progressive poet has emotions which are shared by others who would not call themselves progressive but are not the less valid and not the less valuable for that, and that these can often be most successfully expressed in forms (including free verse) which had no place in the classical canon. Poems like 'Solitude' and 'Despair', which I have already quoted, are good examples of the best that he produced in this style. But in others, the 'modern' trappings seem to be everything. Thus in 'Evening', the overall

impression is one of outlandish, obscure, and pointless comparisons—
'Every tree is like a temple, a ruined . . . temple'. . . . 'The sky is like a
(Hindu) priest. . . . It is as though some magician is seated behind a
curtain. . . .' Here and in other poems Faiz seems to be imitating the
unnecessarily difficult diction, and the fashionable, pretentious,
culturally snobbish and pointless obscurity which characterizes the worst
of Ezra Pound, T.S. Eliot and their imitators, and where what is said,
wherever it is intelligible, seems to be not worth saying. And there is no
doubt that there were, and are, among Faiz's readers, quite a number
who like this kind of poem for exactly these spurious qualities. Faiz
himself evidently liked this poem, for he included it in the selection
which Kiernan translated. Kiernan, perhaps, was less impressed, for he
notes on the comparison of the sky with a Hindu priest, 'I give the
meaning as explained by Faiz, but the image, taken straightforwardly, is
a curious one.'

Faiz's poetic diction, one feels, is often just a bit too much. What is
wrong with it is well illustrated by his remarks already quoted, that the
enforced leisure of imprisonment gave him the opportunity 'to devote
more attention to adorning the bride of poetry.' This pretentious manner
mars a lot of his verse. Many in the audience of a popular poet are
dazzled by poetry that abounds in Persianized vocabulary and Persian
constructions, and Faiz is all too fond of high-flown language; and the
result is sometimes ridiculous, as where the barking of dogs is expressed
as *ghaugha-e sagān* which may be reasonably translated as 'the clamour of
canines.' Even in his best poems, one finds this kind of thing. To describe
freedom's dawn as *shab-gazīdā* ('night-bitten') is disconcerting rather
than striking. If he had left 'the bride of poetry' to exercise her appeal
by beauty unadorned we should have had better poetry.

The content of his verse, too, leaves one with a sense of something
lacking. I have already remarked on his comment that the roots of
youthful love are not deep. Where Faiz is concerned, judging by his
poetry, his love never did become deep. His beloved is, to me, a singularly
unattractive person. In the appealing *ghazal* in *Zindāṅ Nāmā*, which I
quoted above there is a couplet that reads:

The field of love is not a king's court.
Here no one asks your name and lineage.
The lover has no 'name' and love knows no cast.

But if this was Faiz's view of the lover, he seems to have taken a different view of the beloved. His beloved is not simply a woman; she is a lady—a lady with plenty of money and plenty of leisure to spend on make-up, fine clothes and rare perfume, and it is these, rather than any intrinsic qualities (for he rarely mentions any) that Faiz seems to find attractive. No wonder that in 'Freedom's Dawn' it is the restraining arms of rich ladies, reclining in their sumptuously appointed bedchambers (khvāb-gāh) that tried to hold him and his comrades back from participating in the freedom struggle. Nor does Faiz's discovery announced in 'Love Do Not Ask' impress me much. The realization that there are other things in life besides love of women, which must engage a mature man's attention, and that no one can be forever insensitive to the sufferings of the poor and oppressed, is surely not so world-shaking that it needs to be announced with a fanfare of trumpets. However, my rather lukewarm response to this poem reflects my own personal development, in which concern for the poor and oppressed preceded the experience of passionate love for a woman, and it never at any time occurred to me that there was any conflict between the two. I realize that this is not everyone's experience, and that others, who are not lacking in the capacity for wider human sympathies can go through a stage in which these sympathies are dormant, and love for a woman can be so all-consuming that nothing else seems to matter—even in a country where stark poverty confronts one inescapably on every side, as it does not, or need not, in the developed countries of the world. I suppose that I also expected more of a poet who was at home in the ghazal tradition, in which love is all-embracing and it is taken for granted that love of woman (or man), love for humankind, love for God, love for high ideals—all these are aspects of a single, indivisible love. Faiz seems to attain to this realization rather tardily in 'Two Loves', and that too after the relapse announced in 'Poetry's Theme'.

The other of his 'Two Loves', his country and its poor and oppressed inhabitants, is portrayed, like his lady beloved, in terms of external appearances; and in this portrayal, Faiz shows a propensity to dwell upon scenes that evoke disgust rather than on things that arouse sympathy— let alone that admiration and solidarity which are the indispensable basis of the revolutionary social change that Faiz preaches. Thus in 'Love, Do Not Ask' what he contrasts with the charms of his beloved are diseased bodies, with pus flowing from festering sores. In 'Dogs', where dogs are clearly a (not very apt) symbol of miserable, oppressed humanity, the picture is one of people who live and die in filth, begging and stealing in order to live, bearing every humiliation, and when they fight at all, fighting one another.

Ishaque, then, is right when he says that 'the blood and sweat of the working people of Pakistan' is not much in evidence in Faiz's poetry, and that 'his poetry still has to emerge from the drawing room, the school and the college and spread to the streets, markets, fields and factories.' It is in the drawing-rooms and colleges that Faiz felt most at home, where it is my experience that revolutionaries (both those who see themselves as such, only in fantasy and those who are more fully committed) rarely want to know the real human beings whose cause they champion and whose role they seem to see (consciously or unconsciously) as that of admiringly applauding them and doing as they tell them.

Faiz's rather lukewarm style of loving and his concern never to commit himself too unequivocally seems to have entered into his soul, so that even in poems where the expression of stronger feeling would have posed no risk, that feeling is surprisingly absent. His poem on Iqbal, an incomparably powerful influence both for good and bad, says almost nothing, though it was written after Faiz had formed his progressive outlook. A literal translation reads:

> To our country came a sweet-voiced faqir. He came, and passed through— singing his ghazals in his own style. He filled the empty roads with people, and the deserted taverns began to come to life. Only a few had the vision to penetrate to him, but his song went deep into the hearts of all. Now that king in beggar's clothing has gone far away, and the roads of our country are again despondent. A few dear ones have one or two visions, but his song dwells in the hearts of all. The beauties of that song will never fade. Its exuberance, its fervour, its deep feeling—this song is like the fierce flame of a volcano. Caught in its leaping fire, the heart of the wind of non-existence melts [whatever that means]. It is like a lamp that does not fear the rage of the desert wind, like a candle oblivious of the coming of morning.

A poem, in short, that could apply to any poet who exercised a great influence on his contemporaries, and tells us nothing whatsoever about the qualities which made him great and influential, or about Faiz's assessment of him and his message.

Even where we would expect the expression of deeply felt personal emotion, one does not find it—and if Faiz felt it, he did not succeed in conveying it. His 1982 poem in memory of his comrade in imprisonment, Major Muhammad Ishaque, has echoes of Ghalib's lament for his dearly loved adopted son Arif, with its *radīf 'ko'ī din aur'*, and abounds in stilted phrases that convey no real emotion.

Faiz did not rely simply on fortunate circumstances to maintain and enhance his popularity. He and his admirers created myths about his political commitment in which truth mingles with stories which, if not wholly untrue, include substantial elements of 'suppression of the true and suggestion of the false.'

Thus, there is much popularity to be gained outside Pakistan if people know that, in Kiernan's words, Faiz had been jailed 'sometimes', 'in solitary confinement . . . deprived of writing materials', and on one occasion on a charge that could have carried the death penalty. These things make a special appeal in Britain, for once a subject people has actually been victorious in its struggle for independence, the British generally feel a retrospective sympathy for that struggle which they were far from feeling at the time; and in the same way they have a ready sympathy for political prisoners when it is no longer they who are doing the imprisoning. This is a deserved popularity—and it remains unalloyed if one does not know, what is also true, that the conditions in which he lived in jail were, for three-and-three-quarters of his four-year term, not anything like as harsh as Kiernan's words would naturally lead his English readers to suppose. They would be surprised to learn what Faiz's fellow-prisoners, Sajjad Zaheer, and former Major, Muhammad Ishaque, tell their Urdu readers in their foreword to *Zindāṅ Nāmā*. Thus Sajjad Zaheer recalls how, when Faiz's second collection of verse *Dast-e Sabā* was published, 'we got permission from the authorities to hold a party in which all of us prisoners congratulated Faiz on its publication.' Ishaque writes of conditions in Hyderabad Jail, where they were held during the first stage of court proceedings against them:

> The court building was inside the jail. The court sat from 8 a.m. to 12 noon. Saturdays and Sundays were free. In the afternoon, our lawyers would come to consult us from time to time, but the rest of the time was our own. . . . We made our own provision for our meals. Two prisoners . . . who were excellent cooks had been assigned the duty of cooking for us, and we ate in regular style, as though we were dining in the officers' mess. . . . In the evenings we would play volley ball or badminton . . . mushāirās, qavvālīs and dramas generally took place in our compound. When we went to see Sajjad Zaheer on our free mornings, he would entertain us to coffee and biscuits and we would talk about literature and politics.

I have already quoted his statement that in Hyderabad Jail 'we had every bodily comfort which is possible in a jail.' In Montgomery Jail, he says, 'we had pretty well all the facilities we had in Hyderabad.' I shall say more about all this below.

Similarly, the impression has been given that Faiz was forced into exile when Ziaul Haq came to power, though this was not so.

An almost ludicrous example of what can result from this myth-making can be found in Naomi Lazard's introduction, headed 'Translating Faiz', to her recently published translations of Faiz's selected poems.[12] After a greatly exaggerated picture of Faiz's standing throughout the South Asian subcontinent ('Anyone who knows any poetry at all in that vast region knows of Faiz') she says:

> Faiz became a spokesman for his people in another way too. Instead of struggling for a literary career, instead of taking high posts as lecturer or professor, he dedicated himself to teaching illiterate people. He was blasé in his disregard for the blandishments of life. He identified himself with the masses of the poor, the exploited, the victims.

Such statements, based, one must presume, on what Naomi Lazard was told by Faiz himself, can only provoke sarcastic laughter in those who know the truth.

Faiz was also at pains to conceal as far as possible personal habits, which he thought potential admirers would disapprove of. In the sense which 'everyone' bears in such statements, everyone knew that he drank; but he was at pains not to let this general knowledge become more general than it already was. When Kiernan was preparing his translation for publication, I was shown a draft of his introduction in which there was a very mild reference to Faiz's drinking. I spoke of this to Faiz, who told me that there would be no such reference in the finally approved draft; and, sure enough, the published introduction includes no such reference.

All of this has given rise to some bitterness in those progressives who avowed the same political views as Faiz but were denied, or denied themselves, the opportunities to combine this avowal with a life of such material comfort as he enjoyed. One of them told me emphatically, 'Faiz has absolutely nothing to do with the mass of the people.' And another: 'Faiz will never set foot in any house where the floors are not covered with the most expensive carpets.' When he was approaching the end of his self-imposed exile, some young progressives in Islamabad alleged to me that he had now begun to write poetry in which there was nothing to which General Ziaul Haq could object.

I have written these last pages because I think that they deal with an aspect of Faiz and his place in the cultural and political life of Pakistan, which needs to be understood. But having said that I would stress that there are even more important things that should be understood.

Firstly, even if Faiz can be fairly accused of a too wholehearted concern with building his own image and seeking his own safety and comfort, it ill becomes people who have never had to experience imprisonment for their political beliefs, or lived under the threat of a death sentence to adopt a lofty moral tone towards one who has. Those who have not undergone the stress of that experience can only *hope* that if they did, they would have the strength to emerge from it ready to react with more consistent courage than Faiz seems to have reacted. If for most of the years of his imprisonment he lived in relative comfort, imprisonment is nevertheless imprisonment; and moreover, not all his time in prison was spent in such comfort. The solitary confinement in which he had been held for a full three months, Ishaque tells us, 'had had so profound an effect upon him that even after he came to Hyderabad he could not bear to be alone.'

Secondly, the most important thing about Faiz is his poetry. It is Faiz the poet, much more than Faiz the man, that has made a more significant impact on Pakistanis, both in Pakistan and in the numerous other countries where they have settled, and upon thousands of others in the Urdu-speaking community; and there is no reason to think that this impact will not continue many years after his death.

Thirdly, if the best poetry is written by those who, like Mir, for example, live a life in which they consistently feel, think and act as they and their audience would wish them to, and somehow convey this unmistakably in what they write, there are also poets who present themselves not as they are but as they wish they *could* be, and where that aspiration is strongly and sincerely felt, the poetry it inspires is, or can be, good poetry.

And finally, if Faiz's warmest admirers are not the effective revolutionary force one would like them to be, they are nevertheless, in the Urdu phrase—*ghanīmat*—a good deal better than nothing. Faiz's poetry gives their feelings and aspirations the expression that they need and deserve, and it will long continue to inspire others with a hatred of oppression, a sympathy with the downtrodden, and the desire for a better world.

Notes

1. Faiz was not only a poet, but a literary critic of more than average perceptiveness. His collection of critical essays, *Mīzān*, and particularly its outstandingly good article *Sharar* deserves more attention than it generally receives. See Faiz Ahmed Faiz, *Mīzān*, Lahore: Nashireen, 1962, p. 229, Print.

2. The titles of Faiz's eight collections defy translation, and I give their titles in the original mainly for the convenience of readers who know Urdu and already have some acquaintance with Faiz's work. Nearly all—perhaps all—are words quoted from, or based upon, an Urdu or Persian couplet of another poet. *Naqsh-e Faryādī* (which Kiernan translates as *Remonstrance* but which carries something of the sense of an appeal against injustice) combines the first two words of the first *ghazal* in Ghalib's dīvān.

3. *Poems by Faiz*, p. 9 [editor's note: translated by V.G. Kiernan, publication details not mentioned].

4. The introduction is more reticent than one would like, partly for reasons I shall discuss in the essay and partly because *Poems by Faiz* was sponsored by the Pakistan government, and it was evidently thought necessary to tread delicately in order not to jeopardize its chance of publication. All the same it has much useful information.

5. Jointly published by Vanguard Books, Lahore and South Publications n.d.

6. Kiernan gives the date 1943. It seems he worked from a second edition, with added poems (Nos. 14, 15 and 16) which now, in Faiz's collected verse, are included in the second collection.

7. *Dast-e Sabā*, 'The hand of the breeze' aptly translated by Kiernan as *Fingers of the Wind*, is a reference to a couplet of Hafiz which Faiz quotes immediately after his foreword, and which means 'The breath of the breeze of morning will bring fragrance, and the old world will again become young.'

8. The information in this paragraph is taken from an extract from an article prefixed to the complete (or nearly complete) collection of Faiz's verse published under the title of *Nuskhahā'ē Vafā* (roughly, Records of Commitment) by Educational Publishing House, Delhi, 1986.

9. I wonder whether this is in fact so. Both Faiz and Kiernan were in India at the time (as I was), and had the political awareness to understand what was happening. The leaders of the Indian National Congress had resolved to start a mass struggle against the British, but before they could organize it, they were all imprisoned, and the powerful movement which erupted was deprived of their leadership. This is not the situation which this poem describes.

10. *Dast-e Tah-e Sang*, 'The hand (trapped) under the stone'. Kiernan gives it the English title *Duress*. The words are taken from a verse of Ghalib which is quoted in full to form the concluding couplets of one of Faiz's own poems.

11. This is the most deplorable example of the voluntary reticence and self-censorship which is discernible in the Introduction and elsewhere in the book. Iran would almost certainly have vetoed the publication of a book containing such a poem.

12. Naomi Lazard, *The True Subject: Selected Poems of Faiz Ahmed Faiz*, Princeton University Press, 1988, Print. The two quotations are from p. 11.

A FEW MORE DAYS

Original: *Čaṅd roz aur mērī jān* from *Naqsh-e Faryādī* (1941)
TRANSLATOR: DAUD KAMAL

A few days more—my love—only a few days.
We are constrained to breathe this miasmic air
In the trackless jungle of oppression.
Let us try to endure it a little longer—
This wolf-torment, this cobra-grief.
We know that suffering is our ancestral heritage
And we also know that we are helpless.
Captive bodies, chained emotions.
Shackled minds, and strangled speech.
And yet, in spite of all this,
We go on living.
Life is like the tattered coat of a beggar
To which, every day, a new rag of pain is added.
But the epoch of cruelty is coming to an end.
Be patient a little longer—
Our salvation is at hand.

The present is a burnt-out wilderness:
We have to live—but not like this.
The cold-blooded tyranny of our persecutors:
We have to bear it—but not like this.
Your beauty veiled by the dust
Of so many injustices
And the countless frustrations
Of my brief-lived youth.
Moonlit nights—sterility of desire—
The ash-covered contours of the heart.
The body on the torturer's rack.
A few days more—my love—only a few days.

4

TRADITION AND INNOVATION IN FAIZ AHMED FAIZ

Faiz Ahmed Faiz (1911–1984) is widely acclaimed as a significant twentieth century poet of Urdu, and an understanding of contemporary Urdu poetry is not complete without a recognition of the importance of his work. The other major voices of the post-Iqbal period include Josh Malihabadi, Firaq Gorakhpuri, Meeraji, and N.M. Rashed, who had also influenced the contemporary literary scene in their own right in the last few decades. Nonetheless, Faiz gained in popularity over the years, and an understanding of what he had inherited from the tradition, and what he added to it by way of the socio-political content is in fact essential for an overall appreciation of the significance of his contribution to the last fifty years of Urdu poetry.

Faiz Ahmed Faiz was born in Sialkot, West Punjab, received his education at Lahore, and started his career as a lecturer in English. Later, he served in the army for five years, and in 1946 was made Editor of the *Pakistan Times*. In 1951, he was arrested along with some other political and military figures on charges of conspiracy aimed at overthrowing the government, and remained for some time in danger of a death-sentence, but was later released in 1955. He had socialistic leanings from the beginning, and remained an active member of the Progressive Writers' Association during the nineteen-thirties and forties. Faiz published seven collections of poems. His collected works, *Sārē Sukhan Hamārē*, appeared from London in 1982, and *Nuskhahā'ē Vafā* from Lahore and Delhi in 1984. In 1962, he was awarded the Lenin Peace Prize, the first South-Asian poet to receive this honour.

Faiz, in spite of his leftist leanings, was not a rebel poet in the real sense of the word. He was an admirer of the classical imagery of Urdu *ghazal*, and his style bears traces of the language of both Ghalib and Iqbal. He had accepted and assimilated much that was in the tradition and used the classical conventions and imagery with such depth and ingenuity that his poetry reflects at once the heritage of the past and the quest and restlessness of the present.

Faiz was essentially a lyrical poet. He has written both *ghazals* and *nazms*, a comparatively new verse form in Urdu poetry, based on the Western models. Here we will quote from both his *ghazals* and *nazms*, simply to demonstrate his introduction of the *ghazal* imagery to the comparatively new genre of *nazm*.

These lines are from his *qat'a*, 'Because We Live':[1]

hamārē dam sē hai ku'ē junūṅ mēṅ ab bhī khajil
abā-e shaikh-o-qabā-e amīr-o-tāj-e shahī
hamiṅ sē sunnat-e Mansūr-o-Qais zindā hai
hamiṅ sē bāqī hai gul-dāmanī-o-kaj kulahī

Still, because we live, folk in Madman's Alley can laugh at
Shaikh and Shāh and Amīr, mantle and ermine and crown.
We are the heirs of Mansūr the God-crazed, Majnūṅ the smile-crazed; we
Keep from extinction the gay cap and the flower-chequered skirt.

Note the words 'madman's alley', 'Shaikh', Mansūr', 'Majnūṅ', 'gay cap', 'flower-chequered skirt', and 'extinction'. These are all drawn from classical imagery. Majnūṅ is the legendary lover of Lailā, and Mansūr the celebrated heretic who was executed in Baghdad for his boldness and courage to speak the truth in matters of divine love. Here the meanings have been enlarged and they stand for the spirited patriots. The 'gay cap' is the mark of Mansūr, the mystic, and 'flower-chequered skirt' of Majnūṅ, the ideal lover. Hence, 'madman's alley' is here the street inhabited by the socially-inspired patriots. The 'Shaikh and Shāh and Amīr' are conventionally the symbols of the oppressive orthodoxy. Here, therefore, they stand for the soul-less bureaucracy or the imperialists. The anti-colonial message of this short poem is now clear. Faiz has taken all the key words from the repertoire of the classical poetry, and added none of his own; still, he is completely successful in conveying a contemporary social and political idea. At one place, Faiz has remarked:

Let us talk of Farhād and Parvēz, O Faiz
For those who understand will see the truth.

The imagery of the classical *ghazal* was developed and perfected in Persian for love poetry. Later, in the course of centuries, the same imagery was further developed and expanded for the expression of mystical and metaphysical themes. This practice continued for long, and though once in a while, the same imagery was used with socio-political nuances, it was in the twentieth century that a new dimension was added to it by Iqbal, Chakbast, Hasrat and others who sought to make use of classical imagery for political themes. They were followed by Faiz and his contemporaries, who, responding more and more to the demands and stresses of the modern age, used it for socialistic and nationalistic themes, thus broadening its scope and introducing still newer shades of meaning into it. The underlying pattern of such poems is the same age-old love triangle. The first person of the poem is again the *'āshiq* (lover), that is, the revolutionary, the nationalist or the socialist. The *m'āshūq* (beloved) is the country, the society or the people. The third element of the triangle, the *raqīb* (rival), is now the imperialism, foreign tyranny, or the capitalist and the bourgeoisie. Similarly, the set of symbols containing *junūn* (madness), *dār-o-rasan* (scaffold), *maikhānā, sharāb, peyālā* (tavern, wine and cup) and *bulbul* (nightingale) are very common in Faiz's poetry. The following table sums up some of these three-dimensional elements of Faiz's poetic structure:

1.	*'āshiq* (lover) patriot, revolutionary	*m'āshūq* (beloved) country, people	*raqīb* (rival) imperialism, capitalism, tyranny, exploitation
2.	*'ishq* (love) revolutionary zeal	*visāl, dīdār* (union) revolution, social change	*hijr, firāq* (separation) the state of the reactionary controls or oppression
3.	*rind* (libertine) rebel	*sharāb, maikhānā, peyālā, sāqī* (wine, tavern, cup, cup-bearer) sources of social and political awareness	*muhtasib* (censor) the colonial system, the capitalist state, establishment
4.	*junūn* (sublime madness) zeal for social justice	*haq* (truth) socialism	*khirad* (empirical knowledge) capitalism, establishment

5.	*mujāhid* (fighter) freedom-fighter	*zanjīr* (chain) *zindān* (prison) *dār-o-rasan* (scaffold) political imprisonment, or execution	*hākim* (ruler) unjust ruler, colonialist or dictator
6.	*bulbul* (nightingale) nationalist poet	*gul* (rose) political ideal	*bāghbān* (gardener) usurper, or corrupt system

To appreciate further the socialistic and nationalistic implications of the above structure, let us consider the following verses of a *ghazal*:

> *mai-khānā salāmat hai to ham surkhī-e mai sē*
> *taz'īn-e dar-o-bām-e haram kartē rahēṅ gē*
> *bāqī hai lahū dil mēṅ to har ashk sē paidā*
> *raṅg-e lab-o-rukhsār-e sanam kartē rahēṅ gē*

> While yet the Tavern stands, with its red wine
> Crimson the Temple's high cold walls; and while
> My heart-blood feeds my tears and lets them shine,
> Paint with each drop the loved one's rosy smile.

In these lines, the 'Tavern' and the 'red wine', which conventionally stand for divine inspiration, represent the sources of political and social awareness. The 'loved one' obviously represents the masses, or the society. Similar structure is found in the following verses of another beautiful *ghazal*:

> *yehī junūṅ kā yehī tauq-o-dār kā mausam*
> *yehī hai jabr, yehī ikhtiyār kā mausam*
> *qafas hai bas mēṅ tumhārē, tumhārē bas mēṅ nahīṅ*
> *čaman mēṅ ātish-e gul kē nikhār kā mausam*
> *sabā kī mast khirāmī tah-e-kamaṅd nahīṅ*
> *asīr-e dām nahīṅ hai bahār kā mausam*
> *balā sē ham nē na dekhā to aur dekhēṅ gē*
> *farogh-e gulshan-o-saut-e hazār kā mausam*

> This hour of chain and gibbet and of rejoicing,
> Hour of necessity and hour of choice.
> At your command the cage, but not the garden's
> Red rose-fire, when its freshest hour begins.

No noose can catch the dawn-wind's whirling feet,
The spring's bright hour falls prisoner to no net.
Others will see, if I do not, that hour
Of singing nightingale and splendid flower.

This *ghazal* was written in a prison cell in the spring of 1951, when Faiz was facing a death-sentence. The imagery, 'chain and gibbet', 'rejoicing', 'noose', 'net', 'garden', 'wind', 'rose', 'spring', 'nightingale', etc., throughout these lines, is basically classical, but is pregnant with contemporary meanings. So is also the case of the poem, '*Sar-e maqtal*' (At the Place of Execution), where the 'fiery grape' is the desire for freedom, 'street of reproach' is the political prison, 'flask and cup' the national ideal, and so on. Faiz demonstrates how a fine poet can transcend the circumscribing restrictions placed upon him by the conventions, for he has not only infused the conventions with socio-political meanings, but at the same time retained their universal structures—erotic, mystic and spiritual. The different connotations exist side by side, reinforcing each other whereas the 'meaning' is derived either through a familiarity with relations obtaining between elements of these structures, or through the help of some other 'pointer' such as direct expression or the title of the poem itself.

But to say that Faiz is a poet of socialist realism, is just a part of the tale. A close look at the poem, '*Sarod-e shabānā*' (Nocturne), will emphasize this fact:

nīm-shab, čand, khud-farāmoshī
mahfil-e hast-o-būd vīrāṅ hai
paikar-e iltijā hai khāmoshī
bazm-e anjum fasurdā-sāmāṅ hai
ābshār-e sukūt jārī hai
čar sū bē-khudī sī tārī hai
zindagī juzv-e khvāb hai goyā
sārī dunyā sarāb hai goyā

so rahī hai ghanē darakhtoṅ par
čāṅdnī kī thakī hu'ī āwāz
kehkashāṅ nīm-va nigāhoṅ sē
sāz-e dil kē khamosh tāroṅ sē
keh rahī hai hadīs-e shauq-e niyāz

č̱han rahā hai khumār-e kaif-āgīṅ
ārzū, khvāb, terā rū'ē hasīṅ

Midnight, noon, oblivion—
The sum of things all chill and wan,
Desire inaudible;
Listless the fellowship of stars,
Streaming the cataract of silence;
All round a self-forgetting spread;
Life, fragment of a dream—
Earth, all a shadow-play.

Slumbering in the dense woods,
Moonlight's exhausted murmur;
Eyes half-opened, the Milky Way breathes
Legends of thirst of self-surrender
From the heart's unplucked strings
Drifting echoes of exultations;
Longings, dreams, and your charmed face.

The poem functions in two sets of tangible and intangible images. The first stanza opens with the word, 'midnight', then we have a tangible image, the 'moon', and then 'oblivion', originally *khud-farāmoshī* (self-forgetfulness), vague as a state of mind, but quite tangible as an image which involves the 'self'. Considering *khud* (self) as the starting point, let us move on to 'desire', 'fellowship' and 'silence', which again are followed by *bēkhudī* (All round a self-forgetting spread). Then, the poet goes to the source of all activity, 'life', and calls it a 'dream'; hence 'Earth all a shadow-play'. If we try to stretch the imagery a little further, we will see that personal feelings can be identified with something wider. The 'sum of things' originally, *mahfil-e hast-o-būd* (the assembly of old and new) can refer subtly to political ideologies, old or new. Similarly, 'Desire' can stand for the personal choice, and 'fellowship of stars' for the national or political leaders.

Structurally, the first stanza opens with a vague image, 'Midnight', dwells on 'self' as its core, fading eventually, into vagueness, 'dream, a shadow-play'. The second stanza follows the opposite pattern. Beginning as it does with the tangible image of 'dense woods', it soars up the airy 'Milky-Way', and then ends with the tangible 'charmed face'. The imagery in this stanza again is romantic, and the word 'dense' at once revives the memories of black tresses. This is further supported by 'eyes half-opened, the Milky-Way breathes'; and the poem closes with a deep yearning for the beloved. The poem is one of the finest examples of Faiz's subjective moods and his impressionistic style.

As noted by Al-e Ahmed Suroor in the preface to the Aligarh edition of *Zindān Nāmā*, 'Faiz's poetry is oblique rather than direct', a fact which should be kept in mind as we now turn to another excellent poem, *Tanhā'ī* (Solitude):

phir ko'ī āyā dil-e-zār! nahiṅ ko'ī nahiṅ!
rāh-rau ho gā, kahiṅ aur čalā jā'ē gā
Ḍhal čukī rāt, bikharnē lagā tāroṅ kā ghubār
laṛkharānē lagē aivānoṅ mēṅ khvābīdā čarāgh
so ga'ī rāsta tak tak kē har ik rāh-guzār
ajnabī khāk nē dhundlā diyē qadmoṅ kē surāgh
gul karo sham'ēṅ, baṛhā do mai-o-mīna-o-ayāgh
apnē bē-khvāb kivāṛoṅ ko muqaffal kar lo
ab yahāṅ ko'ī nahiṅ, ko'ī nahiṅ ā'ē gā!

Someone has come at last, sad heart! No, no-one is here.
A traveller must be going by, bound some other way.
The starry maze is wavering, night grows to its decline;
About the halls the nodding lamps gutter and go out.
Each highroad drops asleep, worn out listening for steps;
An alien dust has buried deep every trace of feet.
Put out those candles, take away wine and flask and cup;
Close your high doors that know no sleep, fasten bolt and bar;
No-one, no-one will come here now, no-one, any more.

In this poem, personal feeling can again be seen identifying itself with something wider. Kiernan pointed out that the deserted halls are not only the poet's fancied residence, but an old culture or society mouldering away. The next line, 'Each highroad drops asleep worn out listening for steps', alludes to the failing effects of the different strands of the freedom movement. The imagery is further reinforced in the following line: 'An alien dust has buried deep every trace of feet'; The 'alien dust' here refers very deftly to the withering touch of imperialism. (Note that the symbol *ajnabī* is also used for 'foreign yoke' in other poems of Faiz, as in 'A Few Days More': 'Under this load beyond words of a foreign yoke we must submit for a while, not forever submit.') The poem opens with a note of

hope 'Some one has come at last, sad heart', and ends on a note of
dejection 'No-one, no-one will come here now, no-one any more.' It thus
reflects the contemplative and despondent mood of India in the late
thirties and early forties.

Still, Faiz is as deeply concerned with purely personal themes as he
is with the nationalistic and socialistic. Frequently, the two emerge as
poles, pulling him in two different directions. In his poem, *Mujh sē pahlī
sī mahabbat mērī mahbūb na māṅg* (Love, Do Not Ask), he speaks of his
beloved whose 'beauty kept earth's spring times from decay' as one pole,
and of 'men's bodies sold in street and marketplace, . . . with festered
sores dripping corruption' as another pole. One is calling for love, the
other for action. To Faiz, both are dear. He wants to respond to the
individualistic urges, as well as to the call of the exploited society. Hence,
the request, 'Love, do not ask me for that love again.' The emphasis is
on the words *pahlī sī* (that), as individualism completely divorced from
the plight of society is meaningless to Faiz. This cleavage between
human passions and socialistic obligation, or the division of loyalty
between reality and ideal, classical and modern, or love and faith, runs
its contradictory course throughout the poetry of Faiz.

In poems like *Mauzū'-e sukhan* (Poetry's Theme), *Do 'ishq* (Two Loves)
and *Do āwāzēṅ* (Two Voices), he speaks very clearly of this cleavage. In
'Poetry's Theme', speaking of the beloved's 'loveliness . . . languorous
eyes', and the 'henna's delicate stain', he resolves that 'here is the chosen
world of rhyme and dream'. Then, comparing it to 'swarming progeny
and 'hunger wave', he affirms:

yē bhī haiṅ, aisē ka'ī aur bhī mazmūṅ hoṅ gē
lēkin us shokh kē āhistā sē khultē hū'e hoṅṭ
hā'ē us jism kē kam-bakht dil-āvēz khutūt
āp hi kahiyē kahīṅ aisē bhī afsūṅ hoṅ gē
apnā mauzū'-e sukhan in kē sivā aur nahīṅ
tab'-e shā'ir ka vatan in kē sivā aur nahīṅ

Here too are subjects; many more there may be.
But—oh, the slow-parting lips of that sweet wretch!
Oh, those cursed limbs that curve so ravishingly
Tell me where else on earth is such a witch!

No other theme will ever fit my rhyme—
Nowhere but here is poetry's native clime!

But, deeply touched by the suffering of mankind as Faiz is, he cannot be trusted too long for his above resolve. In *Do 'ishq* (Two Loves), he holds the scale once again, this time trying not to tilt it to any one side:

is 'ishq na us 'ishq pē nādim hai magar dil
har dāgh hai is dil mēṅ bajuz dāgh-e nidāmat

—My heart neither this love
Nor that love repents;
My heart that bears every
Scar, but regret.

The *dāgh* (scar) refers to the just or unjust criticism of friends and foes, writers and critics, both literary and political.

This so-called tension between the humanistic and idealistic impulses, or between the devotion to art and country, or to the self and society is nothing new. As suggested by Faiz's translator Kiernan, 'It is the common fate of the progressive movements all over the world'. Wherever the writer is beset with social problems and is given the freedom to speak through his conscience, he will feel the cleavage between duty and choice, the ideal and the practical. But what lends a unique quality to the duality of Faiz's poetry is the fact that besides being true to his personal feelings, and writing lyrical verse of great ecstasy, he has transformed some elements of the classical poetic tradition by infusing them with socio-political meanings.

Speaking of his nationalistic poetry, we have already mentioned that its underlying structure is the same conventional three-dimensional triangle; that is, Faiz speaks of suffering humanity in terms of the beloved of classical poetry. But the reverse is not true. If the conventional triangle in Faiz's poetry is taken to represent both his subjective and socialistic themes, then we will have to assume that there are two triangles functioning on different levels, and the two can never coalesce, that is, Faiz can identify the socialist ideal with the beloved of classical poetry, but not his beloved with the socialist ideal. This unique feature of his duality can be satisfactorily explained only in terms of his deviation from the tradition. Faiz, it should be recalled, appeared on the literary scene when Iqbal was about to depart. Faiz inherited from Iqbal what Iqbal, in his turn, had inherited from Ghalib. Faiz's diction thus bears a clear stamp of the style of both Ghalib and Iqbal. His language is not the common-core Hindustani, but that delicately-decorated medium which re-establishes Urdu's relationship with Semitic and Iranian languages, a relationship which opens to Urdu their 'nostalgic world of rose-garden and nightingale, and goblet and grapes'. Iqbal's majestic voice, though it added new grandeur and charm to Urdu poetry, made it a tool of revivalism. But Faiz, imbued with the spirit of the age, rejected the message of revivalism. As a freethinking man, earnestly desiring to find a solution for the suffering and exploitation of humanity, he turned to socialism, an ideology that offered some hope. However, Faiz is tenaciously rooted in the tradition and, therefore, was not swept off his feet by the winds of political exigencies. Many of his poems remind us of the dreamy monologues of the *ghazal*, and recall the same mood of melancholy. And the captivating musicality of his verse is yet unsurpassed in contemporary Urdu poetry. He is a lyric poet *par excellence*. The humanistic values of Urdu *ghazal* have also saved Faiz from being indignant or violent. Nowhere is he eager to seek the help of the 'midwife' called 'force'. He strongly feels that poetry should come out of its ivory tower and take notice of human misery, but also believes that poetry should serve Beauty and must not be subservient to anything other than the aesthetic or artistic values. Some of these views are not consistent with an ideal left philosophy, and thus, in the strict sense of the term, Faiz is not a 'true believer'. Nor is he a mystic; otherwise he might have reconciled the 'Two Voices' in some obscure way. But is it necessary that the poet must reconcile these two, so-called contrary visions of life, or he should be true to the poet within him, and speak of his internal feelings, riddles and doubts also, as sincerely as he can. Obviously, Faiz has chosen the latter, and in him the two, that is, the ideal and the personal, coexist, one to the fulfilment of the other.

Urdu poetry has thus come a long way from the classical tradition. It has undergone quite a transformation at the hands of Faiz, and he has, in fact, revolutionized its spirit and content, both in the lyrical, as well as in the socio-political sense.

Note

1. All translations of Faiz quoted above are by V.G. Kiernan, *Poems by Faiz*, New Delhi, 1958, Print. Urdu text is from *Harf-Harf*, Rampour, 1965.

MY HEART, FELLOW TRAVELLER

Original: *Mērē dil mērē musāfir* from *Mērē Dil Mērē Musāfir* (1981)
TRANSLATOR: WAQAS KHWAJA

My heart, fellow traveller,
It is again commanded
That you and I be banished
To call in lanes and byways
And turn to unknown places,
To find some loved one's message bearer
And ask of every stranger
News of our home and homeland—
In streets of unknown people
To tend the day to darkness,
A word exchanged with this,
Sometimes that other person.
What shall I tell you of it?
The pain of night is fearful.
This too would be enough if we
Could keep a count of sorrow.
What would we care for dying
Were there no death tomorrow?

5

'ANOTHER ADOLESCENCE':
THE PRISON POETRY OF FAIZ AHMED FAIZ[1]

Introduction

On 9 March 1951, Liaquat Ali Khan, Prime Minister of Pakistan, ordered the arrest of Major-General Akbar Khan, Chief of Staff of the Pakistan Army, his wife, Begum Naseem Akbar Khan, Brigadier M.A. Latif, and Faiz Ahmed Faiz, editor of the left-wing English daily newspaper [the] *Pakistan Times*.[2] These arrests precipitated what came to be known as the 'Rawalpindi Conspiracy Case' in which fourteen persons were tried on charges of treason and conspiracy against the Government of Pakistan. In addressing the Pakistani parliament on 21 March of that year, the Prime Minister stated that the arrests of 9 March and those which followed 'nipped a plot to bring Pakistan under a Communist government administered by military dictatorship'. Had the plot succeeded, 'the country was to be brought under military dictatorship when the existing authorities, both civil and military, had been eliminated.' Further, the government which was to be founded after the *coup d'état* 'was therefore to be patterned on the communist model but under military domination. For this purpose, economic and constitution-making missions were to be invited from a certain foreign country.'[3] While this 'certain foreign country' remained nameless, everyone involved clearly understood that it was the Soviet Union.

Faiz Ahmed Faiz as well as Sajjad Zaheer were well-known not only as leftist political organizers, but also for their literary efforts in Urdu. Twenty years earlier, Zaheer emerged on the Urdu literary scene as the editor of, and contributor to, *Burning Coals* (*Angārē*), a highly controversial collection of Urdu short stories which severely criticized middle and upper middle-class Muslim society and mores to such an extent that the book was banned by the United Provinces legislature and its authors who, in addition to Zaheer, included Ahmed Ali, Dr Rasheed Jahan and Mahmud-uz Zafar were threatened with death.[4] Zaheer was also highly instrumental in establishing the All-India Progressive Writers' Association (AIPWA), the leftist-oriented literary group which, in addition to serving as a fountain-head through which Marxist and socialist realist ideology flowed to the various literatures of India, also functioned as the 'most important front organization created for a specific professional group' by the Communist Party of India.[5]

Prior to 1951, Faiz's reputation as one of the most innovative and gifted young poets to emerge on the Urdu literary scene during the 1940s heyday of the Urdu Progressive Writers' Association rested on a single volume of poems entitled 'Image of Complaint' (*Naqsh-e Faryādī*) published in 1943. Born near Sialkot in 1911, he was the son of a prominent barrister who, having served as chief secretary to Amir Abd-ul Rahman in Afghanistan, went to England where he attended Cambridge University and passed the bar at Lincoln's Inn. Faiz was educated at Scotch Mission High School, Sialkot, then attended Government College, Lahore, where in 1932 he received an MA degree in English literature for a thesis on the poetry of Robert Browning. Two years later he received another MA, this one in Arabic. At this same time, some of his earliest poems were being published in the journal 'Caravan' (*Kārwān*).

In 1936, Faiz accepted an appointment as a junior lecturer at Mohammedan Anglo-Oriental (MAO) College, Amristar. Among his colleagues there were Dr M.D. Taseer, a noted Urdu poet and one of the original founders of the All-India Progressive Writers' Association in London in 1934, who was principal of the college.[6] In addition, Faiz also met Mahmud-uz Zafar, who was serving as vice-principal and a lecturer in history, and his wife, Dr Rasheed Jahan, a gynaecologist, who had set up a medical practice in the city. Through these various friends, Faiz came into close contact with many of the most influential members of the Urdu and Punjabi Progressive Writers' Association. During this same period in the late 1930s, Faiz began what would become a lifelong association with workers' and peasants' organizations in the Punjab. In addition to his college teaching and work in labour organizations, he assumed the editorship of the literary journal *Belles-Lettres* (*Adab-e Latīf*), where a number of his early critical articles on Urdu literature and literary theory appeared.[7]

In 1940, Faiz was appointed lecturer in English at Hailey College of Commerce, Lahore, a post which he held until 1941, at which time he enlisted in the British Indian Army. The precipitating event in this instance was Nazi Germany's invasion of the Soviet Union. By 1944, Faiz rose to the rank of Lieutenant Colonel and worked as editor of the army's Urdu publication in roman script called *Army Newspaper* (*Faujī Akhbār*). That same year he was awarded the honour of M.B.E. (M) (Member of the Order of the British Empire) (Military).

With partition in 1947, Faiz assumed the important post of editor of the liberal English-language daily, the *Pakistan Times*. He was also appointed managing editor of the Urdu daily *Today* (*Imroz*). During his editorship of these two papers, Faiz took the stance of opposing the governmental policies of Prime Minister Liaquat Ali Khan, especially on issues concerning Pakistan's association with the British Commonwealth and the country's pro-American, anti-Russian cold-war policies. Liaqat's Muslim League-dominated government increased its repression of leftist forces to such an extent that the offices of the newly formed All-Pakistan Progressive Writers' Association and of the All-Pakistan Trade Union Federation, of which Faiz was vice-president, were raided. In response to such repression, 'the progressive forces united and on 10 December 1950, formed the All-Pakistan Union or the Defence of Civil Liberties.'[8]

Faiz was one of the seventeen members of its executive committee. In that same year he was also elected General Secretary of the Pakistan Committee for the Defence of Peace. A member of the Pakistan Journalists' Union, he was also the Pakistani representative of the World Peace Council. It was thus in this context and due to these activities that Faiz was arrested in 1951 in connection with the conspiracy case.[9]

The subsequent protracted trial of the various accused was held *in camera*, and special legislation was passed in the Pakistani parliament to deal with the particulars of the different cases. Eventually the various alleged conspirators were sentenced to varying prison terms, Faiz ordered to serve a four-year term in 1953. Because of what was less than solid evidence produced by the authorities against the accused, all of them were eventually released quietly from prison. In truth, the entire affair had been bungled, both by the alleged conspirators, if indeed they had conspired in the first place, and certainly by the Government of Pakistan, which lost a great deal of credibility in the light of agitation against the constitutional validity of the various statutes it enacted in this case.

While Faiz may not have been an efficient conspirator (if, indeed he was a conspirator at all), he was an efficient artist, and prison, oddly enough, was 'To him as a poet . . . a well-disguised blessing.' Faiz's close friend and first English translator, Victor Kiernan, further notes:

> His wartime work had been heavy; he lamented that as soon as a new couplet began to stir in his mind he had to get up and go back to his office. After the war his editorial desk was even more enslaving. He might indeed point to the files of his newspapers, as Lamb did to the ledgers of the East India Company, as his real works. Worst of all has been a social environment prodigally wasteful, everywhere south of the Himalayas, of the time of men whose time is of any value.

Kiernan explains:

> Far more than in the West, a writer's admirers show their appreciation of him by thronging about him and making it impossible for him to write, or to keep any rational plan of work; custom imposes on all alike the same monstrous proportion of talking to thinking as that of sack to bread on Falstaff tavern bills. . . . Prison enabled him to write what for him was a considerable number of poems, in which his ideals took on fresh strength by being alloyed with harsh experience, and which were eagerly devoured by the public, in spite of charges weighing over him.[10]

Faiz himself describes this period of incarceration as follows, and in so doing, gives us at least three clues as to how he views his prison poetry:

> [My] two books subsequent to 'Image of Complaint', 'Hand of the Wind' [Dast-e Sabā, 1952] and 'Prison Narrative' [Zindāṅ nāmā, 1956] are souvenirs of this [four-year] stay in prison. Although basically these writings are related to the mental impressions and thought processes which started with 'My Beloved, do not Ask me for my Former Kind of Love' [Mujh sē pahlī sī mahabbat mērī mahbūb na māṅg, one of the most famous poems in his first collection], prison itself is, nevertheless, a fundamental experience in which a new window of thought and vision opens itself. Thus prison is first like another adolescence when all sensations again become sharp and one experiences once again that same original astonishment at feeling the dawn breeze, at seeing the shadows of evening, the blue of the sky, and feeling the passing breeze.

He continues:

> Second, it happens that the time and the distance of the external world are both cancelled. Even things which are near become very distant, and those

which are far become near. The difference of yesterday and tomorrow is eliminated, effaced in such a way that sometimes a moment seems an immeasurable span of time and sometimes a century appears to be a thing which happened just yesterday. Third, in the tranquillity of separation, one finds greater leisure to attend to the outer adornment of the bride of poetry, in addition to meditation and study.[11]

Thus, in spite of the turmoil which prison brought to his life, including what was doubtless acute anxiety over the fact that during a part of this period he was under the sentence of death, Faiz used his prison sentence to produce many of his best poems.

Dast-e Sabā: 'Hand of the Wind'

As much as any poem in this collection, Faiz's introductory essay 'Hand of the Wind' is an explicit poetic credo. Here in highly metaphorical terms, he insists that one must be able to perceive 'an ocean in a drop of water.'[12] In other words, one must be able to abstract from the particulars of one's own life situation to the generalities and universal aspects of the human condition as it affects all people. For the poet, such an ability to perceive the ocean in a drop of water also entails the grave responsibility of setting the pace for and giving direction to the ebb and flow of the ocean. In other words, the poet must not merely observe and write about what (s)he sees, (s)he must also involve her/himself and struggle fully with the stuff of life and living. Stripping away all the metaphorical language, Faiz then succinctly states:

> What I want to say is that a full comprehension of the collective struggle of human life and a conscious effort to share in that struggle is not only the demand of Life, but also a demand of Art. Art is a part of this Life, and an artistic effort is just one aspect of this struggle.

This demand of the artist remains eternally; therefore, his struggle has no end. His art lies in endless effort and in eternal struggle.

Success or failure in this struggle depends upon the relative prowess of the artist; but most important for him is to remain toiling in this struggle, untired, undefeated, endlessly, eternally.

This introduction, with its demand for struggle against insuperable odds, takes on an additional sense of urgency and irony when one considers that it was written from Central Jail, Hyderabad, Sind, where not only the poet had been confined but also under a possible death sentence.

Thus struggle against tyranny of all kinds, especially that of a political nature, is the dominant theme of both 'Hand of the Wind' and 'Prison Narrative', permeating many of the poems with a genuine sense of indomitable optimism and unfaltering confidence. Such sentiments are expressed in a poetic fragment which opens 'Hand of the Wind':

> If the wealth of tablet and pen were snatched away, what does it matter (to kyā)?
> For I have dipped my fingers into my heart's blood;
> If a seal were put upon my tongue, what does it matter (to kyā)?
> For I have put tongues into the links of my chains.[13]

This fragment sets the tone for many of the poems with political overtones found in this collection. Of course, each poem cannot be considered here individually; we shall, instead, look closely at a number of those which might be considered typical examples of the verse which Faiz wrote during this confinement.

The poem 'Slate and Pen' (Lauh-o-qalam) is notable because it successfully combines traditional Urdu ghazal imagery with contemporary sentiments that express Faiz's plight:

> We shall go on nurturing the slate and pen;
> We shall continue to write about these things which happen to the heart.
>
> We shall gather reasons for the sorrows of love
> And thus remove the desolateness of the times.
>
> Indeed, the bitterness of days will now increase further;
> Indeed, the people of tyranny will continue to practice tyranny.
>
> This bitterness is accepted; this tyranny is endurable to us;
> As long as there is power, then we shall go on providing cures for sorrow.
>
> As long as the wine shop is still standing, then with red wine we
> Will go on decorating the walls and doors of the mosque.
>
> If blood remains in the heart, then we will make from every tear
> Colour for the lips and cheeks of the beloved (pp. 22–23)

The first couplet of this poem restates the point made in the volume's first poem, not only in terms of the general thought content but in terms of the imagery of the slate and pen. 'Those things which happen to the heart' in this context refers not only to love, but also to any other experience of the heart—here a synecdoche for the whole person—may experience, including confinement to jail.

In couplet 2 the speaker states that he will 'gather reasons for the sorrow of love'; that is, he will give full vent to his feelings of love, not only for the beloved, but for his country as well. 'The desolateness of the times' may refer, of course, to the contemporary situation in Pakistan, which, according to the speaker, will be changed because he and others like him will fully express their love for their country and humanity. The speaker, however, is not naïve enough to believe that such changes will occur immediately, for in couplet 3 he acknowledges the continued oppression of the tyrants.

The next three couplets stand together as a unit, each acknowledging the need to struggle against tyranny and oppression, even though the results of this struggle may not be immediately apparent. Here we see Faiz's unique ability, which has been amply demonstrated earlier in many of the poems of 'Image of Complaint', to bring traditional *ghazal* imagery to poems which are fully contemporary in meaning. In couplet 5 he reduces the austerity and hallowedness of sanctified sites like the mosque by having the speaker state that he will continue to decorate the walls and of such places with wine, which, of course, is forbidden to Muslims. Here Faiz draws upon the opposition contained in the images of the tavern and the mosque with which *ghazal* poetry is replete. In couplet 6, variant of the preceding one, the speaker states that he will use his tear, coloured red from his heart's blood, to decorate the lips and cheeks of the beloved, the beloved here a symbol not only for people, but for the homeland as well.

Another important poem in this collection which also expresses sentiments of positive action and hope in light of depressing and disconsolate conditions is 'Two Voices' (*Do āwāzēṅ*). Cast in a dialogue form reminiscent of the great Urdu dialogue poems of Muhammad Iqbal (1877–1938), this poem offers two contrasting points of view relative to the question of people's struggle. The First Voice, sombre and pessimistic in tone, asks:

Now there is no further chance for struggle; the subject of soaring aloft has already ended;
Nooses have already been thrown upon the stars; there has already been a night attack upon the moon;
Why should we now make a pact with these eyes for some future?

Only the business of death remains; whenever we want, we will bring an end to that business.
This is your shroud; that, my shroud; this, my grave; that one, yours
(pp. 24–27)

In response to such a defeatist attitude, Faiz asserts the position of the Second Voice, here offering hope and optimism in light of difficult times and adverse conditions. This voice, possibly that of the poet, not only expresses sentiments similar to those in the initial quatrain of 'Hand of the Wind', but also shares the 'so what' (kyā kyā) attitude of that first poem:

The endless wealth of life is neither your possession nor mine;
If the torch of our heart is wounded in this assembly, if it glitters, so what?
This assembly remains illuminated; if just one niche is laid waste, so what?

In light of such pain and suffering, the Second Voice insists that all people must persist in their pursuit of justice and freedom. The First Voice then offers an account of its vision of present circumstances, which may be intended to be metaphorical references to the general political and social climate of Pakistan in the early 1950s.

Again the Second Voice rejects even more forcefully than before the despondency and questioning doubts of the First Voice. It reasserts its call for positive, forceful action—some of the most violent suggested by Faiz in his poetry in face of such adversity:

While these hands are intact, while heat runs in this blood,
While truth is in this heart, while there is strength in this tongue,
You and I will teach the frenzy of the rebec and flute to
those iron collars and ankle chains,
And teach such frenzy that the tumult of Caesar and of
Xerxes' drumming is nothing before it;
Our every moment is an age; our every future is today.
This evening and dawn, this sun and moon, the stars and more brilliant stars are ours!

The slate and pen, this drum and banner, this wealth and glory are all ours.
(pp. 26–27)

Notable in this last line is the allusion to the 'slate and pen' (*lauh-o-qalam*), the poet's personal weapons in this struggle, which have served as key images in both the initial fragment in this collection, as well as a title for a poem. Another association with this image is that of divine authority who writes all events on the Slate of Fate with the divine pen. Such associations with these images augment the sense of inevitability of the events described and the ultimate outcome as envisioned by the Second Voice.

One of the most moving and powerful poems of 'Hand of the Wind' is 'There Is No Saviour of Crystals' (*Shīshoṅ kā masīhā ko'ī nahīṅ*), which, surprisingly enough, seems to have been generally ignored by some of Faiz's major translators.[14] The phenomenon of post-partition dis-illusionment is highly visible in the literature of the 1950s of nearly all South Asian languages. 'There is No Saviour of Crystals' conveys this frame of mind as effectively as any in the Urdu poetry of the period. The crystals in the title could be the hopes and aspirations all Indians had for their country prior to independence. With independence, however, came partition, and with partition the communal riots and mass slaughter of innocent people in both India and Pakistan. After such blood urges were sated, people in both India and Pakistan settled down to the business of country-building, though not without the spectre of the communal slaughter completely obliterated from their minds. Soon intellectuals and the common person found that opportunism, wealth, and nepotism were the necessary prerequisites for advancing in the new country rather than ability, dedication, and personal worth. Hence, the shattered crystals over which the speaker tells the people of his country not to shed tears. Instead, he observes rather objectively:

What is broken is broken;
How can it be mended with tears
What is broken is thrown away. (p. 60)

He puts the blame for the crushing of such dreams on 'poverty, work, hunger, sorrow'; but these, in turn, are caused by 'the thieves of life' in 'a city of thieves,' populated by:

Some people who
Draw curtains about this [wealth amassed by pillage],
Who auction off
Every mountain, every sea. (p. 62)

The operative word here is 'some' (*kuċh*), and it is significant that the speaker does not make this category universal. He acknowledges a second group.

... who fight
In order to rent those drapes,
To confuse
Every ploy of the thieves of life's wealth. (p. 62)

Hence, the speaker reduces the question of the country's problem to essentially one of the forces of good versus the forces of evil. The poem draws upon the concept of the messiah to put forth the notion that only good people can overcome the evils of others in such situations. In Islam the concept of the messiah carries with it the notable features that the messiah is capable of healing the sick and resurrecting the dead. There is according to the poem, no such messiah for the shattered dreams of disillusionment. People cannot afford to wait the coming of the messiah, but must act on their own to resurrect these dreams. Such an action will require struggle, which the speaker recognizes and meets with the cry:

Rise up! All empty hands
Are called to the battlefield (p. 65)

Another poem which uses the imagery of precious stones is 'To the Iranian Students' (*Irani tulabā kē nām!*), whose title is then qualified with the parenthetical note, '(Who fell in the battle for peace and freedom)'. Two versions of this poem exist. The original was written at the time of Muhammad Mosaddeq's prime-ministership in Iran (3 April 1951–19 August 1953), during which there were in Iran, many anti-British and anti-American as well as anti-Soviet riots in which a number of students were killed.

The second version of this poem was prepared by Faiz for publication in the English-language collection of his poems entitled *Poems by Faiz* and is re-titled 'To Those Students' (*Un tulabā kē nām*; pp. 173–77). Both

versions are cast in the form of a question answer exchange between a
speaker and an Iranian. Revisions are noted in brackets:

Who are these generous ones,
The gold coins of whose blood, drop by drop,
Pour continuously
Into earth's thirsty begging bowl
And are filling up that begging bowl?
O land of Iran! Who are these young men
[O native land of theirs! Who are these young men,]
The extravagant ones,
The gold of whose bodies
In full youth
Is scattered as particles into the dust vainly,
Is scattered about in every quarter . . . ?

The answer comes from an Iranian point of view:

O questioning stranger! These children and youth
Are the newly ripe pearls of that light,
The raw buds of that fire—
Sweet light and bitter fire—
From which has flowered in the dark night of tyranny
The garden of the dawn of revolt . . . ! (p. 52)

Here the Iranian invites all to see the sacrifices which the youth of his/
her country have made in countering tyranny, both internal and external.
In light of the outcome of the events surrounding these sacrifices, the
poem takes on a poignancy that comes from the fact that the tyrants,
both internal and external, were victorious. Similar tyranny in Pakistan
during the 1970s would force Faiz into voluntary exile until the last
months of his life, when ill health forced him to return to Pakistan, where
he died in 1984.

The notion of sacrifice for political ends and other trappings of
persecution and imprisonment suffuse another group of six poems in
'Hand of the Wind'. These include an untitled fragment which begins
'Again Doomsday Has Been Prepared' (Phir hashr kē sāmān), the poem 'The
Time of Neck Chain and Gibbet' (Tauq-o-dār kā mausam), a qavvālī[15] entitled
'The Place of Execution' (Sar-e maqtal), a poem, 'A Sacrifice in Your Lanes'

(*Nisār maiṅ terī galyon kē*), and two companion poems 'A Prison Evening' (*Zindāṅ kī ēk shām*) and 'A Prison Dawn' (*Zindāṅ kī ēk subh*).

The first four of these poems employ traditional imagery, which allows a romantic interpretation of each; however, each poem also carries a distinct political message. The fragment is constructed on an opposition whereby the 'criminals' (*khatākār*) are put on trial for the 'crime of fidelity' (*jurm-e vafā*):

> Again, Doomsday has been prepared in the chamber of passion;
> The judges are sitting the sinners standing;
> See, the crime of fidelity established against so many people!
> All these criminals are standing near the gibbet. (p. 28)

'The Time of Neck Chain and Gibbet' was written in 1951 when Faiz was in solitary confinement. In contrast to the fragment above, the speaker of this poem laments the fact that:

> There is no time for wine or the *sāqī* [cupbearer]; of what use
> Is the season of the graceful movements of clouds on the mountain tops?
> If the company of friends is not available, of what good
> Is this season of the dance for the shadows beneath the cypress and poplar?
> (p. 29)

Faiz contends that the times are strange:

> This is the time of madness (*junūn*), the time of neck chain and gibbet;
> This is the season of determination, the season of freedom. (p. 29)

Here a key term is *junūn*, literally 'madness,' which is rich in its association with the love story of the Arabic lovers Laila and Majūn (literally, 'the mad one') and the idea in mystical, or Sufi poetry that one must pursue the ideal beloved even to the point of madness. The speaker urges others to seize the cage (their own personal prisons), but in so doing should remember that the season of the

> Blooming forth of the fire of the rose [revolution? Reform?]
> in the garden [Pakistan?] is not [yet] yours. (p. 30)

Even though he himself is a prisoner, Faiz has his speaker note:

The drunken, graceful gait of the breeze is not tied down;
The spring season [a brighter future for the country?] is not the captive of
the net [thrown by present-day tyrants]. (p. 30)

Acknowledging that the exact course of the future is undetermined—he
even anticipates execution—the speaker optimistically looks to the season
when this garden will bloom not for him/her, but for others:

No matter if I do not see it: others will see
The season of the blooming of the garden and the singing of the
nightingales. (p. 30)

The poem, 'The Place of Execution' is cast in the form of a *qavvālī*, where
the distinctions between the Ideal Love (i.e., God) and profane love are
sometimes blurred. Here the speaker addresses the evil night that has
prevailed over the entire country; he then looks to better days. The
imagery used throughout is again highly traditional: 'the beauty of
the lovely face' (*jamāl-e rū'ē zēbā*), 'the wine drinkers' (*bādā gusār*), 'the
bubbling of wine' (*josh-e sehbā*), 'wine cup and flask' (*jām-o-mīnā*), and 'the
street of reproach' (*kū'ē malāmat*)—this last the street where the beloved
lives and where the lover receives her reproaches when he enters. All of
these are treated as positive, supportive elements which will give people
the strength to meet the 'troops of rivals and enemies' (*lashkar-e aghyār-o-
a'da*) at the place of execution. The speaker is, of course, implying that the
execution which will take place there is not that of the poets and their
associates, but rather that of the enemies and rivals. Such an execution
is the 'last moment of night' (*shab kī ākhirī sa'at*), but the speaker assures
friends that from such an action they will 'see the light which is hidden
in this hour' and the better future, 'the star which will shine on dawn's
foreheads,' which will emerge from it (pp. 31–32).

In contrast to the allegorical language of 'The Place of Execution' from
which both general and very particular readings and interpretations can
be given, 'A Sacrifice in Your Lanes' is more direct and unequivocal in its
address. Here the speaker once again speaks to his 'country' (*vatan*) as
his beloved:

May I be sacrificed in your lanes, O country, where
It has become the custom that no one should talk with raised head.
If any lover takes a walk (*tavāf*), he must walk
As if to avoid being seen and to guard his body and soul.

Now for lovers, this is the system of captivity and release;
Stone and bricks are tied down, and dogs are set free. (p. 56)

Here the use of the term *tavāf* is particularly significant, for this is a
specialized religious term referring to the circumambulations the faithful
make at a religious site, such as the Kaaba in Mecca. Hence, the speaker
here is equating the beloved—his country—with such a place, and himself
as a 'lover' (*čāhnē vālā*), but also a member of the faithful who make such
religious rounds. He warns such 'lovers' (*ahl-e dil*, literally, 'people of the
heart') to be constantly on guard, for as he notes in an allusion to a story
by the Persian poet Saadi, the stones and bricks (criticism and objections)
which he might throw at attacking 'dogs' (*sag*), or tyrants, are shackled,
as in a paved road. In spite of such dire circumstances, the speaker is
able to see the optimistic side of the situation and uses his typical 'so
what' phrase to express this attitude. He sees the rule of such tyrants as
a short-lived interlude which will be overturned through the 'pledge of
fidelity' (*ehd-e vafā*) of those who love their country:

If today the fortunes of the rival are at their peak, so what!
This temporary godliness is of no consequence;
Those who keep firm their pledge of fidelity to you
Have the cure for the motions of night and day. (p. 58)

The companion pieces 'A Prison Evening' and 'A Prison Dawn' are
significant in that the two of them combine the traditional aspects of
poetry and political messages with the technique of 'mood pictures'
which were special features of certain poems in his first collection, 'Image
of Complaint', where the poems 'Nocturnal Sarod' (*Sarod-e shabānā*), 'A
Scene' (*Ēk manzar*), and 'Sarod' (*Sarod*) are significant examples of this
'mood picture' poetry.[16] 'A Prison Evening' opens with a highly evocative,
sensual image of night, which suggests waiting, anticipation, and the
desire for union with the beloved. Such a mood is also typical of *ghazal*
poetry:

Night is descending step by step
From the curving staircase of evening stars;
A breeze passes by
As if someone has spoken words of love;
Homeless trees in the prison courtyard,

Heads drooping, are lost in making
Designs upon the hem of the sky. (p. 71)

In the second stanza the speaker, as if coming to his senses from such a reverie, realizes that these thoughts are dreams and that the real, live-world situation in which he finds himself is contrary to such dreams. The 'poison of tyranny' (*zulm kā zehr*) is attempting to spread throughout life, and the speaker acknowledges that such people have succeeded in extinguishing the 'candles in the chamber of union' (*jalwa gāh-e visāl kī sham'eṅ*) with the usual 'so what.' Such candles are relatively minor items, he tells us, and are easily extinguished; he then defies the tyrants to extinguish the moon:

A thought continually goes through the heart;
From this moment, life is sweet;
Those who want to mingle the poison of tyranny
Will not succeed today or tomorrow;
If they also put out
The candles in the chamber of union, so what!
Let's see if they can extinguish the moon (p. 12)

Continuing with such moon imagery, 'A Prison Dawn' opens with the moon depicted as a friend beckoning the speaker to awaken from his dreams of the beloved. Just as the first two stanzas of the previous poems were dominated by traditional imagery, the first stanza of this poem is similarly constructed. Here images of the celestial bodies are used to suggest a night of union between the speaker's lover and beloved, if only in the speaker's dream. Such a union is further enhanced with the image of Night and Dawn lying in each other's arms. The remainder of the poem describes the coming of dawn in the prison courtyard. Here the speaker, having just awakened from sleep, mixes the traditional imagery of love poetry, which is indicative of his dream world and union with the beloved, with the stark realities of the courtyard, which could be interpreted as the state of the country under the rule of tyrants:

Far off a gong sounded; disgusted footsteps of
Guards, tortured by yellow starvation, started their rounds,
And the angry, shouting laments of the prisoners
Wander arm in arm with them. (p. 74)

Not all poems in 'Hand of the Wind' contain political messages, overt and covert. There are number of love poems, such as 'To Your Beauty' (*Tumhārē husn kē nām*) and 'Memory' (*Yād*), as well as some *ghazals*, which are purely romantic in nature. 'To Your Beauty' is a greeting from the lover to his beloved from whom he is separated. The poem is rather generalized in its love message, though allusions to the 'times' (*auqāt*) being 'tight' (*tang*) and 'hardships' (*ālām*) as being 'severe' (*sakht,*) and the 'bitterness of time' (*talkhī-e ayyām*) suggest that the reasons for separation are strong, such as imprisonment. He admits to the beloved that it is the memories of her which will enable him to withstand such hardships:

> So long as the light of henna brightens your palms,
> There continues in the world the blandishment of the bride of poetry;
> So long as your beauty is young, heaven is kind;
> So long as you remain, the breadth of our country is our companion;
> Even though the times are tight and hardships severe,
> The bitterness of time is sweet with your memory.
> The poet sends greetings to your beauty (pp. 37–38)

The poem 'Memory' is similar to 'To Your Beauty' in that it is, as the title suggests, built upon the speaker's recollection of the beloved:

> In the desert (*dasht*) of loneliness, O beloved of the world, tremble
> The shadow of your voice, the mirage of your lips;
> In the desert of loneliness, beneath the twigs and dust of distance,
> Bloom the roses and jasmines of your arms.
> Somewhere nearby rises the warmth of your breath
> Smouldering slowly in its own fragrance.
> Far off—beyond the horizon, shining drop by drop-
> Falls the dew of your loving glance.
> With so much love, O love of the world,
> The memory of you has placed its hands on my heart's cheek,
> As though the morning of separation,
> The day of separation seemed to pass, and the night of union has come.
> (pp. 76–77)

While this poem is devoid of any language which would suggest reasons for the separation of the lovers, the use of the term 'desert' (*dasht*) can also evince mystical overtones of Sufism. Here the implication is that the lover is suffering afar from the beloved in much the same way as does the soul separated from God. In order to get to their respective destinations, the lover and the Sufi must traverse this desert of tribulations and difficulties. Yet sustaining the lover here are memories of the beloved, which allow him the illusion of union, even though their separation has just begun.

The poems in 'Hand of the Wind' seem, in the main, politically inspired. The reason for such preoccupation on the poet's part was probably his confinement and the circumstances and uncertainties surrounding his imprisonment. However, these poems offer an interesting contrast to similar political poems in 'Image of Complaint', where the poet was content merely to comment on or describe a particular incident, event, or injustice. The political poems in Faiz's first volume lack the forcefulness of action or the commitment to change, which many of the political poems in 'Hand of the Wind' show. The reason for this difference in tone could be attributed to the numerous significant political events which took place in India and Pakistan between 1943, when the first volume appeared, and 1952, when the second collection was published.

The love poems of 'Hand of the Wind' also have political colouring, for these are mainly concerned with the separation of the lover from his loved ones due to his confinement. In these poems, as well as in the more overtly political ones, Faiz offers the reader a sense of undaunted optimism in light of seemingly overwhelming odds, a faith in the righteousness of his cause, which is also the cause of the people, and finally, a firm belief in his future vindication, which eventually did come, and the destruction of the tyrannical order which placed him in prison. These characteristics are also manifested in many of the poems of Faiz's third collection, *Zindāṅ nāmā*.

Zindāṅ Nāmā: 'Prison Narrative'

Faiz's third volume of poems, 'Prison Narrative', was published in Pakistan in 1956; a year later an Indian edition appeared. This volume contains thirty-three poems, of which only seven are undated. While the poems are not printed in a strictly chronological sequence, one can ascertain from these dates an excellent sense of the order of composition, as well as the place of composition (in most instances Montgomery or Hyderabad jails).

The poem 'Meeting' (*Mulāqāt*) is related in theme and imagery to 'A Prison Evening' and 'Memory' of 'Hand of the Wind'. Whereas the latter two deal with the lover's desire for union with the beloved, 'Meeting' deals with an imagined rendezvous of the lovers; the latter poems anticipate the meeting with the beloved, while the former describes such a meeting. The two poems in 'Hand of the Wind' are charged varyingly with sensual imagery; however, eroticism is sublimated in 'Meeting' to a commentary on the sorrow of the two lovers who are made to suffer at the hands of unnamed forces. Such suffering is then transformed into weapons to be used to free the lovers, and then the weapons are changed into garlands of light, symbolizing hope.

'Meeting' is one of Faiz's most oblique and indirect poems. One key to understanding it, however, is to look upon it as a series of transformations or metamorphoses which occur to a number of the poem's images, particularly the 'tree of pain' and 'grief,' the former a metaphor for the latter, the emotion. Colour imagery here is significant, for black associated with pain and grief, dominates the first stanza but is gradually transformed into 'yellow leaves,' then to pink, a variant of red. The lover's voice emerges from the darkness as 'a stream of blood,' which meets and scatters the beloved's glances described as 'light,/A wave of gold.' In the next stanza grief is smouldering and can 'burst into a spark' due to the 'enflamed' cries of the lover and beloved. Thus black is transformed into red. In the next stanza, grief is depicted as branches from which black boughs have been made into bows; these are then used to shoot arrows of sorrow into the hearts of the lovers. These arrows of sorrow are transformed into axes which will, presumably, be used against those who shot them in the first place; this turning of the oppressor's weapons against the oppressor is a motif that is repeated in several other poems in this volume. In the following lines the transmutation of various light images is delineated:

Here, shattered people will
Find their morning in the ill-fated sky.
Here, where you and I now stand,
Here is their dawn's hope, their horizon;
Here dispersing the sparks of grief,
They become gardens of morning light;
Here, sorrow's axes
Turn to fiery garlands
Of fine-rayed light.[17]

Essentially, the speaker is saying that such grief is transitory and that oppressed people should not lose faith when grief predominates, but should struggle to transform such grief, or any adverse circumstances, into positive results. The final stanza of the poem is a summation of all that has preceded in the poem:

> Night's gift, this sorrow,
> Is now tomorrow's faith;
> Faith, a balm to sorrow
> As morning is to night.
> (Montgomery Jail, 12 October to 3 November 1953)

The poem offers a set of dilemmas, or opposition, which demonstrates even further the notion of transformation and metamorphosis: night versus morning and sorrow versus faith. The 'meeting' of this poem, then, is not entirely that of lovers, as might be surmised from the title. The meeting refers equally to that point at which night meets morning and sorrow meets faith; in other words, the point of transition or trans-formation of the former elements in these on positions to the latter elements.

Another poem which exhibits a similar notion of faith and hope in face of adversity is 'O City of Lights' (*Ai raushnīyoṅ kē shehr*), which opens with a particularly striking stanza:

> All over the grass, the insipid, pale moon is drying up;
> The poison of loneliness is licking the walls;
> The muddied wave of pain—like an ungrateful mist—falls and swells. (p. 47)

The speaker expresses his yearning for the city of lights—Lahore, according to Victor Kiernan—which is described in terms associated with fighting and combat. Here the point is that Lahore is the place where the poet was, in fact, waging war for his cause, as opposed to his jail cell where he cannot fight as effectively or at least not as actively. The poem concludes with a tercet in which he asks the beloveds—whom he calls Lailas, harkening back to the great beloved of Arabic literature—to keep their lamps in that city burning for him, the implication being that one day he will certainly return. Faiz did return to Lahore several times, only to leave again.

A similar sense of yearning and frustration dominates the poem 'We Who Were Killed in Half-Lit Streets' (*Ham jo tārīk rāhoṅ mēṅ māre ga'ē*), one of Faiz's most famous pieces, and which, we are told in a parenthetical remark following the poem's title, was written 'After reading the letters of Julius and Ethel Rosenberg' (p. 53). According to Kiernan, the poem contains an address by the spirit of the Rosenbergs to 'the ideal that they followed in life, and that is personified here as a kind of goddess.'[18] An important point to remember while reading this poem is that the mention of the Rosenbergs is entirely incidental to the spirit of the piece, and that it would maintain itself as a viable poem without this specific reference.

The major image of this poem is the highly sensual image of a woman—Kiernan's goddess—who possesses flower lips, scented billowing hair, and hands of silver. Because of the erotic associations of this woman, it seems that the image is less that of a goddess and more that of an idealized beloved who is also addressed in the intimate second-person *tū* form, as is appropriate to goddesses and beloveds, idealized or otherwise.

Faiz has the speakers in this poem understand their failure in much the same way he himself understands his own imprisonment, which is a result of one of his failures. However, he wishes them to understand, as he does, that there will be others who will pick up where they (and perhaps he) have left off. The personae of the poem accept their death in 'half-lit streets,' a metaphor for the 1950s McCarthy-crazed courts of the United States, where Faiz implies that there is no openness, light of justice, or mercy, but rather stealth, injustice, and murder.[19] Put another way, the Rosenbergs were sacrifices, or martyrs, for their cause.

Faiz deals with other such sacrifices in two other distinctive poems in this volume, 'This Crop of Hopes, O Friend' (*Yē fasl umīdoṅ kī hamdam*) and 'Window' (*Darīčā*), again, two of his best-known works. The former is similar in tone to 'We Who Were Killed in Half-Lit Streets.' Here the sacrifice is a crop of plants—or hopes—which will bear no fruit and must be torn away to make room for another crop:

> Cut them all,
> These wounded plants;
> Don't leave them without water, gasping their last;
> Tear them all away,
> The withering flowers;
> Don't leave them shrivelling on the branch.
> This crop (*fasl*) of hopes,
> O friend, will this time too be ruined.

All the labour of days and nights
Will again prove worthless. (p. 72)

In spite of such frustration, the speaker urges the friend to plan again
for the next crop, which must be fed the compost of blood and the water
of tears. Even if such a crop fails—as the speaker is ready to admit—the
friend must be ready to try to raise yet another, and yet another, crop:

In the crannies and corners of the field
Spread again the compost of your blood;
Again water the soil with your tears:
Again, plan for the next crop,
When once again it will be ruined.
If just one crop ripens, we shall have enough.
Till then, we must try again as we are now doing.

The image of the 'crop' (*fasl*) suggests the idea of the recurrent and
cyclic nature of birth, maturation, and death, an image which is basic to
another 'sacrificial' poem, 'Window':

Crosses bar my window,
Each stained with a messiah's blood,
Each with the hope of union with a god.
On one is sacrificed the rain cloud of spring;
On another a shining moon is murdered;
On a third is crucified a flower branch;
On another the morning breeze is killed.
Every day these gods of kindness and beauty,
Drenched in blood, enter my chamber of sorrow;
Every day, before my eyes,
These martyrs rise up, healed.

A striking feature of this poem, one of the most complex of Faiz's works,
is the use of Abrahamic, and perhaps even Hindu, religious concepts. The
images of 'crosses' (*salībēṅ*) and 'messiah' (*masīhā*) are drawn from the
Christian tradition. These are used to describe the prison bars across the
window of the cell. The crosses separate the prisoner from 'union' (*vasl*)
with freedom outside the cell, as depicted by the images of the 'rain cloud
of spring,' 'a shining moon,' 'a flower branch,' and 'the morning breeze.'
These are the 'gods of kindness and beauty' (*khudāvandgān-e mehr-o-jamāl*)
with whom the crosses of the first stanza desire *vasl*, a term denoting

not only the union of lovers but the sufistic union of the soul with God. These gods daily enter the cell as resurrected 'martyrs' (*shahīd*), only to be crucified, killed, murdered, and sacrificed once again on the crosses the next day.

Here the Muslim concept of the *shahīd* is important, for the belief is that one who is a witness to Islam and dies for one's faith does not die, but lives eternally. The fact that these *shahīds* return cyclically is reminiscent of the Hindu concept of rebirth, for in standard Islam there is only one actual birth, and then life after death for eternity. The regularity with which the *shahīds* return in a cycle of birth and death is also a symbolic re-enactment of the 'bloody' sacrifice of the Roman Catholic Mass, as well as the goat sacrifice at Īd in Islam.

An oblique sense of hope pervades this poem. The speaker is suffering from political persecution, and while he is deprived of freedom, these phenomena of nature, by coming into the cell each day, attempt to assuage the sorrow of imprisonment. That they are sacrificed each day is not as important as the fact that these 'gods of kindness and beauty' return again and again, as if reassurances to the speaker to remain steadfast in his convictions in spite of adverse circumstances. A similar note is struck in 'We Who Were Killed in Half-Lit Streets' with the image of others who will take up the banner of the cause with the passing of people such as the Rosenbergs, and again in 'This Crop of Hopes, O Friend' with the image of the crops which need planting and replanting. All three poems show the poet's recognition of sacrifice for the sake of the cause; they also show that temporary setbacks, as such sacrifices are, must not be allowed to deter right-thinking people in the pursuit of their ultimate cause.

Conclusions

According to psychologists, especially those of a Freudian persuasion—adolescence is preceded by a latency period, a time when children are acquiescent, law abiding, and unemotional, upholders of the status quo, and law and order; in short, that period which parents of adolescent children fondly recall when the child was 'good', and 'well-behaved.' Given Faiz's statement that prison was a 'second adolescence' for him, one could suggest metaphorically, of course, that the nine-year period between 1943, the year of the publication of 'Image of Complaint', and 1952, when 'Hand of the Wind' appeared, as a period of artistic latency for the poet. During this 'latency period,' he was preoccupied with other things and produced very little in the way of major poems.

Prison, however, foisted a 'second adolescence' on Faiz, a period in which his sensitivities and sensibilities, like those of an adolescent, were sharpened once again to the point that he was acutely aware of his environment, however confining it was, and brought to the fore his emotions and affections towards his loved ones, but also towards his activist political causes. For additional insights into Faiz's prison experience, one should read the poems of these two volumes in conjunction with Faiz's prison letters to his wife, Alys, which have appeared in Urdu translation.[20]

Warm, chatty, and informative, these letters in various ways corroborate many of the moods, concerns, and sentiments found in the poetry, but also deviate from them in some cases. These congruences and divergences, however, are a topic for another paper. Because of the 'tranquillity' (Faiz's term) prison afforded him, he was able to write more poems in a shorter period of time than he had done before. The fifty poems of 'Image of Complaint' were written between 1928 and 1942, a period of fourteen years. 'Hand of the Wind' contains forty-one poems, and 'Prison Narrative' thirty-two, for a total of seventy-three poems written within four years, between 1951 and 1955. In terms of simple numbers then, Faiz's poetic output increased dramatically due to imprisonment. If one considers, too, that another nine years passed between the publication of 'Prison Narrative' (1956) and his next volume of poems, 'Hand Beneath the Stone' (Dast-e Tah-e Saṅg; 1965), it is clear that this first long-term prison term, its trauma and injustice aside, was perhaps the most literarily productive period of his life.

Faiz was arrested and held in protective detention one more time [for four months in 1958–59]. He finally went into voluntary exile to Lebanon from 1978, leaving Beirut only at the urging of his friend, PLO leader Yasser Arafat, after the Israeli air attacks in 1982.

During these travails, he continued to write poetry producing his remaining collections: 'The Pinnacle of Sinai Valley' (Sar-e Vādī-e Sīnā, 1971), 'Night's Night' (Rāt dī Rāt; 1975; poems in Punjabi); 'Evenings of the Kings' (Shām-e Shehr-e Yārāṅ, 1978), and 'My Heart, My Traveller' (Mērē dil, mērē musāfir, 1980). His collected works appeared as Sārē Sukhan Hamārē: Kulliyāt-e Faiz in 1983, the year in which he received a nomination for the Nobel Prize for Literature, the year prior to his death. In these he continued to explore, among other topics, the major themes which preoccupied him in the earlier volumes: love in its multifarious guises and permutations, and personal and national freedom, with imagery from his prison days prominent, even persistent.

Notes

1. This paper is based on writing generously supported by the Rockefeller Foundation at its Bellagio Study Center, Lake Como, Italy. (Author)
2. *Manchester Guardian*, 10 March 1951: 5, Print.
3. *New York Times*, 22 March 1951: 7, Print.
4. For a discussion of this incident, together with its ramifications for Urdu and other South Asian literatures, see my [Carlo Coppola], 'The Angārē Group: The Enfants Terribles of Urdu Literature,' *Annual of Urdu Studies* 1 (1981): 57–69, Print.
5. Gene D. Overstreet and Marshall Windmiller, *Communism in India*, Berkeley, CA: University of California, 1960, p. 432, Print.
6. Dr M.D. Taseer was a student in England in the middle of 1930s and participated early on in the establishment of the London Progressive Writers' Association (PWA) in 1934, the forerunner to the Indian All-India Progressive Writers' Association (AIPWA) established in Lucknow in 1936. Tangentially, his wife, the former Christabel George (later renamed Bilquees), was the sister of Faiz's wife, Alys; in fact, Dr and Mrs Taseer introduced Alys to Faiz. For a discussion of this phase of Urdu Literature, see my Carlo Coppola (ed.), 'The All-India Progressive Writers' Association: The Early Phase,' *Marxist Influences and South Asian Literature*, Revised Indian Edition, Delhi: Chanakaya, 1988, pp. 1–41, Print. For an excellent biographical account of Faiz, see Estelle Dryland, *Faiz Ahmed Faiz: Urdu Poet of Social Realism*, Lahore: Vanguard, 1993, pp. 8–32, Print.
7. These letters were published in the collection *Mīzān* (*Scales*), Lahore: Nashireen, 1964, Print.
8. Y.V. Gankovsky, and L.R. Gordon-Polonskaya, *A History of Pakistan*, Moscow: Nauka House, 1964, p. 162, Print.
9. For a detailed account of this entire incident, see Estelle Dryland, 'Faiz Ahmed Faiz and the Rawalpindi Conspiracy Case', *Journal of South Asian Literature* xxvii, No. 2 (Spring-Summer), 175–185, Print.
10. Preface to Victor Kiernan (trans.), *Poems by Faiz*, London: George Allen & Unwin, 1971, Print. The biographical particulars of Faiz's life are drawn from various sources, including Kiernan's preface, my interview with Faiz (see [with A. Jones].*JSAL* 10.1 (Fall 1974): 141–44, Print) and the several excellent introductory essays and interviews in *The Unicorn and the Dancing Girl: Poems of Faiz Ahmed Faiz with Original Text*, Ed. Khalid Hasan, Trans. Daud Kamal, New Delhi: Allied, 1988, pp. xi-lxvi, Print.
11. 'Faiz on Faiz' (Faiz az Faiz), a radio talk which appears as an introduction to Faiz. *Hand Beneath the Stone* (*Dast-e Tah-e Sang*), Delhi: Idara-e Farog-e Adab, 1965, Print. A translation of this essay by Munibur Rahman and me appears in *JSAL* (*JSAL* 10.1 (Fall 1974): 131–39, Print). The quote appears on p. 133.
12. C.M. Naim (trans.), 'Introduction to *Dast-e Sabā*,' *Mahfil—A Quarterly of South Asian Literature*, Print (hereafter Mahfil; superseded by *JSAL* in 1972), [1:1 (Spring 1963), 3;

rpt. 'Eleven Poems and an Introduction by Faiz Ahmed Faiz,' tr. C.M. Naim and me, *Dialogue Calcutta*, 19 (1971). Hereafter 'Eleven Poems.']

13. Faiz Ahmed Faiz, *Dast-e-Sabā* (*Hand of the Wind*), New Delhi: Azad Kitab Ghar, 1953, p. 13, Print. [all poems of *Dast-e-Sabā* quoted from this edition]

14. This poem appears in 'Eleven Poems,' pp. 6–8. For a discussion of five major English-language translators of Faiz's poetry (Victor Kiernan, Mahmood Jamal, Naomi Lazard, Daud Kamal, and Agha Shahid Ali), see my [Carlo Coppola], 'The Language of Faiz and His English Translators,' *South Asia* 14.2 (December 1992): 71–92, Print [another version of the paper: 'Faiz in English: How Five Translators Worked Their Art' included in this book].

15. *Qavvālī*: a type of rhythmic song unique to Urdu, used as a part of a Sufi gathering (*majlis*). Comparable genres exist in other parts of Islamic world.

16. Faiz Ahmed Faiz, *Naqsh-e-Faryādī* (*Image of Complaint*), Amritsar: Azad Book Depot, n.d., pp. 39–40, Print.

17. Faiz Ahmed Faiz, *Zindāṅ Nāmā* (*Prison Narrative*), Aligarh: Anjuman-e Taraqqi Urdu [Hind], p. 30, Print. [all poems of *Zindāṅ Nāmā* quoted from this edition]

18. *Poems by Faiz*, p. 84, note 60. It is significant that Kiernan (and Faiz) did not include this poem in *Poems by Faiz*, to be published in the West, possibly because of its controversial political content.

19. Faiz was refused entry into the United States under the notorious McCarran-Walter Act of 1952, barring all admitted or suspected communists or communist war sympathizers from entering the country. This law was passed at the height of the post-war, anti-communist hysteria. For a discussion of this point, and the works of other poets, Nazim Hikmet, Mahmoud Darwish, Pablo Neruda, Yannis Ritsos, and Pentii Saarikoski similarly barred, see *Poetry East*, 27 (Spring 1989). The translation of seventeen poems of Faiz in this collection are by Agha Shahid Ali, who also guest-edited the entire issue. Mr Ali has published a volume of English translations of Faiz's poetry, Agha Shahid Ali (trans.), *The Rebel's Silhouette*, Salt Lake City, UT: Peregrine Smith Poetry Series, 1991, Print.

20. Faiz's English letters to Alys appear in Urdu translation in Mirza Zafarul Hasan (ed.), *Salībēṅ Mērē Dariče Mēṅ* (*Crosses in My Window*), Karachi, Pak, 1971, Print. Alys Faiz's letters to her husband appeared as *Dear Heart: To Faiz in Prison (1951-1955)*, Lahore: Ferozsons, 1985, Print. Faiz's original English letters cannot be published in English because they were destroyed by termites.* A selection of the letters to Alys appears retranslated into English by C.M. Naim, *Annual of Urdu Studies*, Vol. 5, Chicago, 1985, pp. 117–25, Print. [*Thirty-three of these letters were recently discovered and retrieved. They have been published. See Kyla Pasha and Salima Hashmi (eds.), *Two Loves—Faiz's Letters from Jail*, 1st edn., Lahore: Sang-e-Meel Publications, 2011, Print—Editor]

WE

Original: *Hum log* from *Naqsh-e Faryādī* (1941)
TRANSLATORS: C. M. NAIM AND CARLO COPPOLA

Holding rows of snuffed candles in our hearts,
Frightened by the sun's light, bored;
Tightly holding our darkness in an embrace
Like we hold the limpid thoughts of her charms.

The form of gain and loss; the hew of beginnings and ends
The same futile interest; the same useless question;
Depressed by vapid, present moments;
Sad from past memories; weak from future fears.

Thirsty thoughts, still unquenched.
Burnt out tears, never to reach the eye.
A stiff pain, never to be cast into song,
Caught—concealed in the crevices of the heart.
A vague, confused search for relief;
A greed for wasteland—or prison; a search for garments to rent in rage.

6

FAIZ IN ENGLISH:
HOW FIVE TRANSLATORS WORKED THEIR ART

The 2011 celebrations of the birth centenary of Nobel Prize nominee Faiz Ahmed Faiz (1911–1984) were extensive, not only in Pakistan and India but in expatriate South Asian communities throughout the world, in real time as well as on the internet. Faiz is acknowledged as Urdu literature's preeminent modern poet and one of South Asia's most famous and distinguished writers of the twentieth century. Translations of his works in English were indispensible in bringing Faiz to the attention of a worldwide audience. In this essay I shall examine and attempt to evaluate the English renderings of five of his translators.

In his incisive and often-quoted introduction to Faiz's first volume of poetry, *Naqsh-e Faryādī* (The Image of Complaint, 1943), Urdu literature's ultra-modernist poet and critic N.M. Rashed (1910–1975) described Faiz as 'a poet who is standing at the confluence of romance and reality. His nature urges him to be in harmony with love, but he cannot resist the temptation to cast a glance at the nakedness and bitterness of life through a chink in the door of reality'.[1] Despite his privileged, upper-class background, Faiz was throughout his life, through both his words and his actions, an indefatigable fighter for the world's voiceless and suffering people: Indians oppressed by the British in the 1930s and 40s, African freedom fighters or the persecuted Rosenbergs in cold-war America in the 50s, Vietnamese peasants fleeing American napalm and Agent Orange

This paper, based on research and writing generously supported by the Rockefeller Foundation at its Bellagio Study and Conference Center, Lake Como, Italy, was originally presented at the seminar, 'Abiding Aspects of Faiz Ahmed Faiz', for the annual meeting of Asian Studies on the Pacific Coast, Stanford University, Stanford, California, 29 June 1990. An earlier version of it was published as 'The Language of Faiz & His English Translators', *South Asia: Journal of South Asian Studies*, 15:2 (December 1992), 71–92. Grateful thanks to the South Asian Studies Association (SASA), who also granted permission to reproduce the earlier version of the article.

herbicide in the 60s, or Palestinian children confined to squalid refugee camps in the 70s. In short, he wrote eloquently of the human aspiration for freedom, dignity, and, of course, love.

Anyone who reads Faiz's poetry immediately recognizes several of its outstanding features. His language is highly introspective and symbolic, sometimes simple in the extreme, giving it a strikingly elusive quality. But it is often lush with the traditional romantic imagery of Urdu love (ghazal) poetry: the 'Lover' ('āshiq), the 'Beloved' (mahbūb), and the 'Rival' (raqīb); the 'Nightingale' (bulbul) and the 'Rose' (gul), etc. However, he imbues these old images with new, politically charged overtones. For example, in traditional eighteenth- and nineteenth-century Urdu love poetry the Lover and the Rival vie for the affection of the fickle, often cruel and invariably indifferent Beloved. In the poem Raqīb sē (To the Rival) from Naqsh-e Faryādī, the Lover asks the Rival to join him in putting aside their traditional differences, implying that they work together (as Marxists, one is to assume) to overcome their country's political enemies.[2] In the early 40s, this rewrite of the equation of the traditional love triangle was revolutionary, not only literarily, but politically as well.

Methodology

In order to analyze and critique the work of several of his English translators, I devised the following methodology:

1. First, I have chosen a 'typical' poem, one well-known enough that translators would have to translate it.
2. This Urdu poem is then presented in Urdu, together with a transliteration into Roman script, followed by a highly literal and admittedly awkward English translation I have made for the purposes of discussion.
3. I then examined the structure of the poem as a whole and selected for comment three key words and phrases which are critical to the poem and which provide any translator with a challenge. Three items rather than a larger number have been chosen due to the exigencies of space.
4. Next, the manner in which the five translators have dealt with these three key points is discussed. The five translators have been chosen on the basis of, first, the overall quality of their renderings, and second, their ready availability.
5. Finally, based on this discussion, I have attempted to generalize from this single poem an evaluation of the relative merits (or demerits) of the individual translator's work—in three cases, a whole set of poems, and in two others, that single poem.

For this exercise, I have made several presuppositions—which are, I realize, contradictory—with regard to the art of translation, for, indeed, as the Italian idealist philosopher/esthetician Benedetto Croce (1866–1952) insists, translation is an 'art'. First, translations are impossible but should be done anyway; second, translations—good, middling or bad—are better than none at all; third, as the Italian adage sums up the situation: *Traduttore, traditore* (Translator, traitor); and, finally, Goethe's discerning remark: 'Say what we may of the inadequacy of translation, yet the work is and will always be one of the weightiest and worthiest undertakings in the general concerns of the world'.

A Poem by Faiz

I have chosen Faiz's *Mujh sē pahlī sī mahabbat, mērī mahbūb na māṅg* (From Me, My Beloved, Do not Ask for that Former Kind of Love) from *Naqsh-e Faryādī* as the focus of this essay. It is one of his most famous and, according to the judgement of many critics, one of his finest. An early work dating from the late 30s or early 40s, it is an excellent example of one of the poet's major themes: the romance-vs-reality dichotomy found in much of the early poetry, to which N.M. Rashed alludes in his introduction. Here Faiz couples traditional romantic imagery with contemporary political statement, a device he will use throughout his entire literary career. Faiz himself also acknowledges that this poem was among the first to demonstrate his then-new esthetics based on political and social commitment, or what is termed in Urdu literature of the 30s, through the 70s, Marxist-oriented 'progressivism' (*taraqqī pasaṅdī*).

Each line of the poem is presented three ways:
A in its original Urdu;
B in an interlinear Roman transliteration; and
C a very literal rendering into English.

In order to present the widest range of English meaning possible, multiple synonyms of the single Urdu word or phrase are given, each appearing one after the other separated with a slash mark (/).

Title A: مُجھ سے پہلی سی محبت مری محبوب نہ مانگ

Title B: *Mujh sē pahlī sī mahabbat, mērī mahbūb na māṅg*

Title C: From Me, My Beloved, Do Not Ask for/Beg/Entreat for That
Former/Previous/Earlier [kind of] Love

1 A مُجھ سے پہلی سی محبت مری محبوب نہ مانگ

  B *Mujh sē pahlī sī mahabbat, mērī mahbūb na māṅg*

  C From me, my beloved, do not ask for/beg/entreat for that former/
previous/earlier [kind of] love.

2 A مَیں نے سمجھا تھا کہ تُو ہے تو درخشاں ہَے حیات

  B *Maiṅ nē samjhā thā kē tū hai to darakhshāṅ hai hayāt;*

  C I used to think that [because] you existed, life was brilliant/
resplendent/dazzling;

3 A تیرا غم ہے تو غمِ دہر کا جھگڑا کیا ہے

  B *Terā gham hai to gham-e dehr kā jhagṛā kyā hai?*

  C Your sorrow/sadness/anguish existed, [so] then what was the
wrangling/quarrel/contention of the sorrow/sadness/anguish of
the times/age/world?

4 A تیری صُورت سے ہَے عالم میں بہاروں کو ثبات

  B *Terī sūrat sē hai 'ālam mēṅ bahāroṅ ko sabāt,*

  C From your face came the constancy/stability/permanence of
springtimes in the world;

5 A تیری آنکھوں کے سِوا دُنیا میں رکھا کیا ہَے

  B *Terī āṅkhoṅ kē sivā dunyā mēṅ rakhā kyā hai?*

  C Besides your eyes, what is held/put/placed in the world?

6 A تُو جو مل جائے تو تقدیر نِگوں ہو جائے

  B *Tū jo mil jā'ē to taqdīr nigūṅ ho jā'ē;*

  C [If] you were joined/embraced/clasped [by me], then destiny/fate/
kismet would be overturned/turned upside down/defied;

7 A یُوں نہ تھا، میں نے فقط چاہا تھا یُوں ہو جائے

  B *Yūṅ na thā, maiṅ nē faqat čāhā thā yūṅ ho jā'ē*

  C It was not thus/like this/so; I only wished it were thus/like this/so.

8 A اَور بھی دُکھ ہیں زمانے میں محبت کے سوا

B *Aur bhī dukh haiṅ zamānē meṅ mahabbat kē sivā,*

C [There] are other sorrows/sadness/grief in the world besides love;

9 A راحتیں اَور بھی ہیں وصل کی راحت کے سوا

B *Rāhateṅ aur bhī haiṅ vasl kī rāhat kē sivā*

C [There] are other comforts/pleasures/delights besides the comforts/pleasures/delights of union/caressing/making love.

10 A اَن گِنت صدیوں کے تاریک بہیمانہ طلسم

B *An-ginat sadyoṅ kē tārīk bahīmānā tilism*

C The dark, brutal spells/enchantments/magic of countless centuries

11 A ریشم و اطلس و کمخواب میں بُنوائے ہوئے

B *Rēsham-o-atlas-o-kamkhāb mēṅ bunvā'ē hu'ē*

C Woven/entwined/interlaced into silk and satin and brocade;

12 A جا بجا بکتے ہوئے کوچہ و بازار میں جسم

B *Jā-ba-jā biktē hu'ē kūčā-o-bāzār meṅ jism,*

C Everywhere in the alleys/lanes/byways and markets/shops/bazaars bodies [are] sold,

13 A خاک میں لتھڑے ہوئے خون میں نہلائے ہوئے

B *Khāk meṅ lithṛē hu'ē khūn meṅ nehlā'ē hu'ē*

C Besmeared/besmirched/speckled with dust, bathed/washed/steeped in blood;

14 A جسم نکلے ہوئے امراض کے تنّوروں سے

B *Jism niklē hu'ē āmrāz kē tannūroṅ sē,*

C Bodies emerging from the ovens/stoves/coals of disease/sickness/contagion,

15 A پیپ بہتی ہوئی گلتے ہوئے ناسُوروں سے

B *Pīp behtī hu'ī galtē hu'ē nāsūroṅ sē—*

C Pus flowing from oozing/leaking ulcers/sores/pustules—

16 A لَوٹ جاتی ہے اُدھر کو بھی نظر کیا کیجئے

B *Laut jātī hai udhar ko bhī nazar, kyā kījē?*

C [My] glance returns/retreats/shrinks back from there too; what's to be done?

17 A اب بھی دِلکش ہے ترا حُسن، مگر کیا کیجئے

B *Ab bhī dilkash hai tērā husn, magar kyā kījē?*

C Your beauty is still lovely/attractive/alluring, but what's to be done?

18 A اَور بھی دُکھ ہیں زمانے میں محبت کے سِوا

B *Aur bhī dukh haiṅ zamānē mēṅ mahabbat kē sivā*

C [There] are other sorrows/sadness/grief in the world besides love;

19 A راحتیں اَور بھی ہیں وصل کی راحت کے سِوا

B *Rāhatēṅ aur bhī haiṅ vasl kī rāhat kē sivā*

C [There] are other comforts/pleasures/delights besides the comforts/pleasures/delights of union/caressing/making love.

20 A مُجھ سے پہلی سی محبت مِری محبوب نہ مانگ

B *Mujh sē pahlī sī mahabbat, mērī mahbūb na māṅg*

C From me, my beloved, do not ask for/beg/entreat for that former/previous/earlier [kind of] love

The statement and the structure of the poem seem simple. Rather than continue the type of intimacy the lovers have experienced in the past, the Lover attempts to redefine the relationship in the light of present-day political, social and economic realities. The title of the poem, which is also the poem's first and last lines, demands this redefinition. Rather than catering to the Beloved as a traditional Lover should, this new Lover gently chides her with the statement that she should not ask, or expect, from him the kind of 'love' (*mahabbat*) he and countless lovers before him have shown their beloveds.

The Lover's traditional mental state is suggested in lines 2 through 6, and his posturing, vocabulary and phraseology draw heavily from the *ghazal* lexicon: addressing her in the intimate *tū* (you) form and various allusions to 'pain' (*gham*), the 'sorrow of the world' (*gham-e dehr*), her

'face' (*sūrat*) and 'eyes' (*āṅkhoṅ*), 'springtimes' (*bahāroṅ*), 'constancy'
(*sabāt*), and 'destiny' (*taqdīr*).

Line 7, however, marks a point of critical transition:

یُوں نہ تھا، میں نے فقط چاہا تھا یُوں ہو جائے

Yūṅ na thā, maiṅ nē faqat čāhā thā yūṅ ho jā'ē
It was not thus/like this/so; I only wished it were thus/like this/so.

A simple line, it stands in stark contrast to the elegance and lushness
of the preceding lines, and serves as a bridge to the description of the
horror and suffering to follow. With this line the Lover turns from the
self-absorbed world of romance toward the real, unattractive, frightening
world 'out there'. The latter is described in stark, graphic terms in lines
10 through 15, underscoring the vast contrast with the limited sphere of
life and romance depicted earlier in the poem.

In lines 16 and 17, the Lover poses to the Beloved two questions which
sum up his dilemma:

لَوٹ جاتی ہے اُدھر کو بھی نظر کیا کیجیے

Laut jātī hai udhar ko bhī nazar, kyā kījē?
[My] glance returns/retreats/shrinks back from there too; what's to be
done?

اب بھی دِلکش ہے ترا حُسن، مگر کیا کیجیے

Ab bhī dilkash hai tērā husn, magar kyā kījē?
Your beauty is still lovely/attractive/alluring, but what's to be done?

It is a truism that, sometimes, the right answers are not as important
as the right questions. Here, the Lover does not seem to have any right
answer, but he poses two right questions about what he sees as a choice:
either the Beloved or the real world outside. The questions reflect his
uncertainty about this dilemma. However, the following lines, 18 and
19, are repeats of lines 8 and 9, and the final line of the poem a repeat of
both the title and first line. In the absence of answers to his quandary,
the Lover does seem to imply that, indeed, he will turn his attention to
the 'other sorrows' (*aur bhī dukh*) and 'other pleasures' (*rāhatēṅ aur bhī*)
in that other world.

The Translations and Translators

The translations of this poem, considered in the order of their publication, are taken from:

1 Victor Kiernan, *Poems by Faiz* (bilingual ed; Urdu-English) (London, George Allen & Unwin, 1971)
2 Mahmood Jamal, *The Penguin Book of Modern Urdu Poetry* (New York, Viking Penguin, Inc., 1986)
3 Naomi Lazard, *The True Subject: Selected Poems of Faiz Ahmed Faiz* (bilingual ed; Urdu-English) (Princeton, Princeton University Press, 1987)
4 Daud Kamal, *The Unicorn and the Dancing Girl: Poems of Faiz Ahmed Faiz with original text* (trilingual ed; Urdu-Hindi-English) ed Khalid Hasan (New Delhi, Allied Publishers, 1988)
5 Agha Shahid Ali, *Poetry East,* 27, (Spring 1989)[3]

The full text of each translation is found in the Appendix.

Who are these translators? Four of them are published poets writing in English—Jamal (b 1948), Lazard (b 1936), Kamal (1935–1987) and Ali (1949–2001)—and one, Kiernan (1913–2009), was an academic. The three poets from South Asia (Jamal, Kamal, Ali) speak Urdu as their first language. Of the remaining two—Kiernan, who is British, and Lazard, an American—both speak English as their mother tongue. The poet (Lazard) knows very little Urdu; the academic (Kiernan) was fluent in Urdu, having spent extended time in South Asia during World War II; both had direct access to and input from Faiz himself while making their translations.

Key Passages: 'Sorrow,' Union', and 'Pus'

To carry out this project ideally, we should go through each line of each of the five translations and compare it to the original. Space does not permit such an exercise. However, I am proceeding on the assumption that a discussion of the way translators have treated a few key words and passages of the original poem would give us some indication as to the skill and care with which they have undertaken their task. I have chosen three such items for this discussion:

1 the word *dukh*, which appears in line 8 of the original, repeated again in line 18
2 the word *vasl* found in line 9 of the original and repeated again in line 19 and

3   two lines, 14 and 15 of the original, the key phrase of which is *pīp behtī hu'ī* (pus flowing).

Dukh: Sorrow

Faiz uses two words in this poem which mean 'sorrow'. The first is the Arabic *gham*, appearing twice in line 3:

تیرا غم ہے تو غمِ دہر کا جھگڑا کیا ہے

Tērā gham hai to gham-e dehr kā jhagrā kyā hai?
Your sorrow/sadness/anguish existed, [so] then what was the wrangling/quarrel/contention of the sorrow/sadness/anguish of the times/age/world?

Depending on context, the Arabic word *gham* can also mean 'grief,' 'mourning,' or 'woe.' In the classical love poetry of Arabic, Persian, and Urdu, *gham* is the sorrow/sadness/anguish suffered by the lovers when separated. It is also the sorrow/sadness/anguish the Lover feels when he has been treated badly by the Beloved. In Sufi poetry, *gham* is the sorrow/sadness/anguish resulting from separation from God. At its most mundane, it is the generally sad condition in which one lives out one's life. At its most acute, the *gham* of Sufi poetry can be transformed by the successful mystic into exquisite suffering as ecstatic delight. Significantly, Faiz uses this term early in the poem to describe a traditional love relationship.

The second word for 'sorrow', found in lines 8 and 18 is *dukh*:

اور بھی دُکھ ہیں زمانے میں محبت کے سوا

Aur bhī dukh haiṅ zamānē meṅ mahabbat kē sivā
[There] are other sorrows/sadness/grief in the world besides love;

The word *dukh* is a word of more indigenous, perhaps even humbler, South Asia origins than the loftier Arabic *gham*. *Dukh* is derived from Sanskrit *duhkha*, and, in its Pali form, *dukkha*, is found in the first of the Four Noble Truths enunciated by the Buddha at his first sermon at Sarnath: All existence is suffering (*dukkha*), that is, existential suffering. Thus the connotations of *dukh* are broader, more proletarian, than that of *gham*. To connote the sorrows in the world other than love, some of which are to be graphically depicted a few lines later, *dukh* appears to be a masterful word choice.

English, however, is more limited than Urdu in its connotations of *dukh*. Not surprisingly, many of the overtones of this word are lost in Kiernan's 'torment' for *dukh*:

Our world knows other torments than of love (line 8)

Moreover, the phrase 'other torments than of love', while metrically suitable, is jolting grammatically. Thus it is not entirely felicitous.

Jamal translates *dukh* as 'sorrows':

for there are other sorrows in the world than love (line 13)

The third translator, Lazard, offers 'pain' in the singular, which is simple in the extreme. However, she reconstructs Faiz's line—a simple copulative verb (*hain*) and two clauses 'in the world' *'zamāné mēn'* and 'besides love' *'mahabbat kē sivā'*—into a statement with 'world' (*zamāné*) as a subject of a powerful, aggressive verb, 'to deal out', and 'pain' as the object, suggesting impersonal, uncontrollable fate or chance:

The world knows how to deal out pain, apart from passion (line 10)

Hers is not a translation in the strict sense of the word, but rather a 'transcreation', a translator's successful rendering of the purest, truest sense, if not the exact words, of a foreign-language poet. In fact, with Lazard, numerous examples of such 'transcreations' abound, which, in many ways, make her versions more than 'mere' translations. They can and often do replicate much of the lyricism and many of the refined but elusive turns of language of the original. Faiz was especially pleased to have her as his translator.

Daud Kamal presents Faiz's single line in two lines, with *dukh* translated as 'afflictions':

There are afflictions
Which have nothing to do with desire, (lines 14–15)

The fifth translator, Ali, succinctly offers 'sorrows':

But there are other sorrows, (line 12)

Thus the renderings are 'torments' (Kiernan), 'sorrows' twice (Jamal and Ali), 'pain' (Lazard), and 'afflictions' (Kamal). None of these is fully capable of offering the contrast Faiz achieves with his *gham/dukh* variance. Moreover, Jamal, Kamal and Ali all use the ineffective, bland 'there are/were' construction, thereby diminishing the effect of their translation of *gham/dukh*. Thus, of the five, Lazard's rendering of the entire line is the most notable.

Vasl: Union

Like *gham*, *vasl* is also a powerfully connotative term. It can be glossed as meeting/union/making love, or, progressing metaphorically along this continuum, even copulation or orgasm. In standard love poetry, *vasl* is the union of the lovers, with all that is implied in that meeting. In Sufi poetry it is also used to try to describe—always inadequately and unsuccessfully—the 'ineffable union' (*vasl*) with God. Again, because of the relatively underdeveloped nature of the vocabulary of western mystical poetry as compared to that of the Islamic and Indian traditions, few, if any, of these overtones can be achieved in English.

Kiernan offers the pallid, Victorian 'a fond embrace' for *vasl*:

And other happiness than a fond embrace (line 9)

The second translator, Jamal, is drab with 'other pleasure':

and other pleasure, too (line 14)

Lazard's rendering, 'the realm of love', is better than what either Kiernan or Jamal offers. Equally distinctive and notable is her rendering of the term *rāhat* (pleasure) as 'manna for the heart':

and manna for the heart beyond the realm of love (line 14)

Again, there is, literally, no 'manna for the heart' in Faiz's original. But in the context, especially with its biblical overtones juxtaposed with 'realm of love' (*vasl*), the transcreation is memorable.

Kamal translates *vasl* as 'Raptures', and probably comes closest in meaning to Faiz's word choice:

Raptures
Which have nothing to do with love (lines 16–17)

Here he breaks the single Urdu line into two English lines, offering 'Raptures', capitalized and standing alone in the line, which affords it considerable emphasis. As such, it is a creative and notable equivalent to what would be connoted in Urdu. This translation is as elegant in its simplicity as Lazard's is in its complexity.

Again, the laconic Ali translates *vasl* as 'love':

comforts other than love (line 13)

He has conflated two Urdu lines into a terse single line in English. When the line is repeated towards the end of the poem, he translates the two lines as two (22–23), rather than a single line, as here.

Thus for *vasl* the translators offer 'a fond embrace' (Kiernan), 'other pleasure' (Jamal), 'the realm of love' (Lazard), 'raptures' (Kamal) and 'love' (Ali). Lazard's and Kamal's, for different reasons, are, in this instance, the most successful renderings.

Pīp behtī hu'ī: Pus flowing

If the terms *dukh* and *vasl* cause the translator problems connotatively, the phrase *pīp behtī hu'ī*, literally, 'pus flowing', in lines 14–15 of Faiz's original presents the translator with difficulties that are as much denotative as they are cultural. The idea of 'pus' (*pīp*) in either language is not especially appealing. In fact, it is rather repulsive in both. But, along a continuum of +repulsiveness/-repulsiveness, I submit that Urdu speakers would likely find the word *pīp* less repulsive than English speakers would find 'pus', given the well-known Northern European cultural aversion to most bodily discharges. Thus in English, the word 'pus' is, quite simply, unpoetic in the extreme. The valence of the word in English is negatively powerful beyond what it is in Urdu. Significantly, two poets, Lazard and Ali, do not translate the phrase at all, perhaps preferring to overlook it, realizing its unacceptability in an English lyric poem. Kiernan tones down the original with the more metaphorical 'dripping corruption':

Flesh issuing from the cauldrons of disease
With festered sores dripping corruption (lines 14–15)

Jamal and Kamal are literalists in this instance. Judging from Jamal's word choices and syntax, it seems likely, too, that he had Kiernan's translation in mind when he rendered these lines:

> bodies risen from the cauldron of disease
> pus dripping from their festering sores—(lines 19–20)

Kamal is equally graphic and elaborates by rendering *jism* (bodies) as 'body after body' and *niklē hu'ē* (coming out/emerging) as 'disgorges':

> The furnace of poverty and disease disgorges body after body—
> Pus oozing out of decaying flesh. (lines 24–25)

Of the five versions, only two translate the word *pīp* directly into English, arguably to the detriment of the translation.

Some Final Evaluations

While this short analysis does not give definitive answers about the quality of the translations of this individual poem by these five translators, some general evaluative judgements about the renderings are possible.

Kiernan's translations as a whole are perhaps more workmanlike than literary.[4] He was an historian by training, not a poet, a fact which he readily acknowledges. When no other translations of Faiz existed, his were, obviously, most welcome. However, as more and more of them appear, many made by poets, Kiernan's have assumed a more historical rather than literary significance.

Jamal's translations lack vitality and seem to look too heavily in places to Kiernan's earlier versions. They and most of the pieces in the anthology in which they appear are literal, often wanting in nuance and finesse. Moreover, they seem to have been done in a hurry. More is the pity, because Penguin anthologies, the series in which this Faiz translation appears, attract wide critical attention due to extensive and skillful marketing and advertising. Moreover, because they are reasonably priced and well distributed, these books are readily available to the general reader and are often used as classroom texts. In the hands of a more adept translator-poet, not only Faiz but modern Urdu poetry generally could have been presented more excitingly, more passionately, than they are in this volume. Thus this anthology seems to have been a missed opportunity for Urdu literature.

Daud Kamal would have probably done an excellent job with the Penguin anthology. Degreed from Cambridge, a professor of English, and a poet in English, he was also a scholar of Urdu literature, especially Faiz. In his translations he does not intrude himself into the poetry, either by 'under-translating' (badly translating an especially fine passage or poem), or 'over-translating' (making a rather earth-bound passage or poem in Urdu soar in English; admittedly, this tends to happen less with the best poets, such as Faiz, and more often with second-rate poets). Kamal's sudden death in New York in 1987 was, indeed, a loss not only to Urdu literature, but to a small group of stalwarts in Pakistan who, by writing excellent poetry in English, are establishing a viable, distinctive tradition of English poetry there.[5] In the view of those who have taken the time to learn of his work, Kamal is thought to be much underrated and deserves more credit than he has heretofore received.

This leaves Lazard and Ali. In Lazard's case we have a famous, highly gifted, mature poet who was working under a number of constraints when making her translations. The lack of profound knowledge of the target language need not necessarily be a constraint to a translator. Various poets who do not know a given language, for example, the American poet W.S. Merwin (b 1927), translate successfully in collaboration with a native speaker of that language. Lazard's constraints in translating Faiz had less to do with her knowledge of Urdu and more to do with the less-than-ideal, problematic conditions under which she collaborated with him. They were separated by a distance of about 6000 miles between New York and Beirut. In the pre-Internet dark ages, except for a few face-to-face meetings and the occasional phone call, they had to rely almost entirely on the post for communication. The Israeli invasion of Lebanon, during which Faiz was nearly killed, caused him to depart from Beirut to England and then reluctantly to Pakistan. Finally, his deteriorating health and death brought the collaboration to an end. These problems notwithstanding, Lazard has managed not only to translate, but to transcreate, most of Faiz's best poems, which, because of her close working relationship with him, seem to bear his final imprimatur. Before appearing in book form, Lazard's translations were published in various important 'little' poetry magazines, thereby bringing his works to an important English-speaking, -reading audience. For people who did not know Faiz's poetry, her translations offered a satisfying, sophisticated initial exposure. For people well acquainted with Faiz's original poems, Lazard's renderings may, initially at least, cause a raised eyebrow here and there, especially with its bilingual text (eg 'manna for the heart' for *rāhat*). However, on repeated readings, the refinements she lavished on these pieces become more apparent to the discerning reader. The fact of the matter is, 'manna for the heart' works well within the translation. Moreover, Faiz himself liked it!

Because Urdu was Ali's first language, because he was a practicing poet in English residing in the United states where he had intimate, day-to-day contact with the living language, and because he did not rush into print, his versions may well be the touchstone for English translations of Faiz to date. Ali is sometimes brash with the original text, often working more for those elusive qualities of 'sense' and 'style' rather than mere equivalents. Like Lazard, he sometimes 'transcreates' rather than translates, and like Lazard's, his results are highly effective and affective. Particularly striking are Ali's bold attempts at translating *ghazals,* those 'untranslatable' lyric poems of Urdu whose structure alone, to say nothing of meaning at numerous levels of association and connotation, has made the most capable of translators throw up their hands in despair, resignation and tears.

In the final analysis, Lazard and Ali would have to be judged the most successful of the translators presented here. This is not to say that the others have failed. They each have their own level of success and provide the basis for contrastive analysis with the original and other translations. As Faiz continued to attract additional critical attention, such as that shown in connection with the celebration of his birth centenary, aspiring translators have doubtless studied all of these renderings carefully before undertaking this at-once rewarding, at-once thankless, art.[6]

APPENDIX: FIVE TRANSLATIONS

For the sake of comparison, the three key words and phrase discussed in this essay are presented in boldface in all five translations.

1. Translator: Victor Kiernan, *Poems by Faiz* (London, George Allen & Unwin, 1971)

   #### LOVE, DO NOT ASK

   1   Love, do not ask me for that love again.
   Once I thought life, because you lived, a prize—
   The time's pain nothing, you alone were pain;
   Your beauty kept earth's springtimes from decay.
   5   My universe held only your bright eyes—
   If I won you, fate would be at my feet.
   It was not true, all this, but only wishing;
   Our world knows other **torments** than of love,
   And other happiness than **a fond embrace.**
   10   Dark curse of countless ages, savagery

Inwoven with silk and satin and gold lace,
Men's bodies sold in street and marketplace,
Bodies that caked grime fouls and thick blood smears,
Flesh issuing from the cauldrons of disease
15   With festered sores **dripping corruption**—these
Sights haunt me too, and will not be shut out;
Not to shut out, though your looks ravish still.
This world knows other **torments** than of love,
And other happiness than **a fond embrace**;
20   Love, do not ask for my old love again.

2. Translator: Mahmood Jamal, *The Penguin Book of Modern Urdu Poetry* (New York, Viking Penguin, Inc., 1986)

DO NOT ASK OF ME, MY LOVE

1   Do not ask of me, my love,
that love I once had for you.
There was a time when
life was bright and young and blooming,
5   and your sorrow was much more than
any other pain.
Your beauty gave the spring everlasting youth;
your eyes, yes your eyes were everything,
all else was vain.
10   While you were mine, I thought, the world was mine.
Though now I know that it was not reality,
That's the way I imagined it to be;
for there are other **sorrows** in the world than love,
and other **pleasures**, too.
15   Woven in silk and satin and brocade,
those dark and brutal curses of countless centuries:
bodies bathed in blood, smeared with dust,
sold from market-place to market-place,
bodies risen from the cauldron of disease
20   **pus dripping** from their festering sores—
my eyes must also turn to these.
You're beautiful still, my love
but I am helpless too;
for there are other **sorrows** in the world than love,
25   and other **pleasures** too.
Do not ask of me, my love,
that love I once had for you!

3. Translator: Naomi Lazard, *The True Subject: Selected Poems of Faiz Ahmed Faiz* (Princeton, Princeton University Press, 1987)

DO NOT ASK ME NOW, BELOVED

1   Don't ask me now, Beloved, to love you as I did
when I believed life owed its lustre to your existence.

The torments of the world meant nothing;
you alone could make me suffer.
5   Your beauty guaranteed the spring,
ordained its enduring green.
Your eyes were all there was of value anywhere.
If I could have you, fate would bow before me.
None of this was real; it was all invented by desire.
10   The world knows how to deal out **pain**, apart from passion
and **manna for the heart**, beyond **the realm of love**.
Warp and woof, the trappings of the rich are woven
by the brutish spell cast over all the ages;
human bodies numbed by filth, deformed by injuries,
15   cheap merchandise on sale in every street.
I must attend to this too: what can be done?
Your beauty still delights me, but what can I do?
The world knows how to deal out pain, apart from passion,
and **manna for the heart**, beyond **the realm of love**.
20   Don't ask from me, Beloved, love like that one long ago.

4. Translator: Daud Kamal, *The Unicorn and the Dancing Girl: Poems of Faiz Ahmed Faiz with original text,* ed Khalid Hasan (New Delhi, Allied Publishers, 1988)

DO NOT ASK

1   Don't ask me for that past love
When I thought you alone illumined this world
And because of you
The griefs of this world did not matter.
5   I imagined
Your beauty gave permanence to the colours of spring
And your eyes were the only stars in the universe.
I thought
If I could only make you mine
10   Destiny would, forever, be in my hands.
Of course, it was never like this.
This was just a hope, a dream.
Now I know
There are **afflictions**
15   Which have nothing to do with desire,
Raptures
Which have nothing to do with love.
On the dark loom of centuries,
Woven into silk, damask, and goldcloth
20   Is the oppressive enigma of our lives.
Everywhere—in the alleys and bazars—
Human flesh is being sold—
Throbbing between layers of dust—bathed in blood.
The furnace of poverty and disease disgorges body after body—
25   **Pus oozing** out of decaying flesh.
How can I look the other way?
Your beauty is still a river of gems but now I know

There are **afflictions** which have nothing to do with desire,
Raptures which have nothing to do with love.
30   My love, do not ask me. . . .

5. Translator: Agha Shahid Ali, *Poetry East*, 27 (Spring 1989)

DON'T ASK ME FOR THAT LOVE AGAIN

1   What which then was ours, my love,
       don't ask me for that love again.
       The world then was gold, burnished with light—
       and only because of you. That's what I had believed.
5   How could one weep for sorrows other than yours?
       How could one have any sorrow but the one you gave?
       So what were these protests, these rumours of injustice?
       A glimpse of your face was evidence of springtime.
       The sky, wherever I looked, was nothing but your eyes.
10   If you'd fall into my arms, Fate would be helpless
       All this I'd thought, all this I'd believed.
       But there were other **sorrows**, comforts other than **love**.
       The rich had cast their spell on history:
       dark centuries had been embroidered on brocades and silks.
15   Bitter threads began to unravel before me
       as I went into alleys and into open markets
       saw bodies plastered with ash, bathed in blood.
       I saw them sold and bought, again and again.
       This too deserves attention. I can't help but look back
20   when I return from those alleys—oh, what can be done?
       And you still are so beautiful—what should one do?
       There are other **sorrows** in this world, comforts other than **love**.
       Don't ask me, my love, for that love again.[7]

Notes

1. The introduction is dated from Delhi, 15 November 1941. Unattributed translations
   from the Urdu are by me.
2. '*Raqīb sē*' (To the Rival)
   Come, for linked with you are the memories of beauty
   Which had made our hearts a fairies' abode,
   Recalling which we had forgotten the world.
   We thought time a fiction of Time;
   Those paths where her drunken youth performed an act of kindness
   Know your footsteps,
   Paths where that beauty's caravans pass,
   Worshipped by these, my eyes.
   Those darling winds suffused with the faded perfume of her dress
   Have cavorted with you.
   The moon's glory is also shed upon you from that roof
   Where the throbbing pain of bygone nights lingers.

You have seen that forehead, those cheeks, those lips
Contemplating which we have squandered life.
Those magician-eyes with their lost look have also touched you.
You know why we have wasted away a lifetime.
We share the gifts of love's sorrow—
So many gifts that if I count, I could not finish.
What have we lost in that love? What have we learned?
If I try to explain to someone else other than you, I cannot.
We have learned meekness; we have learned to support the poor;
We have learned the meaning of fear and grief, of sorrow and pain;
We learned to understand the troubles of the oppressed;
We have learned the meaning of cold sighs, of pale faces.
Whenever the helpless sit and cry,
Their tears welling up and drying out,
The falcons come, circling wings outstretched,
To snatch away the beggings of the weak.
Whenever the worker's flesh is sold in the market,
The poor's blood flows in roadways;
Something fire-like bubbles up again and again in the chest.
Don't ask what it is.
I don't even have control of my heart. (75–78)

3. In addition to publishing his Faiz translations in 'little' magazines such as *Poetry East*, Ali twice published them in book form: *The Rebel's Silhouette* (Salt Lake City UT: Gibbs Smith, 1991) and *The Rebel's Silhouette: Selected Poems* (Amherst MA: University of Massachusetts Press, 1995).

4. *Poems by Faiz* is actually Kiernan's second volume of Faiz translations. He also published *Poems by Faiz Ahmed Faiz* (Delhi: People's Publishing House) in 1958.

5. Notable here, in addition to Daud Kamal, are Maki Kureishi (1927–1995), Taufiq Rafat (1927–1998), Shahid Hosain (b 1934), Kaleem Omar (1937–2009), Shahryar Rashed (1948–1998; son of Urdu poet N.M. Rashed), Alamgir Hashmi (b 1951), Imtiaz Dharkar (b 1954) and Adrian Husain (b ?).

6. A number of collections of translations have been published later than those treated here. I plan to address these in a future article. They include: Shiv Kumar, *The Best of Faiz* (2001); Sarvat Rahman, *100 Poems by Faiz Ahmed Faiz, 1911-1984* (2002); Riz Rahim, *In English Faiz Ahmed Faiz A Renowned Urdu Poet, 1911-1984* (2008); Shoaib Hashmi and Salima Hashmi, *A Song for This Day: 52 Poems by Faiz Ahmed Faiz* (2009) and Sarvat Rahman, *Faiz Ahmed Faiz (1911-1984): Presentation for the Centenary of the Poet's Birth: Fifty Poems in Three Languages: Bilingual Translation into English and French from the Original Urdu Written by Hand by the Author* (2011).

7. This early version of this poem differs slightly, but not significantly, from the later version that appears in *The Rebel's Silhouette: Selected Poems* (1995).

PRISON DAYBREAK

Original: *Zindāṅ kī ēk subh* from *Dast-e Sabā* (1952)
TRANSLATOR: NAOMI LAZARD

Though it was still night
the moon stood beside my pillow and said:
　'Wake up,
the wine of sleep that was your portion
is finished. The wineglass is empty.
Morning is here.'
　I said goodbye to my beloved's image
in the black satin waters of the night
that hung still and stagnant on the world.
　Here and there
moonlight whirled, the lotus dance commenced;
silver nebulas of stars dropped from the moon's white hand.
They went under, rose again to float, faded and opened.
For a long time night and daybreak swayed,
locked together in each other's arms.

　In the prison yard
my comrades' faces, incandescent as candlelight,
flickered through the gloom. Sleep had washed them
with its dew, turned them into gold.
　For that moment
These faces were rinsed clean of grief for our people,
absolved from the pain of separation from their dear ones.

In the distance a gong struck the hour;
wretched footsteps stumbled forward on their rounds,
wasted by near starvation, *maestros* of the morning shuffle,
lockstepped, arm in arm with their own terrible laments.
Mutilated voices, broken on the rack, awakened.

Somewhere a door opened,
another one closed; a chain muttered, grumbled,
shrieked out loud. Somewhere a knife plunged
into the gizzard of a lock; a window went mad
and began to beat its own head.

This is the way the enemies of life,
shaken from sleep, showed themselves.
These daemons, hacked from stone and steel,
use their great hands to grind down the spirit,
slim as a feather now, of my useless days and nights.
They make it cry out in despair.

The prisoners,
all of us, keep watch for our saviour
who is on his way in the form of a storybook prince,
arrows of hope burning in his quiver,
ready to let them fly.

7

FAIZ'S LEGACY—LOVE AND REVOLUTION

Faiz was acknowledged long ago as the greatest Urdu poet after Iqbal. Even those who were critical of his progressive, social and political beliefs could not deny him that position, although they always qualified their praise of him by regretting that such a good man should have fallen among the Communists.

In recent years, there have been various ways, among non-progressive admirers of Faiz, to cover up the embarrassing (to them) fact of his being the greatest of the progressives.

One of these is to emphasize the classical style of his verse, although obviously, this classicism of manner does not in any way diminish the unmistakably progressive commitment of his subject matter, and of his lifelong struggle for the cause he had espoused at the very beginning of his career as a poet.

He was a keen student of various traditions of classical poetry in Urdu, Punjabi, Hindi, Arabic, Persian, and English among others and had realized at an early age that it was the content, and not the form which was basic in the art of poetry, that originality had little to do with formal experimentation and was primarily a matter of a profound understanding of human existence in its totality and wholeness.

It was precisely this realization, which had been a necessary element of the spirit of the age in modern Urdu poetry from Ghalib to Iqbal, which impelled Faiz to join the progressive movement like so many other writers of the thirties and later.

His distinctive merit as a progressive poet was, apart from his innovative genius of course, the deep understanding of the world around him and his highly developed insight into the kind of poetry that was needed by a people involved in the conflicts of such a world. His critical essays, written mostly during his formative years, are a testimony to the fact that he had arrived at, and formulated clearly, the essential elements of the poetics necessary for our age, the age of the masses.

Faiz adopted the cause of revolution at a time when revolution was in the air of the subcontinent. He grew up in the midst of the anti-imperialist mass movements of the twenties and the thirties. This was the age of liberation struggles of the people of Asia and Africa, of which the movements in the subcontinent were a necessary part.

Over the entire process which was transforming the consciousness of peoples of enslaved continents, lay the shadow of the October Revolution, so that Iqbal the poet who had influenced Faiz more than any other contemporary poet, was one of the first world poets to welcome it. It is significant to note that the last great poem of Iqbal was *Pus čeh bāyad kard ai aqvām-e sharq (What, then, should be done O nations of the East)*, which was a manifesto of the revolutionary struggle of colonial people against imperialism and its attendant forms of tyranny.

With Iqbal's revolutionary poetry, a poetry of classical dimensions, as the background of literary creative activity, and the whole world of enslaved nations rising in rebellion against masters of various kinds, there was no question of going back to literature of quiescence, withdrawal from struggle or individual self-regard and self-appeasement.

The young writers of the thirties in the subcontinent initiated a movement whose focus was not on the individual poet and his personal fate, but rather on the fate of the poet in the collective world of which he formed a necessary part.

The major contribution of Faiz to modern Urdu poetry, indeed to world poetry, is the concentrated reflection of the experience of the poet as a member of the collective, in the process of revolutionary struggle. This is the secret as much of his fascinating personality as of the elusive, indefinable magic of his poetry. Being the kind of person he was, he chose for himself a task which nobody had performed before.

Iqbal had sung poems of glory to the fact of revolution and given out a clarion call to the people to rise up against the master-classes and tyrants.

Faiz, having joined the people in their rebellion, and having adopted the collective cause as a poet of the revolution, made the transformation of the individual human being and his passage through the infinite variety of situations and moods in this process, the subject of his poetry.

He is concerned, above all, with the experience of the individual human soul in the long and arduous journey of revolutionary struggle. I do not think any other modern poet anywhere, has performed this task so well.

The poetry of Faiz is a kaleidoscopic image of the soul of the individual as a revolutionary. He has sung of his elation and of his despair, of his acceptance, of self-sacrifice and his pain at the sacrifice of the comrades fallen by the way, of his loneliness in the dungeons, and his hope of rescue and the breaking of the walls, of his passionate devotion to the common cause and his suffering, which is his recompense, of his ardent desire for life and its beauty and his realization of death as a necessary end to the struggle.

It is an infinite variety of moods and feelings that are reflected here, all the products of a deeply sensitized creative vision playing on the experiences of the individual who has chosen for himself the path of revolution and is so completely absorbed in his struggle that there is no temptation, not even love, which can cause a distraction.

And yet love is the leitmotif of his poetry. Faiz is one of the great lyricists who seems, from one point of view, to have sung of nothing with greater passion than love. That has made some critics opine that here was a poet of supreme power who also wrote of revolution. The fact, however, is that love and revolution have got fused in his poetry and experience at an integrative level which is rarely to be met with anywhere else in recent times.

In a way this integrative level is nothing new in our classical tradition. In fact it can be said that the Urdu and Persian (Punjabi and Sindhi) poetic tradition is a manifestation of the realization of this integrative level, where love rises above the individual biological craving and transmutes the base metal of selfish desire into a divine urge for world creative endeavour.

This is the way the great classical poets of the Persian language thought of love, and the theme has passed on to the Sufi poets of the mediaeval age in the subcontinent. Mir Taqi Mir, who was exhorted by his father to adopt love as his creed, was to define love as the urge which created the universe.

This theme had fallen from its high creative level to the lower levels familiar to us in later Urdu poetry, until it was sought to be altogether eliminated by Hali and his contemporaries. Even Iqbal, who had given it once again the high level of a creative passion, altogether disassociated it from normal human feelings and desires. Perhaps in him, this was a rebound from the kind of love reflected in the poetry of his mentor, Ustad Dagh.

However, it is only in Faiz that we once again meet the theme of love which is not merely a world-creative force but has been rejoined and infused with the life of common humanity and its simple feelings and desires. It seems to be a realization with the other revolutionary poets of today as well, because a recent poet of Surinam has said that it is necessary to have a profound faith in love for becoming a true revolutionary. In Faiz we see not only this profound faith in love, we see it as the major theme of his revolutionary poetry. He came to realize quite early, the close relationship between the emotion of love and the emotion which impels the revolutionary in his self-sacrificing, humanistic endeavour to change his society. It was even expressed rather blatantly in some of his early poems.

But it was in the course of his experiences in prison that he realized the complete fusion and identification of love as the common desire of the lover for his beloved, and the love as a world-creative and world-transforming passion which embraces the whole of humanity, the whole of life, and the whole of the universe. It is here that his poetry attains its most classical form, and he can identify himself with Khwaja Hafiz whom he quotes as saying:

Every foundation that you see has in it an element of decay,
Except the foundation of love which is without any fracture.

Characteristically, Faiz quoted this verse of Hafiz at the end of his address in Moscow, on the occasion of his receiving the Lenin Peace Award. He spoke in Urdu and gave utterance to thoughts which form the motive force of his activity as poet and revolutionary.

Many persons have pointed out that Faiz was an excellent critic in his early career but then gave up writing criticism. There is some truth in this complaint, although it is not quite correct that he gave up writing criticism altogether.

However, I believe that his criticism, published in his prose collection *Mīzān* was, by and large, an effort to come to grips with the classical tradition, which he was trying to understand and imbibe at the time. Having realized it and attained his identification with it so urgently, he was all the time talking about a critical reinterpretation of the classics of Urdu poetry.

Nevertheless, there are two short pieces that he wrote after the early essays, which are masterpieces in their own right and can be collectively considered as his testament, the essence of his understanding of poetry and of life. One of these was his brief introduction to *Dast-e Sabā* and the other is his Moscow address on receiving the Lenin Peace Prize.

Taken together, they form a most powerful essay on the objectives of progressive literature, one whose force and truth cannot be surpassed. Their value as Faiz's testament, as an expression of his literary and political creed has increased, because all kinds of unrelated ideas are being associated with his name in recent times, especially after his death.

The preface to *Dast-e Sabā* is based on a verse of Ghalib, in which he said that creative vision is not to be regarded as child's play. It has to do with the arduous task of realizing the universal in the particular and the great river in a drop. Faiz takes Ghalib's plea for a deeply philosophical coordination of the poetic profession as his premise to refute the arguments of the aesthetes of his time, for whom poetry was merely peripheral activity. But he goes further and comments that Ghalib's definition of creative vision is incomplete, because the poet is not only required to see the ocean in the drop, but also has to show it to others.

He goes further, and perhaps taking his cue from Marx's thesis on Feurbach, makes an observation about the poet's involvement in the river of life, which makes him responsible for much more than merely seeing the river. He attributes to poetic vision, the task of becoming a factor in changing the river.

From this follows, on one hand, the revolutionary responsibility that Faiz required the poets to shoulder, and on the other, the subjectivity of poetic activity which was the hallmark of his own poetry.

From all this he concludes that the understanding of the collective struggle of the life of humanity, and participation in this struggle, as far as it may be possible, is not merely the demand of life, but also of art. It is a part of his life, and artistic struggle is an aspect of this struggle. This demand is a constant one. Therefore, there is no *nirvān* for the struggle of the seeker after art. His art is an everlasting effort and a perpetual struggle.

How true a definition of the poet's activity we have here, and how faithfully did Faiz adhere to the ideal he had set before himself and others.

So far we have dealt with Faiz's concept of poetic activity as such. In his Moscow address, we find him elaborating the theme of the present struggle in which humanity is engaged. This is a struggle which is not new.

From the beginning of humanity, in every age and every era, contradictory factors and forces have been active, and in conflict. These forces are destruction and construction, progress and decadence, light and darkness, love of justice and hatred of justice. This is the picture even today, and this kind of conflict is still going on.

While the struggles of humanity so far do resemble our present day conflicts, yet there is a difference. Today the forces of war and peace have come to mean the total destruction of human life or its perpetuation, the abrupt and final end of human history or its continuation.

The second difference is that war has become an unnecessary factor in human struggle. The forces of production that have been created by human knowledge and ingenuity are so tremendous that humanity does not need any division of classes into rich and poor, into affluent and the deprived. A new social system catering to the needs of all human beings is not only desirable but eminently possible.

This is no longer a theoretical and utopian ideal, but a matter of practical realization. Through this practice, the frontiers of the struggle for peace and the struggle for freedom have come together.

This is so because the friends and enemies of peace and the friends and enemies of freedom belong to the same camps, are the same kinds of faces. On one side are those imperialistic forces whose vested interests, whose monopolies, cannot be maintained without jealousy and repression, and who are willing to accept the sacrifice of the whole of humanity for the protection of these monopolies. On the other side are those forces who place more value on the lives of human beings rather than on banks and companies.

This clear demarcation between the forces of peace and freedom and the forces of war and enslavement is the basic premise of Faiz's social and political thinking. And, it is for this that he has been struggling all his life.

He believed in the successful conclusion of this struggle, not only because of his deep understanding of the social processes, which have guaranteed the progress of humanity so far, but also because of his immense capacity for loving.

That is why, apart from being a great revolutionary poet, he was a great love poet, and there was no distinction between the two. Love and revolution had become identical in him.

THE MEETING

Original: *Mulāqāt* from *Zindāṅ Nāmā* (1956)
Translator: Yasmeen Hameed

A tree born of pain, this night,
greater in glory than you and I.

Greater in splendour,
for torch-bearing caravans
of myriad stars
trapped in its branches,
have vanished;
moons, in thousands,
in its darkness
surrendered their brilliance.

From this glorious night:
a tree born of pain,
a few moments: its yellowed leaves,
caught in your tresses
are a burning scarlet,
its silence: the dewdrops on your brow,
a diamond string.

(2)

Pitch dark is this night
but in the darkness dazzles
the blood-river
that is my voice,
your eyes: a sparkling gold,
create light.

The pain that seethes
in your verdant arms:

the fruit of this night,
swelled by its own agony,
can fuel into
a spark, a blaze.

All arrows shot
by dark branches,
from my courage I have plucked,
shaped each one
into a stone-axe.

(3)

Dawn of the wretched,
the downtrodden,
is not in the skies;
the bright horizon
is right here,
where you and I stand;
right here the sparks of anguish, of pain
have flowered into the crimson
light of the sky;
right here, daggers
of a killer grief,
row after row,
are a stretch of fiery rays.

From the pain bestowed by this night
has emerged the dawn of faith;
faith, that is greater in glory than grief,
dawn, that is greater in glory than night.

8

TRANSLATING FAIZ

Faiz Ahmed Faiz, the distinguished Pakistani poet, the most important contemporary poet of India and the subcontinent, died in Lahore on 20 November 1984. The last time I saw him was in April when we worked together in London, beginning the translation process of fifteen poems. He was in excellent spirits, looked very fit and trim. Always worrying about him, I now felt relieved. I looked forward to seeing him again in London, perhaps here in New York, perhaps in Pakistan. We talked of someday going to India.

None of this will happen now. I alone will carry the events of our meeting, the decision to translate his poetry into English, the numerous and intense conversations on poetry in general and on his work in particular. I am left with all this and also with the work of translation, which I will continue.

Death is the eggshell that clarifies the poet's work. Though Faiz's poetry is almost unknown in this country, the opposite is true on the other side of the world. For many years the finest musicians have composed music to his poems. When he read at a *mushāirā*, the present-day version of the ancient contest or *agon* in which poets contended in recitations, fifty thousand people and more gathered to listen, and to participate. In our culture, poetry is occasionally set to music but is usually a form of high art, not for popular consumption. In the Hindu and Moslem world it is different. People who barely have an education know Faiz's poetry, not only because of the songs using his lyrics but also the poems themselves, without musical accompaniment. This is testimony to the oral tradition of their culture but also to the universality of his appeal. Faiz, in the years following World War II, in which he fought in the British Indian Army, made himself the spokesman of his people. He was, by the British act of partition, a Pakistani, but his people were the people of all India, Pakistan, the entire subcontinent. Everyone who knows any poetry at all in that vast region knows of Faiz.

Faiz became the spokesman for his people by many and continuous acts of courage and conviction. When he became editor of the *Pakistan Times*, he used that position to speak in prose as well as poetry for peace and social justice. He made himself known as an opponent of oppression. He incurred enmity. In 1951 he was arrested, faced a sentence of death, and was sentenced to four years in prison. This was only one of three sojourns in a cell. Much of his time in prison was spent in solitary confinement.* Some of the poems I have translated were written under those conditions.

Faiz became the spokesman for his people in another way too. Instead of struggling for a literary career, instead of taking high posts as lecturer or professor, he dedicated himself to teaching illiterate people. He was blasé in his disregard for the blandishments of life. He identified himself with the masses of the poor. One incident illustrates that: When we were saying good-bye after our time in Honolulu I asked for his address. He told me I really didn't need it. A letter would reach him if I simply sent it to Faiz, Pakistan. The reason? He had helped found the postal workers' union. They were his people. They knew where to find him anytime.

So this is where Faiz came from when we met in Honolulu in the winter of 1979. We had both been invited to an international literary conference sponsored by the East-West Center. I have an official photograph taken of all the participants. We are fourteen in the photograph, but according to my memory the conference sessions were much more crowded than that. The countries represented were Australia, New Zealand, Fiji, Malaysia, South Korea, Japan, the Philippines, Bangladesh, India, Pakistan, a concentration of Pacific Basin countries, and of course, the United States. Across the bottom of the photograph the following legend is printed: Workshop on the Interaction of Cultures in Modern Literature. We are a casual but unsmiling group, standing in a double line on the lawn, dressed in our summer shirts and pants. Faiz is in the front row. He has a serious expression on his face, almost a frown, the effect of the sun which paid us a rare visit that afternoon. His shirt is not tucked in. A pen is clipped to his shirt pocket. His forehead is high and gleaming.

What the photograph doesn't show lives in my memory, a series of scenes, vignettes, tableaux, the entire montage of those weeks in Honolulu.

---

*Faiz was arrested on 9 March 1951 and was kept in solitary confinement for three months in Sargodha and Lyallpur (now Faisalabad) jails. He was taken to Hyderabad jail in June 1951 for the trial–Editor.

Memory: Faiz at the big conference table smoking cigarette after cigarette, prefacing his remarks with choked laughter. No one was immune to his charm. Very quickly he was established as the spiritual leader of the group. Who was this man whose observations and humour struck such a chord of response in my spirit? When he spoke in his particular variety of English, fluent and cultivated, accented in the most astonishing places, I listened with all my heart.

We got to know each other quickly in the limbo, the never never land produced by a forced stay on a desert island. We were a couple of shipwrecks along with all the others in the swirling sea, clinging to each other for companionship, for continuity, for warmth. From the first day, the clouds burst over our heads. The trade winds went crazy that winter bringing tempests, downpours, driving rains, sudden showers. The rains came again and again. At the same time the automated sprinkler system of the East-West Center turned itself on at its appointed intervals. The conference rolled on and we picked our way, mostly through mud and sheets of rain, to the next session, the next meal, the evening activity. We tried not to get caught in the wide swathe cut by the swish of water from the sprinklers, but we were often slapped with that water as well, as we sloshed across the grass with sodden feet.

I appointed myself guardian to Faiz. He needed one. We had been given rooms in a dormitory building, and while I walked up three flights of stairs to get to mine, Faiz could hardly make it up the two flights to his. His breathing frightened me. Sometimes he had to stop and rest at every tread. I demanded that he be given a ground floor room.

That evening we celebrated this victory by leaving the East-West compound for dinner. We sat in a booth eating pasta that was certainly not *al dente,* and during the course of that meal decided to begin the project of translating his poetry. It was, we noted, a most natural thing to do. After all, weren't we present at a conference being held in honour of the interaction of cultures? I knew by this time that Faiz was one of the great poets of the world. I had read his copy of the translations of his work done by Victor Kiernan. My only question was this: Could I re-create well enough; could I render the passion and quality of his work in English? 'I can try,' I said.

So it began.

From then on, we had no more idle time. Whenever we had a moment, we rushed to his room or to mine, took our places facing each other across a table, and worked. We established a procedure. Faiz gave me the literal translation of a poem. I wrote it down just as he dictated it. Then my real work began. I asked him questions regarding the text. Why did he choose just *that* phrase, *that* word, *that* image, *that* metaphor? What did it mean to him? There were cultural differences. What was crystal clear to an Urdu-speaking reader meant nothing to an American. I had to know the meaning of every nuance in order to re-create the poem.

From the beginning, this work of translation has been a process of discovery for me. I have learned what my own language can and cannot do. I have also learned that I have infinite patience for translation, as I do for writing my own poems. I have learned that it doesn't matter how long it takes, how many transformations a poem must be brought through, until the English version works in the same way that a poem I have written myself works. It must be faithful to the meaning Faiz has given it. It must move in his own spirit, with the same feeling and tone. It must have the same music, the same direction, and above all it must mean the same thing in English that it means in Urdu. I have learned how crucial it is to find the verb, the active way of saying whatever needs to be said, and then to raise the verb to its highest degree, to find the most active verb for the occasion. And I have learned again how necessary it is to throw away those crutches, adjectives on the left hand and adverbs on the right.

Describing the translation process is difficult in the same way as trying to describe the process of writing a poem. It is neither a scholarly nor an academic procedure. There is a great difference between writing *about* poetry and writing poetry. Much of the actual work of writing cannot be described because it is not conscious and it is not controlled. If it were conscious and controlled it would not be poetry. I have to limit myself, therefore, to discussing the conscious part of this process, a vital, but in the end a small part, the concrete wall from which it is then possible to make the leap into poetry.

One of the first poems Faiz gave me is called *Spring Comes*. Here is the poem as Faiz gave it to me.

Spring comes; suddenly all the time returns
all my young days that expired with our kisses,
that have been waiting in Limbo, come back
every time the roses bloom with your fragrance,
and the blood of your lovers.
All my misery returns,

all my melancholy of suffering of friends,
drunken after embraces of women beautiful as the moon.
The book returns replete with the heart's suffering,
the questions left unanswered.
Spring comes.

This is a small poem, delicate, infused with the feeling of a certain, very specific, kind of pain, the old pain that flowers suddenly with the right season, even after a long time has gone by since it made its last appearance. I needed to make each image specific and to heighten the diction in order to make the poem dramatic in English. I asked Faiz what he meant by 'the book' (line nine). He said it was a ledger in which experience is recorded. This was a relatively simple poem to recreate. Here is the final version:

Spring comes; suddenly all those days return,
all the youthful days that died on your lips,
that have been waiting in limbo, are born again
each time the roses display themselves.
Their scent belongs to you; it is your perfume.
The roses are also the blood of your lovers.
All the torments return, melancholy
    with the suffering of friends,
intoxicated with embraces of moon-laden beauties.
All the chapters of the heart's oppression return,
all the questions and all the answers
between you and me.
Spring comes, ready with all the old accounts reopened.

The War Cemetery in Leningrad is an example of a much more difficult problem. A poem of great feeling, written after Faiz visited the site, it is also short, very compact, with not a word or image to spare. Here is the literal text:

THE WAR CEMETERY IN LENINGRAD

These dabs of living blood
are carnations and tulips
sprinkled on the ice cold stone.

Each flower is named for one
of the unforgotten dead,
and of someone who weeps for him.

These men have finished their work;
there is the testament of the flowers
and the woman carved in granite.

She is their mother now;
she makes them all small again,
watches them sleep forever.

Only she is awake, draped in her hard
garland, weaving and reweaving
her other garland of sorrows.

A natural problem that comes up over and over again in translating from
a literal text is the one of making it more specific, since the literal text
is usually a general summation of the original meaning. In the poetry of
Faiz this problem is intensified because his language in Urdu is singularly
devoid of active verbs. Images and passive constructions abound. My
work involves finding active ways of expressing what Faiz has expressed
more passively in Urdu. There is also the problem of a certain construc-
tion that is prevalent in Urdu poetry that is exemplified in phrases such
as these: city of pain, land of isolation, wave of light, disturbance of hope.
These phrases are contained in the poem that follows. The trouble with
this construction is that it becomes boring in English. It has been my
work to change this construction whenever I can into language that is
more active, more specific, clearer. Here is the literal version of *Solitary
Confinement:*

On some distant horizon a wave of light begins to play
and in my sleep the city of pain awakens
and the eye (eyes) become restless in sleep
over the timeless land of isolation
    morning begins to dawn.

On some distant horizon a wave of light is playing,
a snatch of song, a whiff of perfume, a glimpse
   of a beautiful face
pass by like travellers
bringing the disturbance of hope.

I fill the cup of my heart
with my morning drink,
mix the bitterness of today with the poison of yesterday,
and raise a toast to my boon companions
at home and abroad
'to the beauty of earth, the ravishment of lips.'

I wasn't able to eliminate all of the phrases I referred to earlier without
violating the spirit and the meaning of the poem. However, most of them
were transformed into more active constructions. Here is the final
version. I'd like to note here that Faiz wrote this poem out of intimate
experience, when he was a prisoner in solitary confinement. Knowing
this, what is striking about the poem is its almost unutterable sweetness,
a melting sweetness that has nothing to do with sentimentality and is a
million miles away from being saccharine. This sweetness, uncut by
rancour or despair, is characteristic of Faiz's poetry. It expresses the
quality of his heart, a largeness and generosity of spirit. Under the worst
of circumstances something in his essential nature held fast. It is this
quality in his poetry that first struck me.

SOLITARY CONFINEMENT

On the distant horizon a wave of light
begins to play; in my sleep I live
in the city of loss. My eyelids
flutter in their restless dream
as morning moves forward
over the loneliness, the country without borders.

A wave of light is dancing
over that distant horizon.
The merest refrain, the ghost of perfume

the beloved face glimpsed for a moment,
torture me with hope, the final disturbance.

They arrive and leave,
travellers who have no time to stay.

I fill the cup of my heart
with my morning drink, today's gall
mixed with yesterday's bitterness.
I raise a toast to my friends everywhere,
here in my homeland and across the world:

'Let us drink, my dear ones, to human beauty,
to the loveliness of earth.'

Memory intervenes here. Shortly after that spaghetti supper when we
decided to begin this project, Faiz and I ventured out again one evening.
He wanted to find a restaurant that served North Indian food. We found
one. It looked expensive, but we decided to splurge. The stipend we were
receiving, twelve dollars a day for food, wouldn't cover the price of a
meal there, but we were desperate after so many meals in the East-West
Center commissary. In that happy mood brought on by recklessness we
chattered to everyone.

Just as we were about to leave the restaurant a stranger rushed in and
embraced Faiz. The bus boy, a Pakistani, had caught the name, Faiz, and
this news spread quickly. In the weeks that followed we came to know
this stranger well. He is Ijaz Rahman, a physician who has lived and
worked in Honolulu for many years. His hospitality is legendary. From
that night his home was headquarters for Faiz; the Pakistani community
in Hawaii, an enormous one, gathered there to greet their poet, dine with
him, sit on the cushions on the floor of the living room, anywhere, and
just simply be there within voice range of Faiz.

Another poem, *When Autumn Came,* must be read as a political poem.
In Pakistan, under the censorship of the various dictatorships, including
the present one, it is impossible to call things by their right names. This
is a poem that characterizes this situation and calls for its end.

And then one day such-wise autumn came
naked trees of ebony torsos stood arrayed

with yellow leaves of their hearts
scattered all round on roadways.
Whoever willed trampled them underfoot
and not even a moan was heard.
Songster birds of dreams, imaginings,
when they lost their songs
became strangers to their voice,
fell into the dust all by themselves.
And the bird-hunter had not even strung his bow.
Oh, God of Spring, have mercy
Bless these withered bodies with the passion
    of resurrection,
their dead veins with blood.
Let some tree flower again
Let some bird sing.

The passage that gave me the most trouble is the part that begins:
'Songster of birds of dreams, imaginings' down to 'and the bird-hunter
had not even strung his bow.' What was difficult for me was to render
this particular construction that links the loss of their songs to their
becoming strangers (exiles) to their song. Here is the final version:

WHEN AUTUMN CAME

This is the way that autumn came to the trees:
it stripped them down to the skin,
left their ebony bodies naked.
It shook out their hearts, the yellow leaves,
scattered them over the ground.
Anyone at all could trample them out of shape
undisturbed by a single moan of protest.
The birds that herald dreams
were exiled from their song,
each voice torn out of its throat.
They dropped into the dust
even before the hunter strung his bow.
Oh, God of May, have mercy.
Bless these withered bodies

with the passion of your resurrection;
make their dead veins flow with blood.

Give some tree the gift of green again.
Let one bird sing.

The poet who wrote these poems is now dead. He is mourned by millions
of his compatriots. I am still trying to come to terms with this loss. I
have the translations already done, and I am the sole repository now
of our experience together, meeting, finding what bound us as poets
and friends, the continuing work that forged those bonds closer. Faiz
has left the legacy of his work for the world, and to me the legacy of
an extraordinary companionship that leaped across the borders of our
separate cultures. We never could have imagined that January 1979 in
Honolulu, that the conference called in the name of the interaction of
cultures would produce this collaboration.

This fall I embarked on the study of Urdu. My Christmas present to
Faiz was to have been a letter with his name written in Urdu script,
signed with mine, also in Urdu. Instead he is gone. The letter will never
be written.

One final poem. I don't have the original, literal version.

THE DAY DEATH COMES

How will it be, the day death comes?
Perhaps like the gift when night begins,
the first kiss on the lips, given unasked,
the kiss that opens the way to marvellous worlds
while, in the distance, an April of nameless flowers
agitates the moon's heart.

Perhaps in this way: when the morning,
green with unopened buds, begins to sway
in the bedroom of the beloved,
and the tinkle of stars as they rush to depart
can be heard on the silent windows.

What will it be like, the day death comes?
Perhaps like a vein screaming

with the premonition of pain
under the edge of a knife, as a shadow,
the assassin holding the knife,
spreads out with a wing span
    from one end of the world to the other.

Whichever way death comes, or whenever,
in the guise of a disdainful beloved
    who is always cold,
there will be the same words of farewell to the heart:
'Thank God it is finished, the night of the broken-hearted.
Praise be to the meeting of lips,
    The honeyed lips I have known.'

In his poetry, in his steadfast service to his people, in the memories he has left in millions of hearts everywhere and in my own heart, Faiz will continue to live.

IF YOU LOOK AT THE CITY FROM HERE

Original: *Yahāṅ sē shehr ko dēkho* from *Sar-e Vādī-e Sīnā* (1971)
TRANSLATOR: NAOMI LAZARD

If you look at the city from here
you see it is laid out in concentric circles,
each circle surrounded by a wall
    exactly like a prison.
Each street is a dog-run for prisoners,
no milestones, no destinations, no way out.

If anyone moves too quickly you wonder
why he hasn't been stopped by a shout.
If someone raises his arm
you expect to hear the jangling of chains.

If you look at the city from here
there is no one with dignity,
no one fully in control of his senses.
Every young man bears the brand of a criminal,
every young woman the emblem of a slave.

You cannot tell whether you see
    a group of revellers or mourners
in the shadows dancing around the distant lamps,
and from here you cannot tell
whether the colour streaming down the walls
is that of blood or roses.

9

POET AND THE MODERN AGE

The poet in the modern world, as it has always been, is a person with a heart responsive to pain and love. To my mind, being a poet is not a profession; it is a spirit, a state of the heart. When combined with a literary gift, interlaced with destiny, which is a product of character and circumstances, it evolves a phenomenon, referring to which, we not merely pay tribute to a compassionate soul, its flexibility, to the inquiring mind and love's inspiration. We inscribe this lofty name in our hearts and on paper with a capital 'P': Poet. Poets often die young because they are recklessly gallant, because they burn themselves in seething human passions protecting man from evil, misfortune and man itself. Poets are romantics, quixotes of the human race, sometimes regarded with compassion, but condescendingly as spontaneous, sweet but foolish children, since there is little pragmatism in their actions and from the point of view of logic, they are sheer failure. But all the same people go to these alleged cranks, these God's fools, these madmen for advice, help and consolation. Poetry guides and helps like a wise friend, a great visionary. Poets are artisans of blessed words, masters of people's minds, guardians of ideals. Through their powerful words, they make their contribution to social life.

But at times it can be otherwise. General Babar, the founder of the Great Moghul dynasty, was a poet and wrote beautiful *ghazals* in Farsi and Turki. His dramatic life is an example of the incompatibility of bloodshed with inspiration. Here a split ran through the man's heart.

Right Cause

In reality, poetry precisely identifies where, on which side of the barricade, the Truth abides. It sides with the right cause, and even when love dies, when truth is forced to retreat, poetry provides truth with a historical justification and calls on the future generations to fight for the triumph of truth and goodness.

Zebunnisa, a descendant of Babar, was also to become a great poetess. The daughter of a Shah, she lived in the grim Middle Ages and she happened to love a common man. The Shah did not allow his daughter even to think about her beloved. Zebunnisa died at a young age, leaving behind her verses, charged with unbearable anguish and deadly grief. Once I saw her tomb in Lahore: she is buried in a poorly quarter under a tombstone, covered with a threadbare green cloth, reminiscent of first love and fresh grass. I stood there pondering over her bitter lot, and thinking that, despite all, her poetry and her short sad life are a hymn to the glory of love.

Indeed, poets assert virtue not only with their poems, but with their very lives. And sometimes they have to give their lives for it. The great Hungarian poet Shandor Petefi was killed on the barricades of the 1948 Revolution. The night before he had written the 'Patriotic Song', later chanted by the whole of revolutionary Budapest. The next morning he went to the barricades as a soldier and fell alongside with other defenders of freedom and equality.

One of the most striking examples of the humaneness and self-sacrifice of talent is the Great Patriotic War of the Soviet people against Fascism.

In 1941 when the war broke out, many writers went to the front; hundreds of them died defending their motherland, realizing the honest and humane formula of Mayakovsky: 'Perish, my verse, perish like a soldier, like many an unknown one perished in attacks'.

Helping Heart

This code of civic behaviour incarnated in Mayakovsky's line, evolved and became almost aphoristic in the Revolution of 1917. On the battlefields of the Great Patriotic War, young poets, students of the Institute of Philosophy and Literature died: Pavel Kogar, Michael Kulchitsky, Nikolai Majorov and others whose poems were already known and loved. In our hearts and poetry, they will forever remain young. True poets are always where man is in urgent need of a helping heart, where blood is being shed for a righteous cause. In 1936–39 in Spain, many writers fought side by side with the republicans against Italian and German Fascism for the righteous cause of the People's Front. In 1937 at the International congress of anti-Fascist writers, Pablo Neruda and Sesar Vallejo, Oktavio

Paz and Nicolas Guillen, Eric Weinert, Rafael Alberti, Antonio Machado, Hemingway, Erenburgh, Tolstory, Fadeev, Malrzux, Moussinac, Dos Passos, Andersen Nexo, Anna Zeghers and Ludwig Renn, Mate Zalka and Agon Erwin Kisch raised their voices against Fascism. I also cite here the names of the most eminent novelists, since they were great poets who shared the destiny of the Spanish people at the most dramatic moments in its fate.

In 1982, during the three months long siege of Western Beirut, the best of the Arab intellectuals fought together with the Lebanese against Israeli aggression. Many of them were poets and I was fortunate to know some of them personally: the Palestinians, Mouin Besseiso, Mahmud Darwish, and Ahmed Dahbur, and the Iraqi, Saadi Yusef.

The great son of Pakistan, the world-known Faiz Ahmed Faiz was also there. . . .

I was privileged to know quite a few outstanding writers of our time: the Chilean, Pablo Neruda, the Cuban, Nicolas Guillen, the Argentinean, Alfredo Varela, the American, Stanley Kunitz, the Mongolian, Yavuuhulan, the Slovak, Miroslav Valek, the Bulgarian, Lubomir Levchev, the Punjabi poetess, Amrita Pritam, the writers of Urdu, Sajjad Zaheer and Ali Sardar Jafri, and Hindi poets, Shrikant Varma, Agueya, and Bachan.

At the cradle of my own poetic destiny stood the great Soviet poet, Alexander Tvardovsky. I regard my fellow countrymen, the eminent poets, whose friendship was an honour for me, Simonov, Lukonin, Svetlov, Smelyakov, Orlov, as my teachers.

A special place in this galaxy of my brothers in spirit, in torment and joy of creation, belongs to Faiz Ahmed Faiz.

We Love. . . .

My first editor, Michael Lukonin, a poet of the frontline generation who wrote his first lines in the flames of the Second World War, once said: 'We, poets, are not friends. We love each other.' I loved Faiz, his unobtrusive, loving interest in everything his eyes saw and his hand touched, his inspiring fatherly presence in my life. 'Great art is always like great fatherhood', wrote Eugeni Evtushenko. This sums up what Faiz Ahmed Faiz, his poetry, his heroic noble personality has been for me, for my poems, my life.

From the first acquaintance, we developed a kind of silent understanding. We did not talk much, for Faiz was reticent by nature, and bearing in mind my poor knowledge of English, you will be able to understand that it was always easier to remain silent, smiling at each other and communicating like, I think, plants do, or animals and flowers in the woods, like birds and clouds. It was a dialogue of hearts, excelling and superseding an exchange of insignificant words. I translated Faiz's poems, and in the process, learnt to understand him better. I have translated just a few poems of his, but I hope to continue this gratifying work in future. It was difficult, almost impossible, to translate Faiz, because of the differences in style, types of versification and the use of metaphor. Nevertheless, some of my translations are said to be successful.

To me the dearest of the translations is that of his poem about Palestinian refugees charged with the great-heartedness of Faiz, his ability to feel the pain of others as his own. Intensified by the power of the poet's emotional experience, the poem has become a banner of sorrow and pride, flying high over the world, visible to all.

I met Faiz in Moscow, Riga, Tashkent, at international conferences, on preparatory committees, at various discussions, and often informally—at the Writers' Club, at friends' homes, over a cup of tea. But there is one meeting which is still fresh in my memory. It occurred in Karachi, Pakistan, on Faiz's native soil. I had come to Pakistan to attend the jubilee of Amir Khusro. When the Soviet delegation returned from Islamabad, where the function took place, to Karachi, Faiz Ahmed Faiz came to see us at the hotel.

Reverence

During my visit to the Shahi Mosque in Lahore, I had seen how common peasants bowed their heads in reverence at the tomb of the great Iqbal, and it had struck to me that they were praying to him like a saint. When Faiz was coming along the narrow hotel corridor towards us, those who came by bowed and touched his hand, thus expressing their profound respect and filial reverence, and asking as if it were for his blessing. That is what a people's poet, as I see it, should be like. 'Great art is like great fatherhood.'

Faiz is known and loved in my country. I was privileged to participate in Faiz's recitals more than once. Faiz Ahmed Faiz enjoyed great respect in my country; his poetry received wide acclaim. He was awarded the Lenin Peace Prize. Faiz was also the winner of the Lotus Prize for his invaluable contribution to the Afro-Asian writers' movement, of which a number of Soviet writers are also members. Holding Faiz's memorial function was a sad experience.

I remember, when I took the floor, I was thinking what Faiz's prodigious talent, his unique personality could be compared with. I compared him with the Omayyad's Mosque in Damascus. Such a comparison may seem strange, but I will explain what prompted it. A Syrian writer once told me that her Government decided to demolish old buildings around the mosque obstructing the view. Writers protested and wrote a letter explaining that a mosque, unlike a Christian church, should be seen from within. Faiz was a mosque to be seen from within. His inner light, his unforgettable eloquent silence will always remain with me.

VISITORS

Original: *Mērē milnē vālē* from *Mērē Dil Mērē Musāfir* (1981)
TRANSLATOR: DAUD KAMAL

My doors are open.
I am never alone.
First comes the evening—
wistful, sad.
Then the garrulous night
anxious to narrate
her wretchedness
to the stars.
The morning rubs salt
into the wounds of memory.

The noon hides
serpents of fire
in her sleeves.
All these are my visitors.
They come and go as they please.
And I am not concerned.
My thoughts are elsewhere—
over the seas—
bruised, bleeding—
my land, my home.

10

FAIZ AND HIS POETRY TODAY

There are many aspects of Faiz's life and his poetry, which need to be studied. But first of all we must be very clear that Faiz the poet cannot be separated from Faiz the man. In both the roles, his integrity was above doubt. He lived a full life, and what he said in his verse, he practiced. He could be lyrical in his political poetry, and his poetry of love could convey a political message.

Personal integrity demanded courage and Faiz was not found wanting in it. Again, his fearlessness is manifest in both the way he lived and what he wrote. He was never afraid of owning his commitment to his loves and the causes he held dear. He possessed fearlessness of a quality he perhaps, himself could not comprehend. He was as fearless in his actions, in taking resolute stands, as he was in his poetry.

It is very rare that a poet matures without going through a period of apprenticeship. Faiz was such a poet. He emerged in public view as a mature poet and as time passed, he developed that simplicity which comes from complete command over thoughts and words and is the hallmark of a truly great poet and writer.

Faiz's poetry is all the more impressive because he respected the tradition of Urdu poetry, its form. He hardly ever deviated from this tradition. But it is a measure of his greatness that he accommodated within its fold, the ideas and concerns of his age.

Realism

While his poetry matured at an early age, Faiz took some time to temper his enthusiasm for human-kind's deliverance with realism and wisdom. In the beginning, he believed that the paradise on earth that he sought for his people, and in which he believed so passionately, could be quickly attained. It was later on that he began to realize, how long the journey ahead was and how arduous the struggle was going to be. Then he acquired the patience and perseverance of a sage. Likewise, the area of his commitment grew. Of course, his first concern was for his people, his land, but he was equally concerned for the people of Afro Asia and finally for the whole of humankind. That is why we recognize him as not only a Pakistani poet but also as the poet of the entire world.

Eventually Faiz became the poet of Pakistan by whom his country is identified. There are large parts of the world where people know very little about Pakistan, but who have been inspired to struggle for a better future, to acquire a sane outlook on life, to love their fellow beings, by Faiz's poetry.

Since Faiz's genius is many sided, and his poetry has several layers of meaning, it is not easy to translate him, as I realized when I began translating him into Russian. . . . One cannot but agree with Faiz that authentic poetry is untranslatable. However, I could persevere and translate a selection from his entire published verse because of his universal appeal and use of symbols that are not difficult to follow.

Resoluteness

I have often been asked to recall the happiest moments in my long association with Faiz. That would mean recounting every word he spoke, every time he smiled. When I first saw Faiz, I was a very young girl, a student, and was immediately impressed by his seriousness. But he had something about him that enabled one to relax in his presence. And he was a very practical man. Two incidents come to mind. At the Afro-Asian writers' conference in Tashkent in 1958, a serious difficulty arose over the drafting of the declaration. Eventually we turned to Faiz and he soon secured a consensus. He could do so by virtue of his ability to disarm critics with his straightforwardness and clarity of ideas and expression. Of that, I had another experience. What happened in East Bengal in 1971 shocked the whole world. Faiz, of course, knew how to control his emotions. But he was greatly upset when told that a Bengali friend was so angry that he did not even wish to see him.

Faiz insisted on a meeting and when the conversation ended, they were good friends again, and this Bengali writer became one of the staunchest defenders of Faiz.

One may also recall, to illustrate Faiz's resoluteness, an incident towards the end of 1958. Martial Law had been proclaimed in Pakistan and the progressives were among the first targets of the new regime. It was felt that if Faiz returned home, he might be arrested. But when it was suggested that he could stay abroad as long as he liked, his immediate reaction was that he was prepared to pay any cost for staying with his own people. When asked to think the matter over, he agreed to give his final answer some time later, but added that a change of mind was unlikely.

Above All, Peace

To get back to Faiz's relevance to the contemporary world, he is the poet of peace and there is nothing that the world needs today more than peace. The interest of humankind, in his view, is indivisible, and so must be its struggle to spread joy and sense of self-realization. That is why Faiz will never get dated, his message will continue to touch responsive chords in the hearts of men and women who seek a paradise on earth. And when we do find this paradise, we will be able to enjoy the love which Faiz describes as the only thing in the world without blemish.

TO THOSE PALESTINIANS MARTYRED IN FOREIGN LANDS
Original: *Falastīnī shuhadā jo pardēs mēṅ kām ā'ē* from *Mērē Dil Mērē Musāfir* (1981)
TRANSLATOR: MAHMOOD JAMAL

Sweet earth of Palestine,
wherever I went
carrying the burning scars of your humiliation,
nursing in my heart the longing
to make you proud,
your love, your memories went with me,
the fragrance of your orange groves went with me.

A crowd of unseen friends stood by me
and so many hands clasped mine.
In distant lands, on dark lanes,
in alien cities, on nameless streets,
wherever the banner of my blood unfurled,
I've left a Palestinian flag.
Your enemies destroyed one Palestine;
My wounds created many more.

11

THE SKY, THE ROAD, THE GLASS OF WINE: ON
TRANSLATING FAIZ

Many of us have tried to translate Urdu poetry into English. In fact there are more and more of us nowadays, which is an encouraging sign for the future. But there are all too few chances for mutual discussion or for learning from each other's experiences. I want to suggest some thinking points for us all—what can (and can't) we reasonably expect to achieve in a translation? What kind of problems are solvable, and what kind are probably not?

My own experience started with a great desire to translate classical Urdu *ghazal*. I was always looking around for clues to how it could be done. The search was a frustrating one, but I was young, naïve, and hopeful. For various reasons, I did not like most of the translations that I saw. But could I do any better myself? I was not interested in making technically accurate translations that sounded awful in English and/ or did no real justice to the original. Nor was I interested in producing free 'transcreations' that used the Urdu originals merely as jumping-off points for new English poems. I read some translation theory, but I found that it tended to be either extremely abstract and philosophical, or else grounded on specific successes in other languages that were not easy to emulate in Urdu. If practical advice was offered, it was often just common-sensical (the translator was urged, for example, to respond to the needs of the intended audience).

So I began to think about the whole process in quite concrete terms. Naturally (to me at least), I began by asking myself what sort of features of a poem were more 'translatable' than others. One obvious choice: formal features that could be replicated in English. And of all such formal features, repetition was surely the easiest and the least problematical. So, since I wanted above all to work on Ghalib, I began to look for ways

I could translate *ghazals* and preserve the *radīf*. Some *ghazals* obviously had eminently preservable *radīfs*: Mir's '*maiṅ nashē meṅ hūṅ*,' for example, or Momin's '*tumhēṅ yād ho kē na yād ho*,' or Ghalib's '*jal gayā*' or '*mauj-e sharāb*.' In a few such cases, I thought I had some limited success.[1] But most *ghazals*, of course, had unpreservable *radīfs*, or sometimes none at all. And the further difficulties of multivalent 'meaning-creation' (*m'ānī āfarīnī*) and wordplay kept thwarting my best efforts to translate Ghalib, the 'difficult' poet, the one on whom my heart was set.

When I looked at modern poets, however, I felt a bit more hopeful. Since modern Urdu poets so often make a point of avoiding the traditional kinds of complex wordplay, multivalent meanings, subtle allusions, and so on, there tends to be less to lose: starkness, simplicity, deliberate prosiness, colloquial language seem to travel so much better across the language barrier. Moreover, *nazms* as a genre travel better than *ghazals*, since they usually operate in units of thought larger than the two-line *she'r*, and create their own contexts rather than requiring the reader to bring and use so much prior knowledge of the tradition. Thus even when modern *nazms* are complex and subtle (as the best ones often are), they tend to require less background on the part of the reader. The result has been that the poetry I've translated[2] has mostly been modern, and has mostly consisted of *nazms*.

* * *

Of all modern poets, in practice the inescapable, indispensable one is Faiz. He is generally perceived as the hinge between the classical and modern *ghazal*; he is widely known, loved, and even revered. Compared to his great contemporaries, N.M. Rashed and Meeraji, he has been by far the most amply translated: at least five translators have produced whole English volumes of his work, and he appears in countless anthologies. Partly because of this lavish and often high-quality set of translations, I never added my own two cents, though I have studied and taught Faiz's poetry for years.

I first came to know Faiz through Victor Kiernan's very helpful book. Of all the poems Kiernan included, my eye fell on one in particular that seemed born for translation. What a pleasure it was to read it and think how the translation might be done! Here is the poem that seemed to me so relatively translatable:

Raṅg hai dil kā mērē

(1) *Tum na ā'ē thē to har čīz vohī thī kē jo hai*
(2) *Āsmāṅ hadd-e nazar, rāh-guzar rāh-guzar, shīsha-e mai shīsha-e mai*
(3) *Aur ab shīsha-e mai, rāh-guzar, raṅg-e falak*
(4) *Raṅg hai dil kā mērē, 'khūn-e jigar honē tak'*
(5) *Čampa'ī raṅg kabhī rāhat-e dīdār kā raṅg*
(6) *Surma'ī raṅg kē hai sā'at-e bēzār kā raṅg*
(7) *Zard pattoṅ kā, khas-o-khār kā raṅg*
(8) *Surkh phūloṅ kā dehektē hu'ē gulzār kā raṅg*
(9) *Zehr kā raṅg, lahū raṅg, shab-e tār kā raṅg*
(10) *Āsmāṅ, rāh-guzar, shīsha-e mai*
(11) *Ko'ī bhīgā huā dāman, ko'ī dukhtī hu'ī rag*
(12) *Ko'ī har lehzā badaltā huā ā'īnā hai*
(13) *Ab jo ā'ē ho to thehro kē ko'ī raṅg, ko'ī rut, ko'ī shai*
(14) *Ēk jagāh par thehrē,*
(15) *Phir sē ik bār har ik čīz vohī ho kē jo hai*
(16) *Āsmāṅ hadd-e nazar, rāh-guzar rāh-guzar, shīsha-e mai shīsha-e mai*

For purposes of discussion, I give the poem here in the definitive form in which it appears in Faiz Ahmed Faiz's *kulliyāt, Nuskhahā'ē Vafā*, with spacing and punctuation exactly as in the Urdu.[3]

I was encouraged by the very marked formal structure of the poem; anyone who looks at the Urdu will surely see it immediately. Most obviously, line (2) and line (16)—the final line—are exactly the same, and each consists of triple pairs: 'sky limit-of-sight, road road, glass of wine glass of wine.' Within the poem, moreover, these three pairs form basic organizational elements. Line (3) alludes to them in reverse order (altering one for the sake of a crucial rhyme), and line (4) links them to the title of the poem. Line (10) repeats them yet again, and lines (11) and (12) implicitly turn sky, road, and glass of wine into a wet garment-hem, an aching vein, and a mirror changing every moment. Thus by the time they are so starkly repeated in the last line, the trinity of sky, road, and glass of wine have formed an evocative, if deliberately elliptical framework for the poem. I felt that they were a gift from God (or Faiz) to the translator.

Here are the first lines and the last lines of four translations of this poem. I am going to label them A through D, in chronological order; the key will be found in the Appendix.

(A)   Before you came, all things were what they are—
       The sky sight's boundary, the road a road,
       The glass of wine a glass of wine;

       . . .

       And all things once again be their own selves,
       The sky sight's bound, the road a road, wine wine.

(B)   Before you came things were just what they were:
       the road precisely a road, the horizon fixed,
       the limit of what could be seen,
       a glass of wine was no more than a glass of wine.

       . . .

       This time things will fall into place;
       the road can be the road,
       the sky nothing but sky;
       the glass of wine, as it should be, the glass of wine.

(C)   Before you came,
       things were as they should be:
       the sky was the dead-end of sight,
       the road was just a road, wine merely wine.

       . . .

       Stay. So the world may become like itself again:
       so the sky may be the sky,
       the road a road,
       and the glass of wine not a mirror, just a glass of wine.

(D)   Before you came, everything was what it is—
       the sky, vision-bound
       the pathway, the wine-glass.

       . . .

       and once again everything may become what it was—
       the sky, vision-bound, the pathway, the wine-glass.

It is not hard to see that each of these translations obscures Faiz's careful structure of elegant, slightly oblique, paired repetitions. Though (A) preserves strong similarities, only in (D) can the reader guess that the second and final lines of the original might be *totally* identical—and (D) doesn't reflect Faiz's repetition of the three items at all. Moreover, (D) has the problem that 'vision-bound' is most naturally read in English as 'bound by vision' or 'bound for vision' rather than 'the boundary of vision.' Both (B) and (C) introduce a moralizing note: (B) speaks of 'the glass of wine, as it should be, the glass of wine,' and (C) of how 'things were as they should be'; the Urdu offers no hint of any such 'oughtness.' Thus the translators either overlook or consciously ignore the very marked, and conspicuously translatable, formal structure that Faiz has given to the poem.

* * *

Faiz's careful—and carefully unexplained—set of correspondences in lines 10–12 suffers the same kind of damage. Loosely linking his trinity of items, as a group, to a second set of three items, Faiz says:

(10) *Āsmāṅ, rāh-guzar, shīsha-e mai*
(11) *Ko'ī bhīgā huā dāman, ko'ī dukhtī hu'ī rag*
(12) *Ko'ī har lehzā badaltā huā ā'īnā hai*

Sky, road, glass of wine
is some wet garment-hem, some aching vein,
some mirror changing every moment

Here is how the translators deal with it:

(A)   Sky, highroad, glass of wine—
       The first a tear-stained robe, the next a nerve
       Aching, the last a mirror momently altering. . . .

(B)   As for the sky, the road, the cup of wine:
       one was my tear-drenched shirt,
       the other an aching nerve,
       the third a mirror that never reflected the same thing.

(C)   And the sky, the road, the glass of wine?
       The sky is a shirt wet with tears,
       the road a vein about to break,
       and the glass of wine a mirror in which
       the sky, the road, the world keep changing.

(D)   The sky, the pathway, the wine-glass—
      some tear-stained robe, some wincing nerve,
      some ever-revolving mirror.

Since the translators do not take care to preserve the unmediated exact repetitions of these three crucial items throughout the poem, they cannot get the maximum effect from a passage like this. (D) is the closest to the Urdu, though 'wincing' is a facial expression and thus applies to people rather than nerves, 'ever-revolving mirror' sounds like a lighthouse fixture rather than a mirror that actually 'changes' at every moment (as does the surface of a glass of wine), and 'wine-glass' could easily be an empty glass, rather than a full one such as would create a mirror in its liquid surface.

Apart from (D), the other three all feel the need to give the reader extra prompting: (A) through explaining that the 'first' is one thing, the 'next' another; (B) through enumerating 'one,' 'the other,' and 'the third'; (C) through actually making the identifications explicit ('The sky is . . .' and so on). They thus link the three items to their three metaphorical counterparts in a flatter, more pedestrian way than Faiz does. It is easy to imagine their reason for doing so: it might not be entirely evident to the reader that these three new items were meant to correspond one-for-one to the three items in the line before, so it would be better to clarify it a bit.

Yet this whole 'clarification' process, it seems to me, is a fix for a problem that could have been avoided in the first place. Faiz has set up a structure in his Urdu poem that cues any reasonably alert reader to make exactly these identifications. It is no harder for the reader to do this kind of thing in English than to do it in Urdu; English poets routinely expect much more difficult feats than this from their readers. No special cultural background or baggage is involved here—only a genuine, close attentiveness to the language of the poem as it develops. Only because the translators have not reproduced Faiz's careful and systematic formal structure in English, although they easily could have, do they have to insert artificial clues and 'helps' for their readers—and thus in every case make the poem simpler and more prosy, less fluid and mysterious, than the original.

* * *

There are legitimate problems too, of course, that the translators face—problems that cannot be resolved merely by replicating a formal structure. One such problem is the translation of '*bhīgā huā dāman.*' No doubt the sense of '*dāman*' as 'garment-hem,' meaning something like the trailing edge of a long robe, is clumsy to express in English, and the classical Persian-Urdu idiom of a 'wet garment-hem' as a sign of pollution or sinfulness (cf. *tar-dāmanī* vs. *pāk-dāmanī*) does not really come through in English very well. All the translators seem to have decided, however, that the wetness on the garment-hem is that of tears. I don't know of any reason in the Urdu to make such an explicit identification.

If anything, to see the sky as a dirty, stained, bedraggled garment-hem, a garment that has been trailing in the mud, a sign of sin and pollution, seems much more in keeping with Faiz's poem. After all, in the poem there are clear references to moods of exaltation, as well as blood and poison, and no references at all to tears—much less to the kind of endless weeping that would drench a garment. In fact Faiz is not at all a lachrymose poet: when you think of the range of moods he describes in his poems, it is hard to come up with many examples of tears, and easy to find situations in which tears and grieving have been emphatically rejected in favour of more meditative or politically inspirational moods.

Moreover, (B) has decided that the tear-wet garment is 'my tear-drenched shirt,' (C) describes it as 'a shirt wet with tears'; there's no warrant in the poem, however, for turning the sky or a robe or a garment-hem into a 'shirt,' much less 'my' shirt. The sky, after all, is much more like a spread-out cloak or other long flowing garment, than it is like a shirt, so that the altered metaphor becomes much less effective. And since the lover's tears in the *ghazal* world tend most often to be tears of blood, the vision of a possibly blood-drenched garment would rise involuntarily to the traditionally-trained reader's eye. This association of ideas is another reason Faiz is unlikely to have wanted us to think of the sky primarily as wet with (bloody) tears. Translations (B) and (C) have turned an image of cosmic bleakness—the sky as a stained, polluted cloak—into a piece of personal emotional expression—the sky as a shirt wet with tears (presumably shed by the wearer). In the process, they have replaced Faiz's ambiguity—he pointedly does not tell us what the sky is wet with—with an explicit piece of (pseudo-) information.

* * *

If we look at the middle part of Faiz's poem, we see a separate movement of thought, one that involves the basic three items (sky, road, glass of wine) in an intense play of colours:

(3) *Aur ab shīsha-e mai, rāh-guzar, raṅg-e falak*
(4) *Raṅg hai dil kā mērē, 'khūn-e jigar honē tak'*
(5) *Čampa'ī raṅg kabhī rāhat-e dīdār kā raṅg*
(6) *Surma'ī raṅg kē hai sā'at-e bēzār kā raṅg*
(7) *Zard pattoṅ ka, khas-o-khār kā raṅg*
(8) *Surkh phūloṅ kā dehektē hu'ē gulzār kā raṅg*
(9) *Zehr kā raṅg, lahū raṅg, shab-e tār kā raṅg*

In lines (5) through (9), we see that the word 'raṅg,' colour,' is repeated no fewer than nine times, three of them in the final line. This repetition is almost as conspicuous and obtrusive in Urdu as it would be in English; it goes well beyond the creation of end-rhymes, and plainly represents a deliberate, emphatic effect that the poet is creating. Here is how the translators render lines (5) through (6):

(A)   Now golden, as the solace of meeting is,
      Now grey, the livery of despondent hours,
      Or tint of yellowed leaves, of garden trash,
      Or scarlet petal, a flowerbed all ablaze:
      Colour of poison, colour of blood, or shade
      Of sable night.

(B)   your eyes gold
      as they open to me, slate the colour
      that falls each time I lost all hope.
      With your advent roses burst into flame:
      you were the artist of dried-up leaves, sorceress
      who flicked her wrist to change dust into soot.
      You lacquered the night black.

(C)   the grey of your absence, the colour of poison, or thorns,
      the gold when we meet, the season ablaze,
      the yellow of autumn, the red of flowers, of flames,
      and the black when you cover the earth
      with the coal of dead fires.

(D)   Sometimes the golden tinge, sometimes the hue of the joy of seeing you
        sometimes ashen, the shade of the dreary moment—
        the colour of yellow leaves, of thorn and trash,
        of the crimson petals of the flower-beds aglow,
        the tint of poison, of blood, of sable night.

Even without a detailed discussion, it's easy to see that all the translations
have avoided Faiz's incantatory repetition of the word 'colour.'

Perhaps the translators thought 'colour' in English could not be as
evocative as '*rang*' in Urdu? It is easy to sympathize with them, and yet
the attempt could have been an interesting one. It seems to me that the
translators didn't trust the English-reading audience to like what Faiz
actually did in this passage. But what is unlikable about it? Incantatory,
rhythmic repetitions are not exactly unknown or powerless in English
poetry—talented translators like these might have had a go at recreating
Faiz's actual effects in English. Instead, however, they have let that
opportunity pass.

In line (5), moreover, all four translations take *rāhat-e dīdār*, 'comfort
of vision,' the sight of something very pleasant, to mean meeting with
the beloved; this is one possible interpretation, but it still involves
replacing the carefully ambiguous Urdu with a pseudo-specificity that
is in fact misleading. For we notice that line (5)'s apparent opposite
in line (6), *sā'at-e bēzār*, 'a time-interval of disgust/distaste,' pointedly
avoids equating such a time with separation from the beloved (although
translation (C), on its own responsibility, makes this equation as well).
Faiz, as is his wont, is being elliptical here, leaving it for the reader to
assign a meaning to these moods. There is no 'you' in the Urdu—only the
rhythmic enumeration of wildly changing dark and blazing colours and
moods. Versions (B) and (C) have even depicted this 'you' as an active
agent, responsible for creating the colour-changes: in Faiz's Urdu, it's
clear that the lover lives in his own mind, undergoing wild but private
shifts in mood; but in (B) and (C) the lover has been turned into a sort
of helpless victim: the Svengali-like beloved is actively manipulating his
universe.

To varying degrees, all the translations have simply remade the
passage, eliminating Faiz's incantatory repetitions and artificially
'clarifying' his carefully maintained ambiguities into explicit, conventional
phases in a love affair. The Faiz of the translations is much simpler and

more straightforward than the real one. The changes tend to obscure what Faiz was doing in the poem.

* * *

And what was Faiz doing in the poem? The best evidence, I submit, is to be found in these two lines:

> (3) *Aur ab shīsha-e mai, rāh-guzar, rang-e falak*
> (4) *Rang hai dil kā mērē, 'khūn-e jigar honē tak'*

The punctuation is Faiz's, including of course the conspicuous quotation marks around the latter half of line (4). The quotation marks surround a phrase from a famous *she'r* of Ghalib's; and lines (3) and (4), like ten of the sixteen lines in Faiz's *nazm*, are in the same metre that Ghalib used for his *she'r*. And in this one case, the poet substitutes for his otherwise invariable *āsmāṅ*, 'sky,' the phrase *rang-e falak* 'the colour of the heavens,' which both introduces the key term *rang*, and creates an eye catching rhyme (*falak, tak*).

Faiz was a notable Ghalib-lover, of course; the titles of two of his collections of poetry, *Naqsh-e Faryādī* (into which he inserted the *izāfat*) and *Dast-e Tah-e Sang* (from which this poem comes), were phrases from famous verses of Ghalib's. In this case, the original *she'r* is:

> *Āshiqī sabr talab aur tamannā bētāb*
> *Dil kā kyā rang karūṅ khūn-e jigar hotē tak*[4]
> Lover-hood, endurance-demanding; and longing, restless—
> What colour/state would I make of the heart, until it becomes blood of the liver?

Ghalib's now-archaic *hotē tak* has been modernized, by Faiz and almost everybody else, to the current usage *honē tak*. And my clumsily literal translation at least shows the way in which Faiz's line—*Rang hai dil kā mērē, 'khūn-e jigar honē tak'*—is a direct answer to Ghalib's question.

Ghalib poses the question, what colour/state would I cause my heart to be in, how would I manage it, caught as I am between passionate longing and forced endurance, both equally inescapable parts of the lover's situation? Faiz answers, 'It's the colour of my heart,' and embodies the answer in a poem full of vividly shifting heart-colours.

Faiz's title itself, in fact, repeats this phrase: 'It's the Colour of My Heart.' Translation (A) rebaptizes the poem as 'Before You Came'—a translation of the first phrase in line (1) and (B) and (C) follow its lead. Version (D) calls the poem 'The Colour of the Moment,' with even less textual warrant. Thus the translations all deny their readers a piece of important knowledge that the poet obviously meant for them to have: the knowledge that this single phrase embedded in the poem was to be given special importance in interpreting it. Did the translators gain anything through their re-titling that was as valuable as what they lost?

The title-phrase itself, which forms the first half of line (4), calls our attention to the second half of line (4), the directly quoted phrase of Ghalib's: *khūn-e jigar honē tak*,[5] 'until [it] becomes blood of the liver.' This phrase is to be interpreted in the light of *ghazal* physiology: the heart constantly loses blood—because of its numerous wounds and lacerations, and because the lover weeps tears of blood; in the meantime, fresh blood is made in the liver. Thus the heart is an emblem of wild self-consuming passion, and the liver an emblem of fortitude, discipline, endurance. There is also an evocative suggestion of the idiom *khūn-e jigar pīnā*, 'to drink the blood of the liver,' with its wonderfully suitable range of meanings: 'To suppress (one's) feelings, restrain (one's) emotion, or anger, or grief, etc.;—to consume (one's own) life-blood; to vex or worry (oneself) to death; to work (oneself) to death.'[5]

Ghalib's verse, in short, asks how the lover should manage his unbearable, mutually contradictory needs both for wild expression of passion, and at the same time for endurance—which means among other things a kind of stoical suffering in silence. The first line states the dilemma, and the second asks the question, while also making it clear that the question is only a short-term one. For one only has to ask this question, and to worry about a colour/mood (*rang*) for one's heart, *khūn-e jigar honē tak*—until the heart turns completely into liver-blood, until it is ground down between the two millstones of passion and suppression and becomes a mere quivering blob of blood. The single idiomatic expression 'to drink the blood of the liver' carries, as we have seen, the whole range of meanings: one may simultaneously 'suppress (one's) feelings' and 'vex or worry (oneself) to death' for only a relatively short time, because the process itself requires that one 'consume (one's own) life-blood.'

To make the liver a poetic organ in English is a tall order. How have the translators dealt with this complex, multivalent, virtually untranslatable allusion?

(A)   all have taken
      The hues of this heart ready to melt into blood—

(B)   With you the world took on the spectrum
      radiating from my heart:

(C)   Now everything is like my heart,
      a colour at the edge of blood:

(D)   everything bears the colour of my heart
      till all melts into blood.

In all the versions, the heart-liver opposition, so central to what both Ghalib and Faiz were thinking about, drops out entirely. Well, since nobody can really translate Ghalib anyway—as I have been gradually and painfully realizing over the years—why should I be surprised if this complex phrase proves un-conveyable? I as a translator certainly can't do it justice either. I also agree, in literary contexts, with the translators' omission of a scholarly footnote that would identify the phrase as borrowed from Ghalib (though Faiz, through his quotation marks, made a point of his borrowing). In cases like this all translators encounter, I would say, genuine, legitimate, essentially insuperable difficulties. They might as well go ahead and 'transcreate' as best they can.

* * *

Looking at the larger designs of the translations, we can see a tendency— especially in (B) and (C)—to increase the presence of the 'you' in the poem, and to turn the poem into something more like a familiar kind of romantic lyric in English. I would argue that, on the contrary, the organization of the poem around a crucial phrase from Ghalib tends to anchor it in the more austere, tough, pessimistic world of the classical *ghazal*, in which as a rule the beloved is more important for his or her absence than for any other quality.

For this reason I also have some doubts about the translators' reading of the conclusion. The lover says in lines (13) and (14), 'Now that you've

come, stay; so that some colour, some season, some thing/Would stay in
one place.' Line (15), given here in context, is the crucial one. On the face
of it, it would seem to mean literally, 'Again one time everything would
be that which it is.'

(13) *Ab jo ā'ē ho to ṭhehro kē ko'ī raṅg, ko'ī rut, ko'ī shai*
(14) *Ēk jagāh par ṭhehrē,*
(15) *Phir sē ik bār har ik čīz vohī ho kē jo hai*
(16) *Āsmāṅ hadd-e nazar, rāh-guzar rāh-guzar, shīsha-e mai shīsha-e mai*

Yet the translators all blur the 'one time' (*ik bār*). Here is how they render
line (15):

(A)   And all things once again be their own selves.
(B)   This time things will fall into place;
(C)   Stay. So the world may become like itself again:
(D)   and once again everything may become what it was—

They all, as far as I can judge, leave the implication that the lover is
asking the beloved to stay with him from now on, so that the poem
seems to anticipate a kind of reconciliatory 'happy ending,' and possibly
a better future.

My own reading would, by contrast, take the 'one time' (*ik bār*) quite
seriously. The lover has no illusions. He knows that he is doomed—that
the beloved has basically gone, and will not be with him in the future. He
is asking only for a brief moment of respite from his vertigo—a reprieve,
a temporary fix of stability. Let the beloved stay for just a bit, let the
lover 'one time' again see things as themselves rather than as a helplessly
whirling blaze of dark and bright colours, moods, passions.

Of course Faiz has cleverly used *thehernā*, a verb that can mean 'to
stop, rest, pause, cease, desist; to stay, remain, abide, wait, tarry,'[6] so that
he preserves the ambiguity and thus keeps the question at least slightly
and intriguingly open. Here translations (A) and (D) have taken perfect
advantage of the conveniently ambiguous English phrase 'once again.'
Who could say that 'once' is not a satisfactory translation of *ik bār*, and
'again' of *phir sē*? And yet 'once again' can carry a charge of futurity—as
'one more time' cannot. 'My love will be with me once again' and 'My
love will be with me one more time' have very different implications.
I would argue that the anchoring of the poem on *khūn-e jigar honē tak*,
signalled forcefully by quotation marks and by its very title, should sway

our judgement toward the grimmer, less hopeful, more literal reading. After all, the very next poem after this one in Faiz's volume *Dast-e Tah-e Sang* is called *Pās raho*, 'Stay With Me,' and makes it clear that the poet uses *rehnā* as the verb for real 'staying.'[7]

The beloved in 'It's the Colour of My Heart' is envisioned almost as a drug. Before the beloved comes, everything is what it is. Then the beloved comes, and everything is a whirling mass of bright and dark. The lover begs the beloved to stay a while, so that, paradoxically, 'one more time' everything can be what it is. Drugs too first take one *out* of one's normal perceptions of reality; then eventually they become necessary for one to be *in* one's normal perceptions of reality, rather than suffering some wild chaos of withdrawal. All this can come to no good end—except the death of the heart, which may come almost as a relief, as it consumes itself and turns into *khūn-e jigar*. A hopeful, optimistic reading of the conclusion is, I submit, untrue to the Urdu poem Faiz actually wrote; and if the real poem is too bleak to be enjoyed in its own right, why translate it?

* * *

By now it is probably clear that I am urging a kind of middle ground between extreme literalness and free 'transcreation.' It seems to me that we translators ought to try most carefully to understand the original poem very accurately in the Urdu. Then we ought to steer between Scylla and Charybdis. Here are some principles that I suggest for the careful translator who respects and enjoys an Urdu poem:

- Preserve the poem's formal structure as much as possible. (If the poet takes pains to repeat a line in identical form, so should the translator.)
- Maintain the poem's ambiguities and obscurities; do not over explain, do not provide 'information' that the poet has not provided. (If the poet says the sky is a 'wet garment-hem,' don't turn it into 'my tear-stained shirt'; if the poet speaks of a sight that delights the eyes, don't turn it into a meeting with the beloved.)
- Give readers information that the poet clearly wants them to have. (If the poet has used a line in the poem as its title, don't re-title it.)

Of course, it will all too often be impossible to do all this. There will be plenty of situations in which 'transcreation' will be the only option—it is hard to argue that '*khūn-e jigar honē tak*' should be translated literally as 'until it turns into blood of the liver.' Since there are always all too many such impossible situations, why not save the transcreation for those truly hard cases? Why remake the poem unnecessarily, if a great deal of it can be brought over directly into English instead?

Certainly I have no universal solution for the problems of translation, or even for the problems of translating this poem.[8] In an appendix I have given the four translations, (A) through (D), and have added a fifth translation (E), which is my own (unpublished) one. It seemed only fair that I too should have a go, and see how far I could succeed or fail. My heart is with my fellow translators: our task is impossible, but nevertheless it must be done. As Cynthia Ozick recently put it,

> The issues that seize, grab, fall upon, overwhelm, or waylay translation are not matters of language in the sense of word-for-word. Nor is translation to be equated with interpretation; the translator has no business sneaking in what amounts to commentary. Ideally, translation is a transparent membrane that will vibrate with the faintest shudder of the original, like a single leaf on an autumnal stem. Translation *is* autumnal: it comes late, it comes afterward.[9]

Appendix: Translation Texts

(A) Before You Came (tr. by Victor Kiernan)

> Before you came, all things were what they are—
> The sky sight's boundary, the road a road,
> The glass of wine a glass of wine; since then,
> Road, wineglass, colour of heaven, all have taken
> The hues of this heart ready to melt into blood—
> Now golden, as the solace of meeting is,
> Now grey, the livery of despondent hours,
> Or tint of yellowed leaves, of garden trash,
> Or scarlet petal, a flowerbed all ablaze:
> Colour of poison, colour of blood, or shade
> Of sable night. Sky, highroad, glass of wine—
> The first a tear-stained robe, the next a nerve
> Aching, the last a mirror momently altering. . . .
> Now you have come, stay here, and let some colour,
> Some month, some anything, keep its own place,
> And all things once again be their own selves,
> The sky sight's bound, the road a road, wine wine.[10]

(B) Before You Came (tr. by Naomi Lazard)

> Before you came things were just what they were:
> the road precisely a road, the horizon fixed,
> the limit of what could be seen,
> a glass of wine was no more than a glass of wine.
>
> With you the world took on the spectrum
> radiating from my heart: your eyes gold
> as they open to me, slate the colour
> that falls each time I lost all hope.
>
> With your advent roses burst into flame:
> you were the artist of dried-up leaves, sorceress
> who flicked her wrist to change dust into soot.
> You lacquered the night black.
>
> As for the sky, the road, the cup of wine:
> one was my tear-drenched shirt,
> the other an aching nerve,
> the third a mirror that never reflected the same thing.
>
> Now you are here again—stay with me.
> This time things will fall into place;
> the road can be the road,
> the sky nothing but sky;
> the glass of wine, as it should be, the glass of wine.[11]

(C) Before You Came (tr. by Agha Shahid Ali)

> Before you came,
> things were as they should be:
> the sky was the dead-end of sight,
> the road was just a road, wine merely wine.
>
> Now everything is like my heart,
> a colour at the edge of blood:
> the grey of your absence, the colour of poison, or thorns,
> the gold when we meet, the season ablaze,
> the yellow of autumn, the red of flowers, of flames,
> and the black when you cover the earth
> with the coal of dead fires.

And the sky, the road, the glass of wine?
The sky is a shirt wet with tears,
the road a vein about to break,
and the glass of wine a mirror in which
the sky, the road, the world keep changing.

Don't leave now that you're here—
Stay. So the world may become like itself again:
so the sky may be the sky,
the road a road,
and the glass of wine not a mirror, just a glass of wine.[12]

(D) The Colour of the Moment (tr. by Shiv K. Kumar)

Before you came, everything was what it is—
the sky, vision-bound
the pathway, the wine-glass.
And now the wine-glass, the pathway, the sky's tint—
everything bears the colour of my heart
till all melts into blood.

Sometimes the golden tinge, sometimes the hue of the joy of
seeing you,
sometimes ashen, the shade of the dreary moment—
the colour of yellow leaves, of thorn and trash,
of the crimson petals of the flower-beds aglow,
the tint of poison, of blood, of sable night.
The sky, the pathway, the wine-glass—
some tear-stained robe, some wincing nerve,
some ever-revolving mirror.

Now that you're here, stay on
so that some colour, some season, some object
may come to rest
and once again everything may become what it was—
the sky, vision-bound, the pathway, the wine-glass.[13]

(E) It's the Colour of My Heart (tr. by Frances W. Pritchett)

Before you came everything
was what it is:
the sky the limit of sight

the road a road, the glass of wine
a glass of wine.

And now the glass of wine, the road, the colour of the sky
are the colour of my heart
while it breaks itself down
into blood.

Sometimes a gold colour—a colour of eyes' delight
that sooty colour, the colour of disgust
the colour of dry leaves, straw, thorns
the colour of red flowers in a blazing garden
poison colour, blood colour, the colour of black night.
The sky, the road, the glass of wine
are a sodden cloak, an aching vein,
a mirror changing every moment.

Now that you've come, stay—let some colour, season, thing
stay in place.
One more time let everything
be what it is:
the sky the limit of sight
the road a road, the glass of wine
a glass of wine.

Notes

1. Some of these were published as 'Two Ghazals' and 'Stanzas from Ghalib' in *New Letters* 4th ser. 51. Summer (1985): 126–30. Print.
2. F.W. Pritchett, *A Listening Game: Poems by Saqi Farooqi*, 4th ed., Vol. 51, London: Lokamaya Publications, 1987, Print; and with Asif Aslam, *An Evening of Caged Beasts: Seven Post-Modernist Urdu Poets*, Karachi: Oxford University Press, 1998, Print.
3. Faiz, *Nuskhahā'ē Vafā*, Delhi: Educational House, 1986, 365–366, Print.
4. Mirza Asadullah Khan Ghalib, *Divān-e Ghālib*, ed. Hamid Ali Khan, Lahore: Punjab University, 1969, 63, Print.
5. John T. Platts, *A Dictionary of Urdu, Classical Hindi, and English*, London: Oxford University Press, 1930, 497, Print.
6. Ibid., 365
7. Faiz, *Nuskhahā'ē-Vafa*, 367–368 [see note 3]
8. I want to thank my colleague and friend, Shamsur Rahman Faruqi, for his comments and suggestions on this paper.
9. 'The Impossibility of Being Kafka,' *The New Yorker* 11 January 1999: 83–84, Print.

10. Victor Kiernan, trans., *Poems by Faiz*, London: George Allen & Unwin, 1971, 252–255, Print.

11. Naomi Lazard, trans., *The True Subject*, Princeton: Princeton University Press, 1988, 32–35, Print.

12. Agha Shahid Ali, trans., *The Rebel's Silhouette*, Salt Lake City: Peregrine, 1991, 56–57, Print.

13. Shiv K. Kumar, trans., *Faiz Ahmed Faiz: Selected Poems*, New Delhi: Viking Books, 1995, 126–27, Print.

We Who Were Killed in Half-Lit Streets

Original: *Ham jo tārīk rāhoṅ meṅ mārē ga'ē* from *Zindāṅ Nāmā* (1956)
TRANSLATORS: C.M. NAIM AND CARLO COPPOLA

For the love of your flower lips,
We were sacrificed on the gibbet's dry branch,
For the desire of the torches of your arms,
We were killed in halt-lit streets.

Far from our lips—on the gibbet—
Flashed the moisture of your lips,
Your scented hair billowed,
And the silver of your arms gleamed,
When torture's evening fell upon your path,
We followed as we could;
On our lips sweet words; in our heart a torch of sorrow.
Our sorrow was witness to your beauty.
Look! We stood fast to our word,
We who were killed in half-lit streets.

We were fated to fail,
Yet we willed our love.
Who complains if love's affairs end in separation?
More caravans of lovers will pick up banners
And set out anew.
Our steps have shortened the pain
Scattered on their path of desire.
For them, we—by giving our lives—
Made known to all the secret of your love,
We who were killed in half-lit streets.

12

INTRODUCTION: THE REBEL'S SILHOUETTE—
TRANSLATING FAIZ AHMED FAIZ

My first sensuously vivid encounter with Faiz Ahmed Faiz: the voice of Begum Akhtar singing his *ghazals* (lyric poems comprising thematically autonomous couplets united by strict schemes of rhyme and metre). One of the greatest exponents of light classical singing and within that tradition the greatest of *ghazal* singing, Akhtar sang Urdu poets, particularly Faiz, as no one has since her death in 1974, ten years before he died. What other singer can give, the way she did, a raga to a *ghazal* and then make the raga, that melodic archetype, feel grateful for being a gift?

Passion, attachment, something that has 'the effect of colouring the hearts of men'—that is what the Sanskrit term raga literally means. (One interpretation of *ghazal* is 'whispering words of love.') An incipient melodic idea that uses at least five tones of the octave, each raga has 'strict rules of ascent and descent, prescribed resting places, characteristic phrases and a distinct ethos of its own' (Dhar, 84–86). What Begum Akhtar did was to place the *ghazal* gently on the raga until the raga opened itself to that whispered love, gave itself willingly, guiding the syllables to the prescribed resting places, until note by syllable, syllable by note, the two merged compellingly into yet another aesthetic ethos for the Urdu lovers of the South Asian subcontinent. She, in effect, allowed the *ghazal* to be caressed into music, translated, as it were: 'You've finally polished catastrophe,/the note you seasoned with decades/of Ghalib, Mir, Faiz,' I said in my elegy for her (lines 15–17, Ali, 'In Memory of Begum Akhtar,' *Half-Inch*). For unlike so many other *ghazal* singers, who clothe words until they can't be seen, she stripped them to a resplendent nudity. If she clothed them at all, it was in transparent muslins, like the Dacca gauzes; 'woven air, running/water, evening dew' (lines 1–3, Ali, 'The Dacca Gauzes,' *Half-Inch*).

The *ghazal*, a form that in its present shape is eight hundred years old, traces its origins to pre-Islamic Arabia. (Garcia Lorca wrote several *ghazals*, acknowledging in his catholic manner the Arabic influence on Spain.) In its opening couplet, the *ghazal* establishes a scheme that occurs in both lines. As John Hollander says, 'For couplets the *ghazal* is prime; at the end/Of each one's a refrain like a chime: "at the end" (lines 1–2) Having seen this couplet, the reader would know that the second line of every succeeding couplet would end with "at the end" (called *radīf*), the refrain preceded by a word or syllable rhyming with "prime" and "chime" (called *qāfiā*).' Thus, Hollander continues: 'But in subsequent couplets throughout the whole poem,/It's the second line only will rhyme at the end' (lines 3–4). Hollander has done something remarkable here, for he has captured the peculiar fragrance of the form of the *ghazal*, its constant sense of longing. Further, in subsequent couplets, not only has Hollander maintained the form but he has resisted the Western insistence on unity. (His one departure is that he has not maintained syllabic consistency in his line lengths). The form of the *ghazal* is tantalizing because its thematically independent couplets give the poet the freedom to engage in different themes, issues, and attitudes while keeping himself gratefully shackled. Let me offer one more of Hollander's couplets: 'You gathered all manner of flowers all day,/But your hands were most fragrant of thyme, at the end' (lines 13–14).

Before the partition of the South Asian subcontinent in 1947, whereby the states of India and Pakistan were created, Faiz had stayed in our house in Srinagar, the summer capital of Kashmir. Some decades later, Begum Akhtar too was to stay in our home the summer before her death. When I was six or seven, Faiz sent my father from Lahore a copy of his then latest volume—*Zindāṅ Nāmā* ('Prison Thoughts'). My father often quoted Faiz, especially his elegy for the Rosenbergs:

> It's true—that not to reach you was fate—
> but who'll deny that to love you
> was entirely in my hands?
> So why complain if these matters of desire
> brought me inevitably to the execution grounds? (Lines 18–22, 'We Who Were Executed,' *Rebel's Silhouette*)

I must have then begun to internalize Faiz, repeating to myself the Urdu original of this, as well as other passages of his. Without any clear understanding of the lines, I somehow *felt* the words, through their sounds, through my father's rhythmic, dramatic voice. So perhaps my first sensuous encounter with Faiz was not through Begum Akhtar but at home, during childhood.

Poetry was part of the air we breathed. In Srinagar during the summer of 1989 (when my mother helped me to translate Faiz), my grandmother, then eighty-eight, quite by chance quoted Milton during a conversation. In English. Ever since I can remember, she quoted Shakespeare, Keats, and Hardy in English; Hafiz and Rumi in Persian; Ghalib and Faiz in Urdu; Habba Khatun, Mahjoor, and Zinda Kaul in Kashmiri. But I'd never heard her quote Milton. I was ecstatic: once again I didn't need proof of my rights to the English canon (which, in any case, was created in India—i.e., the British established English literature as a subject in the curriculum in India quite some time before its institutionalization in England). Significantly, not only was my training in school in English (I mean that I grew up with English as my first language), but, paradoxically, my first language was/is not my mother tongue, which is Urdu. (I realize that in common parlance and linguistics there is no distinction between 'first language' and 'mother tongue.' But in my case, I grew up breathing Urdu in such a way that it is entitled to being called, at a culturally emotional level, my mother tongue, even though I used and use English for all practical and creative purposes; that is why I call English my first language.) When I wrote my first poems, at the age of ten, they were in English. I did not 'choose' to write them in English; it just happened that way. Naturally.

Someone of two nearly equal loyalties must lend them, almost give them—a gift—to each other and hope that sooner or later the loan will be forgiven and they will become each other's. My double loyalty has, after all, rescued rather than hampered me—by giving me *The Rebel's Silhouette*. In a prefatory note to the book's first edition, I wrote:

Though the poems here are taken from various Faiz volumes, for my selection (which is arranged chronologically) I have chosen to adapt the title of his first volume, *Naqsh-e Faryādī* (*Sketch of the Plaintiff* or *Outline of the Plaintiff* or *Features of the Plaintiff*)—a phrasing that captures the spirit of his entire output. However, because Faiz does not recognize the moral authority of man-made courts, he is a plaintiff only in the courts of the universe. Clearly, a rebel. (*Rebel's Silhouette*, xi)

This explanation reveals my simultaneous love of Urdu and of English. Neither love is acquired; I was brought up a bilingual, bicultural (but never rootless) being. These loyalties, which have political, cultural, and aesthetic implications, remain so entangled in me, so thoroughly mine, that they have led not to confusion but to a strange, arresting clarity. I thus now qualify an assertion I made, at twenty, in a poem:

> call me a poet
> dear editor
> they call this my alien language
>
> I am a dealer in words
> that mix cultures
> and leave me rootless (Lines 1–6 'Dear Editor,' *Beloved Witness*)

Rootless? Certainly not. I was merely subscribing to an inherent, dominative mode that insisted one should not write in English because it was not an Indian language. But in those lines I had implicitly begun to protest this notion of English as alien, questioning the 'they' who 'call this my alien language.' Perhaps I was subconsciously aware that sub continental English needed renewal and reworking, *translation* even, before I and other poets could use it to meet the demands of a 'hybrid' cultural situation. But it was mine, ours.

Why did I choose to translate Faiz? Oh, for a mess of reasons, some of them quite certainly concerned with the poetic ego. Could I make English behave outside its aesthetic habits? But more immediately: When I came to the United States in 1976, no one I met among professors in English departments and, more crucially, among poets seemed to have heard of Faiz (at that time, some people had begun to hear of Nazim Hikmet—a friend of Faiz's and like him a winner of the Lenin Peace Prize for Literature; Faiz had translated some of Hikmet's poems into Urdu). To have to introduce Faiz's name, to explain who he was, seemed an insult to a very significant element of my culture. As Edward Said says:

> The crucial thing to understand about Faiz . . . is that like Garcia Marquez he was read and listened to both by the literary elite and by the masses. His major—indeed it is unique in any language—achievement was to have created a contrapuntal rhetoric and rhythm whereby he would use classical forms (*qasīdā, ghazal, masnavī, qit'ā*) and transform them before his readers rather than break from the old forms. You could hear old and new together. His

purity and precision were astonishing, and you must imagine therefore a poet whose poetry combined the sensuousness of Yeats with the power of Neruda. He was, I think, one of the greatest poets of this century, and was honoured as such throughout the major part of Asia and Africa. (Cover of *Rebel's Silhouette*)

So here was this poet whose work I had grown up reciting and hearing recited by heart, a poet who has continued to be sung by the leading singers of the subcontinent, a poet who was such a master of the *ghazal* that he transformed its every stock image and, as if by magic, brought absolutely new associations into being, and yet—as far as I could discern— he was simply not known in this part of the world. So I made attempts, imbibing some methods that Adrienne Rich and W.S. Merwin (see Ahmad) had adopted in translating Ghalib, the greatest Urdu poet of all time, whom Faiz often echoed; but my attempts were feeble, my results uneven.

And then, quite by chance, I came across five of Naomi Lazard's excellent translations of Faiz's poems in *Kayak*. Because the world—at least of poetry—is delightfully small, a series of coincidences led me several months later to a phone conversation with her and, shortly after that, a meeting in Manhattan. I learned that she had met Faiz at an international literary conference in Honolulu in 1979—one of the times he was allowed into the country. Otherwise, the McCarran-Walter Act had kept him from these shores. As Carlo Coppola says, 'A spokesperson for the world's voiceless and suffering peoples—whether Indians oppressed by the British in the '40s, freedom fighters in Africa, the Rosenbergs in cold-war America in the '50s, Vietnamese peasants fleeing American napalm in the '60s, or Palestinian children living in refugee camps in the 1970s—Faiz wrote painfully, stunningly, and compassionately of the human aspiration for freedom: a hallmark of his verse and, more than once, an excuse to refuse him entry into the United States' (97). On meeting Faiz, Lazard says, she immediately knew she was in the presence of a poet of world stature, one who must be brought to the attention of her compatriots. And so the translation process began, right there at the conference. Lazard writes:

> We established a procedure immediately. Faiz gave me the literal translation of a poem. I wrote it down just as he dictated it. Then the real work began. I asked him questions regarding the text. Why did he choose just that phrase, that word, that image, that metaphor? What did it mean to him? There were cultural differences. What was crystal clear to an Urdu-speaking reader meant

nothing at all to an American. I had to know the meaning of every nuance in order to recreate the poem.

What were these cultural differences? I presume Lazard had to learn the nuances of images that would seem too lush to an American poet—images that recur shamelessly in Urdu poetry, among them the moon, the rose, the moth, the flame. She needed to learn their modern implications as well as their uses over the centuries, a formidable task. For example, the Beloved—an archetype in Urdu poetry—can mean friend, woman, God. Faiz not only tapped into these meanings but extended them so that the Beloved could figure as the revolution. The reader begins to infer, through a highly sensuous language, that waiting for the revolution can be as agonizing and intoxicating as waiting for one's lover. How is the translator to get all of this across? Victor Kiernan, the first to translate Faiz into English, says: 'Of all elements in foreign poetry, imagery is the easiest to appreciate, except when, as often in the Persian-Urdu tradition, it has symbolic and shifting meanings.' Lazard's translation process continued across continents, through the mail; on a few occasions she was able to meet Faiz during his visits to London. When he died, she already had enough poems for *The True Subject*, her volume of Faiz translations; by way of an epigraph, Lazard offers a ring of quotations regarding the true subject:

> Faiz Ahmed Faiz to Alun Lewis, Burma, circa 1943: 'The true subject of poetry is the loss of the beloved.'
>
> Alun Lewis, in a letter to Robert Graves before Lewis was killed, Burma, 1944: 'The single poetic theme of Life and Death—the question of what survives of the beloved.'
>
> Robert Graves, in The White Goddess, Quoting Alun Lewis, 1947: 'The single poetic theme of Life and Death—the question of what survives of the beloved.'
>
> Naomi Lazard to Faiz Ahmed Faiz, Honolulu, 1979 (having read *The White Goddess* many years before and misquoting the line attributed to Alun Lewis): 'The true subject of poetry is the loss of the beloved.'

Someone in a mood to mystify may offer this ring of quotations as yet another kind of translation, one engaged in by destiny. But let me not tempt myself.

Born in Sialkot, in undivided Punjab, in 1911, Faiz came from rustic stock; his ancestors were Punjabi Muslim peasants. His father, however, had served the royal family of Afghanistan and later studied in England, becoming a lawyer after Cambridge and Lincoln's Inn. Unlike his father, Faiz did not travel till much later, but he imbibed the spirit of the 1930s from books and pamphlets and went on to earn a master's degree in English literature and another in Arabic literature. In a sense, he had embarked on his own inner translations and, later, did translate into Urdu the Turkish poet Nazim Hikmet and the Kazakhstani poet Omar Uljaz Ali Suleiman.

A decade before independence, which accompanied the partition of the subcontinent in 1947, Faiz's poems were acquiring the colour of patriotic feeling and socialist passions. (The Punjab had its own branch of the leftist Progressive Writers' Association, which was the literary force at the time, and Faiz was closely associated with it.) By 1939 Faiz had made a definite name for himself as a poet. His socialist vision continued to colour his poetry and also his politics, whereby he saw the Nazi invasion of the Soviet Union in 1941 as a contest in which mankind's destinies were at stake; as a result he joined the army as a lieutenant-colonel, 'solemnly returning salutes from British soldiers' (Kiernan, Introduction to Faiz, Poems, 24) on the Mall in Lahore. After independence, he chose to live in Pakistan and became editor of the *Pakistan Times*. In 1951, along with several leftwing army officers, he was arrested on the charge of planning a Soviet-sponsored coup; he spent four years in prison, mostly in solitary confinement* under the possibility of a death sentence, but was released in 1955. He returned to work on the *Pakistan Times*.

In 1958, he was removed from that post and jailed when Ayub Khan's military government took over. Interestingly, when UNESCO was approaching governments to nominate the representative writers of their countries—so they could be translated into various 'major' languages—Faiz's was the first name Ayub Khan mentioned. That is, by the 1960s, Faiz had become Pakistan's unofficial poet laureate, disarming with his poetry 'some political and even religious prejudice,' writes Kiernan. 'Criticism, even abuse, for his opinions,' however, never ceased 'to come his way, and there are traces of this to be discerned in some of his poems. To be a nationalist writer is easy, to be a national writer hard' (Kiernan, Introduction to Faiz, Poems, 26–27). After translations of his work appeared in Russian, he was awarded the Lenin Peace Prize in 1962. Appointed chair of the National Council of the Arts during Zulfikar Ali Bhutto's primeministership, he lost the position after Bhutto's overthrow

---

*Faiz was in solitary confinement for three months after his arrest on 9 March 1951–Editor.

by Ziaul Haq. He then lived in Beirut until the Israeli invasion of 1982 and edited *Lotus*, the journal of the Afro-Asian Writers' Association. His death in Lahore in November 1984 was reported, sometimes in banner headlines, on the front pages of newspapers in India, Pakistan, the Soviet Union, and throughout the Middle East.

Given Faiz's political commitments, particularly his Marxist/humanist understanding of history, audiences may hastily assume that he was a poet of slogans. His genius, however, lay in his ability to balance his politics with his (in some ways stringently traditional, often classical) aesthetics without compromising either. He once advised a poet to avoid didactic and rhetorical gestures. He also said that

> the future of the *ghazal*, like the future of all poetry, depends above all on the talent of its future practitioners. Pedantically speaking, there is nothing good or bad in any poetic form, but that the poet makes it so. . . . [For] some insight into the future of this much maligned and much admired form of expression, it were best to look at its past. Not the distant past when its excellence was unquestioned but the recent past when its *raison d'être* was first brought into question. This was in the mid-nineteenth century when in Ghalib's phraseology, 'the last candle of freedom anguished by the ending of the convivial night flickered and died'; when the last battle for liberation was fought and lost. In the breast-beating that followed, poetry, which was then synonymous with the *ghazal*, was denounced as one of the factors responsible for this debacle. ('Future of Ghazal Poetry,' 53–55)

But, Faiz emphasizes, the *ghazal* survived and continues to. Faiz's own *ghazals* show the considerable influence of Ghalib, whose great laments reveal a highly personalized grief that historically must be seen in the context of British domination over India and the passing of an age, a way of life, a civilization. One can comfortably argue that it is from Ghalib that Faiz most clearly learned that the *ghazal's* 'rigidity of form is coupled with an equal if not greater freedom in the use of not only Empson's seven but innumerable forms of "ambiguity".' The *ghazal* manipulates the 'meaning of meaning, i.e., endowing a word or sign with a number of concomitant referents explicable only in particular textural or social context' ('Future of Ghazal Poetry,' 55). The form embodies, in Kiernan's words,' 'a kind of stream-of-consciousness, and might prove helpful to Western writers caged in their framework of logic, which they have tried to break out from by discarding metre, and sometimes sense as well' (14). One couplet of a *ghazal* may by political, another tragic, one religious, another romantic, and so on. Comprising at least four couplets, it has no maximum limit. In the hands of a master, this seemingly light form has more grandeur than a sestina and more emotional compression than a sonnet. Ghalib's *ghazals*, for example, reveal a great tragic poet, and Faiz's a great political one (in the most generous, inclusive sense).

Because translating a *ghazal* formally is just about impossible (beyond my powers, in any case), I have adopted loose, free-verse stanzas (along the lines of Merwin's versions of Ghalib; see Ahmad) to suggest the elliptical power of Faiz's couplets. But the magic of the form is missing, often heartbreakingly so. Desperation, however, can lead one to freer ways of approximating magic, and mine led me back to Aijaz Ahmad's edition of the *Ghazals of Ghalib*, a collaboration with Thomas Fitzsimmons, William Hunt, W.S. Merwin, David Ray, Adrienne Rich, William Stafford, and Mark Strand. Ahmad simplified Ghalib into literal versions and added necessary scholarly explanations. He sent this material to the poets and asked them for versions of the ones they liked. What emerged was sometimes spectacular, sometimes magical, sometimes passable—but always interesting. Merwin's and Rich's efforts struck me as particularly compelling, some of which have inspired me in my attempts. They have shown me how one may at times use free verse in translation to capture the essence of a poem, even if the original is in a stringent form. One of my favourite couplets by Ghalib was transliterated by Ahmad, who maintains the passive arrangement of the original:

> To him comes sleep, belongs the mind (peace of mind),
> belong the nights
> On whose arm you spread your hair. (Lines 11–14 'Ghazal XV')

The is how Merwin tackled it:

> Sleep comes to him
>   peace belongs to him
>   the night is his
>   over whose arm you spread your hair (Lines 5–6: 'Ghazal XV')

Adrienne Rich:

> Sleep is his, and peace of mind, and the nights belong to him
> across whose arms you spread the veils of your hair. (Lines 5–6)

William Stafford:

> Sleep comes, peace, quiet of rest,
> for one who holds an arm under your hair. (Lines 5–6)

None of these quite suggests the emotional desperation, however quiet, of the original. How to convey that this person, because of whom your world is in absolute turmoil (the word for 'spreading your hair' evokes that in Urdu), is undisturbed, absolutely in control, asleep peacefully while you are lying restlessly on his arm? Merwin made another attempt:

> He is the lord of sleep
> lord of peace
> lord of night
> on whose arm your hair is lying (Lines 10–13)

Though 'hair is lying' doesn't quite do it, I cannot think of any way his use of 'lord' can be improved upon. It conveys everything, for the passive voice in Urdu is not passive; rather, it can be quite imperious. 'Lord' captures that imperial moment, the control this lover has, his habit of taking for granted the one whose hair is lying on his arm. How I wish Merwin knew Urdu so he could realize his aesthetic victory here; he could then hear Begum Akhtar's rendering of these lines in Raga *Bhairavī* and be put under a spell. This is quite an irony: someone who doesn't know the language he is translating from, can never truly know the extent of his failure or triumph.

Faiz's regular poems (that is, not the *ghazals*) are somewhat easier for me to translate. But how to point out to exclusively English speakers the moment when what they see merely as exotic is actually challenging the 'exotic'? In 'Don't Ask Me for that Love Again,' Faiz breaks radically from Urdu's usual manner of looking at the Beloved, asking that his social commitment be accepted as more important than their love:

> That which then was ours, my love,
> don't ask me for that love again.
> The world then was gold, burnished with light—
> and only because of you. That's what I had believed.
> How could one weep for sorrows other than yours?
> How could one have any sorrow but the one you gave?
> So what were these protests, these rumours of injustice?

A glimpse of your face was evidence of springtime.
The sky, wherever I looked, was nothing but your eyes.
If you'd fall into my arms, Fate would be helpless.

All this I'd thought, all this I'd believed.
But there were other sorrows, comforts other than love.
The rich had cast their spell on history:
dark centuries had been embroidered on brocades and silks.
Bitter threads began to unravel before me
as I went into alleys and in open markets
saw bodies plastered with ash, bathed in blood.
I saw them sold and bought, again and again.
This too deserves attention. I can't help but look back
when I return from those alleys—what should one do?
And you still are so ravishing—what should I do?
There are other sorrows in this world,
comforts other than love.
Don't ask me, my love, for that love again. (*Rebel's Silhouette*, my translation)

This was a revolutionary poem, envied by many Urdu poets who wished they had first brought the socialist revolution into the realm of the Beloved, setting the archetype against itself, as it were. In this poem, Faiz announces that poetry, without dismissing tradition, must take on political themes consciously. Notice that Faiz did not discard the tradition: the poem clearly establishes the importance of the Beloved and her beauty. But its speaker does some plain speaking (almost like Cordelia to Lear), granting love its due, but no more. That Faiz had emphasized political commitment here did not, of course, mean that he would not, in other poems, address the Beloved in the manner of love-poetry, showing how the speaker's life depended entirely on her or him. But often when he addresses the Beloved, he is also addressing a figure that may very well be the revolution—revolution as a lost lover, or a cruel lover refusing to return.

In 'Don't Ask Me for That Love Again,' I took two recognizable liberties. One of the lines, literally translated, could read: 'When there's your sorrow, what is this struggle of the world?' 'Your sorrow' in Urdu can mean both 'the sorrow you've caused me' and 'the sorrow you feel.' Further, 'struggle of the world' does not quite suggest the nuances Faiz was striving for. I enlarged that one line into three:

How could one weep for sorrows other than yours?
How could one have any sorrow but the one you gave?
So what were these protests, these rumours of injustice? (Lines 5–7)

I also bypassed two lines of the original, which Victor Kiernan has translated as

Flesh issuing from the cauldrons of disease
With festered sores dripping corruption—(Lines 14–15)

In my translation, my version of these two lines, had I decided to attempt them, would have come immediately after

Bitter threads began to unravel before me
As I went into alleys and in open markets
Saw bodies plastered with ash, bathed in blood. (Lines 15–17)

Later, I was delighted to discover that in subsequent editions, Faiz himself had deleted those very two lines. Did he also, like me, find them excessive, if not outright gratuitous? There is this kinship among poets, I will insist, this ability at times to see through craft, ironically because of the craft, to the essence.

My translation process, as is clear, was quite different from Lazard's. I knew, both because of her Faiz and because of Merwin's and Rich's Ghalib, that not knowing the original is not necessarily a handicap. Not knowing the original may even be an advantage of sorts as long as one is working with very good literal versions. Merwin, after all, had set a standard for me with one line, against which I had to measure myself. My distinct advantage was that I could hear and say the originals to myself, as I translated, something Rich and Merwin just couldn't do. My particular problem was how to *pretend* that I was not burdened with a dual loyalty, to ignore that I was negotiating the demands of two cultures, both of which I felt in my bones, that I was responding to the sounds of two languages simultaneously. Even though the final product does not show it, I was constantly aware of my dual loyalties. But I decided: Wasn't this absence of a pure agenda an advantage? I had an inwardness with two languages: my loyalty to Urdu made me want to bring across its exquisite power to sway millions of people with its poetry, and my loyalty to English made me (as a poet in the language) want to create poetry in English. To what extent would I compromise

Faiz's voice? I finally attacked the task with no theoretical inhibition, letting each poem dictate itself, which often resulted in my fashioning for Faiz, an English, that is by turns dry and lyrical. But I always heard the music of the original, and that was fruitful, for some people have mentioned that there is a metrical 'feel' to my translation, of which I was quite unaware.

I wrote to Faiz in 1980 in Beirut, where he was living in exile, into which he had been forced by the military regime of Ziaul Haq.* He had 'found a welcome of sorts in the ruins of Beirut. His closest friends were Palestinians' (Said, 50). Besides asking for permission to translate him, I told him that I would be taking liberties with the originals. But what I really did was to bribe him with a sort of home-coming. I reminded him that he had, years before my birth, stayed in our home in Kashmir. I created nostalgia: Begum Akhtar, too, had stayed in our house. I tempted him: I had rare tapes of Begum Akhtar singing his *ghazals* in private concerts. In exactly a month he wrote back: 'I certainly knew your father and I am glad to have news from you. You are welcome to make your adaptations of my poems which I shall be happy to receive. Also some of your own poems and the tape or cassette of Begum Akhtar which you have kindly offered to send.'

My 'Homage to Faiz Ahmed Faiz' underscores my experience as a translator and also reveals some of my strategies for rendering Urdu into English. In one stanza, I incorporated a couplet of Ghalib's in the following manner:

> You knew Ghalib was right:
> blood must not merely follow routine, must not
> just flow as the veins' uninterrupted
> river. Sometimes it must flood the eyes,
> surprise them by being clear as water. (Lines 21–25, *Half-Inch*)

Ghalib's two lines may be transliterated: 'I do not approve of a mere running and loitering in the veins. If it isn't spilled from the eye, then how can it be called blood?' My weaving it into a poem meant explaining it—'You knew Ghalib was right'—paraphrasing it, even.

Sometimes explanation may be the best way to translate. Here is my literal version of one of Faiz's couplets: 'Got an occasion to sin, that too for only four days. I've seen the courage of God Almighty.' I had to fill in

---

*Faiz's decision to leave the country was his own. See Muzaffar Iqbal's conversation with Faiz Ahmed Faiz in this book–Editor.

the elliptical moments and adopted a free-verse stanza, a strategy I have used quite often with the *ghazals*:

> You made it so brief our time on earth
> its exquisite sins this sensation Oh Almighty
> of forgetting you
> We know how vulnerable you are
> We know you are a coward God (Lines 11–15, '*Ghazal*,' *Rebel's Silhouette*)

Will something be borne across to exclusively English readers through my translations? I also hope that those who know both languages will find some pleasure in my moments of literal fidelity to Faiz as well as in those moments (of fidelity, I insist) when I am unfaithful. As for purists, I hope they will be generous and welcome the times when I had no choice but to adjust, especially in the *ghazals*, the letter of Faiz's work—a letter to which I have a visceral attachment. But only in the original Urdu. As Salman Rushdie says in *Shame*, 'Omar Khayyam's position as a poet is curious. He was never very popular in his native Persia; and he exists in the West in a translation that is really a complete reworking of his verses, in many cases very different from the spirit (to say nothing of the content) of the original. . . . It is generally believed that something is always lost in translation; I cling to the notion—and use, in evidence, the success of Fitzgerald-Khayyam—that something can also be gained' (24).

In 'In Memory of Begum Akhtar,' I wrote:

> Ghazal, that death-sustaining widow,
> sobs in dingy archives, hooked to you.
> She wears her grief, a moon-soaked white,
> corners the sky into disbelief (Lines 11–14, *Half-Inch*)

I could use the same words for Faiz. Begum Akhtar comes back to me in strange moments, at times unexpectedly. So does Faiz; often, they come back together.

In a recent poem, 'Snow on the Desert,' I narrate driving my sister to Tucson International Airport in a terribly thick January morning fog. Suddenly, the sliding doors of the fog opened and the sun-dazzled snow, which had fallen all night, blinded us. All the cactus plants were draped in a cocaine-like whiteness. I told my sister to imagine that we were driving by the shores of the sea, for the Sonora Desert was an ocean two

hundred million years ago. At the airport I stared after her plane until
the window was again a mirror. And then,

> As I drove back to the foothills, the fog
> shut its doors behind me on Alvernon,
> and I breathed the dried seas
> the earth had lost,
> their forsaken shores.
> (Lines 52–56 *Nostalgist's Map*)

I thought for weeks that I had nothing to compare that moment with,
nothing to contrast it with. How could I *translate* that moment? Months
later, as I struggled with the poem, I remembered

> another moment that refers only
> to itself:
>
> in New Delhi one night
> as Begum Akhtar sang, the lights went out.
>
> It was perhaps during the Bangladesh War,
> perhaps there were sirens,
>
> air-raid warnings.
> But the audience, hushed, did not stir.
>
> The microphone was dead, but she went on
> singing, and her voice
>
> was coming from far
> away, as if she had already died.
>
> And just before the lights did flood her
> again, melting the frost
>
> of her diamond
> into rays, it was, like this turning dark
>
> of fog, a moment when only a lost sea
> can be heard, a time

to recollect
every shadow, everything the earth was losing,

a time to think of everything the earth
and I had lost, of all

that I would lose,
of all that I was losing. (Lines 57–80 *Nostalgist's Map*)

The only way to translate that moment was to find one more that could not be compared with or to another. But in that untranslatable fraction of time, I did manage a translation by pointing out its impossibility.

Was Begum Akhtar singing Faiz when the lights went out? He is always with me, often in her voice. I have brought them to America with absolute ease, taken them back to the subcontinent, then again brought them back to America. I have not surrendered any part of me; rather, my claims to both Urdu and English have become greater. The way the raga and the poem became the other's for Begum Akhtar, so have Urdu and English become for me. My two loyalties, on loan to each other, are now so one that the loan has been forgiven. No, forgotten.

Begum Akhtar stripped words until they were revealed in the glory of their syllables, each syllable made an integral note of her chosen raga—so often a tantalizingly uncliched Bhairavī. She knew the *ghazal* at its heart has a circularity of meaning, created seductively by its *qāfiā* and *radīf* in couplet after couplet. She knew how to time this circularity so it seemed we were at the stillpoint of the revolving circle, especially when she was interpreting a great poet. No translation can hope to do that. But 'nothing's lost. Or else: all is translation/And every bit of us is lost in it/Or found' (Lines 208–10, Merrill, 'Lost in Translation'). For me, translating Faiz has led to its own moments in which I am sometimes at the stillpoint of the turning circle, sometimes part of its revolution. Sometimes the circle comes to a dazzling halt, and I manage to find my meaning as a translator.

Works Cited

Ahmad, Aijaz (ed.) *Ghazals of Ghalib*, Columbia University Press, 1971, Print.
Ali, Agha Shahid, *A Nostalgist's Map of America*, Northon, 1991, Print.
Ali, Agha Shahid, *The Beloved Witness: Selected Poems*, Viking Penguin, 1992, Print.
Ali, Agha Shahid, *The Half-Inch Himalayas*, Wesleyan University Press, 1987, Print.

Coppola, Carlo, 'Faiz Ahmed Faiz', *Poetry East* (Spring 1989): 96–97, Print.

Dhar, Sheila, 'Hindustani Music: An Inward Journey,' *Temenos* 7 (1986): 83–94, Print.

Faiz, Faiz Ahmed, 'Future of Ghazal Poetry,' *Sonora Review* (Spring 1985): 53–55, Print.

Faiz, Faiz Ahmed, 'Preface,' Trans. Agha Shahid Ali, *The Rebel's Silhouette*, 1st ed., Peregrine Smith, vii-ix, Print.

Faiz, Faiz Ahmed, *Poems*, Trans. Victor Kiernan. Allen & Unwin, 1971, Print.

Faiz, Faiz Ahmed, *The True Subject*, Trans. Naomi Lazard, Princeton University Press, 1987, Print.

Hollander, John, *Rhyme's Reason*, Yale University Press, 1989, 66–67, Print.

Kiernan, Victor, 'Introduction,' Faiz Ahmed Faiz, *Poems*, Trans. Victor Kiernan, Allen & Unwin, 1971, Print.

Kiernan, Victor, 'Iqbal: A Translator's Confessions,' Iqbal Centenary Meeting, Urdu Society, Birmingham, England, 1980, Lecture.

Lazard, Naomi, 'Translating Faiz,' *Columbia: The Magazine of Columbia University* (June 1985): 26–30, Print.

Merrill, James, 'Lost in Translation', *Selected Poems*, Knopf, 1993, 278–284, Print

Rushdie, Salman, *Shame*, Alfred A. Knopf, 1982, Print.

Said, Edward, 'A Mind of Winter,' *Harper's* September 1984, Print.

EVENING

Original: *Shām* from *Dast-e Tah-e Sang* (1965)
TRANSLATOR: AGHA SHAHID ALI

The trees are dark ruins of temples,
seeking excuses to tremble
since who knows when—
their roofs are cracked,
their doors lost to ancient winds.
And the sky is a priest,
saffron marks on his forehead,
ashes smeared on his body.
He sits by the temples, worn to a shadow, not looking up.

Some terrible magician, hidden behind curtains,
has hypnotized Time
so this evening is net
in which the twilight is caught.
Now darkness will never come—
and there will never be morning.

The sky waits for this spell to be broken,
for History to tear itself from this net,
for Silence to break its chains
so that a symphony of conch shells
may wake up to the statues
and a beautiful, dark goddess,
her anklets echoing, may unveil herself.

13

FAIZ AHMED FAIZ AND THE SOVIET UNION

The major part of Faiz's adult life was associated with the Soviet Union. His inclination towards Moscow, Russia and the Soviet Union, which can better be termed as a passion, had its roots in his ideology. Faiz's name had become familiar in the Soviet Union much before he himself arrived there, because, news about the extermination of democratic forces in Pakistan and the Rawalpindi Conspiracy case had already got to Moscow. He was still in jail when Soviet newspapers first began to give headlines about him: *the courageous crusader against capitalism who is being persecuted for his progressive ideas.*

In 1954, famous Indian poet and leader of the Progressive Writers' Association in India, Ali Sardar Jafri, arrived in Moscow. At that time the Progressive Writers' Association had been blacklisted in Pakistan as opposed to India, where it was continuing its activities with good success. The Indians were not at all concerned about Faiz's nationality because he had always been *owned* by them and his poetry was all the rage there.

At one stage, Ali Sardar Jafri had criticized Faiz for the lack of revolutionary fervour in his poetry but later on, upon bidding farewell to the extremist element in progressive writing, he became not only enamoured of the work of his Pakistani friend but also became his most earnest interpreter. In those days, he was so impressed with the poetry Faiz had written in jail that he would be quoting his latest verses and telling his story wherever he went. Whenever the well built, tall and handsome Ali Sardar Jafri went on to recite Faiz's verses in his inimitable style, accompanied by that typical gesture of pushing back his thick black locks with a flourish of the hand, there would hardly be anybody who remained unimpressed. The famous Russian poet Alexi Surkov, who translated numerous poems of Faiz into the language, writes in his preface to Faiz's collection *Sar-e Vādī-e Sīnā*, about his first meeting with

Ali Sardar Jafri. It was in an evening in December 1945 that Surkov first met Jafri at the home of a Russian author, from whom he also got to first hear of Faiz.

> Indian poet Ali Sardar Jafri was humming some verses in a foreign language. The verses, brimming with the finesse of romantic love, the loneliness of incarceration and the rage and fury of a revolutionary fascinated everybody present. This was the poetry of Faiz Ahmed Faiz, who was languishing in a Montgomery prison, far, far away from Moscow.[1]

A couple of months later in 1956, the first Russian translations of some of Faiz's poetry were published in magazines and newspapers, followed in 1962 by complete collections of his translated poems. The collections were all being printed in big numbers, e.g. one hundred thousand copies of a collection of fifty poems were printed in 1983. This was the biggest number printed, while ten thousand copies each, which was the standard for poetry collections in the Soviet Union, were printed of the 1977 and 1985 selections of Faiz. Just the Russian translations of Faiz's books came to more than two hundred and ten thousand copies! Here it needs to be mentioned that Russian translations of his books were normally followed by translations into other national languages, which were immediately seized by avid readers. One of the many reasons for this popularity was not only a general interest in poetry in the region, but also the presence of a reading public hooked to eastern poetry and so, every new name attracted immediate attention. Secondly, Faiz got immense publicity in the Soviet media when he was awarded the Lenin Peace Prize in 1962. This was followed by further recognition in the remotest regions of the Soviet Union as the Pakistani crusader of peace. Thus, vast numbers of readers were naturally drawn to the translations of his work. However the most probable reason behind this popularity was the fact that the translations were undertaken by some of the Soviet Union's best poets who would make efforts to render it in the language of *ghinā'ī* (lyrical) poetry.

There is no doubt that in its Russian form, Faiz's poetry remained the poorer in sonority, form, linguistic license and style, but above all, in the subtle nuances associated with the Urdu poetic tradition. (As it is, it becomes difficult to translate the *ghazal* into a foreign language unfamiliar with Urdu and Persian poetic traditions.) Yet most of the translations of Faiz's poems should be considered successful because they do appear to be the original when read in Russian. Besides, Russian poets find a similarity between their own ideas and sensitivities and those of Faiz, who appears to be a voice like their own. They were impressed by the poetic style, expression and unusual metaphor in Faiz, the translating of which into their own language, they considered an interesting and important kind of poetic experience. (Normally Urdu conversant persons would do a literal translation of the poem and then read out the Urdu original to a well-known Russian poet, so as to give him an idea of the sounds, the rhyme scheme and harmony in the Urdu text. The poet would then give poetic form to the literal translation.) Poets critical of the Soviet system would eagerly take to translating Faiz's social and political poems, because through the language of this Pakistani poet they found a means to express sentiments which they could not do on their own. (It has to be remembered that the Soviet Union practiced a strict code of ideological censorship on speech and writing.) However, it were the subtle poetic innuendoes in Faiz's poetry that collectively impressed his translators as well as his readers.

Thus it can conclusively be said that Faiz Ahmed Faiz, who was introduced to the Soviet Union as a crusader of peace, winning the Lenin Peace Prize, very soon found a way into the hearts and minds of everybody there. As far as Faiz was concerned, he had been a Soviet admirer since his youth. By the second half of the twentieth century, almost half the world had come to associate the Soviet Union as the *answer to the dreams of the world's downtrodden, the defender of world peace, the torchbearer for those who faced coercion and violence* etc. Like the universally respected poets and writers, Lion Feichtwanger, Bernard Shaw, Nazim Hikmet, Andre Gide, Romen Pollan and Anri Barbus who had toured the Soviet Union much before him, Faiz too came here with an open heart. He was greatly impressed by what he saw there and this heightened manifold, his esteem for the country.

Included among Faiz's Soviet friends were also those disenchanted younger poets and writers who would often ask whether he could see no wrong in the political and social system there. Usually he would not get into this discussion but it might not be fallacious to assume that like countless persons from other countries who believed in the communal ends, Faiz too believed in the possibility of a world society built on values of justice and goodwill. Without doubt, he related his own social and political aspirations with the Soviet Union. He was ready to turn a blind eye to the system's shortcomings and failings because he realized that the road to the system being followed by the Soviet Union was wrought with pitfalls and one in which slip-ups were a possibility. All it needed was a bit of adjustment. In fact Faiz points this way in some of his verses:

> Passion, the destination's stairway, led me through
> All the places, where the climbing-rope snapped[2]

This *ghazal* was penned in 1970, after an encounter with a young 'rebel' poet in Moscow, and the reference here to the broken *kamand* (climbing-rope) could well be the poet's acknowledgement of the weaknesses in the Russian system. It seems as if he were trying to encourage his Soviet friends through his poetry.

Faiz became a frequent visitor to the Soviet Union after receiving the Lenin Award (its official name was *Lenin Prize for Efforts Towards the Establishment of Peace between Nations*) which was the biggest Soviet honour that could be bestowed on a foreigner. As all doors opened for him, Faiz got the chance to visit all the Soviet republics and thus experience in person, the life there. This was very unusual, since foreign visitors rarely got to get a view of things behind the curtain. Faiz was the chosen one who could not avoid observing the failings of a system not open to foreigners and yet, in Russian terms, he basically saw it all through coloured lenses.

In spite of his untainted amour for the country, Faiz actually wrote very little on the Soviet subject as opposed to other progressive writers, and if you look closely, you will find few poets and writers who have not written stories or poems about Moscow, Stalin, Lenin and the Red Square. In all the long years of his association with the Soviet Union, he probably wrote only two poems directly dealing with the system. One is *Celebrating the Russian October Revolution* which was actually written under the effect of popular demand on its fiftieth birthday:

> Night, a wounded bird, anguished across the horizons,
> the first ray sparked, of the final dawn;
> then were raised, worn-out curtains, from darkened, sightless eyes,
> hearts put to fire;
> layer after layer,
> doors of the seven skies thrown open,
> turned mirror-like.
> From East to West
> all prison doors are today unlocked,

age-old structures erased,
for the masses' benevolence
to lay their foundation anew;
all bloodied shrouds lifted
from the bosom of time.
The clinking chains
on the feet of slaves
sound the bell for the caravan to proceed;
handcuffs of the oppressed
glisten to form the sword of death.[3]

The Russian connection can be identified even in the poem's title. A composite picture of colossal transformation in the name of freedom has been drawn up through the use of metaphor. In this manner, the poet underlines the universal relevance of the Russian Revolution, of its honourable ends, of which, he had no doubt. The poem contains a favourite and frequently used Faiz's metaphor, *day of judgement;* doomsday, the day all will be judged, the day of resurrection, the day sinners are terrified of but, of which those with a clear conscience shall have no fear! The Russian Revolution has been compared to the first ray of light on the Day of Judgement and has been deemed just as inevitable as the dawning of day after the long, dark night, with the verses stating clearly that this revolution was dedicated to the liberty of slaves and the downtrodden.

The poem has a distinctively progressive colouring with clear echoes of some of Faiz's 'poetry of incarceration'; the echoes of a poetry in which he pondered over the revolutionary process, the Russian communist revolution and the commonalities of movements in nations fighting for their liberty.

For some unknown reason, this poem is not included in any of Faiz's poetry collections. It was many years later, after it had been written, that it was placed in *Mah-o-Sāl-e Āshnā'ī,* his book based on memories and impressions of the Soviet Union. It is also present in the Moscow Chapter of the voluminous 1992 publication on his western references, that were researched and edited by Ashfaq Hussain in Canada. The poem is also present in the book called *Navā'ē Lenin* which is not available now, but needs to be mentioned here. In 1970, along with other books on Lenin, a collection of poems on him by Urdu poets was being put together to celebrate his hundredth birthday. Faiz was requested to write a poem about him, but though he had otherwise, great respect for Lenin's personality and teachings, could probably not accept him as a character in his poetry (as opposed to Allama Iqbal). Hence, he was unable to force his creative jinn. Since in the opinion of the Soviet leaders, no collection of Urdu poetry on Lenin could be published unless it carried a poem by the only Lenin Peace Prize winning Urdu poet, Faiz's poem on the October Revolution was included in *Navā'ē Lenin*.

The Leningrad Cemetery, Faiz's second poem on the Soviet Union, was a call from out of his own heart. One day Faiz visited a Leningrad cemetery to pay homage to the national heroes of the Second World War, where he placed a floral wreath on a communal memorial built into the lap of a huge statue of the motherland. This poem was a more or less impromptu penning of his feelings on the occasion, for the sanctified and solemn pain and anguish pervading the graveyard has been translated into it. The poem, *The Leningrad Cemetery* has been placed in *Shām-e Shehr-e Yārān*.

The Leningrad Cemetery
Translator: Daud Kamal[4]

On cold granite slabs
A sprinkling of flowers
Reminiscent of blood.
There are no names
On the headstones
But every petal is engraved
With its own parable.

The young heroes sleep
Transfigured to the roots
Of their hair.
Only mother is awake—
Massive, with her rosary of stars.
The sky bows down with her.
She is the sky.

Apparently these are the only two poems Faiz wrote on the Soviet subject. Yet the actual situation is somewhat different and he himself explained it thus:

> In the Soviet Union it is possible to enjoy a few days of respite from the vicissitudes of fortune and business of earning one's bread and butter and to

avail of a couple of leisurely and relaxing moments, in spite of commitments. Along with this leisure one can also attain that safe distance from the travails of life and living, so that spectator-like, one can view both with peace. Probably, it is necessary to have that concern as well as a distance, a dialogue as well as a disconnect, an anxiety as well as insurrection to be able to write poetry . . . that one sensibility that the Sufis call a baring of the heart . . . there is no mention of the Soviet Union in poetry written here but all points to the same sensitivity. . . .[5]

In the light of these words, it can safely be said that the poems written in the Soviet Union, specially in Moscow, reflect the poet's heartfelt emotions during his stay in the country and also that the general ambience of the place is juxtaposed in many of his creative outpourings. Many of these sonnets and poems are masterpieces of Urdu poetry. Poems like *Rang hai dil kā mērē*, *Pās raho*, *Manzar*, *Intesāb*, *Sočnē do*, *Sar-e Vādi-e Sīnā*, *Khurshīd-e mehshar kī lau* and *Ṭūṭi jahāṅ jahāṅ pē kamaṅd* as well as *ghazals*, songs and translations of Soviet poets were also written in Moscow. All these contain one or another reference to the Soviet Union, which itself gains a relevant basic identity in the poems of his last days.

Faiz always behaved courteously towards the people whom he met in Moscow and other Soviet cities. This was a part of his personality. His immediate circle of acquaintances with whom he spent most of his time, consisted of literary friends whom he really loved. He had the same feelings even for those who were double-faced. Once, when Faiz commented critically against the Afro-Asian Writers' Movement, the sentence was conveyed by a supposed 'friend' to the Kremlin leadership, who took offence. The 'friend' started avoiding Faiz after this, to the extent of not even recognizing him. Later on when things settled down, he once again approached his dear Pakistani friend, who met him as if nothing had happened, though he was aware of the whole story. It is in view of this attitude that one would like to quote a Faiz verse:

Be it worldly grief, lips of the beloved or the enemy's hand
I have dealt all with love[6]

Indeed Faiz mingled with everyone with equal warmth, never holding anything against anybody. If a reference was made to somebody's discourtesy, a typical response would be, 'One should not give an ear to loose talk. It will die its own death.'

In *Mah-o-Sāl-e Āshnā'ī*, Faiz had this to say about the Soviet people:

> It should not be assumed that only angels totally devoid of human weaknesses
> live here. On getting to know the people, it has brought some measure of
> satisfaction that in this society too, people face unrequited love, hearts are
> liable to get broken, rivalries flourish and daughters and mothers-in-law
> get embroiled in arguments and that wives do nag and husbands are bad-
> tempered. For all these, people have found a way out but somebody has to
> find a way out for GHAM-E DAURĀN; not that it matters because if they do find
> a way out, I wonder what would be the fate of our poet friends?[7]

Faiz preferred this sort of a 'romantic' outlook towards the Soviet
Union and its people. He was not alone in these feelings because the
Soviet Union had generally gained in stature after the defeat of Fascist
Germany. It had come to the forefront as a leader of the *peace and
socialist* camp. Even those leftist western forces who, before the war,
had adopted an openly critical view of the Soviet system as one totally
bereft of democratic liberties, now lapsed into silence, so that one, the
'saviour of peace and socialism' may not suffer a setback and two, that they
themselves may not be labelled as capitalists. Faiz himself realized that
to speak out against the Soviet system was akin to being anti-system and
harming the cause of global peace initiatives and third world countries.
This was the actual political wisdom behind the camaraderie, socialist
thinkers held for the Soviet system of governance. However, there was a
psychological aspect as well to Afro-Asian progressive writers' leanings
towards the Soviet Union. No other country accorded them this kind of
respect and admiration. Neither were thousands of copies of their books
printed anywhere. (It has to be taken into account that in the Soviet
Union, books were published in all its fifteen national languages.) It was
also important that within the Soviet Union, these writers were fully
aware of their individual participation and the effect of their writings on
the movements for national liberty and social justice, in their respective
countries. For lack of better words it can be said that in Moscow, writers
from the developing world reaped psychological rewards. Who would
remain un-affected by all that?

As far as Faiz Ahmed Faiz was concerned, not only was he considered
to be a Marxist and a friend of the October Revolution, of the Socialists
and Progressives, (though this in itself was cause for a major identity
among the Soviet leadership) he was also the winner of the Lenin Peace

Prize. It was because of this status that he was accorded unconditional respect by everybody, from the highest Soviet leadership to villages across the country. There was no shortage of his admirers even in other western and eastern countries, but while there, he was held in esteem only by those who understood his language; here, in the Soviet Union he was popular irrespective of whether people knew his language or not. Faiz was very impressed when the large hall of *Kāshāna-e udabā*, the Moscow Writers' Club, was packed to capacity by people who had come to meet the Pakistani poet and his Russian translators. In those days, countless people were fond of poetry and audiences would listen in silence to Faiz's soft voice. He would recite the poems in Urdu, followed by a renowned poet reading out its Russian translation. They would be poets whose names held deep importance and significance in the history of Soviet poetry. There were senior poets like Isakovsky and Nikolay Tikhonov who translated Faiz as well as other well known ones like Andrei Voznesensky, Alexei Surkov, Yevtushenko, Boris Slutskiy, Derzhavin, Naiman, Rasul Gamzatov and Rimma Kazakova. After each recital, the hall would resound with applause as was customary, instead of *wāh*, *wāh*. The Russian writers would pay homage to their Pakistani counterpart and embrace him, and all the time Faiz would be smiling benignly.

A similar ambience enveloped the *Kāshāna-e udabā* on a cold February evening in 1981. There was a raging snow storm outside, but it was spring time inside the hall. Faiz Ahmed Faiz's seventieth birthday was being celebrated with great pomp and show. There was hardly any breathing space in the hall of the club, where the stage was packed to capacity with seating for those who wished to congratulate him. The speakers greeted Faiz in their own individual styles: some spoke briefly, others in greater detail; some said it in prose, others in verse, some sang, others danced out their greetings, one and all showering Faiz with emotionally charged praises. Each compliment was laden with genuine love and Faiz was fully conscious of the fact. The piano on the stage was piled up with a huge stack of flowers. Faiz appeared to be overwhelmed and his eyes flowed over. Thanking everybody in his speech of acceptance he said:

> Today, I am overjoyed, not because I have turned seventy. The joy is that this evening and the days prior to it have been spent in Moscow and whatever I have achieved or otherwise, is being celebrated in this very city. This city and its people are dear to me for a number of reasons; because here I have made

friends, I have loved; I have written much poetry here, here I have dined with and learnt from the people. Apart from all that, whatever ideology I have acquired has been shaped by friends here. The two things people of this city have taught others, whether outsiders or their co-habitants are the love of peace and the courage to wage battle; to battle not for the sake of battling but for love of peace.[8]

Very often, strangers would welcome Faiz on Moscow streets and greet him. Once an elderly man addressed him on the road thus: 'Are you Faiz Ahmed Faiz, the Pakistani poet? I have one of your books and I love your poetry. Simply love it.' By the time the interpreter had translated what the man said, he had disappeared! On another occasion when Faiz was getting into a car, a young woman approached him nervously and said, 'I love your poems, specially the romantic ones. I want to thank you for them.' One day Faiz was waiting for the hotel lift when a girl came running and shyly presented him with a large red rose and then without saying a single word, ran away. Fans seeking his autograph would constantly be waylaying him at the hotel doors, asking him to write something on one of his Russian books. Faiz never disappointed anyone. His popularity in Moscow can be judged by another small incident when on requiring some medical aid he went to a clinic of the Writers' Union. When his interpreter started to introduce the patient to the young doctor, he immediately cut him short with a smile, saying, 'I am not so ignorant as not to recognize a living classical poet.'

Faiz Sahib would be impressed by such expressions of love by strangers. He would respect them and feel elated after every such manifestation.

During the Moscow sojourn, in the mind of the poet was being fashioned a composite image of the city, as a result of such encounters. However this was no abstract image, but one based on certain individual characters, one embodiment of which was a personality which gained major significance in Faiz's life. This was a petite framed, beautiful and intelligent woman by the name of Maryam Salganik. Like other friends, Faiz too called her Meera. In the meeting of Meera, Faiz's inherent good fortune can once again be detected, for in her he found a truly helpful friend in a foreign land. Maryam Salganik was an appointment holder in the foreign wing of the Writers' Union and possessed a lot of clout. Apart from fluency in English, she had mastery over Urdu and Hindi and was held in high esteem in Moscow's literary circles, because of her vast knowledge about diverse subjects. Meera would understand the slightest hint from Faiz and try to help him out. She was his first translator in Russian and she was also the one who translated Faiz's speech of acceptance at the Lenin Peace Prize ceremony in the Kremlin. How could the poet remain unimpressed by Meera! In all probability the creative jinn that dominated the poet's thinking during the Moscow sojourn, had donned Meera's personality! Thus, it should come as no surprise that Faiz dedicated his 1971 poetic collection, *Sar-e Vādī-e Sīnā* to Maryam Salganik. Once reminiscing about her associations with Faiz, Alys had said that for her, he had become the embodiment of the subcontinent itself. Perhaps the same could be said of Faiz and his association with Meera, in whose personality he could encapsulate entire Soviet Russia.

Actually the renowned writer and translator Maryam Salganik is the same person who introduced the Pakistani poet to her Soviet literary friends, as well as a wide range of readers across the Soviet Union. Later, during Faiz's extensive tours of the region, she continued to act as chaperone even after handing over the responsibility of translation to others, always making sure that he was comfortable in Moscow. She translated Faiz's Urdu and English poetry and prose into Russian and interviewed him for renowned newspapers and magazines. Her conversations with and interviews of Faiz, in publications such as *Ghair mulkī Adab*, *Adabī Akhbār* and *Lotus* always attracted a vast readership. She was also the author of the epilogue in the Russian translation of the jubilee collection of Faiz's verses, published on his seventy-fifth birthday. Here, writing in her signature style, she drew a literary pen-picture of Faiz, while mentioning the basic milestones of his life. To date this is the last collection of Faiz's poetry published in the Russian language.[9]

Faiz was always happy to be in Moscow. Here, he was the centre of attention and accorded great respect in a generally congenial atmosphere, surrounded by friends and admirers. He would feel revitalized and be taken over by the creative process, giving the impression that his creative jinn worked best in the cold northern climes. Barring the universally acknowledged poetry written in jail, the majority of his best poems were penned in Moscow. Of these, it is the poems with a romantic tone that dominate the scene. *Pās raho* was one such poem written in 1963 and was considered by most critics to be the best example of Urdu romantic poetry:

Be Near Me

TRANSLATOR: VICTOR KIERNAN[10]

Be near me—
My torment, my darling, be near me
That hour when the night comes,
Black night that has drunk heaven's blood comes
With salve of musk-perfume, with diamond-tipped lancet,
With wailing, with jesting, with music,
With grief like a clash of blue anklets—
When, hoping once more, hearts deep-sunk in men's bosoms
Wait, watch for the hands whose wide sleeves still
Enfold them,

Till wine's gurgling sound is a sobbing of infants
Unsatisfied, fretful, no soothing will silence,—
No taking thought prospers,
No thought serves;
—That hour when the night comes,
That hour when black night, drear, forlorn, comes,
Be near me,
My torment, my darling, be near me!

Here is another poem written on an evening in a Moscow hotel in 1964;
one rightly deemed a masterpiece of Urdu descriptive poetry:

Vista

TRANSLATOR: AGHA SHAHID ALI[11]

Deserted street, shadows of trees and houses, locked doors—
We watched the moon become a woman,
baring her breast, softly, on the edge of a rooftop.
Below, the earth was blue, a lake of stilled shadows,
on which a leaf, the bubble of a second floated
and then burst, softly.
Pale, very pale, gently, very slowly,
wine that is cold colour
was poured into my glass,
and the roses of your hands, the decanter and the glass,
were, like the outline
of a dream, in focus, for a moment.
Then they melted, softly.

My heart once again promised love, softly.
You said, 'But softly.'
The moon, breathing as it went down, said,
'More, yet more softly.'

The first few lines of this poem are reminiscent of the beginning of renowned Russian poet Alexander Blok's famous poem (the night, the road, the lamp on the road, the shop . . .). In those days, Faiz was a keen reader of the English translations of Russian literature and there is a good possibility that his Moscow poems are coloured with overtones of Russian poetry. However, this hypothesis, which can become an interesting subject for research is beholden to poetic proof.

Faiz's association with Soviet Russia remained the basis of the heartfelt joy and peace of mind pervading his Moscow writings, but later on, it changed to a great extent.

Moscow was not the only place in the Soviet Union where Faiz loved to be. He had special feelings for the Eastern Soviet Republics too, where he would often head. Commenting on his experiences of the Southern regions, Faiz writes:

> In Tashkent and Samarkand, in Almaty or Ashkabad or in Mahach Kila, nowhere have I felt a stranger, because in their mannerisms, in their eating and dressing up and in their lifestyles, the people all appear to be my own brothers. However, Tajikistan takes the cake because here I can converse with everybody directly without the help of an interpreter, for the Tajiks speak Persian and this is not the Persian of the Iranians; it is the Persian we speak. The only difference is that they call it Tajiki and not Persian.[12]

A common thread runs through the culture and traditions of the Sub-continental and Central Asian races. The region and its inhabitants remind Indians and Pakistanis of their age-old ancestral relations. As far as they are concerned, the people of Central Asia readily extend brotherly hospitality to guests from the subcontinent. If these guests happen to be Muslims, and then poets, they will receive a royal treatment. Since Faiz was a Muslim, a poet and a recipient of the Lenin Award as well, the eastern hospitality accorded him, reached a zenith. The First Secretaries of the Central Committees of the Republics (who were like local lords) would hold grand receptions for Faiz in their palaces. The banquets hosted by the rich Presidents of these communal farms could only be compared to those held by rulers of fantasy lands. (The reference is to the same communal farms, designated as the *millionaire farms* and whose number in the Soviet Union amounted to a just a very few. They were under the supervision of the Central Government itself and were the same that were shown to foreign guests as show pieces of the better alternatives of communal farming over the capitalist agricultural system).

Faiz was also accorded grand receptions in the fairy tale republics, especially in Daghistan, from where his dear friend, the doyen of poets, Rasul Hamza (Rasul Ghamzanov in Russian) hailed. Faiz preferred the close circle of his dear friends to the state banquets. Here the food may have been of lesser quality, and in lesser quantity, but the ambience would be more home-like and laden with love and affection. Admirers of Faiz and his poetry (most of them Urdu speaking linguists) would get together in such assemblies and he would repeatedly be asked to recite his poetry, which he readily did. At times he would get tired and become short of breath (his ailing lungs would make their presence felt) but he rarely took a long break. 'How can I refuse anybody's request? These people have come to hear me recite and there is no knowing when we will next be able to get together.'

Compared to the southern republics, Moscow had fewer Urdu and Persian speakers, though even here, there were plenty of people who read Faiz in Russian. I have no idea how, but he would be able to build up a rapport even with them without an interpreter, getting across to people who, far from any knowledge of Urdu or Persian, were totally non conversant even in English. Once, referring to Faiz, the renowned Russian poetess Rimma Kazakova said, 'Poets have their own language; the language of silence.' Perhaps it was in explanation of this mysterious sentence that she wrote a poem in memory of Faiz, which she called *Silence of the Poet*. During her Faiz Memorial Lecture in London in 1986, she read out an English translation of the poem. Here are two stanzas:

O Faiz,
You were a trumpet to my heart
Whose silent calls were clearly, clearly heard!
Although a poor disciple of your art,
I do recall how fine it always felt
To talk to you without saying a word.

O noisy speeches, dull and long—they roar,
How furiously the speakers fan the wind . . .
Not so with you, O Faiz—you were akin
To all of us. Even to utter a word
There was no need: your silence meant much more.[13]

Faiz wrote his impressions about the Soviet Union in his book, *Mah-o-Sāl-e Āshnā'ī*, whose introductory article titled, *Yādoṅ kā Majmū'ā* also supports the subject of the book. This book has also been mentioned before. In its introduction, Faiz wrote:

> This book is neither a journalist's report nor is it an analytical study by an observer. These are the scattered memories of a friend; memories that may not add to the knowledge of those who have already seen the Soviet Union, but for readers who have not had the chance to be here, a visual or two in this rakish album will rouse their interest. And because of it, they may draw near this great land and its people.[14]

Apparently, the chapters of this book, which are something like the different visuals in a compound, appear to be scattered articles, but, actually they are pearls of the one and same string. The book also has a main character, who is Faiz himself and it is through his eyes that readers view this vast country. Each chapter is an article based on the personal impressions of the poet. One can feel Faiz's natural inclination towards shorter genres, even in the composition of the book, or rather in his prose too, one can detect the nuances of his poetic writings. His prose too has colours of the finest of poetic personifications, metaphors and idioms. Readers got to know this peculiar style of Faiz's prose through the letters he wrote from jail.

Commenting on *Mah-o-Sāl-e Āshnā'ī*, a reader writes:

> This collection of memories is an album created not by a photographer but an artist. The background of this visual is delightful but it is the colours filled in by the imagination of the artist that are cause for the inexplicable appeal and enchantment. The fairy tale parameters created by Faiz overwhelm the reader. . . .

And yet it cannot be said of this book that it became overly popular. The basic reason for this was presumed to be the political overtones of the book which was in fact, intentional propaganda. Like the October

Revolution poem on the Soviet subject, which has been mentioned earlier, this book too was written at the request of the Central Committee of the Soviet Communist Party. The truth of the matter is that the book remained incomplete in as far as honouring the request was concerned, because Faiz could not write much on those lines. That is one reason why more than half the book carries either his poems or pictures, not even remotely connected to him. All these amount to a variety of photographs shot by Soviet photographers on different occasions and locations.

Today the one significance of *Mah-o-Sāl-e Āshnā'ī* is that it has been authored by Faiz and is a composite picture of a country that has disintegrated. The book draws up visuals of countless positives of which the Soviet people are rightly proud, but there is not the slightest mention of the failures which, years later in 1992, became the cause for the disintegration and fall of the Soviet Union. Hence, today one can only do bitter sweet analyses of *Khūbsūrat pasmanzar* (the enchanting backdrop) and *Funkār kī jadū'ī rang āmēzī* (the artist's magical play of colours). Now years later, one gets the feeling that initially, Faiz had started writing his memories of those eventful years when living in Moscow, or touring one of the republics was nothing short of a festivity, but his pen appears to have refused to go further on reaching the present. (It has to be kept in mind that the book's year of publication was 1979.) That was also the period when Faiz was beginning to notice the social and political downsides of the Soviet system and towards which he had preferred to turn a blind eye, or those of which he was ignorant. Now his heart and mind were constantly badgered by many questions, and so he could not go on to add more colour to the 'beautiful picture'. The unique, dramatic quality of Faiz's poetry in his last years, appears to be directly related to his not having been able to complete the book. However, this subject is to be dealt with separately.

Getting back to Faiz's numerous tours and his experiences of life in the Soviet Union, it is important to stress the fact that his constant efforts at increasing friendly and brotherly relations between the people of Soviet Union and Pakistan cannot be given enough appreciation. Many Pakistanis considered him the official ambassador in the Soviet Union, and this was not very far from reality. Addressing a conference held in honour of Faiz, Iftikhar Ali, the Pakistani Ambassador in Moscow had said in his opening speech: *It is not me but Faiz who is Pakistan's real ambassador in Russia, because he represents not the government but the people of Pakistan.*

This was a reality and one reason why Faiz's name remains ingrained as a friend in the hearts of all who dwell in the former Soviet Union.

Translated from Urdu by Nyla Daud
Translations of verses at notes 2, 3 and 6 are done by Yasmeen Hameed

Notes

1. Faiz Ahmed Faiz, *Sar-e Vādī-e Sīnā*, Karachi: Pak, 1971, 19, Print.
2. Faiz Ahmed Faiz, *Nuskhahā'ē Vafā*, Lahore: Maktaba-e Karavan, n.d., 453, Print.
3. Faiz Ahmed Faiz, *Mah-o-Sāl-e Āshnā'ī*, Moscow: Dar-ul-Isha'at Taraqqī, 1979, 107, Print.
4. Faiz, *Nuskhahā'ē Vafā*, 551 [see note 2].
5. Ashfaq Husain, *Tahqīq-o-Tartīb: Faiz Ke Maghribī Havālē*, Lahore: Jang, 1992, 814, Print.
6. Faiz, *Nuskhahā'ē-Vafā*, 553 [see note 2].
7. Faiz *Mah-o-Sāl-e Āshnā'ī*, [see note 3].
8. Faiz delivered this extempore speech on the occasion of his seventieth birthday at a grand assembly in February 1978. The speech, which was also recorded at the time, was played in numerous programmes of Radio Russia. However, though it was preserved on audio tape, there is no copy of it now. The author had included the speech in a programme of the Urdu Service of Radio Russia. The content of the programme was preserved and this selection is a part of the same.
9. In April 2011, a new collection of Faiz's verses in Russian translation dedicated to the centennial of Faiz was published in Moscow. The compiler of the collection and one of the translators is Ludmila Vassilyeva. There are two forewords in the book: one by H.E Ambassador of Pakistan in Russia, M. Khalid Khattak and the other by Maryam Salganik.
10. Faiz, *Poems by Faiz*, Trans. Victor Kiernan, Lahore: Vanguard, n.d., 257, Print.
11. Faiz, *Mah-o-Sāl-e Āshnā'ī*, 32–33, [see note 3].
12. Rimma Kazakova, *Faiz Memorial Lecture*, London: Urdu Markaz, 1986, Print.
13. Faiz, *Mah-o-Sāl-e Āshnā'ī*, 5–6 [see note 3].
14. Dr Abdul Qayyum Abdali, 'Mah-o-Sāl-e Āshnā'ī.' *Rooh-e Adab*, vol. 2–3, [Maghribi Bengal Urdu Academy n.d.]: 199, Print.

. . . AND THEN CAME SPRING

Original: *Bahār ā'ī* from *Shām-e Shehr-e Yārāṅ* (1979)
TRANSLATOR: SHOAIB HASHMI

. . . and then came Spring
And it was as if, with the returning life,
There returned, from the world beyond,
All the dreams and all the passions;

All the dreams, and all the passions which had
Lived for love of you,
And which, in death, had found life anew.

And, once more, there bloomed all the roses
Perfumed still with memories of you;
Crimson still with the blood of your friends.

And Spring came too, to all the miseries
The remembered sufferings of old friends
The forgotten pleasures of the nearness of love.

And then came Spring, and opened once again
All the buried chapters of the book of Life!

14

FREEDOM UNBOUND: FAIZ'S PRISON CALL

In the early 1950s, Pakistan's leading Urdu poet and intellectual, Faiz Ahmed Faiz, served a four-year prison term for his role in what came to be known as the 'Rawalpindi Conspiracy'. He was accused along with several army officers and some civilians of allegedly conspiring with communist elements to carry out a military coup d'état against Prime Minister Liaquat Ali Khan's government for its failure to resolve the Kashmir dispute with India.[1] Among those detained with Faiz were the then Chief of General Staff, Major General Akbar Khan, famous for his military exploits in Kashmir, and his wife Naseem Shahnawaz Khan, who was believed to have fanned her husband's political ambitions. The counter conspiracy moves were spearheaded by General Ayub Khan, who had been recently elevated to the rank of Commander-in-Chief of the armed forces. As the first Pakistani to occupy that august position, Ayub Khan had reason to be wary of Akbar Khan's status as a war hero and social connections with left leaning intellectuals. At the time of the arrests in March 1951, Faiz was editor of the Lahore based progressive English language daily, the *Pakistan Times*. His pro-Moscow political leanings at the height of the Cold War, when the post-colonial state was on the verge of aligning itself with the Anglo-American bloc, to say nothing of his vocal and impassioned support for labour causes, provided the state's coercive and intelligence apparatus with a convenient pretext to crackdown on prominent writers and trade unionists and to tighten curbs on pro-peasant and communist activists.

The case against the accused revolved around an eight-hour meeting on 23 February 1951 at Akbar Khan's residence. While the idea of overthrowing the government was discussed, no agreement was reached among the participants to proceed with any such plan. Under the law of the land, a conspiracy requires a plan of execution. The Safety Act (1951) under which the detainees were arrested, circumvented this legal nicety. Despite ample evidence to the contrary, state controls on the creation and flow of information have ensured that the case has come to be remembered as a genuine conspiracy that was tantamount to treason. After being kept in different jails in Lahore, the accused were shifted to Hyderabad jail, where a compound was renovated to serve as the premises for the special tribunal set up to hear the case. The trial started on 15 June 1951 with legal giants like A.K. Brohi leading the prosecution and Huseyn Shaheed Suhrawardy, Manzur Qadir, Mahmud Ali Kasuri along with many others appearing on behalf of the defendants. Unable to pay the legal fees, the accused were abandoned by their legal counsels, leaving Suhrawardy as the lone ranger willing to battle the power of the state until the bitter end. In December 1952, the court concluded its deliberations. With the exception of General Akbar Khan, who was given fourteen years' imprisonment, Faiz and the others were given relatively lighter sentences, though none of the military officers were allowed to resume service after being released.

As the details and intricacies of the eighteen-month long trial have receded from public memory, the 'Rawalpindi Conspiracy' case has been either dismissed as a blunder perpetrated by a few misguided individuals or forgotten altogether. This is especially unfortunate as the unearthing of the plot and its grim aftermath proved to be a watershed in the systematic suppression of independent critical thinking in the newly independent country. The Secretary of the Communist Party of Pakistan, Syed Sajjad Zaheer, a close friend of Faiz and a celebrated trailblazer of progressive Urdu literature in the subcontinent, was one of the more high profile 'traitors' of Rawalpindi. Anticipating the collective amnesia that has virtually erased the Rawalpindi Conspiracy case from Pakistani national consciousness, Zaheer wrote that later generations would remember this period only with reference to the publication of Faiz's anthology of poems, *Dast-e Sabā* (1952) and *Zindāṅ Nāmā* (1956).[2] This was not very far of the mark. Many of the poems in these two collections have served as beacons of popular resistance against authoritarianism in post-colonial Pakistan and are destined to remain so for time immemorial.

What has been less well known is that during the protracted and agonizing imprisonment, Faiz also wrote 135 letters in English to his British-born wife, Alys. Spanning the period 7 June 1951 to 9 April 1955, ninety-two of these were written from Hyderabad prison, eight while he was undergoing medical treatment for an ear and tooth infection in

Karachi, at the district jail and Jinnah hospital, and thirty-five during the final leg of his sojourn as a state guest in Montgomery (now Sahiwal) jail. Faiz doubted the literary merit of the letters and was sceptical of his command over the English language. When pressed by Alys to consider publishing their correspondence, he insisted that it should only be done in Urdu. It took another two decades after his release from prison in 1955 before Faiz got around to reluctantly translating the letters into Urdu at the behest of Mirza Zafar-ul-Hasan, an employee of Radio Pakistan who worked for the Idara-e Yadgar-e Ghalib. The collection was first published in 1976 under the intriguing title, *Salībēn Mērē Darīčē Mēn*, literally 'crucifix at my window', with a cover designed by the renowned Pakistani artist, Sadequain. There have been several reprints ever since. The actual letters were believed to have been destroyed by termites in Faiz's house in Model Town during his exile in Beirut (1978–1981). However a small number (33 in all) were recently discovered among Faiz's papers. It has taken painstaking work and determination to retrieve the original prose and bring into the public domain an important aspect of Faiz's life work and, by extension, of Pakistani history of which the great Urdu poet is such an intrinsic and invaluable part. The letters reproduced in this volume [*Two Loves*: see Sources] are only a few (33), but may lead the reader into Faiz's translations of all 135.

Exquisitely blending the personal and the public, these letters ought to serve as a treasure trove for literary critics looking for rare pointers into Faiz's personality. For anyone interested in Pakistan's political, intellectual and cultural history in the immediate aftermath of independence, there are subtle clues here that are more revealing than may appear at first sight. Escaping the prison censor's hyperactive gaze meant avoiding anything remotely political. Discussing the court deliberations, where the prisoners spent most of their time until the end of 1952, was out of the question. Despite scrupulous self-censorship, the letters often reached Alys at the family residence on 41 Empress Road, opposite Radio Pakistan in Lahore, with entire sentences expurgated. This was adding insult to the injury of involuntary separation. Stoical in his acceptance of prison life, Faiz saw it as a kind of unmasking and enforced character building. Unlike the suffocating atmosphere outside or the agony he had suffered during his interrogation by the police, he was at peace in prison where there were no chains on one's dreams. He came to realize the importance of empathy that gave him insights into his own and other people's weaknesses. The deprivations of life in prison were comparable to what purdah clad women went through and whose mentality he now finally understood. While realizing that the charges against him were very serious, he felt mentally stronger than ever and completely unrepentant. He had committed no moral infraction or broken any law to feel even remotely guilty. Faiz was sure that some meaningless game was being played that would end just as suddenly as it had started. After all, he was neither a thief nor a political leader to be put behind bars in perpetuity.

The one lingering pain he felt was the sorrow of living apart from Alys and his two daughters, Cheemi and Meezo. In one of his typical refrains, Faiz wrote 'things are going on as before and as well as can be expected and I am thinking of you and the little ones and waiting.' Mindful of not causing further pain to his wife by sounding depressed, Faiz wrote about the prison facilities as if he were living in a five star hotel. He joked about the excellent food and wondered how he and his fellow inmates would be able to sustain such a high standard of life once they were released. Occasionally he was more voluble than usual, attributing it to the lack of opportunity to speak about matters of the heart but then also wistfully admitting that communications between them did not remain private. He wrote endlessly about the weather, about the dry heat of dusty Hyderabad, his longing for the monsoon clouds hovering over his beloved city, Lahore, and especially the fresh aroma of the wet green foliage of Lawrence Gardens after a douse of rainfall. Most of the time he wrote about composing poetry, arrangements for the publication of his works and royalties that could pay for the upkeep of his family. In letter after letter, he spoke optimistically about life after prison and the world cruise he and Alys would take together.

Transnational in his intellectual outlook, he delighted in his vast exposure to world literature. While in prison he read widely, including Anton Chekhov, Alphonse Daudet, Havelock Ellis, Friedrich Nietzsche, Henrik Ibsen, William Shakespeare and Alfred Tennyson, to mention just a few. Teaching Ghalib to his fellow prisoners gave him enormous satisfaction, leading him to regret giving up teaching to join the army. He frequently recited his own poetry to his cohorts and was pleasantly taken aback upon discovering that even the prison police were showing signs of becoming a little poetic in temperament. Linguistically gifted, Faiz began taking French lessons from Sajjad Zaheer. He also derived considerable joy from gardening and played tennis and volleyball to stay physically fit. When on 5 January 1953, the court sentenced him to two and a half years in prison, Faiz refused to lose heart. Taking the decision in his stride, he quipped that in the British period there were few decent men in India and Pakistan who did not spend a longer time than that in jail and nothing adverse happened to them. While asking Alys to tell his lawyers to prepare to appeal the decision, Faiz expressed relief that the worst was over. They now at least knew the exact duration of his internment. She ought to think of the remaining thirty odd months of his confinement as if he had gone to do his FRCS in London or was writing a doctoral dissertation. He was only sorry that his old mother had to suffer on his account. But he felt no anger or bitterness whatsoever at the treatment that was being meted out to him and was only grateful for the goodness of life.

Just as Faiz Ahmed Faiz's prison poetry has elicited critical acclaim and popular adulation, these letters written from three different Pakistani jails provide a welter of unique insights into the mind of a prisoner of conscience. An intellectual par excellence, his personality shines through these pages, giving expression to a grim determination, undaunted by adversity, to make the struggle for individual and collective self-improvement the only realistic human goal worth pursuing. Written during a critical and formative phase in their country's turbulent history, the ultimate value of these private epistles will be fully realized when present and future generations of Pakistanis realize the need to go beyond mere appreciation of Faiz's literary corpus to the actual realization of his thought, at once liberating and expansive, whether expressed in his writings or manifested in a life devoid of intellectual and political compromise.

Notes

1. Others implicated in the conspiracy were Major-General Nazir Ahmed, Brigadier Siddique Khan, Brigadier Latif Khan, Air Commodore Mohammad Khan Janjua, Lieutenant-Colonel Ziauddin, Lieutenant-Colonel Niaz Mohammad Arbab, Major Mohammad Ishaque, Captain Khizar Hayat, Major Hasan Khan, Captain Zafarullah Poshni and Mohammad Hussain Atta.
2. Sajjad Zaheer, foreword to Zindāṅ Nāmā in Faiz Ahmed Faiz, Nuskhaha'e Vafā, Lahore: Maktaba-e Karavan, n.d., pp. 195–196.

DEDICATION

Original: *Intesāb* from *Sar-e Vādī-e Sīnā* (1971)
TRANSLATOR: RIZ RAHIM

To today
and today's grief:

Today's grief,
angry at Life's entire garden,
a forest of autumn leaves—
the forest of autumn leaves
that's my country,
a congregation of pain,
that's my country.

To the sad lives of the clerks
to the tired old hearts and voices,
to the postmen, the cart drivers,
the railway workers,
to the illiterate, hungry factory workers,
to the kings, the masters, God's men,
to the peasants
whose cattle are carried away,
whose daughters, kidnapped,
a part of whose crop taken by the landlord
another by the tax collector—
the peasants whose honour is
stomped on and shredded by the powerful.

To the anguished mothers
whose crying children at night
are not consoled by tired, sleepless arms,
children who cannot tell what hurts them,
cannot relax, however much you plead.

To the young girls
whose eyes, like flowers in the window, play
behind the curtain, and blossom only to wilt.
To the newly married,
whose bodies, dressed so often in loveless insincerity,
have gotten bored.
To the widows,
to the houses, the yards and paths, and the neighbourhoods
on whose filthy grounds
the moon does its holy ablutions nightly
and in its shadow complain and sigh
the colourful dresses, clinking bracelets,
fragrant tresses,
the burning smell of the sweat
of their aching hearts.

To the literate people
who, with paper and pencil,
go to their leaders, begging,
hang around them
but don't return home.
To the naïve who,
in their simplicity,
carrying their little torches,
go to places where
night's thick meaningless
dark shadows are being handed out.

To the prisoners
in whose hearts, bright pearls of tomorrow,
burnt in prison's hopeless, oppressive stormy nights,
now shine as stars;
to the future leaders
who like the aroma of a flower
fall in love with their own messages.

15

FAIZ AHMED FAIZ: TOWARDS A LYRIC HISTORY OF INDIA

At its best, the Urdu lyric verse of Faiz Ahmed Faiz (1911–1984) can make available to the reader a disconcerting form of ecstasy, a sense of elation at the self being put in question, giving even the thoroughly secular reader the taste of an affective utopia not entirely distinguishable from religious feeling. It is, at the very least, a paradoxical structure of feeling, given the explicitly Marxist and anti-clerical affiliations of his poetry, which displays a marked interest in the secularization of culture and language. Faiz, who, like Manto, began his writing career in the 1930s, is widely (though certainly not universally) regarded as the most significant Urdu poet of the postcolonial period. His poetry exemplifies some of the central dilemmas of Urdu writing in the aftermath of India's Partition at the moment of independence from British rule. It represents a profound attempt to unhitch literary production from the cultural projects of either postcolonial state in order to make visible meanings that have still not been entirely reified and subsumed within the cultural logic of the nation-state system. Despite his stature as the uncrowned poet laureate of Pakistan during the first several decades of its existence, his is notoriously an oeuvre with vast audiences across what was once North India—the map of its reception seemingly erasing the national boundaries that are the territorial legacy of Partition. Against much of Faiz criticism, I argue here that the foremost theme of Faiz's poetry, which defines it as a body of writing, is the meaning and legacy of Partition. If the problematic of minoritization came to be inscribed in Urdu narrative at the level of genre in a foregrounding of the short story as the primary genre of narrative fiction, in poetry it translated into debates about the meaning and nature, the very possibility, of lyric verse in modernity. In the decades following the 1857 Revolt, for instance, the classical tradition of lyric poetry, and in particular the *ghazal* form, became the site of fierce contention about the prospects of a distinct 'Muslim' experience in Indian modernity and came to be singled out as the genre par excellence of Muslim decline and decadence, as too decorative, subjective, and impervious to nature and (Indian) reality, incapable of the sober intellectual effort and didactic purpose called for in the 'new' world.[1]

The poetry of Faiz exemplifies, for the postcolonial period, the unique relationship of Urdu literary production to the crisis of Indian national culture that is marked by the figure of the Muslim.

The lyric element in Faiz's poetry—its intensely personal contemplation of love and of the sensuous—poses a notorious problem of interpretation: he is a self-avowedly political poet—laurelled in the Soviet Union, repeatedly persecuted by reactionary postcolonial regimes—whose most intense poetic accomplishments are examinations of subjective states. The orthodox solution—shared by critics of many different political persuasions—has been to argue that Faiz merely turns a 'traditional' poetic vocabulary to radical political ends, that we should read the figure of the distant beloved, for instance, as a figuring of the anticipated revolution.[2] I suggest a somewhat different direction here and argue, first of all, that the *political* element in Faiz's work cannot be read without the mediation of the social. Faiz's exploration of the affects of separation and union with the beloved enables us to examine the subject, the 'I,' of Urdu writing. It would be incorrect to assume that Faiz's 'Progressiveness'—his association with the literary culture that carries the imprimatur of the AIPWA—implies a dismissal of the question of identity. The central drama of his poetry is the dialectic of a collective selfhood at the disjunctures of language, culture, nation, and community. In his well-known argument about the relationship of lyric poetry to society, Theodor Adorno suggested that it is precisely the apparent distance of lyric poetry from social determinations that constitutes its social meaning. He held out the paradoxical possibility that its distance from the social actually made lyric poetry an exemplary site for the inscription of social meanings. The more the lyric reduces itself to the pure subjectivity of the 'I,' Adorno argued, the more complete the precipitation of the social within its content will be. The more it immerses itself in that which takes individual form, the more it is elevated to the level of universality but one that is 'social in nature'.[3] In this chapter I elucidate the place of lyric in Faiz's work and its relationship to the social horizon that is brought to a crisis in Partition. It is precisely in those poems that are closest to being 'pure' lyric, that is, those in which the inward turn is most complete, rather than in such explicitly Partition poems as 'Freedom's Dawn,' (*Subh-e āzādī*), that we may glimpse these social meanings in their fullest elaboration.

I wish to explore the possibility that Faiz's love lyrics give expression to a self in partition, that they make visible a dialectic of self and other in which the subject and object of desire do not so much become one as simultaneously come near and become distant, exchange places, are rendered uncertain. The desire for *visāl* or union, takes the form of this dialectic itself. In the years following India's Partition, the problematic of national fragmentation comes to imbue the lyric world of Faiz's verse in profound and explicit ways. But the broader problematic of a partitioned self is already present in the poems of the pre-Partition years, at least as potential, something these poems point to and anticipate. The social truth embodied in Faiz's lyric poetry is that the emergence of the (modern) self is also its self-division. The truth of the self is its contradictory, tense, and antagonistic reality. Faiz makes it possible to think about identity in post-Partition South Asia in terms other than those normalized within the shared vocabulary of the postcolonial states. The purportedly autonomous national selves that emerged from Partition are revealed to be what they are—moments within the dialectic of Indian modernity. And 'Partition' comes to acquire meanings very different from its usual significations, now referring not merely to the events of 1947 (or even of 1946–48) but to a history of social ('communal') identifications co-extensive with the history of the Indian modern itself. The immense popularity of Faiz's poetry in the Urdu-Hindi regions, its almost iconic status as a pan–South Asian oeuvre, is a vague but nevertheless conclusive measure of its success in making available an experience of self that is Indian in the encompassing sense, across the boundaries of the 'communal' and nation-state divides. But this is a staging of selfhood that takes division seriously, refusing to treat it as merely epiphenomenal, as in the unity-in-diversity formula of Indian nationalism. It suggests, in fact, that division, the indefinitely extended separation from the beloved, constitutes the very ground from which union can be contemplated. It is commonplace in Faiz criticism to invoke love of country or nation as an essential feature of his poetry.[4] Faiz himself thematizes this on several occasions, as in the early poem 'Two Loves' (*Do 'ishq*): 'In the same fashion I have loved my darling country,/In the same manner my heart has throbbed with devotion to her' (PF, 166–167).[5] But it is not accidental that neither the criticism nor the poetry itself is unequivocal about what the term 'country' (*vatan*) signifies. It might even be said that to speak of *vatan* and *qaum* (nation or people) in the context of Faiz is to remain meaningfully silent about the objects towards which they point: does love of country or patriotism of Faiz's poetry attach itself to any one of the postcolonial states of South Asia? Does it represent, on the contrary, a hope for the dissolution of these states? What is its stance on Partition, their moment of coming into being? Does it imply a 'civilizational' referent? If so, which civilization—Indic, Indo-Persian, or Islamic? Where exactly, in other words, is the poet's home?

The symbolic vocabulary of Faiz's poetry draws on the stock of traditional, Persio-Arabic images available to the classical Urdu *ghazal*— *barbat-o-nai* (lyre and flute), *lauh-o-qalam* (tablet and pen), *tauq-o-salāsil* (neck-irons and chain), *kākul-o-lab* (lock of hair and lip), *dasht-o-gulzār* (wilderness and garden)—resisting the 'plain' language that had already become more common with some of his contemporaries and is more so with the generation of poets who have followed in his wake. In this sense Faiz's poetry is a living rebuke to the ideal of a neutral 'Hindustani' idiom from which both Arabo-Persian and Sanskritic influences have been excised, an ideal to which the secularist, 'anti-communalist' imagination in South Asia has been repeatedly drawn. Victor Kiernan, his translator and lifelong friend, notes that Faiz 'was repelled by the prospect held up by Gandhi of a united 'Hindustani' language, a nondescript neither Hindi nor Urdu'.[6] The mytho-poetic universe of his work is replete with references to Persian, Arabic, and 'Islamic' sources, although, as Kiernan has noted, 'a fondness for allusion to things Hindu, even religious, has not left him,' an important question to which I shall return.[7] My contention here is that the question of collective selfhood—the meaning of 'nation,' 'people,' 'culture,' 'community'—is at the heart of Faiz's poetry, and not merely in the sense of his political devotion to 'the people' and contempt for their exploitation by neo-feudalism and colonial and postcolonial capital. Faiz problematizes the very notion of nation or people, raising fundamental questions about identity and subjectivity and their historical determinations. More precisely, in Faiz's poetry both the degradation of human life in colonial and postcolonial modernity—exploitation—and the withholding of a collective selfhood at peace with itself—what I am calling Partition—find common expression in the suffering of the lyric subject.

Love and its discontents: The Lyric Poet in the World

In a small number of early poems, one or two of which have something like a programmatic status in his oeuvre, Faiz stages the aesthetic dilemmas of the modern poet. They are meta-poetic texts, for in them Faiz explores the nature and meaning of lyric poetry in modern life. In such poems from the late 1930s as 'The Subject of Poetry' (*Mauzū'-e sukhan)* and 'My Fellow, My Friend' (*Mērē hamdam, mērē dost),* but, above all, in 'Love Do Not Ask for That Old Love Again' (*Mujh sē pahlī sī mahabbat mērī mahbūb na māṅg),* we find the poetic persona torn between the exquisite demands of unrequited love, on the one hand, and the demands of the larger world and its oppressions, on the other. Faiz himself has spoken of these poems as turning points in his aesthetic development, marking a growing sense of dissatisfaction with the dominant, 'romantic' literary ethos of the times.[8] Thus, in the last poem mentioned above, the dominant mood is set by the speaker's request of the beloved not to ask for the kind of love formerly given—*pahlī sī mahabbat*—a singular love, alert to nothing but the beloved's charms and cruelties. The speaker lists the efficacies of this love in which he had formerly believed and concludes the first section of the poem with the confession that 'It was not true all this but only wishing' (*Yūṅ na thā maiṅ nē faqat čāhā thā yūṅ ho jā'ē).* After noting the cruelties of the outer world—its injustice, inequality, and alienation—with which the beloved must compete for the speaker/lover's attention, the poem ends on the note on which it began: 'Love do not ask for that old love again'. In 'The Subject of Poetry', the same tension between the alternative demands on the speaker's senses is maintained, but this tension is approached, as it were, from the other direction. Alternating between the mysteries of the beloved and those of the larger world, the poem ends by affirming that the poet cannot expect to overcome the former as his true theme:

> —These too are subjects; more there are;—but oh,
> Those limbs that curve so fatally ravishingly!
> Oh that sweet wretch, those lips parting so slow—
> Tell me where else such witchery could be!
> No other theme [lit., subject] will ever fit my rhyme;
> Nowhere but here is poetry's native clime [lit., homeland].

> [*yē bhī haiṅ, aisē ka'ī aur bhī mazmūṅ hoṅ gē
> lēkin us shokh kē āhistā sē khultē hu'ē hoṅṭ*

hā'ē us jism kē kam-bakht dil-āvēz khutūt
āp hi kahiyē kahīṅ aisē bhī afsūṅ hoṅ gē
apnā mauzū'-e sukhan in kē sivā aur nahīṅ
tab'-e shā'ir ka vatan in kē sivā aur nahīṅ][9]

These early poems have most often been read as signs of a young poet's political awakening but a politicization that does not lead to an abandonment of concern with the integrity of literary language. Faiz himself has contributed to the authority of this reading.[10] While I do not take this to be an incorrect interpretation, I read the apparent dualism of these poems—interiority (*aṅdarūniyat* in Urdu poetics) and affect versus externality (*khārījīyat*) and the outer world, lyric poetry versus society—somewhat differently, as demonstrating an interest in the relationship between the lyric self of Urdu poetry and the 'wider' world of contradiction and conflict over the meaning of nation and community. I argue that these poems enact, *in a literary-historical register*, the dilemmas and complexities of a 'Muslim' selfhood in Indian modernity. The phrase *pahlī sī mahabbat* points to the problematic of love in the classical Urdu lyric, and the poem comments on the relationship of the modern poet, located in the national-cultural space that is (late colonial) India, to that classical tradition. In Pakistan Faiz has long been spoken of as a 'national' poet, as the national poet during the first forty years of the country's life. I contend that this cannot mean what it usually is thought to mean, that in part the accomplishment, the grandeur and ambition, of his work is precisely that it raises serious doubts about whether the nation-state form can account for the complexities of culture and identity in modern South Asia.

Born early in the second decade of this century in the now Pakistani city of Sialkot, Faiz received an education that was becoming increasingly typical for young men of his regional, religious, and class background—the rudiments of Quranic instruction, Persian and Arabic with the local *maulvi*, modern schooling of the colonial (in his case, missionary) sort, and degrees in (in his case, English and Arabic) literature.[11] According to his own account, Faiz's early reading consisted of a diet of Urdu poetry of the classical period, in particular Mir (1723?–1810) and Ghalib (1795?–1869), and the major nineteenth-century works of Urdu narrative. After finishing his studies at the Government and Oriental Colleges, Lahore—those bastions of modern higher learning for northwestern colonial India—Faiz took up a teaching position at Amritsar, where he was first exposed to Indian Marxism and to nationalist political culture generally, primarily through two colleagues, the writers Dr Rasheed Jahan and her husband, Mahmud-uz Zafar (Mahmud al-Zafar), who had already become notorious for their publications in *Angārē* ('Burning Coals', 1932), the anthology of short stories by four young radical writers that created an uproar for its iconoclastic treatment of sexuality, religious orthodoxy, and other 'social' themes and was finally banned by the colonial government.[12] Faiz's first collection of poetry appeared in 1941, and the last to be published in his lifetime, in 1981.[13] Occasionally Faiz also published widely read volumes of critical essays, letters, and memoirs. In Amritsar, Faiz was drawn into the literary circles that proved to be the core group in the establishment of the AIPWA in 1936, and he subsequently came to be identified as the leading 'Progressive' voice in Urdu poetry while also maintaining his autonomy from that organization and from the Communist Party, never assuming the role of spokesman with respect to either in quite the same way as did a number of his contemporaries, such as Sajjad Zaheer and Ali Sardar Jafri. Jafri once even accused Faiz of equivocating about the goals of Progressive poetry and of 'drawing such curtains of metaphor' (*istiāriyāt*) around one of his poems—'Freedom's Dawn'—that 'one cannot tell who is sitting behind them'.[14] He joined the colonial Indian army after the collapse of the Hitler-Stalin Pact, at a time when the official policy of the Indian National Congress was non-cooperation with the war effort, rose to the rank of lieutenant colonel, and returned to civilian life in 1946 with an MBE (Member of the British Empire). A few years after independence, during which time he rose to prominence in Pakistan as a newspaper editor and labour unionist, he was arrested in 1951 with a number of other radical writers, political activists, and military officers—including Zaheer, one of the *Angārē* writers who was the leading founder of the AIPWA and, after Partition, became secretary general of the newly founded Communist Party of Pakistan—and senior military officers charged with conspiring against the state.[15] The arrests, part of a general crackdown on the Pakistani Left, had a chilling effect on political and cultural life, and marked the beginnings of Pakistan's realignment as a front-line US satellite in the Cold War and as a reliable regional client after the rise of Mohammad Mossadegh in Iran, a role whose price the country continues to pay to this day. After a trial during which the shadow of a death sentence hung over him, Faiz was sentenced to imprisonment and was finally released after spending more than four years in various prisons in Pakistan. In the late 1950s, with the implementation of martial law in Pakistan, Faiz was again in jail, this time only for a few months. Already by the late 1950s he had developed an increasingly international reputation, especially in the socialist countries and many parts of the Third World. In 1962 he was awarded the Lenin Peace Prize, and at the end of his life, in self-imposed exile from Zia's Pakistan, served for several years as editor of Lotus, the journal of the Permanent Bureau of Afro-Asian Writers, which he edited from Beirut, living there for some of the years of that city's devastation, including the months of the Israeli siege and bombardment. In Beirut he composed a small body of what is the most exquisite exile poetry in modern Urdu literature, 'an enactment of a homecoming expressed through defiance and loss,' in the words of Edward Said, who met him in Beirut during those exile years.[16] I turn to this poetry later and argue that it represents an attempt to introduce exile and homelessness into the vocabulary of Urdu verse as a constitutive experience. Read together with the early 'meta-poetic' poems, this later exile poetry demonstrates that, for Faiz, Urdu is, in a strong sense, a homeless literature and culture, that he sees its entire modern history as a series of uprootings and displacements.

The appropriateness of using the term 'lyric poetry' in anything more than a loose and descriptive sense with respect to Urdu writing in general and Faiz in particular is not self-evident and requires some justification. Although Urdu has a number of terms, such as the adjectives bazmīyā and ghinā'īyā, that provide only partial equivalents of the corresponding English term, Urdu poetics makes no extensive theoretical use of such an umbrella concept and proceeds largely in generic terms—and especially in terms of the mutual opposition of the ghazal and the nazm. It is certainly part of the specificity of Faiz's work that, unlike some of his contemporaries, he does not turn his back on the 'classical' poetic genres, the ghazal in particular, with its rigid metre and rhyme schemes, and its set themes centred around the experience of separation from the beloved. He could arguably be credited with having resuscitated this form after half a century of neglect and disdain. In the decades following the suppression of the uprisings of 1857–58, with the collapse of the tottering social structure that had been the basis of the Urdu literary culture of the ashrāf (elites) in northern India, 'reform'—religious, social, cultural, political, and educational—became something like a slogan among these social groupings of what I have termed a process not so much of incomplete as reluctant embourgeoisement, the Aligarh movement of

Syed Ahmed Khan being only the most famous and influential of these reform efforts directed at Muslims.[17] Classical Urdu poetry, and the *ghazal* in particular, became subject, as already noted, to a fierce critique and project of reform within this new literary culture. What is remarkable in the judgement about the *ghazal*, however, is that it was held, in only slightly different form, both by the nationalist 'Hindi' opponents of the dominance of Urdu literary culture and by its Aligarh-connected protagonists and defenders, like Muhammad Husain Azad and Altaf Husain Hali. At issue was therefore a certain language of poetry that, although 'popular', as Hali admitted, was now considered far removed from the everyday reality, including linguistic reality, of the people.[18] This charge against Urdu, which, as we have seen, was at the heart of the early Hindi critique of Urdu, and was vehemently denied by the publicists of Urdu in their defensive moments, was thus not absent from the new poetics being developed in Urdu itself.[19] But for nationalist writers, beginning in the late nineteenth century, the *ghazal* became something like an icon of the vast distances separating the Muslim *ashrāf* from the space of the genuinely popular. Such distrust of the *ghazal* survived into the twentieth century, and indeed into our own times, among both the literary movements committed to the social purposiveness of poetry, including the Marxists of the AIPWA who were Faiz's contemporaries and comrades, as well as their critics and opponents whose commitment to the intellectual demands of modern poetry is in the name of art for art's sake.[20] The Urdu *ghazal* and the constellation surrounding it—metrical structures, histories of composition and reception, Persianate vocabulary and thematic conventions, and the image associated with it of an imperial culture in decline—retain a distinct place in the postcolonial Indian cultural imaginary, from popular 'Hindi' cinema to such a work of Indo-English fiction as Anita Desai's *In Custody*, despite the massive effort in recent decades to denaturalize and alienate Urdu to contemporary Indian culture and society. Perhaps like no other poetic form in northern India, the history of this lyric genre is inextricably linked with the emergence and development of national culture, and in no other form is the question (and the contradictions) of society-as-nation so deeply inscribed, not even in the *gīt*, or 'song', in North Indian languages like Bengali and Hindi that is sometimes said to be the national-popular poetic genre par excellence, most famously in the poetic practice of Rabindranath Tagore.

Even in his practice of the diffuse *nazm* form—whose only possible definition is apparently that it is a non-narrative and 'continuous' poem that is not a *ghazal*—Faiz bridges the divide between these varieties of poetic writing and imbues the lyric world of the former with the non-national forms of affectivity characteristic of the latter. In this essay, I look most closely at a number of poems that are not strictly *ghazals* but apply the concept of lyric to Faiz's oeuvre as a whole, irrespective of genre in the narrow sense. In treating Faiz as a modern lyric poet, however, I am not suggesting that we engage in a search for qualities in modern Urdu verse that are characteristic of the lyric in modern Western poetry. On the contrary, my analysis of a number of Faiz's poems is intended precisely to enable us to explore the specificities of modern lyric in a colonial and postcolonial society. Above all, what the concept of lyric makes possible is the translation, the passage, of Faiz's poetry from a literary history that is specifically Urdu into a critical space for the discussion of Indian literary modernity as a whole. To the extent that Faiz's poetry itself pushes towards ending the inwardness of the Urdu poetic tradition, as I later argue, his work itself implies and requires this critical move.

The past of the self is another country: Lyric subject and memory

I now turn to the theme of separation and union in Faiz's love poetry by working through its elaboration in one of his best-known lyric poems, *Yād* ('Memory'). The poem appears in the collection *Dast-e Sabā* (1952) and has been made hugely popular by the singer Iqbal Bano as *Dasht-e tanhā'ī*:

> In the desert of solitude, my love, quiver   (1)
> the shadows of your voice, your lips' mirage.
> In the desert of solitude, under the dust of distance,
> the flowers of your presence bloom.
>
> From somewhere nearby rises the flame of your breathing,   (5)
> burning slowly in its own perfume.
> Afar, beyond the horizon, glistening, drop by drop,
> falls the dew from your heart-consoling eyes.
>
> So lovingly, O my love, has placed   (9)
> your memory its hand this moment on my heart,
> it seems, though this distance is young,
> The day of separation is ended, the night of union
> has arrived.

[*Dasht-e tanhā'ī mēṅ, ai jān-e jahāṅ larzāṅ haiṅ*   (1)
Tērī āvāz kē sā'ē, tērē hoṅtoṅ kē sarāb
Dasht-e tanhā'ī mēṅ, dūrī kē khas-o-khāk talē
Khil rahē haiṅ, tērē pahlū kē saman aur gulāb

Uṭh rahī hai kahīṅ qurbat sē tērī sāṅs kī āṅč   (5)
Apnī khushbū mēṅ sulagtī hu'ī, maddham maddham
Dūr—ufaq pār čamaktī hu'ī, qatrā qatrā
Gir rahī hai tērī dildār nazar kī shabnam

Is qadar pyār sē, ai jān-e jahāṅ, rakkhā hai   (9)
Dil kē rukhsār pē is vaqt tērī yād nē hāth
Yūṅ gumāṅ hotā hai, garčē hai abhī subh-e firāq
Ḍhal gayā hijr kā din, ā bhī ga'ī vasl kī rāt]   (NV, 184–185)[21]

Dominant in the first stanza is the image of solitude as expanse of
desert or wilderness, expressed in the string *Dasht-e tanhā'ī* (the desert/
wilderness of solitude/loneliness) which opens lines 1 and 3. The
metaphor also governs the second stanza, as the spatial language of
line 5—'From somewhere nearby rises the flame of your breathing'—
acquires a geographical register in line 7: 'Afar, beyond the horizon. . . .'
The dominance of this desert metaphor is sustained in the treatment
of the beloved, at least in the first stanza. There, the solitary subject is
confronted with the 'mirage'-like presence of the object of its desire—'the
shadows of your voice, your lips' mirage.' For the subject, the shadows
and mirage are both signs of the beloved. But whereas a mirage points to
an absent, illusory object, the shadow of an object, although immaterial
in itself, is a sign of the object's physical presence. Placed in combination
with each other, however, each is infused with new meanings. The mirage
becomes something more than illusion, more than a mere projection of
a desire intensely felt, like a vision of water in a parched land; and the
shadow becomes something less than the sign of a physical presence.
The geographical metaphor is fused here with a visual one, and together
they come to signify the manner of the beloved's becoming-present.
What exactly this manner is becomes clearer in the next two lines (3–4),
for here 'the flowers [lit., jasmine and rose] of your presence' are said to
bloom 'under the dust [lit., the withered bushes and dust] of distance.' In
other words, the nearness or presence of the beloved does not cancel out
its distance. And the reverse is also true: the distance of the beloved is
also the mode of its coming near. This theme is developed in the second

stanza. In lines 5–6, the 'flame' (*āṅč*) of the beloved's breathing is said to be rising from somewhere near the speaking subject—*kahīṅ qurbat sē*—and yet, simultaneously, the 'consoling eyes' of the beloved are placed by the speaker 'Afar, beyond the horizon.'

In the third and final stanza, the geographical metaphor is abandoned, and we are within an internal, purely subjective space. This intimate space is signified here by 'heart' (*dil*) or, more precisely, by its 'cheek' (*rukhsār*), which is traditionally a sign of the beloved's beauty and of (the lover's) intimacy with the beloved but here expresses the tenderness of the lover's own heart (l. 10). The inexpressible beauty of this image—a human heart gently caressed by an other's hand, as a lover's cheek is touched by the beloved—is an expression of the desire for an end to suffering, for union, for reconciliation of subject and object. It expresses a desire for the form of reconciliation that Adorno has called 'peace': 'Peace is the state of distinctness without domination, with the distinct participating in each other'.[22] The presence of the beloved continues in this stanza also to be its distance. For the beloved enters this interior realm only as image or 'memory.' In the last two lines (11–12), the poem turns to the intensity of this caress of memory, to its effect upon the subject: the *gumāṅ* (appearance/feeling/illusion) that the 'day of separation has ended, the night of union has arrived.' Like the first two stanzas, therefore, the third stanza also enacts the dialectic of separation and union, in which separation is indefinitely extended, and union, intensely desired and felt, does not cancel out the distance between the subject and the object of desire. It renders uncertain the distinction between them but not in order to appropriate the life of the object in the interest of the subject. The object is also revealed to be a subject and the (desiring) subject an object of (the other's) desire. The beloved is at the same time distant, and hence other, and intimately present to the self as itself. In other words, the self that emerges in the course of *Yād* is a divided one, not at home with itself, desiring reconciliation and wholeness and yet cognizant that its own distance from itself is the very source of its movement and life. It is an uncanny interplay of nearness and distance precisely summed up in a four-line poem titled *Marsiā* ('Elegy') that appears in *Sar-e Vādi-e Sīnā* (1971):

Having gone afar you are near to me,
When were you so close to me?

You will not come now, nor leave,
Meeting and parting [*hijrāṅ*] are now the same to me.

[*Dūr jā kar qarīb ho jitnē*
Ham sē kab tum qarīb thē itnē
Ab na ā'o gē tum na jā'o gē
Vasl-o-hijrāṅ baham hu'ē kitnē] (NV, 438)[23]

We may begin to outline the social meanings of this lyric self by noting
the resonances of the word 'hijr' (separation) in the final stanza of *Yād*
(and of its derivative *hijrāṅ* in *Marsiā*). A transformation of the Arabic *hajr*,
the word is the most frequently used term in classical Urdu poetry for
separation or parting from the beloved. As is well known, the meanings
of this word and those of its paired opposite, *visāl* (union), constitute
one of the central and most familiar problems in Urdu poetics. These
meanings vary not only from poet to poet or era to era but also from
one poetic genre to another, among the works of the same poet, and
often within the same poem itself. Thus, for instance, depending on the
poemic context, the words may signify the dynamics of romantic or erotic
love or of religious devotion. In the Sufi traditions of Urdu (and Persian)
poetry in particular, *visāl* is a sign for mystic union with the divine, for
the desire of the self to become extinct (*fanā*) in a realization of its '*ishq-e
haqīqī* or 'true' love of God, compared to which the love of man for man
is only '*ishq-e majāzī*, inauthentic or 'metaphorical' love. Most typically a
verse may be interpreted at several different levels, in several different
registers, simultaneously.[24] The problematic of 'love' is thus constituted
around an oscillation or productive tension between other-worldly and
this-worldly significations. In latter times this poetic language is very far
indeed from any concrete practice of Sufism. In Faiz, paradoxically, this
religious substratum is again brought close to the surface in order to be
secularized anew.

The secularization of *hijr* in Faiz's poetry is part of the general
secularization of poetic language and purpose which he and his
contemporaries undertake. One aspect of this secularization has been
that the Sufistic eroticism of the vocabulary of the traditional poetic
genres, and the *ghazal* in particular, has acquired political meanings, most
explicitly in militant poets such as Habib Jalib, who was associated with
the world of radical student politics in the 1960s, but also in more serious
poets like Faiz himself. Thus, for instance, *vafā* (loyalty or devotion) and

junūn (madness or intoxication) come to mean political steadfastness and
selfless abandon, the rational and irrational components, respectively,
of commitment. Faiz's most programmatic announcement of the
secularizing impulse of his poetry comes perhaps in 'Prayer' (*Dū'ā*), a
poem written in the mid-1960s:

> Come, let us too lift our hands
> We for whom prayer is a custom forgotten,
> We who except for love's flame
> Remember neither idol nor god—

> [*Ā'īyē hāth uṯhā'ēṅ ham bhī*
> *Ham jinhēṅ rasm-e du'ā yād nahīṅ*
> *Ham jinhēṅ soz-e mahabbat kē sivā*
> *Ko'ī but ko'ī khudā yād nahīṅ*][25]

Prayer may be a 'forgotten' custom for the lyric subject, but its very
knowledge of this fact belies a memory of a living connection to it. The
secular subject contains within itself traces of the life-world signified
here by 'idol' and 'god'. Thus the problematic of an uncannily present
other, which we have seen in 'Memory', is also an account here of the
relationship to the non-modern and the manner in which it becomes
present to the modern subject. Secularism and even atheism live in the
South Asian world in great proximity to the religious, in marked contrast
with the structure of relations within which they have evolved in the
West at least since the eighteenth century. A great deal of Faiz's poetry
performs this proximity, and in this poem, too, secularization is not a
mere rejection of religious experience but rather a wrestling with it. This
is not an expression of a positivistic atheism that wants simply to abolish
the religious impulse in a rationalized culture of struggle and action—
'love' in the sense of political commitment. Instead, what is performed
in Faiz's poetry is the recognition of the immense power of religious
thought and experience for the modern subject. More specifically, the
unorthodox and transgressive energies that are always at least implicit
in the mystical Sufi tradition are turned in Faiz's verse against religious
orthodoxy and its alliance with oppressive worldly authority. A Marxist
and internationalist poet, Faiz is nevertheless immersed in the religious
language of mystical Indian Islam, both in its high cultural elaboration
in the Urdu poetic tradition and as a kind of cultural lingua franca in

South Asia. Faiz's poetry reveals a deep respect and love for this culture and a recognition of the poet's very complex relationship to it. It represents an agonistic embracing of a particular religious tradition—the Indo-Muslim and Urdu poetic elaborations of Sufi expression—in order to produce out of it the resources for modernity; at the same time, therefore, it also points to the worldly basis of religious experience itself. As we have seen with Azad and even Manto, for Faiz, too, the elaboration of a secular social imaginary entails an encounter with the world of Sufi Islam at one level or another (Sarmad the Martyr, the popular cult of Sufi saints, al-Hallaj, and the very vocabulary of classical Urdu poetry). At no point, however, is this merely a nostalgic embracing of a supposedly syncretic religious life as the authentic indigenous idiom of coexistence, and (poetic) modernity appears as a kind of dialectic of the religious and the secular or worldly.

The problematic of *hijr* in the work of Faiz therefore cannot fail to evoke that other narrative-mythological constellation, designated by the related word *hijrat*: the appropriation in Urdu for the dislocations and emigrations that accompanied Partition, especially from the Hindi-Urdu heartland to the territory of Pakistan, of the foundational narrative of Islamic community. It lends to the Partition experience an epic quality and seeks to contain it within a narrative of departure or leave-taking. Faiz explores (and exploits) this historical density of *hijr* as a signifier of relation to place, community, uprooting, and the paradoxes of restoration and return. Although, of course, he himself was not strictly a *muhājir* or Partition migrant—having been born and raised within the territorial limits later claimed for Pakistan—*hijr-hijrat* becomes in his poetry a metonym for the displacements of Partition as a whole, the massive fissure it requires of people, language, culture, and memory coming to be figured as the experience of prolonged separation from the beloved. The political impulse in Faiz's poetry can thus only be understood through the mediation of the social. For the desire for justice, the steadfastness in face of suffering and oppression, and the belief in a new dawn, are complicated by the 'partitioned' nature of the collective subject. In other words, the significance of Faiz's repeated use of *hijr* and its derivatives is that it imbues the lyric experience of separation from the beloved with a concrete historical meaning—the parting of ways or leave-taking that is Partition. If, in Sufi traditions, to speak simultaneously of the pain and joy of *hijr* is to point to a future consummation of love in death or self extinction, then in Faiz this prolongation of separation from the beloved becomes the modality of collective selfhood, its very mode of being in history and the world.[26] It is significant in this connection that, within Pakistan, critics have sometimes complained about the seeming masochism of such prolongation of *hijr* in Faiz's poetry, in marked contrast to the work of his contemporary Meeraji, for instance, where the attempt to project an authentic selfhood not only takes the form of an actualization of union but often is made literal in sexual release. This complaint is significant, for, from within a framework that affirms the terms of Partition, this refusal to grant autonomy to the self (from the whims of the beloved) can indeed only appear masochistic. The lyric subject in Faiz's poetry is located at those borderlands of self and world where autonomy and heteronomy lose their distinctness, where the self is confronted with the uncanny presence of an other that is also self. For Faiz, the end of *hijr* is not a literal union. The sadness of *hijr* echoes the finality of *hijrat*, of leaving your home forever, but it also inverts the implied religious sanction for Partition by re-inscribing the self's taking leave of the (antagonistic) other as a separation from the beloved.

When Faiz speaks of lost companions and almost forgotten friendships, as he does in a number of poems from the 1950s onwards, he is echoing an experience that is common in the entire northern belt that was affected by Partition. Take, for instance, the opening lines of *Pā'oṅ sē lahū ko dho ḍālo* ('Wash the Blood Off Your Feet'):

> What could I [lit., we] have done, gone where?
> My feet were bare
> and every road was scattered with thorns—
> of ruined friendships, of loves left behind,
> of eras of loyalty that finished, one by one.

> [*Ham kyā kartē kis rah čaltē*
> *Har rāh mēṅ kāṇṭē bikhrē thē*
> *Un rishtoṅ kē jo čhūṭ ga'ē*
> *Un sadyoṅ kē yārānoṅ kē*
> *Jo ik ik kar kē ṭūṭ ga'ē*][27]

I suggest that we read 'eras' (lit., centuries) here as a sign of historical time and 'friendships' (lit., relations or connections) and 'loves' (lit., friendships, companionships, or loves) as pointing towards the fabric, the text of culture, difference, and identity in history. The modes and

forms in which memories of the pre-Partition past are popularly kept
alive pose questions of immense importance and interest for scholarship
and have only begun to be explored. In Pakistani cities like Lahore,
Karachi, Hyderabad, and Rawalpindi, which were cleared of their large
Hindu and Sikh populations within months of August 1947, the signs
of these erstwhile residents are ubiquitously present—in the sight of
sealed-off temples, in street and neighbourhood names that continue
in use despite municipal attempts to erase them, in the signs of the
'other's' tongue above doorways in the old quarter of any city. The
memories and stories of older eyewitnesses, the tales travellers tell of
revisiting long abandoned homes, the enormous font of verbal genres—
folk songs, nursery rhymes, proverbs, and popular tales about characters
like Birbal and Mulla Dopiaza—are among the many everyday means of
unsettling the finality of Partition, of disconcerting the self with its own
uncertainty. The paradox at the heart of Faiz reception is that while
he writes poetry that is 'difficult' in some obvious ways and true to the
subjective demands of lyric, it is this enormous font of popular memory
that it seeks to mobilize. We can say of him, as Adorno does of Brecht,
that in his poetry 'linguistic integrity' does not result in poetic elitism
or 'esotericism'.[28] The suffering of the subject in Faiz's poetry, or rather
its pleasure and suffering at being separated from the beloved, echoes in
lyric terms what is already present everywhere in popular experience,
even if in ways that are muted, less than conscious, and fragmentary.

If *hijr* and its derivatives point us in the direction of dislocations and
separations that are collective, such a historical reading of Faiz's lyric
poems is also made possible in other ways. Since *Dast-e Sabā* (1952), an
increasing number of poems in successive collections appear dated by
month and year or by exact date, and many are also marked by place of
composition, which in the case of the poems of *Dast-e Saba and Zindāṅ
Nāmā* (1956) is most often a Pakistani prison. This dating and 'placing'
of the poems is almost always significant. I suggest that we read the
date (or the place name, where it exists, or both) as an extra-poemic,
historical text requiring interpretation, in interaction with which the
poem reveals its meaning. The date functions with respect to the text of
the poem in the manner that Gerard Genette has ascribed to 'paratexts'.[29]
'Elegy,' for instance, is dated 'August 1968,' and 'Prayer' is accompanied
by 'Independence Day, 14 August 1967.' In fact, the month of August,
during which Pakistan and India celebrate their independence from
colonial rule, and Pakistan its separation from India, appears frequently

over the years as the date of composition of numerous poems. The extra-poemic, 'historical' reference here is to the complex text of *national independence-Partition*, lending to these poems a quality of national stocktaking. The pronouns *ham* (we) and *tum* (you, [singular/familiar]) acquire in this context a collective resonance, even as the lyric quality of the poems, their uncompromising subjectivity, produces a sense of deep intimacy, of meetings and partings at the very core of the self, which define its very existence.

Let us take, for instance, 'Black-Out' (*Blaik-āūt*), which appears in *Sar-e Vādi-e Sīnā* and is dated 'September 1965'. The historical reference in the date is to the Indo-Pakistani war of that month, the first full-scale war between the two postcolonial nation-states, which is a watershed in their histories. As C.M. Naim has argued, for Urdu literary culture, in particular, the war proved a turning point, for, with the ensuing suspension of communications between the countries, Urdu literary production and reception began to take place within national spheres in increasingly less contact with each other.[30] The availability of books and journals from the other side of the border, visits of writers and critics, and simultaneous publication of works in both countries, all common in the period leading up to the war, fell sharply in the following years, and indeed has been almost extinct for decades. The year marks the entrenchment of ideological polarization between 'Indian' and 'Pakistani' writers, with increasing self-consciousness about hitching literary production to the cultural fortunes of either the one state or the other. In the wider cultural milieu as well, the war led to a suspension of contacts between the two societies, which had been common and routine earlier, ranging from frequent family visits within divided families to the public availability from across the border of cultural commodities, such as magazines and films. The English loan-word that is the title of Faiz's poem makes reference to the introduction of a new vocabulary of war into Urdu, which, like its technology, is of foreign and Western origin. The poem itself remains faithful to the subjective demands of lyric poetry, with the collective and historical reference made explicit through the title and date of composition:

Since the lamps have been without light,   (1)
I am seeking, moving about, in the dust: I do
not know where
Both my eyes have been lost;

You who are familiar with me, give me some sign
of myself.
It is as if into every vein has descended,
Wave on wave, the murderous river of some
poison,   (6)
Carrying longing for you, memory of you, my love;
How to know where, in what wave, my heart is
swallowed?
Wait one moment, till from some world beyond
Lightning comes towards me with bright hand.   (10)
And the lost pearls of my eyes,
As luminous pearls of new eyes drunk with the cup
of darkness,
Restores.
Wait one moment till somewhere the breadth of the
river is found,
And, renewed, my heart,   (15)
Having been washed in poison and annihilated,
finds some landing-place
Then let me come bringing, by way of offering, new
sight and heart,
Let me make the praise of beauty, let me write of
the theme of love.[31]

Jab sē bēnūr hu'ī hain sham'ēn   (1)
Khāk mēn dhūndtā phirtā hūn, na jāne kis jā
Kho ga'ī hain mērī donon ānkhēn
Tum jo wāqif ho batā'o ko'ī pehćān mērī
Is tarāh hai kē har ik rag mēn utar āyā hai
Mauj dar mauj kisī zehr kā qātil daryā   (6)
Terā armān, tērī yād līy'ē jān mērī
Jānē kis mauj mēn ghaltān hai kahān dil mērā
Ēk pal thehro kē us pār kisī dunyā sē
Barq ā'ē mērī jānib, yad-e baizā lē kar   (10)
Aur mērī ānkhon kē gum-gashtā guhar
Jām-e zulmat sē siyāh-mast na'ī ānkhon ke shabtāb
guhar,
Lauṭā dē
Ēk pal thehro kē daryā kā kahin pāṭ lagē
Aur nayā dil mērā   (15)
Zehr mēn dhul kē, fanā ho kē kisī ghāṭ lagē

Phir pa'ē nazr na'ē dīda-o-dil lē kē čalūṅ
Husn ki madh karūṅ, shauq kā mazmūṅ likhkhūṅ]

The poem opens in darkness, in a state of lightlessness that is external—
'Since the lamps have been without light.' But this absence of light is, as
it were, reflected internally, and the speaker finds himself lost, in search
of himself. The first three lines of the poem are an elaboration of this
metaphor of darkness—darkness as metaphor for forgetting, for losing
oneself. In line 4 the speaker addresses an other being, asking to be
recognized and hence restored to his own (lost) identity. But this other is
also an intimate, who is familiar (*vāqif*) with the latter's identity (*pahčān*).
In lines 5–8 there is a shift of metaphors, and the crisis of the self is
likened to the infusion of an unknown poison—'the murderous river of
some poison' (l. 6)—into the veins, a deluge into which the self—'my life'
(l. 7) and 'my heart' (l. 8)—struggling to keep from drowning, carries its
memories of, and longing for, the beloved (ll. 7–8). In the elaboration of
this second metaphor as well, therefore, we get a shift of emphasis from
externality and the physical to interiority.

In lines 9–13 the poem returns to the metaphor of light or, rather,
returns to the darkness metaphor of lines 1–4 by reversing it into the
image of light as deliverance from the darkness of the self. This section
of the poem opens with the gentle injunction to wait, to be patient—*Ēk
pal ṭhehro* ('Wait one moment')—which is repeated at the beginning
of the next section, lines 14–16. Clearly lines 9–10 contain a primary
allusion—'from some world beyond' and the 'bright hand' of lightning—
to the (here Quranic) story of Moses on Mount Sinai, an allusion made
explicit in the title poem in this collection, *Sar-e Vādi-e Sīnā*, written on
the occasion of the 1967 Arab-Israeli War. But here I again stress the
manner in which this image is secularized: *us pār*, unlike 'beyond' in
English, is more suggestive of a horizontal gesture, directed towards the
horizon, than a vertical one, towards the heavens, which the strictly
religious image would require. The light that restores comes, in other
words, from beyond the horizon—an orientation we have already seen
in the poem 'Memory'. The feeling produced by the phrase 'from some
world beyond' is of a neighbouring world that should be unknown, and
yet is half familiar and vaguely remembered.

The spatial register in which these images, and indeed the use of
space in 'Memory', become meaningful is the very opposite of state
territoriality or of a geography whose scale is larger than human. There

is something small scale and intimate about it. It suggests distances that
are traversable by human beings. It is a register to which Faiz repeatedly
turns in order to convey a sense of a place both not so far away and yet
not so close as to be indistinguishable from *here*. I suggest that we read
this complex spatial imagery as a means of exploring, within the terms
of lyric poetry, the connections between culture and geography or,
more precisely, the process through which the nation-state converts its
territory into a *national* geography. Here Faiz is able to render a human
geography that traverses the boundaries, and escapes the territorial
logic, of the nation-state. In a number of essays and lectures from
the 1960s, to which I return below, Faiz raises the basic geographical
conundrum faced by Urdu writing in Pakistan: the historical 'home'
of Urdu—Delhi, Uttar Pradesh, Hyderabad—lies beyond the territorial
confines of the country. In his lyric poems this question is echoed by the
predicament of a dislocated, displaced lover, often depicted as imagining
union with a beloved left behind in a world—nearly but not completely
forgotten—somewhere beyond the horizon. In lines 14–16 of 'Black-Out',
the metaphors shift again, and the dominant image is once more that
of a river, a broad and mighty river, and the struggle of the self to keep
from drowning. But this river, which could consume the self, is also the
means to its restoration, to the healing of its wounds. In fact, in order to
be restored to itself, in order to find a riverbank (*ghāṭ*), the self must be
bathed in this poison and become extinct (*fanā*). Having come to know
annihilation, it is born anew. That Faiz uses reaching a *ghāṭ* as an image
of restoration and healing is not insignificant. It is an Indic (rather than
Persio-Arabic) word and image, with a clear reference both to the Hindu
sacralization of bathing in river waters as a means to purification and
to the ritual cremation of the dead. Furthermore, *fanā* points to the Sufi
goal of extinguishing the self in the (divine) object of the self's desire. But
in its secularization here it has a utopian impulse, signifying an end to
the self's suffering. This combination of these images—the one clearly of
'Muslim' origin, the other 'Hindu'—is an attempt, in this poem occasioned
by the war of 1965, to keep open possibilities of collective selfhood which
that event was closing off. Nothing is more natural to a nation-state
than going to war, and it may be argued that this particular war was a
key moment in the realization of the nation-state form in postcolonial
South Asia. That is certainly how it was perceived in contemporary Urdu
writing, and, aside from Faiz's own poems of that moment, Ahmad Faraz's
Maiṅ kyūṅ udās nahīṅ is among the more famous literary responses to the

dilemmas it posed. But even in Faraz's poem, there is a slipping into the terms provided by the structure of national citizenship, as the speaker singles out and names the Pakistani cities of Sialkot and Lahore, both on the border with India and both threatened with occupation, and bemoans their suffering.[32] In Faiz's work, on the contrary, the insight about the war as interpellative event is held onto steadfastly, and, above all, suffering never becomes an alibi for a reification of the self. The functioning of lyric in Faiz's writing as a whole is as an abrupt flash of memory—not a fully formed recollection but rather an instantaneous sensation, of the self in motion, in dialogue with an other that is, uncannily, also self.

The final two lines of 'Black-Out' offer a glimpse of reconciliation and restoration. Having been washed in poison and made anew, armed with 'new sight and heart,' the self becomes capable once again of 'praise of beauty' and of writing of 'the subject of love.' This resolution is highly significant, for it comments on the seemingly dualistic movement of programmatic poems like 'Love Do Not Ask for My Old Love Again' and 'The Subject of Poetry,' discussed earlier in the chapter, and opens it up to the influence of a third term.[33] If those early, pre-Partition poems suggest an internal tension or, as it were, poemic indecision between the aesthetic autonomy of love and lyric, on the one hand, and the material predications of the (lyric) subject, on the other, these closing lines suggest that the earlier duality was not simply the opposition of lyric self and society but rather that the identity of the social was at stake all along in each of its terms. Thus it is not simply the material environment of the lyric self that poses the problem of the social; the interior world of affect itself raises questions about collective identity. The closure of that lyric world is a figure for the illusion of autonomy of Urdu literary culture and identity as a whole. And the coherence of that world is disturbed by the uncanny appearance of the other. To suggest that the lyric self in modern Urdu can no longer be contained within the world defined by love's intoxications is to insist, in historical retrospect, that the claim to autonomy of that world is itself socially determined, that it is a moment within the contradictory movement of a larger whole. Thus in neither of the two early poems is the lyric sensibility simply cancelled and overcome by a higher sensibility. The two are held in an indefinite, dialectical tension, with the result that while the first term is forced to open itself up to the second, larger term, it does not simply submerge its identity within it. The poems announce an end to the isolation of the lyric

subject or, rather, an end to the illusion of its isolation. But they do
not cancel out the distance between the interior world of subjectivity
(*dākhilīyat*) and the outer world of objectification (*khārijīyat*). To the
extent that these poems are programmatic works, therefore, this is not
simply in the sense that they announce an aesthetic of commitment. They
are essays, in the etymological sense, in literary and cultural history.
They explore the relationship of the lyric in Urdu to the larger history
of social and 'communal' contradictions that is the history of the Indian
modern itself, raising questions about the 'subject' of Urdu writing in
the double sense of the word, a duality that the word *mauzū'* shares with
its English equivalent. What these poems make visible is the social life
of the lyric subject—the subject as it appears in classical Urdu lyric—its
isolation now appearing as its mode of being in the (Indian) world.[34]
In the closing lines of 'Black-Out,' the impossibility of sustaining the
purely lyric sensibility is finally explicitly linked to the vicissitudes of
collective and national selfhood. What forces the lyric self to look beyond
itself, to other pleasures and sufferings than those of love, is therefore a
recognition of its own fragmented reality. The lyric as an aesthetic mode
will become possible once again only when the wounds of the self are
healed and it is whole again. In other words, the lyric, and the 'purely'
aesthetic in general, are held up as a utopian possibility linked to the
end of the antagonisms, and hence suffering, of the collective subject.

In *Sipāhī kā marsiā* ('Soldier's Elegy'), another poem from this period
and dated 'October 1965'—that is, marking the end of the war—this
refusal to reify self and other is given a novel turn. The poem, in the
voice of a parent (perhaps mother) addressing the parent's dead son,
abandons 'high' Urdu vocabulary altogether, and turns to an idiom
whose resonances are, I would argue, 'Hindavi,' in a generalization of the
function that *ghāṭ* performs in 'Black-Out':

> *Uṭho ab māṭi sē uṭho*
> *Jāgo mērē lāl,*
> *Ab jāgo mērē lāl,*
> *Tumrī sēj sajāvan kāran*
> *Dēkho ā'ī rain andhyāran . . .* (NV, 412–414)

> [Stand up, get up from the dust
> Wake up, my son
> You wake up now, my son

Look, to make your bed
Dark night has arrived . . .]

The linguistic effect here is untranslatable into English. (A very partial
parallel would be a poem about the Second World War written in Middle
English.) It is as if, in this moment of crisis for collective selfhood,
modern Urdu becomes inadequate as a vehicle for grief. Made possible
here by the linguistic displacement is an exploration of the communal
and nation-state conflict in terms of the dissonances of language and
language history. 'Hindavi' is, of course, a term with a complex history of
usage as a name for spoken or poetic language over the centuries, and, as
Shamsur Rahman Faruqi has noted, among its overlapping and sometimes
contradictory references are those to the poetic tradition of the late
seventeenth and eighteenth centuries that today is exclusively referred
to as Urdu.[35] I use it here, however, in the more familiar contemporary
sense of the wide range of vernacular poetic practices that are often
excised from official histories of Urdu as too vernacular, that is, not
Persianized enough, to be considered an antecedent for the 'classical'
literary Urdu that emerged in the seventeenth and eighteenth centuries
but is embraced within modern Hindi literary culture as the mediaeval
font from which modern, shudh, or 'pure,' Hindi has evolved.[36] This
dissonance of literary histories, in which perhaps the most emblematic
name is that of Amir Khusro (1258–1325), poet and follower of the
Chishti Sufi saint Nizamuddin Auliya of Delhi, is one of the more fraught
issues in the history of the Hindi-Urdu conflict over the last century
and a half. The poem opens up a window on the vast linguistic-literary
vista—Braj, Avadhi, Bhojpuri, Dakhni, Maithli, Rajasthani, to name just
a handful of the vernacular language forms that the northern region
(and its southern outposts) have produced over the centuries—that
has been occluded from view in the standardization of rival 'Hindi' and
'Urdu' registers, each of which has its own distinct place *within* this
range of language and literary practices, despite disavowals of filiation
and descent in the one instance (that is, in modern Urdu) and claims to
being the encompassing linguistic and literary form in the other (that
is, in modern Hindi). Faiz therefore undermines here, within a linguistic
register, the claims for an autonomous Muslim (and hence Pakistani)
selfhood, on the one hand, and an autonomous Hindu-Indian self, on
the other. He places the language that is conspicuously absent from the
poem, namely, modern 'high' Urdu, in a line of descent from the lingua

franca of fourteenth-century northern India. Or, rather, the surface
of modern language is peeled off to reveal submerged sounds and
meanings. To turn to 'Hindavi' in order to articulate the grieving voice
of the modern self is to reveal affinities beneath the surface of modern
Urdu that are disavowed in its official history. If *this* poem can belong to
the canon of Urdu, and of Pakistani, literature, then the linguistic and
cultural configurations of self and other are not what the postcolonial
nation-states, in this moment of self-definition through war, require
them to be. This linguistic displacement makes it impossible for the poem
to be canonized as an elegy for a *Pakistani* soldier alone. But it does this
not through disavowals of difference—'we are all the same'—but rather
precisely through a careful elaboration of the text of linguistic, cultural,
and historical discontinuities.

Faiz returns to the themes and motifs of 'Soldier's Elegy' in a poem
dated 'September 1975'—pointing to the tenth anniversary of the war
of 1965. The poem, *Morī araj suno* ('Hear my plaint'), is accompanied by
a dedication to Amir Khusro and opens with a series of citations from
the Hindavi verses attributed to the latter, each in a plaintive mode,
asking for recognition, for the attention of the other, for deliverance and
restoration. In other words, Faiz provides a clue here about how we may
read that earlier poem as well. Unlike in the former poem, however, here
modern Urdu provides the dominant discourse, with the Hindavi in the
subordinate position of citation, a mode appropriate to *remembering* the
war and the crisis of self it had precipitated a decade earlier. The language
of the rest of the poem, following the lines in Hindavi, is the 'normal'
language of Faiz's poetry, with words and phrases from the citations
inserted. The overall effect of the poem is therefore again to resist a
reification of self and other, to disconcert the self with a recognition of
the sameness of the other, without collapsing the distinction between
them. The poemic present, signified by *ab* ('now'), points to the moment
of the modern, specified by the self's apperception of itself in the other.
As in so many of Faiz's poems, modernity is the putting into motion of
self and other.

Impossible narratives of the nation

In the 1960s, as he became established, despite official distrust and
harassment, in the role of something like a national poet in Pakistan,
Faiz became a key figure in a wide-ranging public debate about the

problem of 'culture' in Pakistan, among other leading participants such as Muhammad Hasan Askari, Saleem Ahmed, and Jamil Jalibi. The question of the distinctness or identity (*tashakhkhus*) of Indian Muslim culture had, in fact, informed a large number of his writings on Urdu literary history as early as the 1930s. But now, in a number of essays and lectures, Faiz turned to the post-Partition situation and developed a theory of the three-dimensionality of national culture, sometimes using the English 'culture' but more often the Urdu *tahzīb*.[37] The latter word, unlike *saqāfat*, is closer to 'civilization' than to 'culture' in the sense of the arts, or even of 'folk' culture. In fact, in defending his choice of terms, he made it clear that what he has in mind is precisely the sense of collective selfhood, essence, and destiny that is implied by 'national culture.' The three dimensions of the culture of a people or nation—the word he most often uses is *qaum*—are its length (*tūl*), breadth (*arz*), and depth (*gahrā'ī*). The first of these terms refers to the historical expanse of the culture of a nation, the question of when historically a nation locates its beginnings; the second refers to its geographical extension, that is, to the geographical home of the national culture; and the third is a measure of the extent to which the given cultural complex penetrates society as a whole—the problem, in other words, of hegemony. Each of these 'dimensions' poses a set of problems for Pakistan, all of them interconnected, but while the problem of 'depth'—differences of culture by class, region, and the rural-urban divide—is one the country shares with numerous other nations in the world, the first two imply unique problems with no clear solutions. Faiz's contributions to this debate assume that if Pakistan is to continue to exist as a separate state—these writings predate the breakup of Pakistan and the creation of Bangladesh—these solutions must be found. He insists upon the importance of culture in the work of nation building and proposes a vast project of national cultural production, distribution, and exposition, constantly clarified and informed by historical, linguistic, and literary research into the history and mutual relations of each of the linguistic and literary formations in the country, always with an emphasis on what is common to them and unifies them rather than what is distinct and therefore divisive. But it is his formulation of the historical and geographical 'dimensions' of Pakistani 'culture' that is of most interest to us here.

The question of national culture in Pakistan is characterized, first of all, according to Faiz, by a problem that arises as soon as one tries to specify the point of origin of the culture to which Pakistan as a nation-state is heir. If this beginning is located in the earliest settled culture known to have inhabited the territory that is now Pakistan, namely, the Indus Valley or Harappan civilization, then all the intervening stages and influences—from the Vedic-Aryan to the Buddhist and Greek—must also be included in 'our' cultural heritage. This means, of course, Faiz told his readers and audiences, that the cultural prehistory of Pakistan, a state created in the name of the cultural distinctness of Indian Muslims—is not distinguishable from that of post-Partition India. All Muslim countries, Faiz points out, trace their history to some pre-Islamic culture: Egypt to Pharaonic times, Iraq to Babylon, even Arabia to the so-called *jāhilīya* (Age of Ignorance). But if pre-Islamic, Indic culture is also our own, does that not negate the very basis of the demand for Pakistan? If, on the other hand, 'our' history begins with the arrival of Islam on the Indian subcontinent, that is, if we see as our ancestors the Muslim conquerors, traders, and divines who brought Islam to India, then are we not faced with the problem that the cultures of these various Muslim invaders—who include Iranians, Afghans, Arabs, and Central Asian Turks—must also be considered 'our' heritage, surely a notion that confounds the very idea of nation?

Similar difficulties arise if we approach the problem of national culture along the 'dimension' of geography. If the culture of Pakistan is simply the culture or succession of cultures that have been produced within the territory that is now Pakistan, then aside from the problem of 'regional' differences—and, of course, Pakistan consisted then of two segments separated by a thousand miles—what becomes of the culture that was produced, as Faiz puts it, 'over there' (*vahāṅ*): '[the] national language of West Pakistan, it has been decided, is Urdu, whose real homeland [*aslī dēs*] is not this side of Wagha but that side of the Jamna, and its most venerable [*buzurg-tarīn*] poets and writers are asleep [*mahv-e khvāb*] far from our borders. Similarly, the preparation and development of our music, painting, architecture, and other arts also took place in centres that Mr Radcliffe did not include within our boundaries [*hudūd*]'.[38] In this passage we see, first of all, the geographical register we have already identified in Faiz's poetry: the border post of Wagha, here coming to stand in for the border between the two countries as a whole, is on the site of an old village on the outskirts of Lahore, the city where Faiz lived for much of his life both before and after Partition. (During the war of 1965 Indian troops crossed the border at Wagha and threatened to enter Lahore.) Second, Faiz highlights the arbitrariness of the nation-state boundaries in question, and hence the discontinuities of national history, by referring to the English barrister who produced the eponymous 'Award' that marked the territories of the two newly partitioned countries. If the territorial basis of a nation-state is so clearly the result of an arbitrary colonial decision, can an effort to answer the question of national culture within the confines of territory produce anything but arbitrary results? If, on the other hand, we loosen the territorial requirement and look beyond the borders of Pakistan for the sources of its culture, then on what basis can this extension be made? The 'Indic' basis leads to the problem already identified; the 'Islamic' basis threatens to extend the search indefinitely and make the notion of a distinct Pakistani nationality (*Pākistānīyat*) meaningless.

The solutions Faiz proposes to this conundrum vary from writing to writing and often contradict one another. On one occasion he says that Pakistan's cultural history extends five thousand years, four thousand of which 'we' share with 'them'—he alternates between 'Hindus,' 'Hindustan,' and 'Bharat'—and the last one thousand 'we' do not; another time he claims that every cultural accomplishment of any Muslim culture is, by virtue of 'our' being Muslims, also our own. And sometimes he steadfastly refuses to offer answers, saying that they can be provided only in the future. Faiz's confused and contradictory answers to the questions he himself raised are in themselves meaningful. They highlight a number of narrative difficulties that Pakistan as nation-state poses. The underlying question that Faiz's efforts all seem to point towards is this: What kind of national narrative can Pakistan produce? He argues repeatedly that national culture (*qaumi tahzīb*) is not 'a natural characteristic or something one is born into' (*fitrī aur paidā'ēshī sifat*) but rather a 'wilful and creative act' (*irādī aur takhlīqī amal*), a set of meanings produced in narration.[39] This creative effort was not undertaken, he notes, when the demand for Pakistan was raised and now has become unavoidable.

The confusions and contradictions Faiz points to, together with his clear-sighted perception that national belonging is a 'creative' act, already hint at what is made clear in his poetic works: that Pakistan cannot become the site for the elaboration of a narrative that is strictly national—in other words, a narrative that posits the existence of an autonomous subject marked by the attribute of 'Pakistaniness'. Put differently, it cannot deliver what Etienne Balibar has called 'the two symmetrical figures of the illusion of national identity,' namely, the sense of a collective destiny, whose contours, furthermore, are already visible, however imperfectly, at the moment of origin.[40] Such a narrative would assume the continuous and autonomous existence of a 'Muslim' self finally realized in the form of the Pakistani nation-state. There were, of course, numerous attempts at producing such a synthesis in the decades after Partition; among the better-known scholarly works in English are Aziz Ahmed's *Studies in Islamic Culture in the Indian Environment* and Ishtiaq Husain Qureshi's *The Muslim Community of the Indo-Pakistan Subcontinent*.[41] As an essayist, Faiz demonstrates concisely the confusions and contradictions into which such a framework falls. As a poet, he allows the perception that not only can a 'Muslim' or 'Pakistani' self not be attributed with an autonomous development, that its very meaning is incomprehensible without reference to the self whose development is the theme of the *Indian* national narrative, but that this meaning consists precisely in undermining the resolutions and syntheses, the narrative twists and turns, through which that 'Indian' self is produced.

Towards a lyric history of India

As we have seen, the poetic programme Faiz announced early in his career envisioned orienting the lyric subject towards the larger world. I have argued that some of his most ambitious and effective poems are a series of exercises precisely in ending the isolation of the lyric subject or, rather, in ending its illusion of isolation. They take the form of imbuing it with the recognition that what it takes as object, as the larger world of things, is itself subject and in dialogue with it. This dialectic of inner and outer worlds, I have argued further, carries collective and historical resonances; it is an enactment of the relationship of 'Muslim' culture and identity to the emergence of a wider 'Indian' modernity. The self absorption of the lyric subject in classical Urdu poetry, so widely and repeatedly condemned since the nineteenth century, becomes for Faiz a social fact. And if that lyric subject—and its locus classicus is the *ghazal*— appeared to be, as Azad and Hali had argued, addicted to fantasy and impervious to reality and nature, that judgement could itself be explained in terms of the emergence of the horizon of 'nature' and 'reality' that we call the nation. Hali had been very clear in his *Muqaddama-e She'r-o-shā'irī* (Introduction to Poetry and Poetics, 1893) about what he had in mind when he recommended *naičaral shā'irī* (natural poetry): 'By 'natural poetry' is meant that poetry which, in terms of both words and meanings, is in accord with nature and habit . . . [in accord with] the everyday form of the language, because this everyday speech carries for the inhabitants of the country where it is spoken, the weight of nature [nēčar] or second nature [saikiṇḍ nēčar]'.[42] Therein lies the *modernity* of his and Azad's critique of classical lyric: it seeks to reorient writing within an emerging national experience organized around such terms as the indigenous and the vernacular, with the fatally necessary corollary that it enter the field of contest and conflict over the meaning of community and nation. In this sense, Faiz is indeed a descendant of these nineteenth-century reformers—and we should recall that his early formation took place in a milieu where the writings of *na'ī raushnī* (The New Light) had acquired canonical status—with the crucial difference that for him this project is to be carried out not through didactic poetry, as it is for Hali, but in terms of the lyric itself.[43] What is the nature of the modern (Indian) self? That is the question underlying the reorientation of the Urdu lyric subject in Faiz's poetry, and it is this same question that informs his periodic essayistic forays into the realm of 'Pakistani culture.'

The enormous paradox of Partition for Faiz is that it requires a rewriting of the self in the name of whose preservation it had been demanded. It is a paradox that he sometimes figures as the collision of different, inner and outer languages of self, as in this couplet from a *ghazal* dated '1953':

The heart as such
had settled its every doubt
when I [lit., we] set out to see her
But on seeing her
the lips spoke love's unrehearsed words
and everything changed everything changed[44]

[*dil sē to har mu'āmlā kar kē čalē thē sāf ham
Kehnē mēṅ un kē sāmnē bāt badal badal ga'ī*]

I suggest that we read the pathos of this couplet, this sense of the impossibility of saying what you mean, as a response to 'public' languages of selfhood and identity. Here Faiz points to the excess that cannot be contained within the categorical structure of the nation-state, within which 'Muslim' is placed at the cusp of a fatal dilemma: it can signify either 'a separate nation' or 'an Indian minority.' Faiz's entire lyric oeuvre is a refusal to accept the terms of this fixing of identity and an attempt to put the self in motion. The narrative element in this couplet—the self setting out with confessional intent to encounter an other but finding its own words becoming alien, producing meanings other than those intended—must be read in a collective and historical register as an interpretation of the history of conflict over the meaning of nation and communal identity and, in particular, as an interpretation of the history of Muslim cultural separatism. Faiz is indeed a descendant of the writers and intellectuals of the New Light who, a century earlier, postulated for the first time the distinctness of a 'Muslim' experience in Indian modernity. But, with historical retrospection, he bathes that assertion itself in the subdued light of pathos, pointing to the twists and turns, the re-routings and misfirings that mark the passage from that moment to our own. This *ghazal*, composed in 1953, is a comment on India's Partition from this side of the cataclysmic event, filled with infinite sadness at what Indian Muslim 'nationhood' has finally been revealed, in the cold light of statehood and 'sovereignty,' to mean. Faiz distils that historical pathos into the subjective language of the *ghazal*, giving it the form of the lover's sadness at the impossibility of saying, when face to face with the beloved, exactly what you mean.

The recurring image in Faiz's poetry of an ever elusive totality that is no less real for its elusiveness shares something of the melancholy of Adorno's concept of a contradictory whole whose 'movements' are visible only in the 'changes' of the fragments: 'The whole cannot be put together by adding the separated halves, but in both there appear, however distantly, the changes of the whole, which only moves in contradiction'.[45] This concept of the dialectic is an attempt to comprehend totality in late modernity, once 'the attempt to change the world,' as Adorno put it, has been missed.[46] The 'lateness' of the contemporary world for Adorno thus resides in the fact that it is the aftermath of a disappointment, a kind of dénouement once the utopian hopes generated by modern European history have suffered a catastrophic defeat. Hence the series of questions that Adorno directs at contemporary culture: Is it possible to write poetry after Auschwitz? Is philosophy possible once the chance to realize it in a transformation of human existence has been missed? Is it possible, or even desirable, to defend the subject in an age when it is besieged on all sides by the forces of mass culture and mass destruction? Postcolonial culture is, of course, itself constituted by an aftermath and marked by the 'late' acquisition of the cultural artefacts of the European nineteenth century:

national sovereignty, the popular will, the demand for democracy. In postcolonial South Asia, this moment is also that which follows the partitioning of northern Indian society. Frantz Fanon argued long ago that in order to be transplanted to the colonial setting, 'Marxist analysis should always be slightly stretched'.[47] The 'lateness' of postcolonial culture itself requires a stretching of the concept of late modernity, its uncoupling from the narrative of economic overdevelopment and over-consumption and its opening up instead to a comprehension of the aftermath of decolonization. Faiz is certainly not an 'Adornian' poet in the sense in which Celan, Beckett, or even Mann might be spoken of as Adornian writers.[48] But my purpose here is to rethink and expand what it means to write in and of the vistas of 'lateness' that Said and others have identified in the constellations of Adorno's thought. Faiz is the poet of a late *postcolonial* modernity, a poet who directs the energies of negative thinking—the heterodox mystical gesture of *inkār* (refusal) to which his poetry repeatedly returns—at the congealed cultural and social forms that constitute the postcolonial present. For Adorno, the concept of lyric poetry has a referent that is 'completely modern,' and 'the manifestations in earlier periods of the specifically lyric spirit familiar to us are only isolated flashes'.[49] Faiz, however, turns to the traditional Urdu lyric itself and extracts from it a vocabulary for the elaboration of the relation of self to world, individual to totality. He elaborates an experience of modern Indian selfhood that seeks to escape the cultural logic of the nation-state system inaugurated at Partition, that paradoxical moment of realization through re-inscription, of success through failure. He does this, furthermore, by immersion in the Indo-Islamic poetic tradition, with its deep relationship to Sufi thought and practice, and its long involvement in the crisis of culture and identity on the subcontinent. This is the larger meaning of Faiz as an Urdu poet with an immense audience across the political and cultural boundaries implemented by Partition. His is not an appropriation of the fragment from the position of totality, but neither is it an attempt to reconceive the fragment itself as a totality. His is the oeuvre of an aftermath once the chance to achieve India, to 'change the world,' as it were, has been missed. He confronts the fragment itself with its fragmentary nature, making perceptible to it its own objective situation as an element in a contradictory whole. To put it differently and more explicitly in historical terms, we might say that 'Faiz' is another name for the perception, shadowy and subterranean for the most part but abruptly and momentarily bursting through the surface of language and experience from time to time, that the disavowal of Indianness is an irreducible feature of Indianness itself.

Words out of place: Urdu as a literature of exile

Towards the end of his life, Faiz returned to a number of these themes and motifs—the search for a definition of the self, the other who comes bearing the meaning of self, the meaning of place and home, the relation of modern poetry to the classical antecedents—and combined them into a multifaceted image of exile. In conclusion, I turn to one of these late poems, written during the period of his own exile from Zia's Pakistan. Much of the work contained in the collection *Mērē Dil Mērē Musāfir*, the last to be published in his lifetime, dates from this period and was composed in London, the Soviet Union, and Beirut. The book itself is dedicated to Yasser Arafat, and a number of poems in it invoke the figure of the Palestinian as a quintessential figure of exile. I concentrate here on 'Dil-e man musāfir-e man', the opening poem in the collection, from whose first line the latter takes its title. The title of the poem is difficult to render into English, but perhaps 'My Heart, My Fellow Traveller' might be an adequate working translation.

A recurring poetic structure in Faiz's work is literary citation, as in 'Hear my plaint' above, namely, the insertion into poems of phrases and even entire lines from one or another of the classical masters, often from the *ghazals* of Ghalib. More often the citations are not the exact replication of a literary precedent but rather recall an original in some specific way.[50] It is a technique that poses unique problems of rhyme scheme and metre, since the *ghazal* in particular follows one or another from a relatively small set of strictly defined metrical schemes and an absolutely inflexible rhyme scheme (aa–ba–ca).[51] Among Hali's critiques of the genre is exactly the charge that what unifies it is rhyme and metre rather than the elaboration of a single continuous (*musalsal*) theme. Hence its popularity and its institutionalized reception in the form of the *mushāirā*, where an audience can enthusiastically and loudly anticipate the end of a verse before the poet has finished reciting it—all features of Urdu poetry and poetic reception that Hali considered inimical to modernity.[52] In the present poem Faiz turns this seeming limitation— the mnemonic quality lent to the *ghazal* by metre and rhyme—to his advantage by replicating, towards the end of the poem, the metre and rhyme scheme of one of Ghalib's most famous *ghazals*.[53] This formal citation is accompanied by citation at the level of content: lines 14–15 and 18–19 are slightly amended versions of the first and second hemistich, respectively, of the eighth couplet of Ghalib's *ghazal*; furthermore, lines 10–13 also echo a couplet from a *ghazal* by Ghulam Hamadani Mushafi (1750–1824).[54] The exact parallels with Mushafi and with Ghalib are as follows:

FAIZ	MUSHAFI
10. *Sar-e kū'ē nā-shanāyāṅ*	1. *Tērē kūčē is bahānē,*
11. *Hamēṅ din sē rāt karnā*	*mujhē din ko rāt karnā*
12. *Kabhī is sē bāt karnā*	2. *Kabhī is sē bāt karnā,*
13. *Kabhī us sē bāt karnā*	*kabhī us sē bāt karnā*
FAIZ	GHALIB
14. *Tumhēṅ kyā kahūṅ kē kyā hai*	1. *Kahūṅ kis sē maiṅ kē kyā hai*
15. *Shab-e gham burī balā hai*	*shab-e gham burī balā hai*
18. *Hamēṅ kyā burā thā marnā*	2. *Mujhē kyā burā thā marnā*
19. *Agar ēk bār hotā* (NV, 613–614)	*agar ēk bār hotā*

The dominant affect of this poem is the pathos of recollection. Faiz produces an image of exile as a constant effort to remember, expressed in the latter half of the poem in the effort to 'remember' literary antecedents. Lines 1–9 constitute the first section of the poem, in which the idea of exile is introduced and elaborated upon. The idea itself is introduced in lines 1–4, as the speaker addresses his own self—'my heart' (*mērē dil*)—with the intimation that it is 'again' ordained that 'we' leave home (*vatan*—country/homeland). The word *phir* here is significant, for it introduces the idea of repetition, establishing this as only the *latest* in a long series of exiles. And its relationship to *vatan* suggests that we are concerned with repetitions in *historical* time. Lines 5–9 offer an elaboration of the idea of exile: to be in exile is to wander in search of some *yār-e nāma-bar* ('friend bearing a missive') and to ask 'every stranger' (*har ik ajnabī*) for the way back to the home one has left behind. *Yār* could simply mean someone who is known or familiar, the opposite of stranger, but it is also a conventional poetic term for the beloved; and *ajnabī* signifies both stranger and foreigner. Thus to be in exile is both to be in constant search of the familiar/beloved who comes bearing a letter (*nāma*), a message, from home, and to interrogate strangers about the identity of the place that is one's own. To be in exile is to engage in a constant effort to remember, to rediscover, a self that is at home.

If the first half of the poem introduces and elaborates the theme of exile as remembrance or recollection, the rest of the poem is an *enactment* of that exile. This enactment takes the form, as I have already noted, of the textual effort to 'remember' classical literary antecedents. Let us consider the Mushafi parallels first. Lines 10–11 echo the first hemistich of Mushafi's couplet. Line 10 shares nothing lexically with the first half of the hemistich, but it recalls it metrically and semantically. *Kūčā* and *kū* are both 'street.' But if in Mushafi it is the beloved's street ('your street'), in Faiz it is a street inhabited by 'strangers.' Line 11 is nearly identical with the second half of the hemistich, except that the first-person singular pronoun *mujhē* is replaced by the plural form, *hamēṅ*—a substitution in line with Faiz's preference for the first-person plural, a preference that, as I have argued, lends to the language of selfhood a collective resonance. Lines 12–13 are identical with the second hemistich. If in Mushafi's couplet the dominant image is that of the speaker-lover lingering in the street of the beloved in the hope of catching sight of her, randomly engaging passers-by in conversation, in Faiz's poem the speaker finds himself in an unfamiliar street, searching for his own identity, for *himself*, among strangers. One of the relationships with the classical lyric that this poem enacts, therefore, centres around the identity of the self: the specificity of the modern in this poem is to *open up* the question of selfhood, to display the self in motion, searching for itself in and through 'some' other.

The 'Mushafi' segment of the poem (lines 10–13) is followed immediately by two lines that echo the first hemistich from Ghalib's couplet. The difference between the two rests in that Faiz replaces the openness of the quest for the other—*Kahūṅ kis sē maiṅ* ('to whom should I say')—with a definite addressee—*tumhēṅ kyā kahūṅ* ('what should I say to *you*?'). Lines 16–17 are, lexically speaking, original, but they echo the Ghalib couplet, and the *ghazal* from which it is taken, in terms of rhyme and metre. Their function is therefore to interrupt the expectations of the reader, or rather to fulfill them only in part, by postponing the second hemistich, or its echo, until lines 18–19. And here the only displacement of the original is in the substitution of the first-person singular *mujhē* with the plural form, *hamēṅ*, a substitution that lends a collective resonance to the language of selfhood, as we saw in 'Black-Out.'

The last six lines of the poem therefore give the impression of a run-on 'Ghalib' *ghazal* couplet (ab–b), with an extra 'second' hemistich. Alternatively the last four lines together suggest the first couplet of a *ghazal* (aa).

The choice of poets to 'echo' here is significant. Mushafi is among the important poets of the late eighteenth and early nineteenth centuries, who spent much of his creative life in Lucknow, although whether he belongs to the 'Lucknow School' of poets is open to question in a way that it is not with respect to such later Lucknow-resident poets as Shaikh Imam Bakhsh Nasikh (1771–1838) or Khwaja Haider Ali Atish (1778–1847), the latter a student of Mushafi's.[55] He was credited, by the British Orientalist scholar of Urdu Grahame Bailey, with being the first poet to use the word 'Urdu' as the name of the language of his poetry.[56] Ghalib's poetry, of course, represents the culmination of the rival 'Delhi School.' He is the final eminence of the period in Urdu literary history that ends with the uprising of 1857, and a transitional figure between the 'classical' tradition and the 'moderns,' like Azad and Hali. Between them, therefore, these two poets signify in Faiz's poem the classical heritage of the modern lyric poet. Together they constitute an image of 'home' for the poet in exile. But they are both literary ancestors who lie 'asleep,' to borrow the image Faiz uses in the essay I cited, 'that side of the Jamna,' rather than 'this side of Wagha.' In this imaginative homecoming, in other words, the poetic consciousness in exile finds that home itself is a form of displacement, figured here in the disorientations of inter-textual echo.

Thus the subject of Urdu (lyric) writing is for Faiz, in a strong sense, a homeless one. Faiz's poetic intent here is to confront the subject with its own displacements and, in the larger context of his oeuvre, to propose that its reorientation towards the 'larger' world, which constitutes its modernity, also means a critique of forms of existence premised upon notions of being, as it were, at home. To adopt a secular relationship to the world is to renounce the possibility of such an existence. Urdu for Faiz cannot be normalized as the language, literature, and culture of a (Muslim) nation-state. But nor is it assimilable to the contours of a 'minority' (Indian) literature. The gesture that properly expresses the ambivalence of this position at the cusp of nation and minority is the look always directed elsewhere and, as in so many of Faiz's poems, towards the horizon, which serves as a figure for the limits of normalized perception. For it is there, just beyond the limits of what it is permissible to perceive, that the self encounters its own incompleteness and manages to capture the fleeting perception that what it had taken to be its outer boundary is a line of internal division, that its own truth, its wholeness, takes the form of an unresolved contradiction. Partition appears in Faiz as a defining feature of the self itself, the manner in which a collective self has been produced in modernity. The collectivity-in-antagonism pointed to here is therefore both nation and not nation. For although it is the project of the nation-state in South Asia to normalize its emergence from colonial rule as the realization of autonomous national selves, a project against which Faiz's entire oeuvre is directed, it is by working through, rather than simply disavowing, the partitioned national experiences of postcolonial South Asia that this larger self-in-contradiction can now ever even be perceived.

In this sense, then, for Faiz, modern Urdu writing can only be a writing of exile, a writing that seeks constantly to displace the relationship of language and self to place. The selfhood that it takes as its subject, in both senses of that word, is not a self at home. Furthermore, Faiz's poetic practice insists, and demonstrates, that that is precisely Urdu's vocation, its special meaning and place in the panorama of Indian cultures. The powerful tradition of lyric poetry in Urdu, long accused of its indifference to properly Indian realities, is revived and given a new lease on life in Faiz and his contemporaries not because they infuse old words with new meanings, as the intentionalist cliché in Faiz criticism would have it, but because in their practice it becomes a site for the elaboration of a selfhood at odds with the geometry of selves put into place by Partition. In his lyric poetry, Faiz pushes the terms of identity and selfhood to their limits, to the point where they turn upon themselves and reveal the partial nature of postcolonial 'national' experience. In this sense, Faiz may be said to be situated somewhere very close to Manto and Azad, even though he is quite distant from them, and they from each other, on an ideological spectrum, with vastly different tastes in politics, religion, and even literature and culture. What these major writers from the middle decades of the century bring to Urdu literary history, from very different directions and points of origin, is the essentially exilic thrust of their writing, or, more precisely, their oeuvres consist of forms of elaboration that do not consecrate the nation-state as the natural horizon of culture and community. The ongoing process of the partition of Indian culture and society becomes the occasion and means in their writing for an exploration of the mediated production of selves and the fissures and displacements out of which their sense of wholeness is produced. These are, we should note, *vernacular* forms of displacement, by which I mean that they do not simply replicate the antinomies of colonial culture—local versus cosmopolitan, indigenous versus modern—and view the great indigenizing machinery of nation and nation-state as itself a product of the colonial world. One aim here has therefore been to attempt to rescue the problematic of exilic consciousness—*gharīb ul-vatanī*, as Azad so beautifully called it for his Friday audience in Delhi in 1947—from the stultifying contemporary debates between what we may term, on the one hand, postmodern globalists and, on the other, national localists, a debate in which neither side seems capable of recognizing and comprehending these exercises in vernacular modernity.

Notes

1. The standard work in English on these debates in the late nineteenth century is Pritchett, *Nets of Awareness*.

2. See Agha Shahid Ali, 'Introduction: Translating Faiz Ahmed Faiz', in Faiz Ahmed Faiz, *The Rebel's Silhouette: Selected Poems*, rev. ed., trans., Agha Shahid Ali, Amherst: University of Massachusetts, 1995, xiv, Print; and V.G. Kiernan, 'Introduction to Poems by Faiz', in Faiz Ahmed Faiz, *Poems by Faiz*, trans. V.G. Kiernan, Lahore: Vanguard, 1971, 40, Print. This work will be cited as PF.

3. Theodor W. Adorno, 'On Lyric poetry and Society,' ed. Rolf Tiedemann, *Notes on Literature*, Vol. 1, New York: Columbia University Press, 1991, 42, 38, Print.

4. See, for instance, Syed Sibte Hassan, 'Faiz Kā Ādarsh,' *Faiz Ahmed Faiz: Tanqīdī Jā'izā*, ed. Khaleeq Anjum, New Delhi: Anjuman-e Taraqqi-e Urdu, 1985, 119, 121, Print.

5. In matters of translations, I have set the following principles for myself: wherever possible, I work with Kiernan's translation, the 'literal' one if I am engaging in a line-by-line analysis, as this is closest to the original in terms of line content, and the 'non-literal' where the object is to convey a sense of the whole, in either case altering the translations as necessary. Where a poem or fragment is not available in a Kiernan translation, I either provide my own 'literal' translation or turn to the more freely translated versions of Agha Shahid Ali (see note 2) or Naomi Lazard—see Naomi Lazard, trans., *The True Subject: Selected Poems of Faiz Ahmed Faiz*, Princeton, N.J: Princeton University Press, 1988, Print—depending, again, on the specific purpose at hand.

6. See Kiernan, introduction to PF, 38. On Gandhi and Urdu, see chap. 3 of Aamir R. Mufti, *Enlightenment in the Colony: The Jewish Question and the Crisis of Postcolonial Culture* [refer to Sources].

7. Kiernan, Introduction, *PF*, 38.

8. See Faiz Ahmed Faiz, 'Faiz-az Faiz,' *Nuskhahā'ē Vafā*, Lahore: Maktaba-e-Karavan, 1986, 308–311, Print. This work will be cited as NV.

9. See Faiz, *PF*, 90–95, and Faiz, *NV*, 89–91.

10. See Faiz, *NV*, 308–311.

11. This biographical summary is based on the following sources: Kiernan, *Introduction to PF*. Khaleeq Anjum, 'Faiz Bītī,' *Faiz Ahmed Faiz: Tanqīdī Jā'izā*, 14–37, Print; Faiz, 'Faiz-az Faiz,' *NV*, 307–314; Faiz, 'Ehd-e Tiflī Sē Unfuvān-e Shabāb Tak,' *NV*, 489–97; Faiz Ahmed Faiz, 'Bačpan Kī Qirat Sē Josh Kī Buzurgī Tak,' *Mata'-e Lauh-o-Qalam*, Karachi: Danyal, 1985, 112–21, Print.

12. See Carlo Coppola, 'The Angārē Group: The Enfants Terribles of Urdu Literature,' *Annual of Urdu Studies* 1 (1981): 57–69, Print.

13. *Naqsh-e Faryādī* (Remonstrance) was published in 1941, to be followed, during his lifetime by *Dast-e Sabā* (Fingers of the Wind [1952]), *Zindāṅ Nāmā* (Prison Thoughts [1956]), *Dast-e Tah-e Sang* (Duress [1965]), *Sar-e Vādē-e Sīna* (Mount Sinai [1971]), *Shām-e Shehr-e Yārāṅ* (Twilight over the city of Friends [1978]), and *Mērē Dil Mērē Musāfir* (My Heart, My fellow Traveller [1981]. His late and previously uncollected poems have been collected as *Ghubār-e Ayyām* (Dust of Days [1984]). The first four translations here are Kiernan's, the rest are mine.

14. Quoted in Azmi, *Urdu Meṅ Taraqqī Pasaṅd Adabī Tahrīk*, Aligarh: Anjuman-e Taraqqī-e Urdū, 1972, 109, Print.

15. See Hasan Zaheer, *The Times and Trial of the Rawalpindi Conspiracy 1951: The First Coup Attempt in Pakistan*, Karachi: Oxford University Press, 1998, Print.

16. Edward W. Said, 'Reflections on Exile,' *Granta* 1984: 160, Print. Faiz appears briefly in Mahmoud Darwish's memoir of the Israeli siege. See Mahmoud Darwish, *Memory for Forgetfulness* (Translated and with an introduction by Ibrahim Muhawi), Berkeley: University of California, 1995.

17. On the early years of Aligarh movement, see, Lelyveld, *Aligarh's First Generation*; on a particular strain of religious neo-orthodoxy, see Barbara Daly Metcalf, *Islamic Revival in British India: Deoband, 1860–1900*, Princeton, NJ: Princeton University Press, 1982, Print; and an intriguing study of culture and space by Faisal Fatehali Devji, 'Gender and the Politics of Space: The Movement for Women's Reform, 1857–1900', in *Forging Identities: Gender, Communities, and the State*, ed. Zoya Hasan, New Delhi: Kali for Women, 1994, 22–37, Print.

18. See Altaf Husain Hali, 'Muqaddama-e Sh'ēr-o-Shā'erī,' ed. Dr Waheed Qureishi, Aligarh: Educational Publishing House, 1993, 116–17, 153–154, 158, 178–185, Print. On the popularity of the *ghazal*, and hence the greater importance of its 'reform' (islāh) than all other genres of poetry, see 179.

19. For a full-length account of these debates, see Frances W. Pritchett, *Nets of Awareness: Urdu Poetry and Its Critics*, Berkeley: University of California Press, 1994, Print.

20. See Gopi Chand Narang, *Sākhtīyāt, Pas-sākhtīyāt, aur Mashrīqī Sheriyāt*, Delhi: Educational House, 1994, 9, Print.

21. Regrettably, Kiernan did not include this very beautiful poem among his excellent translations. Agha Shahid Ali has a lovely interpretation, although not in his Faiz volume. This translation is my own. I have tried to keep it as literal as possible—with almost no attention to metre or rhyme scheme—and to remain true to the content of the lines, even at the cost of syntactical awkwardness, as in lines 9 and 10. The punctuation and capitalization in the original are, of course added. (Urdu lacks the latter and makes sparing use of the former.) My analysis stays close to the original,

with the translation meant merely as a rough guide for readers unfamiliar with the Urdu.

22. Theodor W. Adorno, 'Subject and Object,' eds. Andrew Arato and Eike Gebhardt, *The Essential Frankfurt School Reader*, New York: Continuum, 1982, 500, Print.

23. Faiz, *NV*, 438. Again the translation is mine, the literal meaning my immediate goal, with some attention to rhyme scheme.

24. For the classical *ghazal* and its symbolic and thematic universe, see Ralph Russell, 'Chapter 2,' *The Pursuit of Urdu Literature: A Select History*, Delhi: Oxford University Press, 1992, Print; and Annemarie Schimmel, A *Two-Colored Brocade: The Imagery of Persian Poetry*, Pt. 2, Chapel Hill: University of North Carolina, 1992, Print; on the erotics of *ghazal* imagery, see Annemarie Schimmel, 'Eros—Heavenly and Not So Heavenly-in Sufi Literature and Life, *Society and the Sexes in Medieval Islam*, ed. Afaf Lutfi Al-Sayyid-Marsot, Malibu, Undena Publications, 1979, 119–41, Print.

25. See Faiz, *PF*, 276–277, for Kiernan's rendition, which I have altered slightly; and Faiz, *NV*, 429.

26. See Schimmel, *Eros—Heavenly and Not So Heavenly—in Sufi Literature and Life*, 134–135, [see note 24].

27. This evocative, but largely free, translation is Agha Shahid Ali's. See Faiz, *The Rebel's Silhouette*, 85 and Faiz, *NV*, 524–525.

28. Adorno, 'Lyric Poetry and Society', 46, [see note 3].

29. See Gerard Genette, *Paratexts: Thresholds of Interpretation*, trans. Jane E. Lewin, Cambridge: Cambridge University Press, 1997, Print; and Georg Stanizek, 'Texts and Paratexts in Media,' *Critical Inquiry 32* (Autumn 2005): 27–42, Print.

30. See C.M. Naim, 'The Consequences of Indo-Pakistani War for Urdu Language and Literature,' *Journal of Asian Studies* 38.2 (February 1969): 269–283, Print. Also see Aijaz Ahmad, 'Some Reflections on Urdu,' Seminar 359 (July 1989), 29.

31. This is a slight modification of Kiernan's translation. See Faiz, *PF*, 268–271. Also, in Faiz, *NV*, the lineation is slightly different, and Kiernan's line 12 is broken into two after 'siyahmast' and line 16 after 'ho ke' (see 409–410).

32. Ahmad Faraz, 'Maiṅ Kyūṅ Udās Nahīṅ.' *Nāyāft*, Lahore: Mavra, 1989, 29–30, Print. The title itself is ambiguous and could be translated as either 'Why Do I Not Grieve?' or 'Why I Do Not Grieve'. I am not concerned here with the explicitly jingoistic verse that was produced in response to the war. For a discussion of some of this work and its context, see Naim, 'The Consequences of Indo-Pakistani War for Urdu Language and Literature.'

33. Kiernan translates the title 'Mauzū'-e Sukhan' as 'Poetry's Theme'. This leaves out the grammatical and philosophical senses that *mauzū* shares with 'subject'.

34. For a rather different reading of 'Mujh sē pahlī sī mahabbat' by an orientalist 'lover' of the classical *ghazal* tradition, see Russell, *The Pursuit of Urdu Literature*, 230–231 and 243–244, Print. In line with his literal readings of Urdu poetry in general, Russell notes sarcastically that he is not impressed with the discovery 'that there are other things in life besides love of women' (243). His entire chapter on Faiz would be laughable—he considers Faiz a second-rate poet—if it did not border on the scurrilous, accusing Faiz of self-promotion and political insincerity and cowardice.

35. See Shamsur Rahman Faruqi, 'Chapter 1', *Early Urdu Literary Culture and History*, chap 1, Delhi, Oxford University Press, 2001, Print.

36. Some of these matters are discussed in chapter 3. Aamir R. Mufti, *Enlightenment in the Colony: The Jewish Question and the Crisis of Postcolonial Culture* [refer to Sources].

37. This summary of Faiz's views on the problem of 'Pakistani culture' is based on the following essays, lectures and interviews: 'Pakistanī Tahzīb kā mas'alā' and 'Jahān-e nau ho raha hai paidā,' in Faiz Ahmed Faiz, *Mīzan*, Karachi: Urdu Academy Sindh, 1987, 87–96, 97–101, Print; Faiz, 'Ghalib', *Mata'-e Lauh-o-Qalam*, 134–139, Print; and the four lectures and one interview collected in Faiz Ahmed Faiz, *Hamārī Qaumī Saqāfat*, ed. Mirza Zafarul Hasan, Karachi: Idara-e Yadgar-e Ghalib, 1976, Print.

38. Faiz, *Pakistanī Tahzīb kā mas'alā*, 94, Print [see note 37].

39. Ibid., 94–95.

40. Etienne Balibar, 'The Nation Form: History and Ideology,' in Etienne Balibar and Immanuel Wallerstein, *Race, Nation, Class: Ambiguous Identities*, New York: Verso, 1991, 86–87, Print.

41. For an example of the form such contortions take today, see Aitzaz Ahsan, *The Indus Saga and the Making of Pakistan*, Karachi: Oxford University Press, 1996, Print.

42. Hali, *Muqaddama-e Sh'ēr-o-Shā'erī*, 158, Print [see note 18].

43. Faiz himself argues that much of what Hali is credited with having originated in poetry—the turn to 'nature,' the rejection of 'artificial' affect, the rejection of abstraction and esotericism—can in fact be traced to Nazir Akbarabadi, who wrote almost a century earlier. Hali's uniqueness lies in the national (*qaumī*) nature of his poetry and poetics. See his important essay, Hali, 'Nazir aur Hali,' Faiz, *Mīzān*, 169–70, 179–83, Print.

44. The English here is a modification of Agha Shahid Ali's very free but lovely translation. See Faiz, *The Rebel's Silhouette*, 30, [see note 2].

45. Theodor W. Adorno, 'The Fetish Character in Music and the Regression of Listening,' trans. Arato and Gebhardt, *The Frankfurt School Reader*, New York: Continuum, 1982, 275, Print.

46. Theodor W. Adorno, *Negative Dialectics*, trans. E.B. Ashton, New York: Seabury, 1973, 3, Print. On Adorno and lateness, see Fredric Jameson, *Late Marxism: Adorno, or the Persistence of the Dialectic*, London: Verso, 1990, Print; and Edward W. Said, 'Adorno as Lateness Itself,' *Apocalypse Theory and the Ends of the World*, ed. Malcolm Bull, Oxford: Blackwell, 1995, 264–281, Print.

47. See Frantz Fanon, *The Wretched of the Earth*, trans. Constance Farrington, New York: Grove, 1979, 40, Print.

48. I am grateful to Stathis Gourgouris and Eduardo Cadava for elucidating the need for this clarification.

49. Adorno, *On Lyric Poetry and Society*, 40 [see note 3].

50. See Kiernan's notes to selections 10, 32, 47, 48, 49 and 54, in PF.

51. See Muhammad Abd-Al-Rahman Barker and Shah Abdus Salam, *Classical Urdu Poetry*, Vol. 1, Ithaca, NY: Spoken Languages Services, 1977, xliv, Print.

52. Hali speaks of the 'unbearable confinements' (nā qābil-e bardāsht qaidēṅ') of rhyme scheme in the *ghazal*. See Hali, *Muqaddama*, 178–179 [see note 18].

53. Radif (refrain) 'hota'. See Mirza Asadullah Khan Ghalib, *Dīvān-e Ghālib*, Aligarh: Educational House, 1991, 63, Print.

54. I am grateful to Tahsin Siddiqi of the University of Michigan, Ann Arbor, for his help in identifying this couplet from Mushafi.

55. See Carla Petievich, *Assembly of Rivals: Delhi, Lucknow and the Urdu Ghazal*, Delhi: Manohar, 1992, x, xvi, n. 14, Print; and Annemarie Schimmel, *Classical Urdu Literature from the Beginnings to Iqbal*, Wiesbaden: Otto Harrossovitz, 1975, 191, 198, Print.

56. See Amrit Rai, *A House Divided: The Origin and Development of Hindi/Hindavi*, Delhi: Oxford University, 1984, 32–33, Print.

TWO LOVES

Original: *Do 'ishq* from *Dast-e Sabā* (1952)
Translator: Victor Kiernan

Fresh yet in memory,
Sāqī, rose-sister,
Those days whose bright mirror
Reflects her face still;
Those moments like opening
Blossoms, of sight of her,
Moments like fluttering
Heartbeats, of hope for her—

Hope of fulfilment
Come to end heartache,
Hope of love's night of thirst
Ending at last:
Sinking, those sleepless
Stars that rained sorrow,
Dawning, that destined
Joy so long waited—

Oh, this rooftop the sun
Of your beauty will gild,
From that corner its rays
Red as henna will break,
From this doorway your steps
Like quicksilver gliding,
By that pathway your skirt,
A twilit sky, flowing!

Fevered days too
I have known, separation's
Pangs, when lament was
Smothered in anguish,

Each night's dark burden
Crushing the breast,
Each daybreak's arrow
Piercing the soul.

Lonely, how many
Ways I remembered you—
Wretched, how many
Refuges caught at,
Pressing the wind's cool
Hand on hot eyelids,
Round the moon's cold neck
Throwing these arms!

So I have loved that
Mistress, my country,
Heart no less ardent
Beating for her:
This love too a pilgrim,
Seeking its haven
Now in a curving cheek,
Now a curled lock.

To that sweetheart too
Soul and flesh, every fibre,
Have called out with laughter,
Cried out with tears;
No longing of hers,
No summons unanswered,
Her griefs all transmuted,
Her sufferings made light;

Never devotion's
Prompting unheeded,
Never the trumpet
Left to ring hollowly—
Ease and indulgence,
Worldly distinction,

All the shrewd huckster's
Counsels forgotten.

What others on that road
Meet, I have met with:
Prison-cell solitude,
Marketplace calumny,
Priestly anathemas
Thundered from pulpits,
Threats and revilings
From places of power,

No barbed dart of insult
By strangers omitted,
No mode of upbraiding
By near and dear spared.
—My heart neither this love
Nor that love repents;
My heart that bears every
Scar, but of shame.

16

FAIZ AHMED FAIZ AND N.M. RASHED:
A COMPARATIVE ANALYSIS

Faiz Ahmed Faiz (1911–1984) and N.M. Rashed (1910–1975) are two of the most celebrated twentieth-century Urdu poets. Born within a year of each other, both poets began their literary careers at Government College in Lahore in the 1930s, yet took seemingly opposite literary paths. Commenting on their critical reception, Asif Farrukhi recently observed, 'the two of them still seem to be interlocked with each other like Siamese twins, the kind of colliding and contrasting pairs Urdu critics love to compare, right from Mir and Sauda to Zauq and Ghalib and Nasikh and Atish down to Anis and Dabeer.' Whereas Farrukhi sees Rashed as the 'closest parallel to Faiz,' most Urdu critics instead see them as fundamentally different.[1]

When contrasting Faiz and Rashed, critics frequently rehearse a favoured dichotomy used to understand modern Urdu literature that divides writers into two camps—progressives, who favour 'art for life's sake,' and modernists, for whom art is for art's sake alone. Faiz is always taken as representative of the former, while Rashed is frequently grouped with the latter. These categories of *adab barā'ē adab* (literature for literature's sake) and *adab barā'ē zindagī* (literature for life's sake), as well as of *taraqqī pasaṅd* (progressive) and *raj'at pasaṅd* (retrogressive), were first developed in the 1930s and 40s by the generally secular nationalist and frequently Marxist critics associated with the Progressive Writers' Association. They have had a remarkable staying power.[2]

As this paper will argue, this distinction does not really hold when measured against the work of either poet. But that does not mean it should be discarded, because the distinction became central to the ways that both poets thought about their own work and, especially, the work of the other. This essay therefore considers the role of literary interpretation in literary production, meaning, it will look at the way that poets shape their own work in accordance to the way it is received. In the case of Faiz and Rashed, their critical appraisals of one another are unusually revealing. Discussion of the way they understood one another, and the role played in that understanding by progressive criticism, form the first sections of this paper. Then, I will turn to their poetry itself, and consider two thematically related poems to see how these critical distinctions and the poets' assessments of each other fare when confronted with their texts themselves.

Faiz on Rashed

In a speech made shortly after Rashed's death in 1975, Faiz states that while at Government College, Rashed showed him the possibilities of poetry and greatly influenced his own style. Faiz describes Rashed's voice as always separate and individual, both on account of his temperament and the fact that 'he would not stay at one place.' While it might seem that Faiz is commenting on Rashed's peripatetic lifestyle, Faiz clarifies here that he is talking about Rashed's poems—how they would change even in the course of one volume, let alone over two or three. As to their different styles, Faiz reports that he would say to Rashed, 'whatever the topic is, you make it a thesis,' to which Rashed would retort, 'no matter what the topic, you make it a *ghazal*.' Rashed would then say, 'no matter how complex and deep a topic . . . you abbreviate or simplify it before presenting it, so that people would understand it and people could praise it,' and Faiz would respond in turn that 'whatever you present, we can't simplify'.[3] Through this dialogue, Faiz outlines an opposition that many of the poets' critics would recognize. Unlike Rashed's, Faiz describes his own language and poems as more simple and oriented towards the common man.

On a more sombre note, Faiz continues by noting the length of time Rashed had spent outside of Pakistan, since joining the United Nations in 1952. Faiz speaks of the 'distance' between the poet and his public as a loss, not only to the Urdu literary community but also to Rashed himself. 'When a man is overseas,' Faiz states, 'then his own self (*zāt*) cannot stand in for society (*anjuman*) and, in a way, his own self becomes a separate country.' Instead of focusing on his own society, such a poet becomes at once too preoccupied with 'looking inside his self' (*darūṅ bīnī*) and too prone to transcendent pronouncements. Rashed's cosmopoli-

tanism, Faiz asserts, left him disconnected from the specific concerns
of his people. He became focused on his own estranged self and on the
'international problems' of man in an almost existential manner, devoid
of any particularity.[4]

Faiz's argument is organized around a distinction between 'outer-
looking' (jahāṅ bīnī) and 'inner-looking' (darūṅ bīnī) poetry that is a
central dichotomy of progressive literary criticism. The opposition
between the inside and the outside is also frequently marked as that
between the 'zāhir' (evident) and the 'bātin' (the hidden, or internal).
The progressive critics who translated the principles of Soviet socialist
realism into Urdu frequently used these terms, inverting their usual
Sufi connotations. When applied to the interpretation of classical Urdu
or Persian poetry, the 'zāhir'—the outward depictions of wine drinking,
rakishness, and lust—are contrasted to the more privileged 'bātinī'
meaning of such verse—the internal, spiritual meaning of otherwise
disreputable statements. Progressive critics, reversing this evaluation,
argued that writers should focus on the 'real' entirely, and not on psychic
life. 'Darūṅ bīnī' was therefore as much a sign of European bourgeoise
decadence as of an excessively mystical or escapist 'oriental' under-
standing—a product of literature's relationship to the feudal court—as
earlier outlined by ashrāf literary reformers, such as Hali and Azad.[5] For
socialist realist critics—and certainly not all progressives were of this
persuasion—a focus on the real allowed for the exposure of the dialectic—
the processes of history—without a thorough theoretical understanding
of the Marxist philosophy of dialectical materialism.

Faiz adopts the categories of progressive criticism when he describes
Rashed's late poetry, composed for the most part outside of South Asia.
Unlike his own work, Faiz sees Rashed's poetry in general as difficult to
understand. He explains this complexity as a result of its being more
inner-focused than outer-focused. Finally, he attributes this feature to
Rashed's own physical and mental distance from his people.

N.M. Rashed wrote of Faiz in 1941, and 1950, and 1969, and the pro-
gression in these statements shows not only Rashed's changing opinion
of the other poet but also the increasing role of the categories of pro-
gressive criticism in his analysis. In each treatment, he sets Faiz against
these categories and puts forth a theory of literary creation at odds with
them. In the process, the categories of progressive criticism remain the
ground against which Rashed articulates his own position.

In his 1941 introduction to Faiz's first collection, *Naqsh-e Faryādī*, Rashed describes Faiz as standing at the 'junction of Romance and Reality'—driven by love but induced to stare at 'life's nakedness and bitterness.' Rashed characterizes Faiz's earliest work as especially concerned with beauty while lacking a direct connection with life. He sees this feature as common to most of the writers of their generation.

In the volume's later poems, Rashed sees a noticeable change. Faiz did not 'say goodbye to romanticism and take the progressive road,' but instead showed maturity in his thoughts, as though he 'entered a world in which the shadows are deeper and the path rockier.' Rashed argues that Faiz's poetry is purposely not a revolt against tradition. The 'worn-out symbols' of the executioner and the rival appear in his poetry, and there is no major break with traditional metres and rhymes. Yet Faiz's poems appear to Rashed as completely different and disconnected from those of tradition. Rashed attributes this in part to Faiz's appreciation of beauty, which he argues was absent in the traditional poets, whom he states praised beauty but could not experience it. Faiz instead wanted to create a paradise of beauty, which he comes close to but from which he would then withdraw to look at life in all its ugliness. Rashed describes Faiz's early poetry as the story of retreating from this *'tilismī haqīqat'* (illusory reality). He concludes that Faiz is not a centrally ideological poet but a poet of experiences, and he joins those strong experiences with beautiful words.[6] By emphasizing the categories of both experience and beauty, Rashed disrupts a reading of Faiz's poetry that would use the terms of progressive criticism.

In 1950, Rashed wrote an English article for Ahmed Ali's *Pakistan PEN Miscellany* in which he describes Faiz's poetry in decidedly negative terms. He writes:

> Faiz Ahmed Faiz is fundamentally a poet with an introspective romantic bent of mind and a keen poetic sensibility, who has abandoned himself to the so-called 'leftist realism.' In his early poetry, particularly in his *Tanhā'ī* (Loneliness) and *Mauzū'-e Sukhan* (Theme of Poetry) he stands out as an imagist who is almost sensuous, but the ideological change that came over him some eight years ago has brought about a noticeable decline in his poetic expression. Although he has all along been suffering from a cleavage within himself, yet he is one of the few poets of our age who had once successfully fused their personal experiences with a social philosophy of life. Today neither his experiences are immediately personal nor his philosophy of life varied and original. He had an undoubted capacity for writing poetry of permanent

value, but since he has identified himself with the group of writers who only speak under the inspiration that comes from outside he has been lost to the cause of poetry.[7]

In this statement, we see a very clear condemnation of art written for the sake of ideology in, of course, the context of the Cold War.

Rashed's charges against Faiz's artistic production, however, seem to be more ideological than based in any substantial way on an analysis of Faiz's poetry itself. Rashed's description of Faiz as 'lost to the cause of poetry' for writing 'under the inspiration that comes from outside' marks an absence of personal experience in Faiz's poetry. While fermenting in Rashed's 1941 introduction, this critique becomes much more explicit by the 1950s. Writing under 'outside' influence, Rashed argues, limits the effectiveness of the artist's work by establishing a limitation on his freedom of personal expression.

Rashed's final major statement on Faiz is found in an interview with American Urdu scholars for the journal *Mahfil* that also formed the preface, in Urdu translation, for his 1969 *Lā=Insān* (X=Man). In it, Rashed states that he still stands by his 1941 statement that 'Faiz stands at the junction of romanticism and realism.' He adds that Faiz 'borrowed the whole complex of symbolism, myth and even phraseology' from the Persian and Urdu *ghazal*, but unlike the traditional poet, he did not seek a 'personal catharsis.' Rather, he worked to 'awaken first within himself and then in the mind of his reader a pain and pathos which would link his experience with the experience of mankind as a whole.' Rashed here adopts a universalist rhetoric found in much of his writing from the 1960s onwards. He adds that Faiz also reaches this universal level by recharging the 'clichés of the Persian and Urdu *ghazal*' so that the 'solitary suffering of the disappointed romantic lover is transformed into the suffering of humanity at large.' Unlike the 'traditional poet' Faiz thus writes 'with a clear awareness of a multitude behind him'.[8]

While in 1950 Rashed had condemned Faiz for falling in line with 'leftist realism,' in this later interview he states that while Faiz is indeed a 'Progressive poet' he has not made his poetry 'serve a functional purpose.' Unlike other Progressives, Faiz does not resort to 'oratorical outbursts' or make himself accessible to ordinary readers through 'the idiom of everyday speech, or by more direct expression, or by simple oratory.' Instead, Faiz uses the 'familiar phraseology of the *ghazal*' and images that are 'largely ornate' to approach his reader in such a way that he manages to 'create a single emotional experience'.[9]

Rashed concludes that Faiz gains an approach to his readers on two levels simultaneously. The first is 'the level of the ordinary lyrical poet, with a direct emotional appeal.' The second level is that of 'a socially conscious poet, in terms of a political metaphor.' Rashed adds that 'his reader has thus to make a slight mental adjustment to arrive at the underlying meaning of his poetry, particularly when Faiz's poetry is not a poetry of intensely subtle personal experience, which the ordinary reader would find difficult to share with him'.[10] Rashed's criticism of Faiz is that the reader just has to make a *slight* mental adjustment to understand his poetry, while in his own poetry, Rashed believes, individual, personal experience itself produces an encounter with difference that compels the readers towards critical reflection.

Whereas Faiz saw Rashed's poetry as too internally focused, Rashed saw Faiz's poetry as limited by its lack of personal experience. Rashed grounded his entire critical apparatus in opposition to what he understood as the overvaluation of 'external' influence in progressive criticism. In his early 1941 assessment, Rashed described Faiz as able to join personal experience with a social philosophy in a way that compromised neither beauty nor individuality. By 1950, Rashed viewed Faiz as too driven to outside forces at the expense of his own personal interpretation. In his last statements from the 1960s, Rashed evaluated Faiz's poetry as still somewhat lacking in the breadth of personal experience and limited by its sentimental ornateness but still able to form a bridge between lyrical experience and universal human suffering.

The Speaking Subject

While Faiz and Rashed are frequently held as fundamentally opposed, a comparative study of their poetry often reveals remarkable similarities in their message, if not their style. In the section that follows, I will compare two poems thematically that address the topic of speaking truth to power. Though a small sample, an analysis of even two poems can complicate the categories of progressive criticism as applied to these poets.

The poem by Faiz, *Bol* ('Speak'), from his first collection, is among his best known. The poem reads:

Bol

bol, kē lab āzād haiṅ tērē
bol, zabāṅ ab tak tērī hai
tērā sutvāṅ jism hai tērā
bol kē jāṅ ab tak tērī hai
dēkẖ kē āhangar kī dukāṅ mēṅ
tuṅd haiṅ sholē, surkh hai āhan
kẖulnē lagē qufloṅ kē dahānē
pẖailā har ik zanjīr kā dāman
bol, yē tẖoṛā vaqt bahut hai
jism-o-zabāṅ kī maut sē pahlē
bol, kē sač zindā hai ab tak
bol, jo kučẖ kehnā hai keh lē[11]

Speak

Speak, for your lips are free
Speak, for your tongue is still yours
Your long-suffering body is yours
Speak, for your life is still your own
Speak, for in the blacksmith's shop
The flames are fierce, the iron red
The mouths of locks have begun to open
The skirt of every chain is outspread
Speak, this little time is enough
Before the death of the body and tongue
Speak, for truth is still alive
Speak, say what must be said

Using relatively simple language, Faiz's poem is instantly accessible to a wide-range of both Hindi and Urdu speakers. The poem is a *pāband nazm* ('bound' verse), which has an accessible metre. Its message is perfectly clear: don't be afraid to express yourself; the time to speak is at hand. The images of the blacksmith's shop—of locks opening their mouths, and of chains spreading out their *dāman* (garment's skirt), as if in supplication, amidst blazing flames and hot iron—bring to mind an urban proletariat, their labour, and their tools. They point to the social collectivity of 'the oppressed,' whose time for freedom has come. Yet the poem does not clearly identify who is addressed; it leaves it open to the listener's social imagination. This flexibility is one of the reasons this poem remains so popular today. Although the Progressive critic Ali Sardar Jafri would at one time accuse Faiz of being an 'unprogressive poet' (*ghair taraqqī pasaṅd sha'ir*) for 'putting curtains of metaphors into his poems such that no one knows who is sitting behind them,' part of the strength and appeal of Faiz's poetry is exactly this metaphorical instability, the resolution of which is left open to the listener.[12]

Rashed's poem *Harf-e Nāguftā* ('The Unsaid Word') is on a similar theme. He composed it in the early 1960s and added it to the fourth edition of *Iran Mēṅ Ajnabī*. It reads:

Harf-e nāguftā

harf-e nāguftā kē āzār sē hushyār raho
kū'ē-o barzan ko,
    dar-o-bām ko,
        sholoṅ kī zabāṅ chāṭti ho,
vo dahan-basta-o-lab-dokhtā ho—
  aisē gunah-gār sē hushyār raho!

shehna-e shehr ho, yā banda-e sultāṅ ho
    agar tum sē kahē: 'lab na hilāo
lab hilāo, nahīṅ lab hī na hilāo
    dast-o-bāzū bhī hilāo
dast-o-bāzū ko zabān-o-lab-o-guftār banāo
    aisā kuhrām mačā'o kē sadā yād rahē,
ahl-e darbār kē atvār sē hushyār raho!

in kē lamhāt kē āfāq nahīṅ—
    harf-e nā-gufta sē jo lehzā guzar jā'ē
      shab-e vaqt kā pāyāṅ hai vohī!
hā'ē vo zehr jo sadiyoṅ kē rag-o-pai mēṅ samā jā'ē
    kē jis kā ko'ī tiryāq nahīṅ!
āj is zehr kē baṛhtē hu'ē
    āsār se hushyār raho
harf-e nā-guftā kē āzār se hushyār raho![13]

The Unsaid Word

Beware of the sickness of the unsaid word
If as the streets and lanes,
    the doors and rooftops

are being licked by a tongue of flames,
someone would have a closed mouth and sealed lips,
    beware of such a sinner!

Whether it's the city's sheriff, or the king's henchman,
    if he says to you, 'Don't move your lips'
move your lips, no, not just your lips
    move your fists and arms as well,
make your fists and arms the tongue and lips of speech,
    raise a cry that will be remembered forever,
beware of the ways of the people of the court!

Their moments have no horizons—
    a moment that passes with an unsaid word,
        is itself the end of the night of time!

Alas, it's that poison which, if it enters the veins and fibres of centuries,
    has no cure!
Today beware of
    the advancing symptoms of this poison,
beware of the sickness of the unsaid word!

Rashed's poem, like that of Faiz, is a call for protest. It is an *āzād nazm* (free-verse poem), but it still has a discernible metre, with variations, and obvious rhyming elements. In the first stanza, the devastating 'tongue of flames' points, through synecdoche, to any injustice perpetrated against a populace. The 'sinner,' whose mouth is closed and whose lips are literally 'sewn together' (*lab-dokhtā*), suggests someone who silently ignores this injustice. The message of the second stanza is clear: if you are being oppressed and an authority tells you to remain quiet, speak up and revolt. Yet the offices of the authoritarian characters referred to, the '*shehna-e shehr*' and the '*banda-e sultān*,' which I translate as city's sheriff and king's henchman, are not terms from the contemporary world. They refer instead to a past world of feudal monarchies, as does the stanza's final line, '*ahl-e darbār kē atvār sē hushyār raho!*' (Beware of the ways of the people of the court). This stanza's final line cautions that one must be wary of monarchs and courtiers, the '*ahl-e darbār*,' referencing a stereotype of the feudal court, rife with assassinations and duplicity.

The final stanza explores the consequences of not speaking out. These consequences have something to do with time. The moments of unsaid words 'have no horizons,' that is, no limits. Words that are not spoken do not rise into history and establish their eventness, their temporality. Instead, they seep, unrealized and unspoken, into the past, like a poison for which there is no antidote. While the second stanza with its feudal nomenclature appears to be set in the mediaeval past, the third stanza proposes a universal, transhistorical continuity for the demand for dissent; when flames of injustice are burning the populace and yet people are silenced by authoritarian structures, people must rise up, seize the moment, and bring their protest into history. Despite its different level of abstraction and more complex vocabulary, Rashed's poem shares the same message as that of Faiz's: don't be afraid to speak up right now.

The formal differences of these two poems suggest the question of the presumed audiences for these works, and—in a slightly different register—their relationship to the categories of progressive criticism. One way in which modern Urdu poets have come to be categorized by literary critics is in terms of traditions. Through this strategy, Faiz is linked to a 'musalsal rivāyat' (continuous tradition) that runs from 'Mir to Firaq,' in which, to quote Aftab Ahmad, 'the language of common speech (rozmarrā ki bol čāl) has a fundamental position. It is familiar and idiomatic, flowing and easily accessible, and has the traits of the living language of everyday speech.' Rashed, by contrast, is linked to a tradition of difficult (mushkil-pasaṅd), intellectual (aql-parast), and Persianate poetry associated with Ghalib, Iqbal, and Bedil.[14] The invention of new literary traditions and schools for Urdu poetry has been a preoccupation of Urdu literary critics since the late nineteenth century. Though taking literary traditions as an exclusive form of categorization does not necessarily make for good analysis, the underlying point made by the reference to tradition is of some use in understanding the reception of these two poets. While Faiz's poetry, in general, is certainly not 'common speech,' Faiz's poetry does settle neatly within a horizon of expectations about what Urdu poetry should be, as he in general draws heavily on the vocabulary and imagery of the Urdu ghazal. Neither bombastic nor harshly realistic, it frequently uses sensuous language to explore subjective emotional states. In his own words, 'The construction of beauty is not just an ornamental action; it is also a utilitarian one',[15] and for Faiz, 'The true subject of poetry is the loss of the beloved'.[16] Yet frequently in orthodox progressive readings of his poetry, every mention of the beloved is viewed only as a symbol of the revolution. This approach can certainly be supplanted by more heterodox readings, such as Aamir Mufti's recent reading of Faiz's poetry as focused on the meaning and legacy of Partition.[17] Indeed, part of the political significance of Faiz's poetry is that, despite or perhaps because of its use of *ghazal* imagery, it is accessible to a variety of readers, and not bound to the fixities of the nation-state.

The poetry of Rashed, on the other hand, is marked by a continuous evolution in form and a greater rejection of the *ghazal* and its sensuous language. Yet despite Rashed's later claims to be writing of the situation of 'modern man,' his poetry remained oriented towards a particular audience, who had access to his more belletristic language and whom he envisioned as largely to be found in Pakistan. However, even in his complex diasporic late poetry, Rashed is working allegorically, seizing elements from Urdu poetic tradition and, rendering them in a new context, disruptively investing them with new meanings that aim to upset traditional understandings.

While Faiz has typically been treated, following progressive criticism, as a poet concerned with the politics of 'external' social life, Rashed has been frequently and unnecessarily excluded from such a reading.[18] And yet, a poem such as 'The Unsaid Word' has both an explicit political message—a call to expression—and a covert critique of the forms of expression available at present. Otherwise, what are we to make of his establishing continuity between pathological feudal forms of government and contemporary political conditions? This poem could as surely be read as a critique of present politics as that of Faiz.

Similarly, while in Urdu literary criticism, Rashed seems to be universally accepted as a pillar of Urdu modernism, the question remains, what of Faiz? While no one would ever deny that Faiz is a modern poet, the place of his literary production within the field of literary modernism in Urdu has generally been ignored. Yet the literary production of Faiz— and, one may argue, of the Progressive movement as a whole—is by its very nature a modernist enterprise; it is no less of an attempt to seek new modes of expression than is Rashed's poetry.

Conclusion

Both Faiz and Rashed have been ill served and frequently misrecognized by progressive criticism. Faiz is read as a poet concerned with the external world of society above all. Rashed is considered obsessed with poetic form in itself with no connection to reality. In understanding each other's poetry, both writers make reference to the categories of

progressive criticism. However, they do make some headway in advancing
an interpretation of each other's poetry beyond these categories.

In describing Rashed's poetry, Faiz emphasizes the differences in their
style. Faiz sees Rashed's poetry as resistant to simple explanation—a
statement that is by no means universally true but that does certainly
describe a considerable amount of Rashed's literary output, particularly
from his later years. He interprets this feature of Rashed's poetry as a
product of his 'inner looking' or introspection into the self, which he
attributes to the author's experience living abroad. But Faiz fails to see
that Rashed's poetry continues to draw on both collective experience
and literary conventions, although perhaps more obliquely than his own.
Despite his physical distance from Pakistan and his own universalistic
rhetoric, Rashed's poetry remains embedded in Urdu literary tradition.
He continues his relationship with his Urdu literary community through
an allegorical disruption of literary conventions.

In 1950, Rashed accuses Faiz of being overly ideological. But both
earlier and later, he contradicts himself to insist that Faiz is not a
fundamentally ideological poet but instead focused on individual
experience. Rashed's description of Faiz joining lyrical individual
experience with collective suffering steps beyond the most common
reading of Faiz, which values most, his image as a poet of the collective.
In a 2011 article in *Tehelkā*, for example, Javed Akhtar writes of Faiz, 'The
·word *maiṅ*, 'me', never made an appearance in his poems'.[19] This claim
is obviously not actually correct; Faiz made no real effort to avoid the
personal pronoun. What Javed Akhtar seems to really value is something
closer to Rashed's interpretation of Faiz's poetry, which focuses on the
manner in which he represents the collectivity through his own personal
experience.

An example of this individual but also collective experience is found
in Faiz's short poem *Mērē dard ko jo zabāṅ milē* (If My Pain Would Find a
Voice):

merā dard naghma-e bē-sadā
mērī zāt zarra-e bē-nishāṅ
mērē dard ko jo zabāṅ milē
mujhē apnā nām-o-nishāṅ milē
mērī zāt ko jo zabāṅ milē
mujhe rāz-e nazm-e jahāṅ milē
jo mujhē ye rāz-e nihāṅ milē

mērī khāmshī ko bayāṅ milē
mujhe kā'ināt kī sarvarī
mujhe daulat-e do jahāṅ milē

My pain, a song without a voice
My self, a speck without a trace
If my pain would find a voice,
I would discover a trace of myself
If my self would find a voice,
I would discover the secret of the world's order
If I found this hidden secret,
If my silence would find message,
I would have sovereignty over the universe,
I would find the treasures of both the worlds.

In this short poem, Faiz celebrates individual experience, describing its necessity. For, as he writes, the individual's experience of suffering is what opens up the possibility for a transformative self-awareness.

This awareness is first of the individual self, the 'I,' not of the collective. However, an appreciation of the individual reveals the nature of the 'outer' world—the 'world's order' (*nazm-e jahāṅ*)—while also unveiling the other 'inner' world, as well. In this poem, as well as in oeuvre on the whole, Faiz clearly transverses the internal and the external, the individual and the collective. And so it would be a mistake to see this poet as ignoring the individual in favour of the collective; in fact, what he does is to articulate the relationship between the two.

Though the categories derived from progressive criticism do not encapsulate the work of either poet, they remain important as a historical fact. They were constitutive of the discourse through which both poets understood their own work and that of their contemporaries. And, they provided terms for both poets to write against. In his poetry and commentary, Rashed insists that through an encounter with a poet's subtle, individual personal experience a reader's critical consciousness can be raised. His disruptive use of Urdu poetic tradition, however, implies a collective experience. For his part, Faiz insists on his address to and comradeship with the common man. However, he does so largely through lyrical depictions of individual experience. Faiz did not consider breaking with conventional poetic language as imperative as did Rashed, who increasingly sought new modes of expression. But Faiz's poetry, like progressivism as a whole, still represents a degree of formal and thematic experimentation that can be more productively understood as a part of Urdu modernism, than its opposite.

While Urdu modernism remains vital to the Urdu literary community, offering extraordinary pleasures, the clarity of hindsight must now prompt a re-evaluation of the terms of Urdu literary discourse. In particular, the division between progressive and modernist poets seems increasingly to be unhelpful to the interpretation of poetry—especially, it seems, the poetry of the most reassured exemplars of these positions. This essay attempts to consider again what role that division might play in a revisionist view of that crucial historical period.

Notes

1. Asif Farrukhi, 'Among His Contemporaries,' *Dawn Centenary Special, Dawn* (13 February 2011): 23, Print.

2. For the history of the Progressive Writers' Association and its criticism, see Khalil ul-Rahman Azmi, *Urdū Mēṅ Taraqqī Pasaṅd Adabī Tahrīk*, Aligarh: Educational Book House, 1996 [1957], Print.

3. This article is a transcript of a commemorative address given by Faiz at the Pakistan National Centre, Lahore. All translations are my own. See: Faiz Ahmed Faiz, Address, N.M. Rashid, Pakistan National Centre, Lahore, December 1975, *Kitab*, 3rd ed., Vol. 10, 20–21, Print.

4. Ibid., 21–22.

5. For Hali and Azad, see Frances W. Pritchett, *Nets of Awareness: Urdu Poetry and Its Critics*, Berkeley: University of California, 1994, Print.

6. N.M. Rashid, 'Muqaddama-e Naqsh-e Faryādī,' *Maqalāt-e N.M. Rashid*, ed. Shima Majid, Islamabad: Al-Hamra, 2002, 375–81, Print.

7. N.M. Rashed, 'On Some Urdu Poets of Today,' ed. Ahmed Ali, *Pakistan PEN Miscellany*, (Kitab Publishing: Karachi), 1950: 92, Print.

8. N.M. Rashed, 'Interview with N.M. Rashed', *Mahfil*, vol. 7, 1971: 8, Print. See also N.M. Rashid, 'Ēk Musāhibāh,' *Lā = Insān*, Lahore: Al-Misal, 1969, 23–26, Print.

9. N.M. Rashed, 'Interview with N.M. Rashed', pp. 8–9.

10. Ibid., 9.

11. Faiz Ahmed Faiz, 'Bol,' *Nuskhahā'ē Vafā*, Lahore: Maktabah-e Karavan, n.d., 81, Print.

12. Sardar Jafri, 'Taraqqī Pasandī kē B'āz Bunyādi Masā'il,' *Shahrah 2*, Print. Quoted in Khalil Ul-Rahman Azmi, *Urdu Mēṅ Taraqqī Pasand Adabī Tahrīk*, Aligarh: Educational Book House, 1996 [1957], p. 97, Print.

13. N.M. Rashid, 'Harf-e Nāguftā,' *Irān Mēṅ Ajnabī*, 4th ed., Lahore: Al-Misal, 1969, 74–75, Print.

14. Aftab Ahmad, 'N.M. Rashid: Shā'er-o-Shakhs,' *N.M. Rashid: Shā'eroṅ kā Shā'er*, Lahore: Mavara, 1989, 55, Print.

15. Faiz Ahmed Faiz, 'Na'ē Chirāgh.' *Adab-e Latīf*, September 1954, Print. Quoted in Khalil Ul-Rahman Azmi, *Urdu Mēṅ Taraqqī Pasand Adabī Tahrīk*, 138, Print.

16. Faiz Ahmed Faiz, trans. Naomi Lazard, *The True Subject: Selected Poems of Faiz Ahmed Faiz*, Princeton, NJ: Princeton University Press, 1988, Print.

17. Aamir Mufti, 'Towards a Lyric History of India', *Boundary 2* 31.2 (2004): 245–74, Print.

18. In more recent scholarship produced in connection with Rashed's birth centenary in 2010, this is not necessarily the case. See, for example, Fatah Muhammad Malik, *N.M. Rashid: Siyāsat aur Shāʿerī*, Islamabad: Dost Publications, 2010, Print.

19. Javed Akhtar, 'Do You Dare Snuff Out the Moon,' *Tehelkā Magazine*, 12 February 2011, Web, 5 August 2011, http://www.tehelka.com/story_main48.asp?filename=hub120211DO_YOU.asp, Vol. 8, Issue 6.

ON MY RETURN FROM DHAKA (Bangladesh III)*

Original: *Ḍhākā sē vāpsī par* from *Shām-e Shehr-e Yārāṅ* (1979)
TRANSLATOR: AGHA SHAHID ALI

After those many encounters, that easy intimacy,
    We are strangers now—
After how many meetings will we be that close again?

When will we again see a spring of unstained green?
After how many monsoons will the blood be washed
    from the branches?

So relentless was the end of love, so heartless—
After the nights of tenderness, the dawns were pitiless,
    so pitiless.

And so crushed was the heart that though it wished,
    it found no chance—
After the entreaties, after the despair—for us to
    quarrel once again as old friends.

Faiz, what you'd gone to say, ready to offer everything,
even your life—
Those healing words remained unspoken after all else had
been said.

---

* Revisited after the massacre.

17

'LET THEM SNUFF OUT THE MOON': FAIZ AHMED FAIZ'S PRISON LYRICS IN *DAST-E SABĀ*

In our society, for a whole lot of people, getting sent to jail is not something out of the ordinary or unexpected, rather it is a part of their lives. (Faiz Ahmed Faiz, 1985, 117)

At 6:30 a.m. on 9 March 1951, a group of policemen arrived at the house of Faiz Ahmed Faiz, editor of the liberal *Pakistan Times* and one of the nation's most prominent poets. Faiz's wife Alys woke to the sound of loud voices repeatedly calling her husband's name. 'I crossed the verandah, and looked down over the parapet into the garden below,' she wrote later. 'I could see armed police—plenty of them—they had surrounded the house' (Faiz, Alys 1993, 133–4). The elections for the Punjab Assembly were scheduled for the next day, and Faiz told Alys that he suspected the police only intended to detain him long enough to assure his silence until after the elections. Before he could tell her anything more, the men pried open the doors and the upper courtyard of the house was suddenly filled with policemen, 'their rifles at the ready' (ibid., 134).

The officers did not know the exact charges but insisted that Faiz come with them. He refused to leave until he could consult with Mazhar Ali Khan, his colleague at the *Pakistan Times*. By the time Khan arrived at the house, a warrant had been produced for 'indefinite detention without trial under the Bengal Regulations of 1818' (ibid.)—an outdated law created by the British to hold anti-government elements. Khan assured Faiz that this was merely a short-term election detention and that he should go quietly. After he was allowed to gather bed linens and a few clothes, Faiz was loaded into a jeep and taken to Sargodha jail, but the superintendent of the all-women's prison had not been informed of Faiz's arrival.

While the superintendent was on the phone trying to straighten out the matter, Prime Minister Liaquat Ali Khan came on the radio with an important announcement. He said that a conspiracy to overthrow the government had been uncovered and the leaders of this intended coup arrested. They were identified as Major General Akbar Khan, Chief of General Staff, his wife Nasim Akbar Khan, Brigadier Muhammed Abdul Latif Khan, Commander 52nd Brigade and Station Commander Quetta, and Faiz Ahmed Faiz. In his statement, the Prime Minister declined to 'disclose publicly the details of the plans of those who were implicated in the conspiracy,' citing national security concerns, but he asserted that they had intended to use 'violent means' to disrupt 'the stability of Pakistan' (Zaheer 1998, 1, 13; Faiz, Alys 1993, 148).

The news must have come as a shock. Faiz's political leanings were no secret, but he was no revolutionary. If anything, his politics were fiercely unpredictable—seemingly guided only by his personal convictions. He had tested his poetry readers in undivided India in 1943 by openly criticizing Gandhi in the poem 'To a Political Leader,' but when Gandhi was assassinated in 1948, Faiz risked the scrutiny of the Pakistani government by travelling to India to attend the funeral. He consistently supported leftist causes, but refused to join the Communist Party. He took high-profile positions as the vice president of the Trade Union Federation of Pakistan and as secretary of the Pakistan Peace Committee, but remained close with many of the country's top military leaders, with whom he had become friends when he served in the Moral Welfare Directorate of the Indian army during the Second World War.

Faiz had been the new nation's most visible writer, as both poet and journalist, in the years following the 1947 Partition of British India into India and Pakistan, and he had initially supported his new nation as described by Quaid-i-Azam Mohammed Ali Jinnah. However, after witnessing the communal violence in Punjab during the Partition, the assassinations or mysterious deaths of the leaders who led Pakistan to independence, the corruption and social intolerance, and the tyrannical rule of the police in Punjab, Faiz's early enthusiasm for the possibilities of a Muslim state quickly faded. He assumed the editorship of the *Pakistan Times* in 1947, where, V.G. Kiernan writes, he 'made use of prose as well as verse to denounce obstruction at home and to champion progressive causes abroad; he made his paper one whose opinions were known and quoted far and wide' (Kiernan 1971, 24). Until that very morning, however, Faiz had considered himself immune from government oppression.

The prison superintendent finally found a cell in solitary confinement for Faiz and ordered him away. For the first time, Faiz realized he would be tried for conspiracy to overthrow the government. By the next day, the London Times would characterize him as some of 'the most dangerous and influential leftist figures in Pakistan' (10 March 1951). Over the next two years he would face trial before a secret tribunal that held the power to condemn him to death before a firing squad; he would also compose the remarkable poems of his second book, Dast-e Sabā ('Fingers of the Wind').

* * *

In coining—or at least popularizing—the term 'poetry of witness,' Carolyn Forche acknowledged that this new way of categorizing poetry 'presents the reader with an interesting interpretive problem' (1993, 31). Twentieth-century poetry of witness resisted the traditional division of 'personal' and 'political' poetry by forging a new style that wedded the two, reclaiming the right of subjective points of view to speak in opposition to the unified voice of society or the imposed voice of those in power. By the very act of opposing, however, the poet of witness enters into a dialogue, overt or covert, with his oppressor, and thus the language (the style, the form, even the imagery) of the poem is partly dictated by the conditions under which the work is written. As poet Gregory Orr writes in the introduction to Poetry as Survival:

> Human culture 'invented' or evolved the personal lyric as a means of helping individuals survive the existential crises represented by extremities of subjectivity and also by such outer circumstances as poverty, suffering, pain, illness, violence, or loss of a loved one. This survival begins when we 'translate' our crises into language—where we give it symbolic expression as an unfolding drama of self and the forces that assail it. This same poem also arrays the ordering powers our shaping imagination has brought to bear on these disorderings. Thus the poem we compose (or respond to as readers) still accurately mirrors the life crisis it dramatizes, still displays life's interplay of disorder and order. (2002, 4)

The conundrum is that the crisis reflected in lyric poetry takes a necessarily individuated form—the very distinguishing feature of the lyric—thus complicating the task of determining overtly the crisis it represents. If, however, as Orr suggests, the lyric 'still displays life's interplay of disorder and order,' then it must not only be possible but imperative to read the lyric poem in light of the context of its production.

In his seminal essay, 'Lyric Poetry and Society,' Theodor W. Adorno contends that this is especially important because the content of lyric poetry is 'essentially social in nature' (1974, 57). The use of private imagery and individual expression is paradoxically what distances and binds the reader to the poet by showing that the unknowability of each individual is perhaps the most singular trait we share. This interplay refuses what Adorno calls 'vague feelings of universality and inclusiveness' (ibid.); the poet beckons us to bridge the human divide by filling in context and historical background on our own, bringing the poem back to the instant of its creation. Adorno writes:

> Such a precisely specifying cast of thought is not at odds with art and does not add merely external commentary—it is in fact required by every linguistic creation. A poem's indigenous material, its patterns and ideas, cannot be exhausted through mere static contemplation. (Ibid.)

In the case of poetry of witness, such historicized readings become even more important as the 'indigenous material' may not be entirely of the poet's choosing. Because it speaks in opposition to other voices, the lyric of witness is not the voice of the poet alone but the voice of the poet in dialogue. As such, Forche writes, '. . . it will take many forms. It will be impassioned or ironic. It will speak in the language of the common man or in an esoteric language of paradox or literary privilege. It will curse and it will bless. . . .' (Forche 1993, 46)

Furthermore, in the case of prison writings, the context of a poem's production is inseparable from its content and thus crucial to its interpretation, as material demands placed on the poet often determine defining features of the work. Miguel Hernandez's famous poem 'Lullaby of the Onion,' for example, cannot be reasonably understood without the biographical information that he was imprisoned at the time and had learned that his wife had only bread and onions to eat, souring her breast milk and giving their newborn child, colic. Without this information, these lines would be inscrutable: 'Fly, child, on the double moon of her breast;/though saddened by onions, /be satisfied.' So essential, in fact, is this external context that nearly every edition that includes the poem—in Spanish or in translation—features the head note provided by Hernandez's first editor.[1]

As significant as the imposed imagery of prison life are the quotidian material demands of writing under such circumstances. One could not offer a full, legitimate interpretation of the dense, crystalline gulag short stories of Russian writer Dmitry Stonov without knowing that he was denied writing materials and was forced to use a contraband pencil nub to compose his stories in a miniature script on the inside of his unrolled cigarette papers. Is it any wonder that, in contrast to the great Russian epics of the period, Stonov's stories are highly distilled vignettes?[2]

Likewise, when Faiz was confined to solitary, his pen and paper confiscated, he composed qit'as—a four-line rhymed form that he could memorize and recite. Later when he could commit his poems to paper, Faiz's writings that were sent outside the confines of the prison walls were subject to rigorous censorship. Thus he was forced to develop a covert system of images and metaphors, often drawn from the traditional forms of Persian and Urdu poetry, that would seem harmless to the unthinking eyes of the censors.

On 12 March 1984, less than six months before he died, Faiz revealed something of this private cosmology when he addressed the Asian Study Group at the British Council in Lahore. The left-leaning newspaper the *Dawn* reported that although he was 'ostensibly lecturing on the cultural and social background of the classical *ghazal* and the evolution of contemporary Urdu literary movements,' Faiz instead seemed to be laying out 'a discourse on the subtle art of evading censorship.' In the lecture, Faiz contended that

> an entire range of symbols evoked in the Urdu *ghazal* have transcended successive historical periods, each time acquiring new meanings to reflect changing political, economic and social realities. Faiz then demonstrated why traditional symbols like *čaman* (garden), *sanam* (idol), *sayyād* (captor) and *qafas* (prison) are valid today and how they can be used as a means of escaping censorship. He said that when a poet speaks of *ehd-i-junūṅ* (period of obsession) or *čaman kī udāsī* (sorrow of the garden) he or she is actually referring to oppression and injustice.[3]

Thus, the poet has left a partial key to unlocking the complicated imagery of his most lyric poems.

As Aamir Mufti suggests, however, the images in Faiz's prison poetry must not be interpreted as representative—and thus universalized—lyrics about the condition of incarceration. They must instead be read in the context of their particular historical moment of production as exemplars of

> some of the central dilemmas of Urdu writing in the aftermath of the Partition of India at the moment of independence from British rule. [Faiz's poetry] represents a profound attempt to unhitch literary production from the cultural projects of either postcolonial state in order to make visible meanings that have still not been entirely reified and subsumed within the cultural logic of the nation-state system. (1997, 183–4)

Furthermore, by publishing the poems in *Dast-e Sabā* in the rough order of their composition, Faiz invites us to read the psychological evolution of his productions as they relate and respond to the shifting conditions of the nation-state system they oppose.

His earliest poems in *Dast-e Sabā* may be categorized loosely as poems of defiance, followed by a middle period of remembrance, and finally a time of loneliness and despair. Careful historical examination of the events shaping the composition of these poems provides much insight into this progression as the Rawalpindi Conspiracy trial dragged on for nearly two years and the likelihood of Faiz's conviction became increasingly certain. These events, however, do not fully define the poems, and it is equally fascinating to read the unfolding argument of Faiz's work as he develops a system of setting the true country of Pakistan—the nation promised by Jinnah before Partition—in opposition to the realized totalitarian nation-state. Thus, his poems occupy the singular space of a lyric that does not speak for the subjugated one against the oppressive many, but rather for the many ruled against the ruling few.

For the first three months of his imprisonment, while he awaited trial, Faiz was held in solitary confinement at Sargodha, then later at Lyallpur (now Faisalabad). No visitors were allowed, and he was denied all reading and writing materials. To pass the time, Faiz would recite poems he had committed to memory by Ghalib or Iqbal. Sometimes he would listen to the stories of the man in the adjacent cell, who would spin tales of genies, demons, fairies, and saints. The only poems he composed during this period were *qit'as*—a form he could memorize or (according to his fellow inmates) scrawl with chunks of coal on the walls of his cell. Not surprisingly, these brief poems fluctuate between pure defiance and extreme loneliness. The best known of these is also the poem that Faiz claimed as his first prison composition:

> Why should I mourn if my tablet and pen
> are forbidden,
> when I have dipped my fingers in my own
> blood until they stain?
> My lips have been silenced, but what of it?
> For I have hidden
> a tongue in every round-mouthed link of
> my chain.[4]

Bravado, however, would frequently give way to longing. In another poem of this period, Faiz addresses an unnamed, absent lover. By this time, he already advocated the use of stock imagery from Persian love poetry as a way of averting the temporal—an idea fully realized later in a poem titled 'Any Lover to Any Beloved.' Nevertheless, it is hard not to believe that Faiz had his wife, from whom he was not only separated but held incommunicado, specifically in mind when he wrote:

> Of the long days when I knew you could
> not come,
> don't ask if I thought of you or missed you
> very much.
> Your memory alone fills the wellspring of
> my mind
> but it is not the same as your lips, your
> arms, your touch.

Even here, the imprisoned lover instructs his beloved not to ask of his longing, because—he implies—he refuses to long for her on the days when he knows that she is impossibly separated from him, and thinking of her only reminds him of his forced isolation. Thus, even in the love poems of this period, Faiz's righteous defiance pervades.

Alys, however, left to care for their two daughters, could not afford to fly in the face of officials. Rumours and conflicting accounts of Faiz's mistreatment inside the prison were excruciating, but she had to continue to have faith in his safety and work through channels to arrange a visit. 'Those who came to see us brought tales of horror,' she later remembered. 'He was being tortured, he was on lie detector, he had gone out of his mind' (Faiz, Alys 1993, 48).

There was good reason to fear. On 28 April the government announced that the Parliament in a secret session had passed the Rawalpindi Conspiracy Act of 1951, appointing a Special Tribunal to try the conspirators. The act declared that the trial would be held outside of Pakistan's usual legal system, and, as such, several special provisions were included, stipulating that: (1) convictions would be determined by the government appointed Tribunal, not by a jury; (2) the Tribunal would have the power to convict the accused of crimes not included in the list of charges, and all statutes of limitation on previous crimes were repealed; (3) the proceedings would be closed to the public, and the accused would be forbidden to speak to anyone but their counsel or face prosecution under the Official Secrets Act of 1923; and 4) the convictions of the Special Tribunal would be exempt from appeal or future revision and could only be overturned by pardon or reprieve from the Governor-General.[5]

In late May, Alys was at last permitted to see Faiz at Lyallpur (now Faisalabad), where he was still being held in solitary confinement:

> He looked well, pale but cheerful, but was distressed at the sight of me. You are thin, pale. Remember I depend upon you now, be of good cheer and courage—we have a battle to fight. The girls clung to him. We said goodbye and the long trial began. (Faiz, Alys 1993, 49)

On 4 June, all those accused under the Rawalpindi Conspiracy Act were officially charged, boarded onto a specially commissioned train under armed guard, and then transferred to the Hyderabad jail. The walls of the prison were raised higher in preparation for their arrival. Additional police were hired to guard the jail. All gates were electrified. But when Faiz wrote to Alys on 7 June, he made it sound as if they were honoured guests.

> How grandly we travelled! We had everything—the only thing missing was a brass band! The moment we boarded the train it felt as if all our troubles had vanished. The joy of travelling, the pleasure of seeing the world again, the elegant meal—so many delightful things happened to us all at once. For the first time since that distant day when they suddenly took me away from home, we had a really delicious meal—roast chicken, pulao, fruit cocktail, and

ice cream. (Unfortunately, I didn't have an appetite.) But the best thing of all was to have some human company—the most cherished thing in the world—something we had been denied for so long. . . .

Our home in the jail is not bad. We have enough to eat. It doesn't get too hot either. Anyway, the worst days are over. Whatever else may happen, I need not fear being put into solitary confinement again. Nor is there any reason to fear further interrogation by the police. My life and my self-respect are intact. Now I can put before me your picture—and the children's—and smile. My heart no longer aches thinking of you the way it used to. I am now more than ever convinced that in spite of everything life is wonderful—and also very lovely. (Faiz 1985, 118)

This ebullience appears to have been real. Among those brought to Hyderabad with Faiz was Major Muhammad Ishaque, an old friend, who had been arrested on 27 April. He later remembered being 'relieved' when he saw Faiz for the first time in jail, after months of 'rumours and strange agonizing stories' about the brutal treatment he was receiving at the hands of the police. 'He had the same smiling face and the same glitter in his eyes,' Ishaque wrote. 'Around him was the same aura of the smiling Buddha and all-embracing love which is so familiar to all those who know him' (Ishaque 1989, 44).

For a brief time, this joy of 'human company' brought a spark of creativity. On June 14 Faiz wrote to Alys, 'I have just finished my sixth poem after being arrested. That means I have written twice as much in the past three months as I had written in the previous three years' (1985, 119). But soon inspiration was subsumed by constant talk of the upcoming tribunal, meeting with lawyers, preparing for a defence. '[It] becomes hard to engage in quiet reflection,' he told Alys. 'Besides, we are now busy preparing for the trial and there is little free time available' (ibid.). Once the trial began, however, Faiz's attention returned unexpectedly to his poetry. 'Human mind works so strangely!' he wrote to Alys on 24 June:

For the past three months my mind constantly worried about this case. But now that the case has started, I feel not the slightest interest in its proceedings. Again and again I remind myself that it's a very grave matter and that one should take it quite seriously. But my heart remains unaffected. It all appears like an unreal and totally silly play which will one day come to an end as suddenly, and without reason, as it started. Like my arrest and imprisonment, this case too has no cause or justification. (Ibid.)

Soon after the official commencement of the trial, Alys was notified that she could come to Hyderabad for her first visit, but before she could start out she received a telegram from Faiz saying only, 'Don't come yet.' Inside the prison, the accused men had been told that they could only see their families through an iron grate. The prisoners refused to leave their cells to attend the trial. After a brief standoff and interruption of the proceedings, the prisoners were allowed to see their families in locked meeting rooms monitored by two armed guards. All conversations would be transcribed (Faiz, Alys 1993, 50).

When Alys at last received word to come, she crossed the Sindh desert alone in the middle of summer in the crushing heat of a second class railcar until she arrived at last at the station and was taken to the jail gates.

> So this was Hyderabad and these were the grey prison walls, and here in the compound was the whipping post. I was to grow to know it all so well. The dreary Dāk bungalow, where the lawyers stayed and where food was cooked for us on payment. The cool desert breeze after nightfall. The Victoria carriage which would take me to the jail gates. The sound of the bolts being drawn, the small door through which I entered. The Superintendent's room, the arrival of the CID officers. The arrival of Prisoner No. 13. Can't you change your number? Make it 12B? Faiz laughed, and asked what difference a number made. It hardly did. (Ibid.,51)

After the first visit from Alys—with its mix of joy and longing—Faiz composed this *ghazal* of self-encouragement:

When time starts to heal memory's scars,
I make excuses to think of you for hours.

When the words of my beloved break into flower,
every woman begins to brush out her hair.

When I walk down your street, even now,
I see old friends in place of where strangers are.

When exiles whisper of their homelands to the wind,
tears fill the eyes of the morning hours.

When our lips are sewn closed,
the air rings still louder with these songs of ours.

When prison doors lock me behind night's bars,
inside my heart, O Faiz, it is bright with stars.

This poem is written in the strictly formal style of the Persian *ghazal*, attending to all the requirements of the form: the parallel structure (which translates as anaphora, though the reflexive structure of Urdu arranges those repetitions at the end of each couplet in the original), a rhyme introduced at the end of each of the first four lines and repeated at the end of each following couplet, and use of the poet's name in the final couplet. Other more stylistic conventions are also followed; the second line of each couplet complicates or contradicts the first line, and each individual couplet could potentially stand apart as its own poem.

Choosing this form, Faiz allies himself with a form that extends back to the seventh century. Hundreds of Persian poets—Hafiz and Rumi best known among them—wrote in this form from 1100 to 1500; its dominance as the major mode of love poetry in the region could be likened to the preponderance of love sonnets in English for the two hundred years following. Predominantly used for love poetry or for spiritual contemplation reached by drinking wine, the form is nevertheless almost always melancholy. The very name derives from what Kashmiri poet and Faiz translator Agha Shahid Ali called 'the cry of the gazelle when it is cornered in a hunt and knows it will die' (Ali 2000, 3). Aside from its topical history, the form also encourages grand associative leaps from one couplet to the next—a style that Ralph Waldo Emerson famously complained was like the unstrung beads of a necklace, but which Ali called 'ravishing disunities,' adding that despite their apparent disparity, 'there is a cultural unity—created by the audience's shared assumptions and expectations. There is a contrapuntal air' (see Padgett 1987, 87; Ali, 5). These shared assumptions create the specific context in which the poem is written; thus, it must be remembered that the poems of this period were written for three defined audiences: his fellow inmates, his friends and family on the outside, and the general readership of Pakistan. These audiences were not only aware of the long history that Faiz was writing in, but also the social moment he was describing. As such, the lyric gesture in these poems is not an expression of isolation, so much as recognition of a degree of intimacy beyond the need for exposition or even narrative.

Though it may seem hard to believe, prison officials at Hyderabad allowed Faiz to give readings to his fellow inmates twice a month.

Muhammad Ishaque, who lived in the cell next to Faiz's, was entrusted with bringing the poet's notebooks to each reading, a charge he carried out with great pomp and mock pageantry:

> When the other companions saw us walking in a procession, a wave of happiness used to spread all round. This was because in jail, the occasion of the recital of Faiz's fresh poetry was tantamount to a festival. Then we walked in a style that provided a humorous occasion for merriment. Faiz Sahib sauntering smilingly, anxiously and coyly trudging along and I, like a formidable villager, stiff necked, with my nose high up in the air, looking over the heads of others, proved quite a sight. Not until Faiz Sahib was seated and had been presented the book of verses with due decorum, did I relax or smile. (Ishaque 1989, 47)

These sessions may have begun with great humour, but the seriousness of Faiz's verses soon shifted the tone. Poem's like 'The Execution Yard (A Song)' were clearly intended to stoke the political fires of his fellow inmates:

> Where the road of longing leads us, we will see tomorrow.
> This night will pass, and this too we will see tomorrow.
> Don't fear, my heart; we will see day's shining face tomorrow.
> Let the drinker's thirst for wine slowly sharpen:
> we will see how long they deny the fierce grapevine tomorrow;
> we will see how long they refuse the cup and flask tomorrow.
> Let the summons come to the assembly from the Street of Scorn:
> we will see who is stopped by idle threats tomorrow;
> we will see who is strong enough to return tomorrow.
> Today men of heart go to test their spirits and their faith:
> let them bring an army of enemies, we will meet them tomorrow;
> let them come to the execution yard, we will join the spectacle
> tomorrow.
> No matter how heavy this last hour may seem, my friend:
> we will see the light hidden tonight shine brightly tomorrow;
> we will see the morning-star sparkle as today edges into
> tomorrow.

Though it may seem remarkable that guards allowed such poems to be read, Faiz was able to avoid repercussions by the use of certain stock images from Persian and Urdu poetry.

In 'The Execution Yard,' the familiar character of the drinker is positioned as the central figure of the poem, though he can clearly be read as the accused inmates. Likewise, calling for a summons 'to the assembly from the Street of Scorn' would appear to be a direct appeal for the people of Pakistan to revolt against the General Assembly, but, in fact, 'the assembly' and the 'Street of Scorn' are familiar tropes in Urdu poetry. As V.G. Kiernan writes:

> So much of the spirit and tone of Urdu poetry derives from Persian tradition that this ancestry must often be kept in mind, even when a poet like Faiz is alluding to quite contemporary matters. Verse forms and metres, besides diction, have helped to preserve continuity; and, still more strikingly, a common stock of imagery, which can be varied and recomposed inexhaustibly. (1971, 32)

Thus, the poem's tropes are predicated on a scheme of acknowledged fictions which Faiz then works to reshape into a new but still recognizable context. The assembly, familiar to readers as the fictive circle to which all poem's are recited, can double for the direct reference to the General Assembly. 'The poet's world,' writes Kiernan, 'is an imaginary city . . . [and] in this city there is always a *kū'e malāmat*, or 'Street of Reproach' (ibid., 34), which in earlier times referred to the wrong side of town where the prostitutes and dancers and poets lived, but which could be read more literally as the restless streets of Pakistan.

So effective was this subversion, that the censors permitted Alys to carry copies with her from Hyderabad, always with 'the pompous rubber stamp, 'Passed by the Censor, Rawalpindi Conspiracy Case Tribunal,' then the Registrar's signature, plus the date' (Faiz, Alys 1993, 45). When she returned, friends gathered to hear news of Faiz's well-being and listen to his latest poems. Alys remembered, that 'poems were copied as they came, and it was obvious to all that this was to prove the richest period in Faiz's poetry. Magazines vied for the poems, and they were bargained for, couplets were on everyone's lips' (ibid., 52). Though the rhetoric heated up within the sealed courtroom, Faiz grew increasingly serene. He joked with Alys on 2 July:

> I sometimes fear I might turn into a saint by the time I get out of the jail. Nothing bothers me. All the lies, the deceits, the false accusations which used to bother me so much in the past—now when I think of them I only laugh. In fact, in a way, I find delight in them. . . . These days, after the evening meal,

I teach my friends Ghalib's poetry. I find it very enjoyable. I don't mean to boast but I think I'm a very good teacher. I should never have left the job at the college and joined the army. Well, I'm now resolved that when this stupid case is all over, I shall only read and write. (1971, 32)

Though he often felt the urge to write during those first days of his confinement, it had been impossible for Faiz to preserve the poetry that came to him. Now he was able to record his memories of the experience in longer, more complex poems written in alternating rhymes, such as those in 'Ghazal':

> Among the sun's cooling embers, the evening star turns to cinder.
> Night unfurls its curtain, cloistering the devout.
> Will no one shout in defiance?—nearly a lifetime has passed,
> since heaven ordered the caravan of day and night driven out.
> To quell memories of friends and shared wine,
> they outlaw the moon by night and disallow the day its clouds.
> But the morning breeze comes again tapping the prison door:
> *Dawn is breaking—tell your heart not to doubt.* (1954, 49)

Such poems show his growing mastery and manipulation of the stock imagery of the evening star, wine drinkers, and the prison door. Faiz found prison life to be 'a fundamental experience' (1989, 29), which had the unexpected effect of focusing and concentrating his talents—an experience he later likened to being in love:

The first thing is that, like the dawn of love, all the sensations are again aroused and the mistiness of the early morning and evening, the blue of the sky, the gentleness of the breeze return with the same sense of wonder. And the second thing that happens is that the time and distances of the outside world are negated; the sense of distance and nearness is obliterated in such a way that a single moment weighs on the mind like the day of judgement and sometime [*sic*] the occurrences of a century seem to be like the happenings of yesterday. The third thing is that in the vastness of separation, one gets more time for reading and thinking and for decorating the bride of creativity. (Ibid.)

The trial, however, would prove gruelling. The accused were forced to spend 'hours of sitting as prisoners on our haunches before the Special Tribunal,' Syed Sajjad Zaheer later remembered, 'hearing the statements of the witnesses, the arguments of the lawyers, and the legal hair-splittings of the learned judges' (1989, 41). All the time they were aware of the Prime Minister's growing desire to see them executed; in their rallies, in government pamphlets, and in editorials run under banner headlines in special issues of newspapers, the men Ishaque called 'the toadies of the government' were 'demanding . . . our death by a firing squad' (Ishaque 1989, 45).

In mid-July, Faiz's brother Tufail came with his wife Sarwar and their two daughters to visit him at Hyderabad. Tufail had been unwell but was desperate to see his brother. The arduous journey by train across the desert, however, had taken its toll; on the morning of 18 July, while still in the city, Tufail suffered a fatal heart attack during his morning prayers. A call came to the *Pakistan Times,* and Mazhar, Faiz's replacement there as editor, was forced to tell Alys the news that Tufail had died from 'heartbreak' (Faiz, Alys 1993, 55). By all accounts, Faiz was never again completely lighthearted, and Ishaque believed that Tufail's death was the reason 'that in the latter part of *Dast-e Sabā,* there is no such abundance of passion and zest, which is found in the first part' (Ishaque 1989, 50).

Instead the poems of the middle period turn more toward poems of sorrow and remembrance. No longer defiant, poems such as 'These Days of Manacle and Stake' employ a different rhetorical strategy though they share formal similarities to the earlier poetry:

These days of waiting lie down every path.
These days of spring are not really the days of spring.
These days of praying for bread weigh on my heart.
These days of suffering test the beloved's beauty.
Bless the moment that brings a dear friend's face to mind:
these days quiet the disquieted heart.
When there is no wine, no one to share it, what use
these days of watching clouds move over the mountain?
If no friends are allowed, what good
these days when shadows dance among the cypress and chenar-trees?
The scars of my heart ached like this long ago, but now
these days away from friends are something different.
These days are days of ecstasy now, of manacle and stake now.
These days are days of free will now, of coercion now.
The cage is under your command, but you do not command
these days when the garden brightens into rose-fire.
No trap can stop the dervish of morning breezes.
These days of spring can't be made prisoner by a snare.

No matter that I can't see it myself. Others will see
these days of the brilliant garden and the singing nightingale.

The poet no longer challenges his oppressors, as he did in 'The Execution
Yard,' to 'bring an army of enemies, we will meet them tomorrow.'
The insistence of personal freedom has devolved now to asserting the
dominion of nature over the dictates of petty rulers. Faiz concedes now
that 'the cage is under your command' and that the august days of spring
would arrive and pass without him.

Then on 16 October 1951, the unexpected occurred. Just as Prime
Minister Liaquat Ali Khan was expected to make an important
announcement before a large crowd gathered at the Municipal Park
in Rawalpindi, he was assassinated by Saad Akbar. The assassin was
immediately riddled with bullets by the Prime Minister's bodyguards,
leading to speculation that his guards were party to the murder.

There was brief hope that Khan's death could be an opportunity to halt
the conspiracy trial. Progressives within Pakistan and around the world,
including Paul Robeson and Howard Fast in the United States, sent letters
to Nazimuddin to appeal for Faiz's release. Instead, scrutiny was stepped
up in the Rawalpindi Conspiracy; the fact that the murder took place in
Rawalpindi, after all, only seemed to confirm their guilt. On 28 October,
the day of their tenth wedding anniversary, Alys wrote to Faiz to tell him
that she was under constant surveillance:

> The general public censures the CID and the police very strongly for Liaquat's
> death and they in their turn circulate all kinds of rumours which no one of
> course believes. In the normal way, upon my return, the 'guests' are at the
> gate. Sitting two at a time, sometimes even three—and yet they couldn't save
> Liaquat! (Faiz 1985, 122)

Faiz sank deeper into despair, but once again he turned—through his
poetry—to remembrances of the past, rather than events of the day.
Most famously, he composed that summer a poem that would come
to symbolize Pakistan's long struggle for independence and true self-
rule. 'The Dawn of Freedom (August 1947)' turns back to the moment
of Partition and with knowledge of recent events asks whether the
'severing' of Partition was the solution to Muslim problems after all:

> This leprous daybreak, this night-bitten dawn.
> this is not the dawn we awaited with longing sighs;

this is not the dawn that drew our friends on
believing that, somewhere in the desert of these skies,
they would find the resting-place of the stars,
somewhere find where night's sluggish tides reach shore,
somewhere find the boat of heartache and drop anchor.

When we friends set out by the secret byways of youth
how many hands bid us stay, pulling at our hems!
From eager bedchambers in the palace of truth,
sweet arms kept crying out, flesh calling us to come;
but dearer was the seductive face of daylight,
dearer still her robe aglow with sprites:
my longing seemed to buoy me, my weariness grew light.
It is said that the division of day from night is done,
it is said our goals are realized and unflawed;
but only the ways of our hurtful leaders are new-sprung,
collective joy decreed, the anguish of separation outlawed.

The fire in our livers, the burning in our hearts, the riots in our eyes—
this severing cannot cure any of these.
When did that dear morning wind arrive—and must it go yet?
The lamps on these byroads have not left its breeze;
no one has come to lighten this night's heavy load yet,
our heart's inheritance has not been bestowed yet.
Come with me, come, our goal lies down the road yet.

Though clearly the most overtly political and direct poem of Faiz's prison
years, 'The Dawn of Freedom' still relies on a number of stock metaphors,
most significantly *hijr*—translated here as 'the anguish of separation.' As
Aamir Mufti eloquently argues:

> the desire for justice, the steadfastness in face of suffering and oppression, and
> the belief in a new dawn, are complicated by the 'partitioned' nature of the
> collective subject. In other words, the significance for me of Faiz's repeated
> use of *hijr* and of its derivatives is that it imbues the lyric experience of
> separation from the beloved with a concrete historical meaning—the parting
> of ways or leave-taking that is Partition. (1997, 202)

This notion began to surface even in Faiz's letters during this period.
Responding to Alys's anniversary letter, he wrote her on 30 October:

You have mentioned how alone you are. I know how hard it must be for you. How heavy must be these hours of separation. One can't wipe them off one's mind. But one can certainly lessen the pain by recalling how good were the days that are gone—and how good will be the days that shall come. At least, that's what I do. Since the day the gate of the jail was locked shut after me, I sometimes unravel the past to its very warp and woof. Then weave it together again in diverse manners. At other times, I try to catch the coming days in my imagination—then design with them all sorts of futures. It's a useless pastime—that I know. Dreams can never be set free from the chain of the realities. But at least for a short while one can use one's imagination to lift oneself out of the surrounding mire. Escapism is bad, but when one's hands and feet are tied down it's the only way to freedom. Thanks to such thoughts I now find the bars of the prison insignificant and illusory. Very often I don't even think of them. (Faiz 1985, 122–123)

This conflation of the beloved with the beloved country-through the conventional theme of *hijr*—allowed Faiz to take his familiar imagery to new heights. If the true country of Pakistan, 'the dawn we awaited with longing sighs,' has not yet arrived, then he may address his nation with the same sense of longing he feels for his absent wife. This union of the personal and political is most manifest in the poem 'Two Loves,' which begins with the extremely conventional gesture of addressing *Sāqī*, the wine-bearing muse of Persian poetry, in exclamatory declarations of love, before revealing midway the poem's central conceit:

Oh rose-like Sāqī, fresh yet in my memory
    are those days whose bright mirror still vibrates with her;
those moments we met, like an opening flower,
    the moments, like fluttering heartbeats, I waited for her-
Lo!—hope, roused by the sad heart's good luck;
    lo!—that love's night of heartache had come to end;
lo!—that those sleepless stars of sorrow were sinking,
    that promised joy so long dormant had awakened.

From this rooftop the sun of your beauty will rise,
    from that corner its rays red as henna will dawn,
from this doorway your steps like quicksilver will flow,
    by that pathway your twilit dress will blossom!
Fevered days too have I known, separation's pangs,
    when lament was forgotten in the soul's sorrow,

each night's dark load so heavy, the heart was crushed,
    each morning's flame piercing it like an arrow.

In solitude, how could I keep from thinking of you?
    What refuges did my sad heart not seek?
Sometimes I felt the hand of the morning-breeze on my brow,
    sometimes I put my arms around the moon's neck.

II

In this same way I have loved my darling country;
    in this same way my heart has pounded with devotion to her;
in this same way my passion has sought the respite of a resting-place,
    in the curve of her cheek, in the curls of her hair.

In this same way, to that sweetheart world, my heart and eyes
    have called out with laughter, cried out with tears.
All the demands of her summons I have fulfilled;
    I made light every pain and calmed every fear.
No bidding toward ecstasy ever went unheeded,
    never did the bell's echo return to the tower alone.
The heart's ease, creature comforts, a station in life,
    all the connivers shrewd advice, forgotten.

What befalls all travellers on that road befell me,
    a solitary prison cell, my name ridiculed in the market;
self-anointed holy men from their pulpits thundered,
    dictators roared from their seats of power.
No treacherous arrows were spared me by strangers,
    no scorn was omitted by those most esteemed,
but my heart feels shame neither for this love nor that love;
there is every scar on this heart but the scar of shame.

By using only loose rhyme and discarding the incantatory traditional
forms he had previously favoured, Faiz places the emphasis firmly on his
subject matter—the division of the lover from the beloved in section one
and the division of the beloved country in section two. The poem is not
only literally partitioned into halves, but the middle octave is cleft for
the dramatic effect of interrupting the lover at the height of his fervour–
asking: 'What refuges did my sad heart not seek?'—in order to insert:
'In this same way I have loved my darling country; in this same way my

heart has pounded with devotion to her.' The insistent repetition of 'in this same way' conjures the *ghazal*, but in this case the parallel structure is used to emphasize the thematic similarities of the two halves of the poem. As the poem closes, Faiz returns to the defiant stance of his earliest prison poems, claiming that though he is confined to 'a solitary prison cell, my name ridiculed in the market,' his heart 'feels shame neither for this love nor that love'—meaning the love of his wife nor the love of his unrealized dream for post-Partition Pakistan.

The late poems of *Dast-e Sabā*, composed in the first nine months of 1952, thus, become its most fully realized. Relying less on traditional structures and predetermined rhetorical turns, the poems aspire to more imagistic inventiveness and are, at times, strikingly unpredictable, as in the poem, 'Prison Nightfall':

> Rung by rung, night descends
> its spiral staircase of stars.
> A breeze passes gently by,
> as if words of love had been whispered.
> Trees in the prison courtyard, like exiles
> with heads bowed, are absorbed
> in embroidering arabesques on the skirt of the sky.
> On the crested roof are glittering
> the beautiful fingers of moonlight,
> dissolving star-shine into dust
> and washing the blue sky into white.
> In the green corners, dark shadows collide
> as if the ache of separation
> might eddy and fill my mind.
>
> But one thought keeps running through my heart—
> how sweet these moments are. Though
> there are those who may concoct tyranny's poisons,
> they will have no victories, not today or tomorrow.
> So what if they douse the candles in rooms
> where lovers meet? If they're so mighty,
> let them snuff out the moon.

In describing the Spanish poets of this same era, Robert Bly has written, 'Difficult poetry of the true and vigorous sort does not move from idea to idea, from mind to mind, but moves from the anguished emotions to the intellect and back' (2001, XV). A poem like 'Prison Nightfall' is exactly what he means. The poem is far from narrative, but its tropes link in intuitive linear ways—what Hart Crane called 'lyric logic'—so that the images are neither scattered like beads from an unstrung necklace, nor strung too tightly together. After this impressionistic succession, the poet feels as if *hijr* ('the ache of separation') 'might eddy and fill my mind.' Again the mention of separation, the invisible spectre of Partition, moves the poem from the personal to the political.

Interestingly the closure of 'Prison Nightfall' returns to the rhetorical turn of 'These Days of Manacle and Stake,' but with greater success. Here the poet allows that rulers may be able to 'douse the candles in rooms where lovers meet,' as he granted earlier that 'the cage is under your command.' However, rather than baldly asserting 'you do not command these days when the garden brightens into rose-fire,' comparing their small power to nature directly, Faiz instead challenges these rulers to demonstrate their superiority: 'If they're so mighty, let them snuff out the moon.' The parallel structure is more fully realized as well—showing their power over a candle but not the moon, rather than over a prison cell but not the rose garden.

The promise of these stylistic advances in the last poems of *Dast-e Sabā* is fulfilled in the poem, 'Bury Me Under Your Streets.' Shuttling brilliantly from rhetoric to image, from argumentation to emotional evocation, it moves, as Bly says the best difficult poems do, 'from the anguished emotions to the intellect and back':

> Bury me under your streets, O my beloved country,
> where today men dare not pass with heads held high,
> or where lovers of you who wish to pay tribute,
> must fear for their lives and come around on the sly.
>> Good men suffer this new law and decree
>> where stones are locked up and dogs run free.
>
> It is too much for tyranny's trigger-happy hand,
> if your name is invoked even by extremists.
> When power-starved men are both accuser and judge,
> who will defend us, where can we seek justice?
>
>> But man somehow spends the days he must spend,
>> away from you, as mornings come and evenings end.

As the prison grating darkens, my heart remembers
that somewhere under these stars, you brush out your braids.
When the links of my chain begin to shine, I think
that somewhere day breaks over your sleeping face.
    I live, in short, in the fantasies of nightfall and dawn;
    I live in the shadow of walls, in the gate's closed palm.

This is the same war tyrants and true men have always fought;
their tactics are not new, and neither are ours.
They have always set fires and we turn them to flowers;
their tricks are not new, and neither are ours.

    That's why I don't complain about my fate;
    or let my imprisoned heart start to quake.
If today I am away from you, tomorrow we'll be together;
this separation of one night is nothing to us.
If today our enemies ride high, playing god, so what?–
their reign of four days is nothing to us.
    Only those who hold to their vows under such scrutiny
    are safe from night-and-day's endless mutiny.

The poem's opening phrase, 'Bury me under your streets,' means literally, 'let me be a sacrifice to your streets' (*Nisār maiṅ tērī galyoṅ kē*). A common Urdu phrase ('Let me be a sacrifice to—') is usually completed by some expression of religious devotion, but here Faiz uses the structure ironically, preferring to be a sacrifice not to some higher power but to the streets of his beloved country. Stanza two continues with the direct address of poet to his country, but stanza three shifts to the personal and the addressee is now the beloved, whom the poet imagines in her bedchamber and he sits confined in his cell. Stanza four seems to return to addressing the country, but in the concluding stanza five, that shift is called into question. The climactic lines—'If today I am away from you, tomorrow we'll be together; this separation of one night is nothing to us'—can be read equally literally as an assurance to the poet's lover or to his country. The 'reign of four days' would seem to apply most directly to the four years of Pakistani government, but even this is reduced to the human level of two lovers separated by but a few days. The final couplet puns on the word 'vows,' meaning either marriage vows or vows of allegiance to the mother country, and asserts that these principles alone are enough to undo 'night-and-day's endless mutiny.' Returning again to the natural world, Faiz implies that mere men cannot 'snuff out the moon,' but those who hold to their vows of love will survive the succession of daybreaks and nightfalls and the succession of nation-states.

On 22 December, *Dast-e Sabā* was released at a well-attended ceremony at the Argentina Hotel in Lahore. The book begins with a short introduction by Faiz himself, a small polemical on the responsibility of the artist. Though he never overtly mentions the circumstances of his arrest or imprisonment, he wonders whether Ghalib's famous statement that 'an eye which cannot perceive an ocean in a drop of water is not a discerning eye' would not now bring him under scrutiny as 'a supporter of propaganda in literature. If instructing a poet to perceive an ocean in a drop is not an obvious attempt at propaganda, then what else is it?' Faiz, however, asserts that mere perception of a hidden ocean is no longer enough:

> The poet's work is not only perception and observation, but also struggle and effort. A full comprehension of this ocean of Life through the live and active 'drops' of his environment depends upon the poet's depth of perception. To be able to show this ocean to others depends upon his control over his art; and his ability to set in motion some new currents in the ocean depends upon the fire in his blood and the zeal of his passion. Success in all three tasks demands continuous toil and struggle. (1963, 3–4)

Within the walls of Hyderabad, the prisoners also learned of the publication of *Dast-e Sabā*. Syed Sajjad Zaheer remembered that 'we had heard these poems from the lips of Faiz himself and had also read them repeatedly, but all those prisoners who had a literary taste were overjoyed at the publication of the volume' (1989, 41). The inmates obtained permission from the prison officials to throw a party. Though the outcome of their trial was increasingly certain, they celebrated that some part of their story would be known. Within a few months all fifteen men charged in the Rawalpindi Conspiracy trial were convicted of crimes of varying seriousness. Though none in the end were sentenced to death, all were eventually sentenced to additional years in prison, including Faiz who would not be officially freed until his sentence expired in April 1955.

Many years later, however, Zaheer refused to dwell on the particularities of the trial or his imprisonment; he insisted:

Long after the people forget all about the Rawalpindi Conspiracy Case, the Pakistani historian, when he comes across the important events of 1952, will consider the publication of this small book of poems as a most important historical event.

Notes

1. For Hernandez's poetry see, Genoways 2001.
2. For Stonov's short stories see, Stonov and Darrell 1995.
3. 'How a Poet Escapes Censorship,' Dawn, 13 March 1984< http://dawn.com/events/ Mughal/1984.htm>
4. All translations are my own, based on the literal translations available in V.G. Kiernan's text and literary translations by Kiernan, Agha Shahid Ali, Shiv K. Kumar, and Naomi Lazard.
5. Zaheer (1998) reprints the entire Act, 305–309.

Works Cited

Adorno, T.A., 'Lyric Poetry and Society,' Telos 20, Summer (1974): 56–71, Print.

Ali, Agha Shahid (ed.), Ravishing Disunities: Real Ghazals in English, Middleton, Conn: Wesleyan University Press, 2000, Print.

Bly, R. 'Preface,' The Selected Poems of Miguel Hernandez: A Bilingual Edition, ed. Ted Genoways, Chicago: University of Chicago, 2001, Print.

Faiz, Faiz Ahmed, Dast-e Sabā, Amritsar: Azad Book Depot, 1954, Print.

'Introduction to Dast-e Sabā,' Mahfil: A Quarterly Magazine of South Asian Literature I (I) 1963: 3–4, Web.

'Faiz to Alys to Faiz: Some Prison Letters,' Annual of Urdu Studies 5 (1985): 117–125, Print.

Husain, Imdad (ed.), 'Faiz on Faiz: From Dast-e Tah-e Sang,' An Introduction to the Poetry of Faiz Ahmed Faiz, Lahore: Vanguard, 1989, Print.

Faiz, Alys, Over My Shoulder, Lahore: Rahmat Shah Afridi, 1993, Print.

Forche, C. (ed.), Against Forgetting: Twentieth-Century Poetry of Witness, New York: W.W. Norton & Co., 1993, Print.

Genoways, Ted (ed.), The Selected Poems of Miguel Hernandez: A Bilingual Edition, Chicago: University of Chicago, 2001, Print.

Ishaque, M., 'The Story of the Prison House', in Introduction to the Poetry of Faiz Ahmed Faiz, ed. Imdad Husain, Lahore: Vanguard, 1989, Print.

Kiernan, V.G. (ed.), Poems by Faiz, London: George Allen & Unwin, 1971, Print.

London Times, 10 March 1951, Print.

Mufti, A.R., Enlightenment in the Colony: The Jewish Question and Dilemmas in Post-Colonial Modernity, PhD Diss., Columbia University, 1997, Print.

Orr, G., Poetry as Survival, Athens: University of Georgia, 2002, Print.

Padgett, R. (ed.), The Teachers and Writers Handbook of Poetic Forms, New York: Teachers and Writers Collaborative, 1987, Print.

Darrell, Kathryn and Stonov, Natasha S. (eds.), In the Past Night: The Siberian Stories of Dmitry Stonov, Lubbock: Texas Tech University Press, 1995, Print.

Zaheer, Hasan, *The Times and Trial of the Rawalpindi Conspiracy 1951: The First Coup Attempt in Pakistan*, Karachi: Oxford University Press, 1998, Print.

Zaheer, Syed Sajjad, 'Foreword to Zindāṅ Nāmā', in *An Introduction to the Poetry of Faiz Ahmed Faiz*, ed. Imdad Husain, Lahore: Vanguard, 1989, Print.

FREEDOM'S DAWN

Original: *Subh-e āzādī* from *Dast-e Sabā* (1952)

TRANSLATORS: BAIDAR BAKHT AND KATHLEEN GRANT JAEGER

This pock-marked daylight, this morning that reeks of night.
Is not the morning we looked for
Is not the morning the good companions longed for
When they set forth across the wasteland by starlight,
Seeking the shore of night's dead ocean,
Some anchorage for the vessels of grief.

Starting out, those friends
Found traps on young blood's mysterious highways;
Allurements called from the land of pleasure,
Arms beckoned, lips blew a kiss.
But the face of morning was their heart's desire,
The thighs of daylight gleamed near.
Tense with desire, they knew nothing of weariness.

People say that the light and the darkness are parted.
People say that feet and destination have met.
The afflicted are far better off, people say.
The pleasures of union are blessed,
The rigours of parting forbidden.

That fire in their hearts, that longing in their eyes
This 'blessed union' will never assuage.
When did the breeze of morning rise,
Where did it go?
On the roadside the lamp glows, just the same.
The night hangs heavy, just the same.
Our hearts and eyes still look for salvation,
Let us move on now,
We have yet to arrive.

18

FAIZ GAVE US THE LIVING WORD*

What are the criteria with which to judge a poet? Where does he stand in our history? What part did he play in moulding our minds and in enriching our culture? Where does he stand in our *poetic tradition? What was his message? How did he relate* himself to his milieu? How did he relate himself to humanity? What manner of man was he? This last question is answered first by Professor Karrar:

Faiz was a great man and since he was a great man, he was a great poet.

After this, Professor Karrar gives a brief outline of the Urdu poetic tradition:

There are three main strands—the *qasidā*, the *masnavī* and the *ghazal*. *Qasidā* was the poetry of the court. It was not so much about monarchs as about monarchy. In the *masnavī* came the *dāstān*, the *qissā* and the work of the *sufis*. *Ghazal* is the central strand of the poetic tradition in Urdu poetry. To the *ghazal*, which is the soul of the Indo-Muslim culture, Faiz gave a new lease of life. The soul of Indo-Muslim culture was love. Love outside of your self. The *ghazal* rejects deceit and pride and simulation and dissimulation, and keeping up appearances. The *ghazal* represents universal brotherhood, but this brotherhood is God-centred. But there was a kind of passivity in this brotherhood in classical Urdu poetry. Since the *ghazal* grew up as a genre in mediaeval India, it was pervaded with a great deal of fatalism. There was repression and there was nothing you could do about it. The world was as it was and there was nothing you could do to change it. The Indo-Muslim culture that grew up around the *ghazal*, rejected pomp and ceremony and tended to accept things as they were. There was a conscious attempt, however, to achieve chastity and accuracy in expression. Sufism became a rigorously practiced vocation and you worked equally hard to achieve catholicity in culture.

Desire for Change

When poetic sensibility turned away from this classical tradition, acceptance of things as they were, gave way to a desire for things as they ought to be. The fatalism of the classicists was replaced by the optimism of the inheritors of the classical tradition. Not for them the pessimism, that the world could not change. Change was possible, achievable. Even faith began to give way to ideology and poets began to dream of putting a stop to repression. Acceptance of things as they were, was replaced by a commitment to social change. Now poets began to dream of revolution, of peace.

Look at Faiz against this background. He retains chastity and accuracy and the music of expression, but with the beauty of expression is born a new purpose, a new direction. The imagery is the same but Faiz gives it new meaning, new power. A tradition survives if it lends itself to internal change but when it shuts itself against change, it dies.

How to evaluate this internal change? One way, according to Professor Karrar Husain, is to make a comparative study of great poets. The poetic tradition was trudging along the beaten path when Iqbal appeared on the scene. He deviated from it and set up a magnificent structure in the manner of Milton's Paradise Lost. After Iqbal, it was impossible for the *ghazal* to remain the same. Change had started with Ghalib but not to the extent that Iqbal wrought. But Iqbal spoke to his people from a pedestal. He even admonished them, sometimes with affection, sometimes in anger. Faiz, on the other hand, is one of us. Let us go, he says, and he doesn't go alone. There's great love, great acceptance in Faiz, of fellow human beings.

Iqbal's Worldview of Islam

Iqbal takes a worldview of Islam and, gathering building material from various sources, sets up an imposing structure. At places, there is complete integration between philosophy and verse and at places verse gives in to philosophy. This gives birth to contradictions. Sometimes he even becomes paradoxical. He does all this in order to achieve a certain objective, but in order to do so, he deviates from the Urdu tradition. You can now think of Hafiz, Urfi, and Naziri but not of the Urdu tradition. T.S. Eliot once said of Milton that he wrote no language. Professor Karrar recalled, and returned to Faiz.

Faiz is committed to an ideology but this ideology does not stand up and bite. There is a complete fusion of vision and ideology in Faiz. He rejuvenates both language and imagery. A poet is an artist also, only the material he uses are words. He considers the limitless possibilities of words. The call for revolution had been given before Faiz by Majaz and Josh. But there was much romanticism in it. Revolution was part of romanticism in Majaz. Josh was a giant among men. Very lovable, with childlike innocence. Even his love is the love of the revolutionary. But in Faiz, there is as much concern for the beloved as for the world in which he lives. In Iqbal it is different. His theory of love is different. In his crusade, he forgets that woman too, lives on earth. This is so with Milton. Both ignore woman in a manner that it becomes a problem for them in the end.

To be a Worthwhile Poet

To be a worthwhile poet in Urdu, knowledge of the Persian tradition and at least one European language, preferably English, is necessary. And if you are thinking of the Hereafter, a smattering of Arabic, too, wouldn't be such a bad idea. Those who seriously aspire to become poets would do well to read Sufi poetry from the Punjab and Sind and elsewhere.

Faiz and his generation were influenced by the English romantic poets, particularly Byron and Shelley. If you are shallow, you are swept off your feet by this kind of external influence. You cannot just quote this French critic or the other as you are quoting from the scriptures and be done with it. Living criticism is always in response to a living problem. Europe has lived through the era of affluence. The Industrial Age is gone. Today, Europe is in the post-Industrial age. And the Europeans have seen through the meaninglessness and the absurdity of crass materialism. They have lived through wars and the world stands again on the verge of disaster. But materialism still has a great deal of attraction for us. We are following it like men possessed.

Commitment

This is not the case with Faiz. In him, there is commitment for a certain objective but with detachment, at a distance away from his own self. This is *jihād* (struggle) with an insight, an objective. Struggle without purpose is violence. If there is no purpose, no meaning, no objective to and for your struggle, it means you don't have a spine. In Faiz, language changes of its own and merges into thought.

What was his message? This is a very beautiful world and when you realize that this is a beautiful world, you begin to have a certain sanctity for your own body. It becomes something sacred. And love is the spring of this beautiful world. When you realize this, you ask yourself: What has man done to man? What sort of repression is this? Your body, your honour, your faith, everything is for sale. If you want to keep your faith intact, you have to sell your body. All this makes Faiz greatly sad, but out of this sorrow is born love for the immortal man, man who will never perish. He does not pity the disinherited. He respects them for they are the inheritors of history. The meek shall inherit the earth. They are not the dispossessed. Sovereignty belongs to them and Faiz identifies himself with them. He is certain that repression will disappear one day. Be on their side if you can, so that the world really becomes beautiful and the dignity of man is revived. Humankind has been dishonoured. And then he invites them: The way to victory is difficult and dangerous but that is what will make the final triumph that much sweeter. This is the sum total of his message.

Patriotism

One last thing: How is Faiz related to his milieu? There are many who claim, they are the ultimate patriots. What sort of patriotism is this? Patriotism means love for the people and not for a piece of land. War propaganda is not patriotism. It has brought much misery to the world. This kind of patriotism is a crime against humanity. Love for the motherland should mean identification with the pain and misery of the people, with the desire to improve their quality of life. What is all this talk about *jihād*? The first pre-requisite is the establishment of a polity based on justice and harmony. There is no moral merit in self-defence per se. If one of you dies, he is a martyr and if one dies on the other side, he is dispatched to hell. There is a distinction that the poets make between caprice and love. What do men who love, have to do with men who covet?

The Living Word

The short-sighted think that survival lies in affluence and in arms. The fact is that when nations are about to fall, there never is dearth of affluence. After all, India was called the golden sparrow when it was gobbled up by the imperialists. A nation which does not have the living word is not a nation. We are grateful to Faiz because he gave us the living word and it was heard by the whole world. We identify ourselves with Faiz.

Note

* From notes of the First Faiz Memorial Lecture, Faiz Foundation, Lahore, 6 February 1985. The name of the transcriber is not mentioned. This writing was also later reproduced in *Lotus*, Issue 59, 1988.

IN YOUR OCEAN EYES

Original: *Jab tērī samandar āṅkhoṅ meṅ* from *Dast-e Tah-e Saṅg* (1965)
Translator: Shiv Kumar

The fringe of day, dusk
where the two hours of time meet—
neither night nor day, neither today nor tomorrow.
One moment eternal, another just smoke—
on this day's fringe, for a moment or two
the fervour of lips,
the ardour of arms,
this union of ours, neither true nor false.
Why say a false thing.
When in your ocean eyes
will sink this evening's sun
then everyone will sleep blissfully in his house
and the traveller will wend his way.

19

SOCIALISTS*

Socialist verse, though quite abundant, is seldom high in quality. Any ideology is good enough for poetry, provided it is supported by adequate art. The greater part of socialist verse is deficient in this respect. It suffers from another limitation as well: it is written according to a formula which circumscribes the poet's range. Life is wider than any creed, however comprehensive, and when a poet ties himself down to a prescribed code, he forfeits his freedom and limits his range. Literature, when it hedges itself with 'isms' and ideologies, surrenders its birthright, namely, to express freely the entire personality of the writer. Lest this be construed as an acrimonious approach to socialist poetry, I hasten to point out that this was no less the bane of communal and nationalist poetry that was being written before the Partition.

Very pertinent in this respect is Jazbi's advice to his associates. He writes:

> Engles is of the opinion that the more hidden a poet's social and political views, the more appealing they would be. As viewed by him, the real object of the writer is to eradicate certain superstitions and create doubt in regard to the eternal validity of the present order. And this can also be done without presenting a direct solution of the point at issue to the reader. And in some cases, it is not necessary to suggest with whom the author's sympathies lie.
>
> For some time past, there has grown a tendency in the Progressive writers which is largely based on narrow-mindedness. Our poets and writers have begun to think that to write of beauty and love is a sin in the Progressive writers' religion which may not be forgiven. Progressive is only another name for politics, and outside it, whatever enters literature is anti-Progressive. If this trend takes root, our writers would continue to shrink more and more.

The course of Progressive writing shows that this counsel of perfection has been studiously ignored.

I remember someone once telling me that according to the official socialist formula, love is a bourgeoise sentimentality. If this be true, and a socialist must rise above this most common human frailty, then Faiz Ahmed Faiz is no better than an outsider; for with him the worship of beauty at the purely physical level is the be-all and end-all of life. The function of Faiz as a poet is to celebrate beauty, dwell on its charm and bask in its sunshine. Like the English poet Rossetti, he is enthralled by it, but whereas with Rossetti, the flesh is the symbol of a higher reality and a stepping-stone to it, with Faiz it is the ultimate reality. He is of the sense sensuous. Notice with what joy he lingers on the human body, its form and shape and contours—the soft shapely arms, cheeks, eyes, hands, lips. He is also intensely alive to colour and light, but these sensations, too, for the most part, pertain to the human body and such appurtenances as clothes, ornaments, or such aids to beauty as henna, rouge, antimony, etc. He is one of love's lovers, and to portray that glamorous world, he has a set of images which he uses with success in that world.

The difficulty arose when he turned socialist, adding a new province to his verse. With this new theme, so different from his earlier interest, he should have evolved a style appropriate to it. This is what Faiz failed to do. In fact, so great was the obsessive force of his erotic imagery that he applied it whole-sale to his socialist verse. Let his theme be what it may, he insensibly slips into that dream world. Consequently, in Faiz's socialist verse, there is often a clash between style and subject matter. In fact, the style interferes with the latter and dissipates the effect he is eager to produce. The female image is everywhere in one form or another, with its motion, and colour, and accessories. This imagery, which is in place in his love poetry is felt to be an intruder in his socialist verse.

To illustrate how his engrossing interest in the female image or human body in general dominates his imagination and gets the better of his judgement, I would refer the reader to two of his poems, *Ham jo tārīk rāhoṅ mēṅ mārē ga'ē* (We who were Killed in Darksome Ways) and *Mērē hamdam mērē dost* (My Companion, my Friend).

In the first, Freedom is apostrophized as a beautiful woman. The poem is for all practical purposes a *ghazal* in which the steadfast and adoring lovers dwell on her beauty as love's martyrs. So great is the emphasis on her tantalizing charms and their unsatisfied yearnings and travail that the reader is likely to miss the horror and pity of the situation. Here are the opening verses of the poem:

تیرے ہونٹوں کے پھولوں کی چاہت میں ہم
دار کی خشک ٹہنی پہ وارے گئے
تیرے ہاتھوں کی شمعوں کی حسرت میں ہم
نیم تاریک راہوں میں مارے گئے
سُولیوں پر ہمارے لبوں سے پَرے
تیرے ہونٹوں کی لالی لپکتی رہی
تیری زلفوں کی مستی برستی رہی
تیرے ہاتھوں کی چاندی دمکتی رہی

In our longing for the flower of thy lips
We were crucified on the dry branches of a gibbet.
On gibbets—away from our lips,
The redness of thy lips continued to glow;
The intoxication of thy ringlets rained fragrance;
The silver of thy hands continued to gleam.

More interesting still is *Mērē hamdam mērē dost*. It shows how on the slightest excuse, love, the *leitmotiv* of his verse, comes to the forefront and monopolizes attention.

روز و شب، شام و سحر میں تجھے بہلاتا رہوں

میں تجھے گیت سنا تا رہوں ہلکے شیریں

آبشاروں کے، بہاروں کے، چمن زاروں کے گیت

آمدِ صبح کے، مہتاب کے، سیاروں کے گیت

تجھ سے میں حسن و محبت کی حکایات کہوں،

کیسے مغرور حسیناؤں کے برفاب سے جسم

گرم ہاتھوں کی حرارت میں پگھل جاتے ہیں

کیسے اک چہرے کے ٹھہرے ہوئے مانوس نقوش

دیکھتے دیکھتے یک لخت بدل جاتے ہیں

کس طرح عارضِ محبوب کا شفاف بلور

یک بیک بادہءاحمر سے دہک جاتا ہے

کیسے گلچیں کے لئے جھکتی ہے خود شاخِ گلاب

کس طرح رات کا ایوان مہک جاتا ہے

یونہی گاتا رہوں، گاتا رہوں تیری خاطر

گیت بنتا رہوں، بیٹھا رہوں تیری خاطر

Day and night, morn and evening, I would entertain thee;
Sing thee songs, light and sweet—
Songs of waterfalls, springtide, gardens;
Songs celebrating dawn, morn, and planets.
Tell thee stories of love and beauty;
How the snow-white bodies of proud damsels
Melt with the heat of hands,
How the restful familiar features of a face
Undergo a sudden change?
How the transparent glass of the sweetheart's cheek
Becomes suddenly aglow with red wine;
How the rose bough itself bends for the rose gatherer,
And the hall of night is filled with fragrance;
Thus will I sing and sing to thee;
Sit weaving songs for thee.

Faiz wrote the poem to say that not by dallying with poetry, but by strong self-effort (the use of hands) alone, we can break the chains that bind us. But while dilating on the theme, his predominant sex interest asserts itself and he gets absorbed in it for its own sake. Faiz is surely adept in love's arena, and his findings are, no doubt, revealing. But surely, this is no place for them. It is significant that while he slurs over the other objects that might interest the reader, he luxuriates in those pertaining to sex. Fine as these lines are, they are, strictly speaking, irrelevant.

This is not to underrate Faiz or deny that he has some very strong points. He has an eye for colour and his poems are full of images that sparkle and coruscate. He is also alive to sense impressions related to eye, ear, touch, and smell, although they have a limited range, revolving round human body or my lady's boudoir. He has also a capacity for felicitous and concentrated epithets. His words are aptly chosen and have a strong pictorial quality; sometimes single words flashing forth, whole pictures:

ان دِسکتے ہوئے شہروں کی فراواں مخلوق

کیوں فقط مرنے کی حسرت پہ جیا کرتی ہے

The teeming millions of these gleaming cities–
Why are they consumed by a longing for death?

Or take the following. Here are hard, incisive, rasping images that have the force of strong physical impact:

سالہا سال یہ بے آسرا جکڑے ہوئے ہاتھ

رات کے سخت و سیہ سینے میں پیوست رہے

جس طرح تنکا سمندر سے ہو سرگرم ستیز

جس طرح تیتری کہسار پہ یلغار کرے

اوراب رات کے سنگین و سیہ سینے میں

اتنے گھاؤ ہیں کہ جس سمت نظر جاتی ہے

جا بجا نور نے اک جال سا بُن رکھا ہے

دور سے صبح کی دھڑکن کی صدا آتی ہے

For years on end, these helpless manacled hands
Grappled with the hard black breast of the night.
It was like a bit of straw warring with the sea,
Or a butterfly attacking a mountain,
And now in the hard black breast of the night
There are so many gashes
That look where you like,
There is a network of light.
And from afar you hear the heart-beats of the morning.

حسنِ محبوب کے سیالِ تخیل کی طرح

اپنی تاریکی کو بھینچے ہوئے لپٹائے ہوئے

Like the fluid image of the beauty of the beloved
Hugging their darkness to their hearts and clinging to it.

One of his most successful poems is 'Africa Come Back'. Here, the language is creative and the images powerful and luminous. It was composed in an exultant mood, the subject being the awakening of Africa from its age-long stupor into full vigour. Note how well all this is reflected in the stately rhythm, reminding one of a triumphal march. Another poem, equally successful and one of the finest lyrics in the language is *Yād* (Remembrance) composed in jail.

دشتِ تنہائی میں اے جانِ جہاں لرزاں ہیں

تیری آواز کے سائے، ترے ہونٹوں کے سراب

دشتِ تنہائی میں، دوری کے خس و خاک تلے

کھل رہے ہیں ترے پہلو کے سمن اور گلاب

اٹھ رہی ہے کہیں قربت سے تری سانس کی آنچ

اپنی خوشبو میں سلگتی ہوئی مدھم مدھم

دور — افق پار، چمکتی ہوئی قطرہ قطرہ

گر رہی ہے تری دلدار نظر کی شبنم

اس قدر پیار سے اے جانِ جہاں رکھا ہے

دل کے رخسار پہ اس وقت تری یاد نے ہات

یوں گماں ہوتا ہے، گرچہ ہے ابھی صبحِ فراق

ڈھل گیا ہجر کا دن، آ بھی گئی وصل کی رات

In the desert of loneliness are trembling
The shadows of thy voice and the miracle of thy lips.
In the desert of loneliness, beneath the rubbish, dust, and loneliness
Are blossoming the roses and jasmine of thy side.
I seem to feel somewhere near me the warmth of thy breath,
Kindling gently in its fragrance.
Far off beyond the horizon, glistening drop by drop

Falls the dew from thy enchanting eyes.
Life of life so lovingly hast thy memory now
Laid its hand on the heart's cheek
That despite its being the morn of separation, I have begun to feel
That the day of separation has declined,
And the night of union has already come.

His most intriguing poem is *Tanhā'ī* (Loneliness). Neither in its treatment
nor theme is it a typical Faiz poem; for his poetry for all its sombre
shadows is streaked with light; and here we have the quintessence of
despair. In form and treatment it reminds one of Walter de la Mare's
Listeners. What did Faiz have in mind while composing it? Is it no more
than the transcript of an experience, or has it a deeper meaning? As I see
it, it is built on two complementary ideas; first, that the genius of the East
has exhausted itself and is not likely to have a new lease of life; second,
that the old landmarks have disappeared under the pressure of foreign
domination. The last verse clinches his gloomy forebodings. As hinted
above, the poem is no more than the expression of a mood, for Faiz, as a
socialist, believes in the ultimate triumph of his cause.

The poem is a masterpiece of economy and suggestion. Especially
remarkable is the way in which, with three bold images, the dying
candles, the dusty road, and the vanishing stars, he has created an
atmosphere of tense and prolonged expectancy, ending in utter despair.
Here is the poem:

پھر کوئی آیا دلِ زار ! نہیں، کوئی نہیں   سو گئی راستہ تک تک کے ہر اک راہگزار

راہرو ہوگا، کہیں اور چلا جائے گا   اجنبی خاک نے دھندلا دیۓ قدموں کے سراغ

ڈھل چکی رات بکھرنے لگا تاروں کا غبار   گل کرو شمعیں، بڑھا دو مے و مینا و ایاغ

لڑکھڑانے لگے ایوانوں میں خوابیدہ چراغ   اپنے بے خواب کواڑوں کو مقفل کر لو

اب یہاں کوئی نہیں، کوئی نہیں آۓ گا

Sore heart of mine! Has someone come again?
No, none, O none!
Some wayfarer perhaps; he will go somewhere else.
The night is far advanced,
The dust of stars has begun to disperse.
The lamps all sleepy
Stars flickering in the hall;

And tired of their long vigil the roads have gone to sleep.
The alien dust has bedimmed the footprints.
Put out the candle, remove the wine, the wine bottle and the cup.
And your sleepless doors, make fast,
No one, no one will come here now!

It is interesting to compare it with Hardy's *Nobody Comes*:

The leaves labour up and down
And through them the fainting light
Succumbs to the crawl of night
Outside in the road the telegraph wires
To the town from the darkening land,
Intone to travellers like spectral lyre
Swept by a spectral hand.
A car comes up, with lamps full-glare,
That flash upon a tree;
It has nothing to do with me,
And hangs along in a world of its own,
Leaving a blacker air;
And mute by the gate I stand again alone,
And no one pulls up there.

Note

* Excerpt from 'Twentieth Century Urdu Literature'.

LAST NIGHT YOUR LOST MEMORY . . .

Original: *Rāt yūṅ dil mēṅ terī kho'ī hu'ī yād ā'ī* from *Naqsh-e Faryādī* (1941)
TRANSLATOR: MAHMOOD JAMAL

Last night your lost memory
Came to me
As spring comes quietly upon a wilderness
As a cool breeze
blows gently across desert sands
As a sick man
without reason finds relief.

20

FAIZ

Is it really possible to write about Faiz? To encompass in a few pages what was really a lifetime spent near him, as part of him, a lifetime of over four decades? No. From the wide spectrum of those years—years of joy, sorrow, struggle; years of prison, years of exile, years of bearing and bringing up children, of trying to come to terms with an environment so far removed in social and cultural terms from that of one's beginnings—one must, nevertheless, endeavour to construct a picture as fulsome and satisfying as the passing of the years was.

When I came to India in 1938, I was not new to the cause, which was uppermost in the Indian mind—the cause of India's independence, freedom after centuries of colonialism. I had in London been near to such people as Sajjad Zaheer, Iqbal Singh, Mulk Raj Anand and had worked in my spare time with Krishna Menon in the India League. My coming to India and meeting Faiz in Amritsar was really no accident. I came as a sister-in-law to Dr Taseer's house where, weekend after weekend, intellectuals gathered. Poetry, politics, culture were topics which were discussed far into the night, and when beddings were spread out on the floor of the wide drawing-room, it meant that the next day there would be much more to follow.

Faiz, then in MAO College as a teacher of English, was a regular visitor. He was kind to the young English girl who had so much to learn; there was so much, which astonished her, so much which displeased her, yet so much that was a marvel of interest and beauty. Faiz, as did others, helped to sort things out, and gradually I found that this somewhat taciturn, quiet poet had a fund of stories not told to all, and a pleasing sense of humour.

We walked in the evening. Autumn had set in and winter followed, and in those sunny days and cold, starry nights, our friendship became something special. Faiz was a poor man then. His family had lost its fortune when his father died, and leaving the palatial house in Sialkot, not far from the ancestral paternal village of Kala Qadir, they moved to live in humble circumstances in Lahore where Faiz finally finished his MA in English from Government College, and his MA in Arabic from the College of Oriental Studies. He was ready then to help support a large family of widowed sisters and orphans. To me there seemed to be no end to his responsibilities, and when finally we spoke of marriage, I knew it would be a formidable undertaking. He was the sole wage-earner in the house, and his salary ended before it began!

He was already a poet and even in his days as a student in Government College when he participated in *mushāirās*, A.S. Bokhari turned to Sufi Tabassum saying, 'A young poet to be watched.'

MAO College at that time was staffed by men of academic distinction and of progressive political views. It was here, as Faiz told me, that he first undertook a serious study of Marxism as a philosophy and ideology with such people as Mahmud-uz Zafar and Rasheed Jahan.

I taught in a school-cum-college in the heart of the city of Amritsar, travelling by tonga from the Civil Lines to Katra Mahan Singh, winding in and out of narrow lanes, passing filthy gutters, and ending up in front of the Rosemary School and College. Here I taught English to senior school-girls, and French as an optional subject to one shy Hindu girl, who never raised her eyes to meet mine, and who finally, by nothing short of a miracle, passed her FA!

I was getting to know India and Faiz, listening to him recounting his experiences with the underground groups of workers whom he taught at night. Extraordinary—he met up with some of his pupils decades later in Southall, near London, as expatriates!

But life was hard for his family. Money was scarce, girls and boys were growing up and had to be sent to school and, later, college. Raw materials, rice, ghee and wheat came from the village to the house, and his mother, a grand matriarchal head of family, managed to keep the life of this hard-hit family going at a regular pace. I lived through all this later, when I was wedded into this poor but proud family.

Our marriage was delayed because of the orthodox views of the family, and Faiz made it clear that for us to marry against his family's wishes would isolate us; he was needed by his family, and he needed them. Finally, most opposition was overcome with the help of an understanding sister, and the date of our marriage was set—October 1941. Taseer had, by this time become Principal of the SP College, Srinagar, which meant that our marriage would take place in Kashmir.

On 26 October 1941, the grand *barāt* arrived: Faiz, carrying the wedding-ring and a small suitcase with cloth to be tailored for the *valīmā*, held later in Lahore, accompanied by his younger brother, Inayat, and a Communist worker, Naeem, then in Lahore. What a small wedding-party! No wonder that Rafi Peer's nieces and nephews complained. No band, no blare of trumpets, just three people.

We were married on the evening of 28 October, and the *nikāh* was performed by Sheikh Abdullah. A special contract was drawn up, similar to the one drawn up by Allama Iqbal, who performed the marriage ceremony of my sister and Dr Taseer. We had no money, we were really poor, luxuries were few, and a long life lay ahead. We moved to Lahore and Faiz took up a none too congenial job as a lecturer in English at the Hailey College of Commerce. We shifted from the city to a more congenial area near the canal and set up house. Faiz continued his political work, wrote poetry, brought out his first book, earned extra money with All India Radio, and I tried as best I could to come to terms with a large family, a new language, a spartan existence and the hope of raising a family.

We had made friends before our marriage in Simla, where I took up a teaching job with a delightful couple, Colonel and Amina Majeed Malik, and they remained friends for the rest of our lives. Amina now is near and dear to me, and through her comforting spirit, I have weathered storms—of imprisonment and now of the loneliness without Faiz.

The war had by now entered a dangerous phase. The Japanese army was moving towards India, Calcutta had been bombed. The Soviet Union was actively involved, and the progressives were encouraged, in fact directed, to take part in any way they could in the struggle against the advancing tide of fascism. Majeed asked Faiz to join the propaganda front of the British Army. It was a hard decision to make, but one which was unavoidable. We moved to Delhi and Faiz went into uniform. We soon met up with the NCO progressive elements in the British Army and study circles began in our house. I remember years later, in 1951, when our house was being searched by the police after Faiz's arrest in the Rawalpindi Conspiracy Case, that the police found a large volume of closely-written notes on Marxism. In spite of long questioning and endless threats, I kept the secret of the BOR soldier who had entrusted it to me years before!

They were dangerous but exciting times in Delhi. Faiz travelled to many parts of India and, of course, continued his political work and contacts.

Salima was born in Delhi in 1942 and a new life of responsibility began. With lack of accommodation all round, we moved into tents; then found a small apartment in Karol Bagh near Dr and Mrs Saleemuz-Zaman, who have remained friends since then. Tilly passed away in 1985 leaving a terrible void, but Saleem, now 87, meets me whenever I am in Karachi, or when he is in Lahore. Most of our friendships have been life-long.

Moneeza was born in Simla in 1946; for my poor mother-in-law a bitter blow—she did so want a grandson. She eventually had nine granddaughters! But she was always kind to me, although we were worlds apart. I do know that she realized the problems of being married to a poor man. The army pay made life easier, but responsibilities did not diminish. Shafqat was a niece whose battle for education I fought—she was taken out of school in her eighth class. But we persevered and finally she graduated. It was a long and arduous fight.

Two children, the war ended, Partition on the way as seemingly the only solution to a free India. Our future lay in Pakistan, and Faiz accepted an offer from Mian Iftikharuddin to take up the editorship of the *Pakistan Times*. So Lahore it was to be, new career as a journalist. A career, which was to land Faiz forever, on the wrong side of every government, until Bhutto came along. But his reputation for fearless journalism grew, and the Progressive Papers Limited stood as the best dailies in Asia.

My mother and father arrived from England for a holiday just before Partition. It was a joy to have them with us. They decided to take a house in Kashmir for the summer and bring us all together. On the day I was to leave to join them and the Taseers, all hell broke loose in Lahore. Rajgarh was aflame—there was news of riots everywhere. Faiz took us as far as Rawalpindi, and then we set out by bus for Srinagar, myself and two little girls, one just ten months old. It was a long and tedious journey, but at last, we made it. It was a sad and dreadful summer. The children fell ill with whooping cough, were hospitalized, my mother grew very sick and news from the Punjab was appalling. We faced each new day with trepidation.

At last, Faiz arrived to see us and decided that we should be nearer each other, since Kashmir might be cut off. We travelled down to Murree—two sickly children recovering from whooping cough and a harassed mother. It was here that I saw the true tragedy of what was happening near at hand. A group of us, young women, decided that we would help the Sikh families left behind in Murree to leave for India. We managed to hire at least five buses, and on the appointed day, early in the morning they were loaded with men, women and children. The caravan was to leave from the main shopping centre, travel to Rawalpindi, where the contingent would entrain for Lahore, onwards to Amritsar. They were well supplied with food and water. Between Murree and Rawalpindi there is a small village—a hill stream runs through the main street. It was here that the caravan was held up and massacred to the last child, and their bodies strewn along the village street. The stream ran red. Had we done wrong? Should we have taken the matter into our own hands? Was the fault ours? To this day, I do not know. We acted in good faith. We gathered in the evening in terrible dismay, mourning. Our diaries were full of names and addresses of the victims' relatives. . . .

Soon after this, we were sent for by Faiz. Let us all be together, he wrote. The letter came by a special messenger. We entrained at Rawalpindi. I wore a *burqā* and carried a Quran—I was after all an English-woman travelling alone—and massacres were going on everywhere. We were all gripped by terror. By that time, train after train was arriving in Lahore piled high with bodies—madness was rampant.

Life was hazardous. We worked in the refugee camps, nursing, feeding, searching for mother, father, child—families had been separated. It was chaotic. But for my parents it was too much, and they decided to leave for Europe. We never met again. Faiz's long bout in prison prevented any travel, and both my parents passed away. I had tried to get away to London to see my father when he was critically ill, meaning to avail of a delegate's ticket to a Peace Conference in Vienna. But the Government refused to allow me to leave—I had made the stupid mistake of switching my British passport for a Pakistani one on the advice of my lawyers. But I hasten. . . .

Gandhi was assassinated and the world stood aghast. Faiz travelled to India to take part in the funeral—a courageous act in those days. The reputation of the journals grew. I took over the women's and children's pages of the *Pakistan Times.* On 9 March 1951, time stood still. Suddenly tragedy struck. The infamous Rawalpindi Conspiracy Case was concocted, and Faiz, along with important army officers, was arrested. He remained in solitary confinement for months while others were arrested. The RCC Act was passed through Parliament and a Tribunal was set up for a secret trial in the jail of the desert city of Hyderabad, Sind.

Our little world seemed to have collapsed. I worked full time in the *Pakistan Times,* sold my car, bought a bicycle and started life as a mobile working journalist. By that time, Dr Taseer had passed away and my sister, too, had three children to support. It looked like devastation. But courage returned, and the long struggle was on.

At long last we were allowed to visit Faiz in the Central Jail, Hyderabad, travelling for 24 hours in a dusty, hot third class compartment. We met under strict police surveillance. We needed legal help. Money was borrowed and a lawyer engaged. The trial began. Long years ahead. I dreaded the day, and longed for the night and oblivion. I wondered how I would see it through—it was Faiz's courage which sustained me. Faiz and I have published our letters of this long period—he translated his into Urdu, mine are in the original English. These two books are the story of two years of separation. It is the story, too, of the richest period of Faiz's poetry, written during those years in prison—poetry of optimism, of hope, courage—an inspiration to us all.

When the sentence was passed, after this so-called trial was over, Faiz was moved to Montgomery (now Sahiwal), nearer home—a three hours' journey, and we settled down to wait out the four years' sentence. Friends had rallied and now it was easier, we could now count the years, the months, the weeks and the days—tick them off and say, yes, we shall see it through. The girls grew up, grey hair arrived—how much strength did we need? What were our reserves?

Then a constitutional crisis shortened the sentence. Parliament was prorogued over a legal battle, and the RCC Act was declared null and void. We filed petitions for release, they were accepted, and I rushed by car to Montgomery to bring Faiz back. But by the time I arrived, the jail gates had been shut for the night and by morning he had been re-arrested under the infamous Detention Act—as had all other prisoners. Yet another legal battle—the prisoners were finally released on bail. The struggle was nearing its end. Bail was eventually lifted, and Faiz was asked to rejoin the *Pakistan Times.* He then led a journalists' delegation to China.

In 1958, with no small amount of difficulty, he journeyed to Tashkent to the Afro-Asian Writers' Association's meeting. It was while he was there that Pakistan was usurped—General Ayub Khan led a coup d'état. All progressives were arrested, the jails were full, and the *Pakistan Times* and other papers attached to it were taken over.

Faiz travelled to London, saw through the release of his film *Day Shall Dawn*, then returned. He was arrested in Lahore on 15 December 1958. So began another long period of prison. But it ended. Again no job, although I was still working in the *Pakistan Times* and hating every moment of it.

These were the days of Governor Kalabagh in the Punjab. Faiz was requested to take over the Arts Council, Lahore with certain restrictions and conditions. He said no, no conditions, freedom of action or nothing. Agreed. Things went well; he brought new life to the Council.

Yet, slowly but surely it came under the surveillance of the CID—staff members were harassed and Faiz realized that working like this was impossible. He tendered his resignation to the Chairman, Justice Rehman, who took it up with the Governor. A commitment was made that there would be no more intimidation. It was then that Faiz suffered a mild heart attack through overwork and mental strain. He was looked after by Dr Seltzer.

Then came the announcement of the Lenin Peace Prize. The press was in an uproar! Welcoming, condemning and what have you. Faiz sat it out and made his plans. Salima was already almost packed for her higher studies in UK. As the uproar subsided a little, General Ayub Khan granted permission for Faiz to leave for Moscow.

Then followed a period of comparative peace. We all lived in London for two years. I signed a contract for a two years' teaching assignment, Moneeza went to school and Salima to her university. Faiz travelled, was relaxed and happy. But he grew homesick as did we all. Faiz finally left for Pakistan, to take up an interesting assignment in Karachi; Moneeza followed after her O levels, and I after completing my contract. Salima stayed on to finish her degree.

Karachi was for us, a haven of peace, work and good friends. Faiz established an excellent complex of school, college, orphanage and clinic for the Haroon family. I set up a nursery school for Amina; Moneeza joined Kinnaird College in Lahore. Salima returned, married Shoaib, and joined the National College of Arts in Lahore. Moneeza trained in television and married the man of her choice.

Then came the tragedy of East Pakistan, and 90,000 Pakistani prisoners of war in India. By now, Bhutto was Prime Minister of Pakistan and he invited Faiz to take over the newly formed Pakistan National Council of the Arts. We moved to Islamabad and I was offered a contract with CEF. I accepted, and life seemed a little easier—three grandchildren into the bargain!

But then, gradually the opposition press began a campaign against Faiz, and through this against Bhutto—a Communist as his cultural adviser! Eventually, Faiz asked to be relieved and to go to Lahore. He was appointed Consultant to the Ministry of Culture. We had managed to build a small house, and I started a nursery school along with friends. Again, we seemed at peace for a while. But no, it seemed never to end. Came the Zia takeover and Faiz realized that work now with this government would be out of the question. He asked to be relieved and sought permission to leave, to avail himself of the many invitations piling up. This meant a period of self-exile—and another period of separation. But we accepted it as the only answer to continuing harassment, and absence of any meaningful work.

But the appointment as Editor of *Lotus* magazine was in the offing, and Faiz decided that he would accept. It meant Beirut. We were both in Moscow when the final offer was made. We found ourselves in Beirut. There we lived and worked in close contact with the Palestinians and were able to travel without restriction. I think, on the whole we were happy, although our family and friends were far away. Our small apartment overlooking the Mediterranean was our home for two years, until the Israelis struck. At that time, I had gone back to Pakistan for a short holiday, but it proved to be a final break with Beirut. I look back and know that these two years were 'growing years' for us both—writing, travelling, meeting some of the world's bravest people—above all knowing Arafat and the Palestinians.

All shattered when the Israelis reached Beirut. Faiz managed to travel to Damascus with UN personnel at the risk of his life, since he was a marked man, and had no diplomatic passport. Our apartment was bombed, many precious books and possessions destroyed. Sabra and Shatilla later massacred. Beirut became for us but a courageous memory.

When I later joined Faiz in Moscow, I knew how stricken he was by this tragedy. But he went on—writing, travelling—there seemed to be no end to the demands on his time and he, not willing to rest... When his collection came out in London, he had already been hailed as a legend in his time.

My love for him knew no bounds, and we had now decided to accept the fact that the pace of our lives should slacken. *Lotus* had shifted to Tunis—but Mouin was gone, and there was his grief-stricken family. Faiz and I went to Tunis. After Beirut, it seemed barren, un-rich, and the

Palestinians scattered. . . . Tunis it had to be, but not to live in, to visit as the need arose and as the work for *Lotus* demanded.

Our last memorable holiday together was in Alma Ata in the summer of 1984—it was beautiful, peaceful, the world seemed responding to our need for well-earned rest. Faiz was at work on a translation into Urdu of an Arabic story. He finished it, put down his pen and said, 'You know, darling, nobody can write Urdu like I can!' I told him, then he should write more. He said he would. We laughed. Our interpreter came into the room. 'Oh, you both look so happy', she said. She was called Vera. She was beautiful. We have had so many lovely interpreters, it is difficult to remember them all—Vera, Natasha, Mila, Bella, Tanya, Marina. . . .

I know there are gaps in my reminiscences; as I said at the beginning, one cannot hope to encompass life with Faiz in pages, even millions of words. Our small house is crowded with bits and pieces we have gathered during our travels. Even as I raise my eyes, I can see clay horses from Bokhara, delicate green glass from Lebanon, ceramics from GDR, more ceramics from Daghistan, the porcelain elephant from Vietnam, the box from Damascus. . . .

We have instituted the Faiz Foundation to pay tribute to his memory and to many others like him, men of courage and of love. For the past two years, we have held a Festival on 13 February in Lahore—Faiz's birthday. Salima and I have just returned from Scandinavia—Faiz has been translated into Swedish now, and the publishers invited us to launch the books in Norway, Denmark and Sweden. How graceful and loving they all were. It was a moving and overwhelming experience—as life itself has been with Faiz.

ANY LOVER TO ANY BELOVED (2)

Original: *Ko'ī 'āshiq kisī mahbūbā sē* (2) from *Mērē Dil Mērē Musāfir* (1981)
TRANSLATOR: NAOMI LAZARD

Today, if the breath of breeze
wants to scatter petals in the garden of memory,
why shouldn't it?
If a forgotten pain
in some corner of the past
wants to burst into flame again, let it happen.
Though you act like a stranger now—
come, be close to me for a few minutes.
Though after this meeting
we will know even better what we have lost,
and the gauze of words left unspoken
hangs between one line and another,
neither of us will mention our promises.
Nothing will be said of loyalty or faithlessness.
If my eyelashes want to tell you something
about wiping out the lines
left by the dust of time on your face,
you can listen or not, just as you like.
And what your eyes fail to hide from me—
if you care to, of course you may say it,
or not, as the case may be.

21

A LIFE DEVOTED TO PEACE

Faiz haunted almost the entire adult life of the generation to which I belong.

When we came out of school, with pretensions of being intellectuals and idealists, we found Faiz and N. M. Rashed, among the poets, and Saadat Hasan Manto, Ismat Chughtai and Krishna Chandra, among the short story writers, dominating the contemporary literary scene, striking a posture of affront and iconoclasm, which shocked their seniors but fired the imagination of their contemporaries and the younger people.

I still vividly remember the experience. Manto, Ismat and, to some extent, Rashed, were like a thunderclap, frightening yet exciting; but Faiz and Krishna Chandra were like meteors or comets, which quietly shot across the skies, yet irresistibly riveted your attention. Faiz's poetry specially had the capacity to get under your skin, take your psyche into its grip and even before you knew what was happening to you, change your entire outlook on life.

Enormously Exciting

The appearance of Faiz Sahib's first collection of verse *Naqsh-e Faryādi* in the early forties, when I was still in school, was a memorable experience. His poems, *Mujh sē pahlī sī mahabbat mērī mehbūb na māṅg*, or *Phir ko'ī āyā dil-e zār? Nahīṅ ko'ī nahīṅ*, or *Bol kē lab āzād haiṅ tērē, Bol zabāṅ ab tak tērī hai*, opened up new vistas of perception. While, at the time, one had little realization of how profoundly the event was affecting oneself, one had the gut feeling that something enormously exciting was happening and that one's way of looking at poetry and literature was no longer going to be the same.

I still sometimes relive that intense emotional reaction when I first discovered Faiz. I remember how any irresponsible or flippant reference to Faiz's poetry, like the parodies of Furqat Kakorvi, angered me and even brought tears to my eyes.

Soon Faiz was to establish a sort of personal association with our family. Towards the latter part of the Second World War, he had come to live in Delhi, after he had been commissioned into the Army PR set-up. One hardly expected to see Faiz in the uniform of an army officer. It seemed incongruous, and one was still too immature to understand the rationale of how the war had suddenly become a peoples' war. However, in due course, because of my father's past close and long association with Lahore and with Faiz's old college and several of his mentors, Faiz visited our home in old Delhi.

But I did not really get to know Faiz in a personal sense until I had moved to Lahore after partition, where he was then editing the *Pakistan Times*. Until then, we had looked upon Faiz, as one would call it now, an 'Urdu medium' type. One's admiration for him suddenly deepened when one discovered that he had become the editor of an important English language daily, even though there was hardly anything Westernised about him.

Thorough Native

Indeed, from the time of my earliest association with Faiz, this fact always intrigued me that while being perfectly at home in the European society, Faiz never adopted a Westernised style of life. His wife was English-born, he began his life as a teacher of English in a college in Amritsar, he edited an English language newspaper and edited it most capably in competition with the *Civil and Military Gazette*, whose editor then was a true-blue English-man; he spent a great part of his life travelling in the West, and yet he remained a thorough 'native' all his life.

A poet of Urdu, Faiz could well have changed over to writing poetry in English if he had cared to, and yet he did not. For reasons of convenience, he frequently wore a suit while travelling abroad, and yet you could see that he felt most comfortable, the moment he changed into his favourite kurta-pyjama. His command over the English language was impeccable. In fact, he had the gift of being able to express himself in English most vividly, with utmost frugality of words, rather a rare quality, and yet he left it to Victor Kiernan to translate his poems into English. All this, undoubtedly because he felt proud of being able to express himself in a language which was his own, and which had

a robust poetic tradition and was proud of his undying love for the
cultural milieu to which he belonged. His home, where his English-born
wife ruled, was the home of a Pakistani, of a Lahorite, in fact, and never
made you feel like an alien.

I do not of course believe that Faiz Sahib was ever a firebrand Marxist.
He certainly felt for the under-dog and was greatly pained by any act of
injustice or suppression, regardless of where it happened. He was equally
deeply moved by the execution of the Rosenbergs, as the ruthless and
sad end of Pablo Neruda, the persecution of the Black people in South
Africa and the unending injustices and miseries heaped upon the people
of Palestine. And he had the rare capacity for immortalizing his personal
protest in poetry in a language which steered clear of text book clichés
and was relevant not only to the incident immediately that inspired it,
but to humanity at large. That is the reason why Faiz's poetry never
seems dated.

Faiz's association with Leftists went back to the early thirties, when
he was a young lecturer at MAO College in Amritsar and came under the
influence of Professor Mahmud-uz Zafar and his wife, Dr Rasheed Jahan,
both card-holding party members. He was also in the vanguard of the
Progressive Writers' Movement and until shortly before his death, chief
editor of *Lotus*, the official journal of the Afro-Asian writers' organization.

A Humanist

Yet I always felt that for a revolutionary, Faiz's poetry was remarkably
devoid of any rhetoric or polemics. He was perhaps more of a humanist
and a dreamer. His genuine admirers, however, often felt disconcerted
at the fact that many of his close associates could not be considered
reconcilable to his ideological orientation. But Faiz was too indulgent
or lethargic to discriminate. Faiz's company was undoubtedly a status
symbol.

Faiz lived in Karachi for several years in the late sixties, as did I. That
was when I had the opportunity to see him frequently and in the circle
of his close admirers and friends. Two or three aspects of his personality
left a lasting imprint on my memory. Firstly, while being a pioneer, and
indeed an unrivalled 'prophet' of modern poetry, he never looked upon
the traditionalists with contempt, or even indifference. On the other
hand, he treated them with admiration and respect. He had a respect

for age, which most other younger poets who achieve even a modicum of success at *mushāirās*, discard at the first opportunity.

Secondly, he never behaved like a celebrity. He certainly liked to be sought after, to be admired and fussed over. But he had no snobbery. And he also had hardly any sense of discrimination about whom he met and whom he congregated with. His circle of friends and fans was always diverse, motley and heterogeneous, not always the most desirable. He could suffer dilettantes and upstarts and even cads, who, he knew, would join the chorus of his critics and detractors, if that brought any material advantage to them.

Thirdly, I found that Faiz had a true love for the classical heritage of Urdu poetry; for the poetry of Dard, Mir, Sauda and Ghalib. One of his great ambitions in life was to edit a selection of classical Urdu poetry, and he felt sorry that he could never quite find the time to get down to it. His love and admiration for Ghalib particularly was demonstrated not only by the repeated hark-back to Ghalib's verses in many of his well-known poems, he also devoted considerable time and attention to an institution called Ghalib Library in Karachi, which had a very modest beginning, and which, in fact was situated in a part of Karachi that could not be called progressive, and always had a preponderance of writers and pseudo-poets who demonstrate little admiration for poets like Faiz, and had the Furqat Kakorvi-like attitude towards him.

No Rancour

And lastly—and this was the most baffling—I got to discover Faiz's total incapacity for acrimony or rancour. Even towards those, who openly labelled him as a *surkhā* (red) or a stooge of someone or the other, and there were many who would do so whenever it suited them, in any way, and often in a language that hurt him deeply.

Faiz would remain placid and tolerant. He never stooped to argue or remonstrate, and met all hostility with his enigmatic smile. While in Karachi, I used to write a regular column for an English daily and had made several valiant attempts to take on some of Faiz's critics, whose manner had been consistently obnoxious, if not obscene. But Faiz himself had remained quite unmoved. Once, quite exasperated, I asked Faiz as to why he did not react to what was being published not only about him but also about his close family? He looked rather surprised at my sense of outrage and said in Urdu: *Kyā hu'ā? Kyā likhā jā rahā hai!* (What is the matter? What are they writing?) I said: *Kamāl hai, itnā hangāmā ho rahā hai aur āp kuch̲ kehtē hī nahīṅ.* (This is strange. There is such an uproar and you don't react to it?) He said: *Bhā'ī, ham to paṛhtē nahīṅ. Tum ko taklīf hotī hai to tum bhī na paṛhā karo* (*Bhā'ī*, I don't read these things, and if they upset you, you shouldn't either.)

In the end, I must confess that in spite of our long association, and in spite of my having been with him in some of the closest and most intimate companies, I cannot really claim to have known Faiz very intimately. Indeed, I believe that virtually no one really could claim to have known Faiz very intimately, and most of those who do so, are only flattering themselves.

The fact is that Faiz lived several lives at various levels. On the surface, he was a very human person, who liked good company and other good things of life. At another level, he was the sensitive, socially committed intellectual, who suffered with the underprivileged and the exploited.

And then, deep within himself, he lived an inner, highly introspective, highly intense life, something no one else, not even those closest to him, could really share. It was this Faiz that smouldered from within and wrote great poetry, the poet that led a restless life, a life that drove him from one place to another, from one set of admirers to another, even making some people believe that he had self-exiled himself. There could have been nothing more absurd; for what he was supposed to have exiled himself from was something to which he was deeply attached, that is, Pakistan and Lahore, to which he returned again and again and which was in his bones and blood, and where he preferred to breathe his last.

In the final analysis, I believe Faiz remained all his life something of an enigma, an outsider, someone who may have physically, and perhaps even emotionally, belonged to the people or places where he happened to be at any given time, but who nevertheless remained remote, inaccessible, eluding even those who were closest to him. It was this Faiz who lived a restless, nomadic life, in a spiritual, if not always physical, sense—and it was this remote, inaccessible restless Faiz who wrote:

Ham kē t̲hehrē ajnabī itnī mudārātoṅ kē b'ād
Ph̲ir banēṅ gē āshnā kitnī mulāqātoṅ kē b'ād

Mērē dil, mērē musāfir,
Huā ph̲ir sē hukm sādir,
kē watan-badar hoṅ ham tum,

dēṅ galī, galī, sadā'ēṅ,
karēṅ rukh nagar nagar kā,
kē surāgh ko'ī pā'ēṅ,
har ik ajnabī sē pūchēṅ,
jo patā thā apnē ghar kā

To me, this was not instant poetry, as some would have us believe. An incident or event may have been momentarily the immediate motivation for it. This clearly was the wail of an outsider or the covenant of a great creative artist with himself, to never give up his quest for true peace and tranquillity, even though true peace and tranquillity may forever remain an illusion, like the *unqā* (phoenix) of the Urdu *ghazal* tradition.

TO THE RIVAL

Original: *Raqīb sē* from *Naqsh-e Faryādī* (1941)
TRANSLATOR: VICTOR KIERNAN

Round you my memories of that fair one twine
Who made my heart a fairies' nursery,
Caught in whose toils I called this busy age
An old wives tale, and let the world go by.

Familiar with your feet too are those paths
Her youth time deigned to tread, drunk with youth's pride,
While as her beauty's pageant passed, these eyes
Gazed on it worshipping, unsatisfied.

With you too have those darling breezes played
Where fading perfume of her dress still hangs,
On you too from her roof has rained that moonlight
Haunted by long-done nights and bygone pangs.

You who have known that cheek, those lips, that brow
Under whose spell I fleeted life away,
You whom the dreamy magic of those eyes
Has touched, can tell where my years ran astray.

Such gifts as love and love's keen anguish bring,
Gifts beyond counting, side by side we earned:
To whom else could I speak of what that passion
Cost me, or through that passion what I learned?

I learned of misery, helplessness, despair,
I learned to be the friend of suffering creatures,
I came to know the torment of the oppressed,
The truth of sobbing breath and livid features.

Wherever now the friendless crouch and wail
Till in their eyes the trickling tears grow cold,
Or where the vulture hovering on broad pinions
Snatches the morsel from their feeble hold—

When labourers' flesh is sold in chaffering streets,
Or pavements run with poor men's blood, a flame
That lurks inside me blazes up beyond
All power of quenching; do not ask its name.

22

FAIZ IN LONDON

Lonely but Never Alone

London is one city Faiz has always returned to. The only time he decided to make his home abroad, he chose London. This was in the early sixties. But he went back. The poem *Yār āshnā nahīṅ ko'ī ṭakrā'eṅ kis sē jām..kis dilrubā kē nām pē khālī sabū kareṅ* was written during those days. I like to imagine it was in a pub. And I like to imagine that when the lines came to him, Faiz was alone.

But that is what I like to imagine, because Faiz is never alone in London. He is always surrounded by people. People he knows and people he does not know. I have never been able to tell the difference, because for him no strangers exist. His warmth and concern for people—friends, foes, strangers—is like London rain which falls on everyone, making no distinction.

Faiz knows his way around in London. Actually, his sense of direction, like his memory for names and faces, is quite uncanny. London is a city without end; especially if you get lost, which I often do in its eastern and south-western stretches. I remember a few summers ago, driving Faiz to somebody's house beyond Crystal Palace. I got lost. My London A to Z seemed to confuse me further. For a time I kept pretending that, being a Londoner, by circumstance if not by choice, I knew exactly where I was going. Faiz surveyed the area nonchalantly and told me to proceed straight, then take a couple of turns and, well, we soon were where we were supposed to be. In explanation, because I did need one, he said that he had been to the house before.

And once, actually only last year, I was driving him to Highgate and I got on to a dual carriageway leading in an entirely different direction. I thought Faiz had not noticed, till he said to me, 'If you don't take a right turn soon, we will end up in Oxford'. But then Faiz should know London.

He has been coming here since he was a young man, though I know many people who should know London as well as him, but who cannot guide you from Knightsbridge to Regent Street.

I think this winter something happened which changed the London that Faiz has always come to. It will never be the same place again for him. He may not perhaps even want to come here as often as he used to. It will be hard for him to accept that one of his best-loved friends and someone who was so much of London for Faiz, he will not be able to see again because Mohammad Afzal died somewhat suddenly one cold day in February this year.

Faiz always used to stay with him. It was only recently that he started putting up with Majid Ali and Zehra Nigah in their Knightsbridge flat. I think Afzal was not really well and Faiz did not wish to impose himself. Last summer, though, Alys did stay at Afzal's when Faiz went to Canada, having been wanting to go there for a long time. I did not know Afzal in Lahore. He left Pakistan before my time. But I had heard of him and his brave contribution to the trade union movement. I always found him an acerbic man with a dry, almost cynical sense of humour. Also, a bit quiet and even somewhat impatient with what he did not like.

I asked Faiz. 'No, that is not so. You see, Afzal hasn't been too well for some years and has had to change his habits and go on a diet. That makes him irritable at times. But he is not what he might appear to be now. He used to be a live wire and tremendously committed.'

I have met people like Afzal abroad. Committed people who wanted Pakistan to become a progressive, enlightened and tolerant state, but who gave up to come and live in a foreign country. And though over the years, their cynicism grew, while physically their lives became more comfortable, they somehow diminished as men. Afzal was such a man; but he and Faiz had a profound relationship. They could sit in a room for hours and not speak. But yet, they were in communication. This alchemy, only an old and intensely shared friendship can produce.

So Afzal is dead. Faiz was in London when it happened, but I wasn't, so I don't know how he took it. A friend says he was shattered, became very quiet, did not want to talk about it and flew back to Beirut in great sadness. I do believe that because I have seen him and been with him in a similar situation. That was when Sufi Ghulam Mustafa Tabussum died.

Limitless Sorrow

Faiz took it very badly. He fell into a strange silence, not a silence born of resignation and acceptance, but one of limitless and inconsolable sorrow. I began to talk about Sufi Sahib, the way he was, the evenings spent with him, his poetry, his humour, his lifelong poverty and his cheerful, mystic acceptance of it, and so much more and so many things that he was to so many of us. Finally, Faiz spoke, 'We were merely amateurs. He was the master. When one was in doubt, one would go to him. Language, idiom, diction, syntax, usage. Now that he is gone, who does one go to!' Faiz, as all his friends know, never uses the first person singular. He either uses its more impersonal plural form or the third person indefinite. What he was saying was that he had now been left without an *ustād* whose word on the craft of poetry he could accept.

'Malāmatī Sūfī'

When Faiz is in London, there are a number of people he phones as soon as he has installed himself. With the utmost humility, I should state that I have been among them. The phone rings. I pick it up, 'Hello?' I inquire. 'Bhā'ī, Faiz', the voice says. 'When did you come?' I ask because he is not expected. 'You are the first one I have called', he says. And no matter what one is doing or what engagements there are, one goes to be with him. I have always recognized the privilege that being in his presence confers. He is a man of immense affection. He is without malice. Ashfaq Ahmad once called Faiz a *malāmatī sūfī*. The amount of abuse and calumny he has taken in his life, without retaliating, should certainly place him in the mystic order.

It is not that Faiz is unaware of the people who want to sit at his feet when he is around and who make nasty, small-minded remarks about him when he is away. There is some one in London—and he is one of many such—who prefixes every sentence with '*bha'ī*. Of course, every time he says that to me, I watch my back, waiting for the dagger to be plunged in. Once I heard him say that Faiz had waned as a poet and really had nothing left to say and what he was saying, he was saying badly, a shadow of the poet that was. He was being equally dismissive of the new collection of poems by Faiz.

Next time Faiz came to London and I went to see him, I found my 'brother' grovelling at his feet. That evening we went to the BBC Club and spent a long and lovely time there. Poetry flowed and the conversation was good. At some point I remember telling Faiz, what I had heard the man who could not be made to sit in a chair in Faiz's presence, say about him and his poetry. Faiz smiled inscrutably. 'Don't get upset', he said, 'I have had this sort of thing said about me from certain quarters for more than forty years. It does not matter at all.' 'But do you know how double-faced and hypocritical these people are?' I insisted. Since Faiz never abuses anyone and does not co-author abuse, he merely smiled and kept quiet.

Immense Patience

Faiz has immense patience and when he is in London, it can be taxed to breaking point. There is a friend who, over the years, has developed to a fine art his inability to listen to any one when he himself is talking. The disquieting bit is that as long as he is around, he is talking incessantly. No pauses, no full stops, no commas even. He just goes on talking. And it could be anything that is occupying his mind on the day of the encounter. Soviet foreign policy, the vagaries of English weather or a comedy called 'No Sex Please, we are British.'

Faiz got caught one evening with him at the BBC and suffered him in uncomplaining silence, punctuated by faint-hearted attempts to jump ship, for well over two hours. That beat my record which, in my reckoning, was an all-time high at sixty minutes.

Crank Versifiers

In London, as I have no doubt, elsewhere, he has to suffer crank versifiers. There is one I know who has recently published a collection (at his own expense, needless to say) of poems for which a succession of 'opening' ceremonies have been held, as if it were not a book of poetry but a garage. When Faiz is in London, he not only takes many calls from him, but, in addition, has to receive him and actually listen to his poetry for extended periods, a crucifying experience without question. I, who am not a poet but read poetry and, perhaps, understand it a bit, would sooner start howling and commit physical violence than listen to such mindless drivel. Faiz does it with a quiet grace which defies description.

Politicians

Faiz is not an admirer of politicians in general. He has no illusions about them. He has known too many of them over too long a period of time. But there are exceptions. With Mian Iftikharuddin, his relationship was very special. He feels that Mian Iftikharuddin was the first person to see the obscurantist hell-hole Pakistan was moving towards. He tried to fight a rearguard action but was defeated by a miscellany of interests whose sole motivation was personal aggrandizement and unprincipled pursuit of power. Had the Azad Pakistan Party been allowed to build itself on the wreckage that the Muslim League became almost immediately after independence, the course of Pakistan's history might have been different.

Suhrawardy

Faiz also speaks with deep affection about Huseyn Shaheed Suhrawardy. I reminded him that after Suhrawardy died, a Western newspaper (I can't remember which) wrote that there were two links which joined East and West Pakistan: Suhrawardy and the Pakistan International Airlines. The Paper wondered how long the airline alone could keep the country together.

The late Mumtaz Hasan used to say 'If this is the west wing and that is the east wing, then the question arises; where is the bird?' I asked him if he knew the answer. In case he did, he chose to keep it to himself.

Faiz has invested his entire life, sometimes it seems to me, in the maintenance of friendships. There can be no lessening of affection for those who have once been admitted to his friendship. Whenever he is in London, he keeps an evening free to spend with Faizul Hasan Chaudhry, 'Hamid Akhtar's Ludhiana crowd,' as he described it to me, and his family. I could not go with him last time for some reason, but the summer before, when his children came from Lahore and there was a big family reunion in London, we spent a long evening at Faizul Hasan's house in Ealing.

Faiz at the time was unwell in Beirut and though medical tests later had shown everything in order, he was put on a drinks and cigarettes quota. So while we sat in Faizul Hasan's house, half of us on the floor, the rest here and there, Faiz was constantly being supervised, mostly by Alys and when she was not looking (which lapse she committed but occasionally) by Salima and Moneeza.

Compulsive Smoker

Faiz is a compulsive smoker. Unlike most of us, he has no brand loyalties. He will smoke anything. He puffs or drags at his cigarette in rapid-fire fashion and before it is half smoked, he buries it absent-mindedly in the ashtray. Hardly has he snuffed one out when he begins to reach for another. I think he smokes almost unconsciously. It does not seem as if he enjoys it.

But with Alys in full, hawk-eyed control and Salima and Moneeza playing the sheriff's deputies rather effectively, Faiz's style was being constantly marred, but he was submitting to the disciplinary admonitions of the women rather well, I thought. I kept teasing him. 'You should have seen him in Beirut. He was really unwell', Salima said. '*Bha'i ko'i aisi bhi bāt nahiṅ thī*', Faiz said. He always talks about himself with imprecision, almost as if he were talking about someone else.

The Russians

One day, last winter at Majid Ali's house, someone was trying to tell Faiz how much influence he must exercise with the Russians. I think he was asking him to persuade them to pull out of Afghanistan or bomb Diego Garcia or something equally mindless. 'Let me tell you one thing', Faiz said. 'The Russians talk politics seriously or allow access of a political nature only to members of the Party. I am not a member of the Party; never have been. That is very important to them. If you are a member of a fraternal communist party, you are treated differently. You are then on another wavelength. You may call it a hang-up or whatever, but to them the Party is the prime thing. I am accorded respect and extended many courtesies because I am a poet and winner of the Lenin Peace Prize. However, politics, they only talk to or discuss with Party members'.

To someone else who thought a person like Faiz could flit in and out of Moscow when fancy took him, he said, 'No, they are very formal, very correct about these things. They have to invite you for you to go. You don't show up at Moscow airport one afternoon and say, 'Hi, Sasha, I'm here. Come pick me up. I am in the lounge.'

The Poet and the Man

I never saw so much of Faiz in Pakistan as I saw of him in London. For one thing, when I moved to Lahore, he was living in Karachi and when he moved to Lahore, I was living abroad. I have known Faiz since I was a little boy. He was a friend of my father's through Dr M.D. Taseer. Taseer and my father, the late Dr Noor Hussain of Kashmir, were close. Their friendship went back to the late twenties or the early thirties.

One of my first memories is of Faiz in our house in Gulmurg, Kashmir. 'He would go to bed with his shoes on,' my mother once told me. So between us has thus existed an almost father-son relationship or bond of love. But that is describing it too simply. The fact that after 'partition' we settled in Sialkot is another link with Faiz. That city is in his bones. That is where he grew up and went to school and later to college.

Early Days

In London, we have talked so much about his early days in Sialkot. He was taken to Maulvi Mir Hasan and Maulvi Mohammad Ibrahim Sialkoti by his father when a little boy. Faiz learnt Arabic in Maulvi Mir Hasan's *maktab*; later also at Murray College. From Maulvi Ibrahim he learnt the Quran, *hadīth* and *fiqh.* He told me that Maulvi Ibrahim was perhaps one of the greatest scholars of Islamic learning in India at the time.

Faiz began to memorize the Quran as a child and was able to commit nearly half of it to memory. In any case, he knows it better than half of our *mullās* put together and quotes from it often.

Some years ago, Faiz said that he wanted to return to Sialkot and live there. He felt a tremendous nostalgia for the dark, winding, pebbled streets where he played as a boy. People in Sialkot, of course, still think of him as a native son. One of Faiz's closest boyhood friends was Khwaja Ferozuddin Faiz who died some years ago. Faiz often remembered him in London. Khwaja Ferozuddin was not a poet, but the friendship between the two was so deep that he adopted Faiz's name as part of his. In Sialkot, he was also affectionately known as Feroz 'Tommy,' perhaps because of his fair complexion and his dapper manner.

Joins GC

Faiz told me during one of our forays around London that when he came to Lahore to join Government College, he wrote an essay in English which was so outstanding that it was adjudged to be the best, and even put on the college notice board for everyone to read. He remembers that the next time they were given a test, he wrote what he thought was a highly erudite, knowledgeable piece. He was quite shocked to find that he had scored very poor marks. His teacher, an Englishman whose name I forget, called him in. 'The first thing you wrote was original. It was your own. This time you were merely reproducing what you had read elsewhere. You were not being yourself. Well, you don't have to do that. You have an original mind. Don't reproduce what others have said and written.' I don't think Faiz has.

I have asked him several times in London to put together an anthology of classical Urdu poetry. He told me that he did one several years ago. The manuscript (of which there was only one copy) was taken by a woman who was then living in New York. She has since got married and in the process lost the manuscript. Poetry and marriage obviously make poor companions.

Iqbal

Faiz is a great devotee of Iqbal, but of the living Iqbal, not the fossil he has been turned into by hacks, pseudo critics, self-styled ideologues. Faiz often talks about doing an Iqbal selection with a long introduction. 'Iqbal's real views on Islam and other fundamental questions are contained in his English writings. That was perhaps the reason Iqbal put them in English, beyond the reach of the obscurantist'. It is another matter that the majority of our obscurantists is English-speaking.

He told me that when he was a very young boy, his father took him to the annual session of the Anjuman-e Islamia, Sialkot, where Iqbal was among the assembled luminaries on the stage. Faiz recalls that he was made to recite the Quran. 'I was so tiny that I had to stand on something to be visible. After I had finished, Iqbal patted me on the head very affectionately and said something like 'What a nice, clever boy you are.' My father, of course, knew him well.'

Faiz is lonely. He misses Pakistan immensely. The number of offers he has rejected over the last few years would have tempted lesser men. Last year, the Jawaharlal Nehru University kept after him to accept a visiting professorship. He consistently refused. Visiting India is different, he told me, but accepting an arrangement of the kind that has been offered, would be embracing permanent exile as an act of volition. At one point last year, when I was looking for work in London, or elsewhere, someone suggested that I could have a job in Delhi or Bombay. I asked Faiz, 'No, not that. Go to Iceland or anywhere else, but once you take employment in India, then you have cut the cord, the umbilical cord with Pakistan.'

Beyond Redemption

I do not write this in an effort to assuage Mr Majid Nizami, or the Qureshi brothers and their likes, because they are beyond redemption and as Faiz once said to me, 'Those whom God Himself decides to mislead, no man can help.' I merely recall this to record something that Faiz told me on two occasions with such finality. And he is not the sort of man who makes final judgements. That is something he leaves to God, to the people and to history.

One day, last year, Faiz asked me to pick him up in the morning, late morning, that is. Of course, the way he says these things is very Faiz like, such as, 'Bha'ī kal ā jānā, hāṅ yehī ko'ī gyārā bārā bajē.' He was staying at Majid Ali's, which is next to Harrod's, a place Faiz never visits. He is not a shopper. I have never seen him shop. And to say that of a Pakistani in London is to place him in some sort of a Nobel Prize category.

It materialized in the forenoon. It was a nice day. We dutifully had a couple of quick ones. 'Let's go and see a movie,' Faiz suddenly said. That really got my goat, because I had never thought of Faiz as a moviegoer. 'You don't see movies, do you? I mean not really,' I asked. It turned out that in Beirut, for want of better entertainment, he had become something of a moviegoer. In any case, we set out looking for a movie to see.

We were not in luck. They all started too late or too early. Finally, finding ourselves in the Euston Road area, we decided to eat. Faiz told me of a place where you could eat čāt, pūri-halvā and drink honest-to-goodness Punjabi lassī. He said he had been there once. So after having successfully beaten the London one-way system (which a friend of mine describes as the ultimate imperialist conspiracy against the masses), we entered a place called 'Dīwānā!' Faiz was absolutely thrilled with the name. 'That is really delightful, Dīwānā!' I thought of all the havoc this word had wrought in Urdu and Persian poetry, Faiz himself being responsible for some of it.

We ate quite a good deal, drank, what turned out to be as Faiz had promised, honest-to-goodness Punjabi lassī, and generally had a good time. When you are with Faiz, you get used to being accosted by strangers. Faiz meets all of them as if he had known them for years. He may not always remember names, but he almost never forgets a face.

Nostalgia

When Faiz is in London, his nostalgia for Pakistan intensifies, because London has so many reminders of Pakistan: the people, the restaurants, the old imperial link. I think one of the ways in which he sublimates his nostalgia for Pakistan and particularly for Lahore, is to visit places which, our friend Athar Ali of the BBC once described as '*Pure Mozang.*' One such pure Mozang of London is a *kebāb* and *tikkā* place in East London called (what else?) the Lahore Kebab House.

Faiz told me about it. Last time he was in London, or perhaps it was the time before last, when he was on his way to Moscow to attend his seventieth birthday celebrations, he kept saying that one place we should eat at, some evening, deserved to be the Lahore Kebab House.

I have two friends in East London, Dar and Durrani. Dar is a big, strong, handsome Kashmiri from Sialkot who is in the wholesale garment trade and something of a '*dādā*' of the area. He is a Faiz admirer. So I phoned Dar and he said nothing would delight him more. We landed in the Lahore Kebab House quite late, beyond their normal closing hours, except that Dar had ensured that it was open. It was absolutely like being in Lahore. Had we for a moment managed to forget that we were in London, we would have stepped out and repaired to Maula Bux for a *Banārsī pān*.

Famous Pub

Earlier, Durrani, who runs a fur and leather coat business, had taken us to the famous East London pub, 'Jack the Ripper'. The area is not very greatly changed from old Jack's days. Inside the pub, there are framed facsimiles of the newspaper pages of those days, describing in blood-curdling detail, the surgeon like handiwork of Mr Ripper. There is also a large plaque, dedicated to the mad and mysterious murderer, outlining his exploits in the area. Nobody knows who Jack the Ripper was, because he was never caught. However, East London has not forgotten him and, in fact, done honour to his gory memory. We toasted Jack the Ripper after Faiz had read everything about the celebrated gentleman, since all are agreed that he was a gentleman and, what is more a titled one. Long live the British upper classes!

Faiz came to London a few weeks before his seventieth birthday. 'You have reached the biblically-ordained age of three score and ten,' I said. Someone asked him who the rather personable young lady was that he had gone to lunch with a day earlier. 'Before I disclose the identity of the personable young lady in question,' Faiz replied, 'may I state for the record that I have retired from this department.' Naturally, nobody believed him. To women, he has always been a charmer.

Whenever Faiz comes to London, he always takes a short trip to Birmingham. He stays with a couple, Badr and Nasreen, that he has grown increasingly fond of over the years. And then, Saleem Shahid Batra lives there as well. (I wonder how many still remember the late Hafeez Hoshiarpuri's famous *ghazal*, allegedly inspired by or dedicated to Saleem Shahid or Razi Trimzi or both.) Zia Mohyeddin and Naheed also live in Birmingham now. They moved from London after Zia began to produce his fortnightly programme on ATV 'Here and Now.'

This time I offered to drive Faiz in an old Toyota I had. 'We should go through Oxford,' Faiz said, 'It is a nicer drive and there is an old friend in Oxford from my Delhi days that I have been meaning to look up.' We got out of London around eleven o'clock. It started to snow. The M-40, which leads you to Oxford was quite treacherous and I did not have snow tyres. The car wasn't pulling too well either, some water having gone into the plugs, but Faiz seemed to be paying no attention to our hazardous and slow progress.

I believe he is like that. Alys told me that when a bomb blasted an apartment building next door to theirs in Beirut, Faiz did wake up briefly and having noticed everything more or less intact, at least in their apartment, promptly returned to sleep. But I must come back to our drive to Oxford. I had a cassette player in the car in which I fed Taj Multani's scintillating rendition of Khwaja Farid's *kafis*.

We kept listening and the snow kept falling. Suddenly Faiz said to me, 'This is poetry of a very high order.' 'Yes, indeed,' I said. There is a line in one of the *kafis*, '*ishq hai sāḍā pīr*. It really seemed to have moved Faiz. I rewound the tape and played it again. 'Listen to it carefully,' Faiz said. 'You notice that one of the greatest poets of the Punjab has no hesitation in making profuse and liberal use of Persian and Arabic words. This is what people like Najam Hosain Syed lose sight of or do not understand. They advocate the purity of the Punjabi language. If only they would listen to or read its great masters.' I said that Khwaja Farid had even used an English word in a *kafi*, the line being '. . . *dukẖāṅ dī* appeal *ai*.' 'That is the point,' Faiz observed. 'To the poet, the supreme thing is poetry. He is not a grammarian or a lexicographer. Language is something that is his tool, his material which he uses to create. It is subservient to him, not he to it.'

We arrived in Oxford in one piece. The car had not conked out and Khwaja Farid had stayed with us through the driving snow and sleet, a far cry from the burning deserts where he had created poetry of such intensity and splendour. We found the house we were looking for. Faiz found it, in fact. He told me he had been there once years ago. His friend turned out to be a lady in her sixties who had lived in Delhi during the War. She married Guy Wint, the author who died some years ago. She has a daughter by him, Indira Joshi, the actress.

Charming Woman

Mrs Wint turned out to be a charming woman. She is a Buddhist, has been one for years. She teaches Buddhism and Comparative Religion in Oxford. She is an accomplished contemplative. We had a lunch of bread and cheese. Faiz and she talked about old times. They had so many memories and friends to share. Mrs Wint must have been a good-looking woman in her time. 'So she was,' Faiz told me later. 'Quite the toast of Delhi.' She used to work in the psy-war department of the Government of India. 'Keep in touch, Faiz. It is good to see you,' she said as she stood outside her charming little house waving goodbye.

In Birmingham, as elsewhere, Faiz's tribe was on the flourish. People came to know he was in town and would walk in unannounced but welcome. Every time he comes, there are so many he touches with his grace and affection. His reservoir, unlike OPEC's, is non-depletable.

Athar Ali and I spent a long and sentimental evening with Faiz almost on the eve of his seventieth birthday. We went to a pub in Knightsbridge called Turk's Head. It is a very nice place, where they always have a log fire in winters. There was nothing Faiz wanted more than to be in Lahore on the day. 'What do the children say?' Athar asked. 'What they say is not really helpful. They say, do what you really wish,' he answered.

In His Bones

The evening rambled on. But it was being in Lahore on his birthday that was on Faiz's mind. 'That's where all my friends are.' He talked about

Abdullah Malik, Hamid Akhtar, Mazhar Ali Khan and Tahira, Syed Wajid Ali (who aided and abetted by Syed Abid Ali, had made Faiz an 'honorary' Shia when they took him to Karbala Gamey Shah to recite his powerful *marsīā*) and so many others. Lahore is embedded in his bones. It is, as it always was, his city of lights.

At one point I said to Faiz, 'You know how much you are loved. You are and you have always been much more than a poet.' The evening was deepening and we were all growing a little sad. And that is when I saw it. Faiz's eyes grew misty and his voice changed. 'Well,' he said with some difficulty, 'I don't know why so much of people's affection has fallen to my share. One is only a poet, after all.' We said no more. Faiz did not go to Lahore. He was honoured at ceremonies in Moscow and Beirut, the latter arranged by Yasser Arafat himself. But Lahore is where he wanted to be. He was so profoundly touched when he heard of the ceremonies that had taken place in Pakistan, and Lahore especially.

Faiz once said to me, 'It is not that one has no fight left. It is only that I am not as young as I once was, and it is difficult to take physical punishment when you are older. The soul is willing but the body is not.'

Intense Commitment

The intensity of Faiz's commitment to freedom, equality, justice and humanity has always burnt bright. He has always been a fighter; but everyone must fight after his own fashion.

It is true he is not an instant jack-in-the-box rhyme monger like some. If the test of patriotism is writing *tarānas* for the genre invented by Altaf Gauhar during 1965, called *millī mausīqī* or some such, then Faiz is neither a poet nor a patriot. But who has written with more pain, love and hope about Pakistan and the elusive goddess of freedom than Faiz?

His great poem on the 1965 war *Uṭho ab māṭi sē uṭho, ab uṭho mērē lāl* remains one of the most moving works of its kind in any literature. Those who attack Faiz as lacking in what they consider patriotic commitment, are the same conscience-sellers, who were celebrating the great Islamic victories of Yahya Khan's tigers in East Pakistan in 1971, when Faiz was writing one of the most chillingly prophetic poems in our language *Sajē to kaisē sajē qatl-e 'ām kā mēlā*.

The sycophants who castigate Faiz, it must not be forgotten, are the same men who were dancing in the streets with roses in their buttonholes, celebrating Ayub Khan's 'victory' in 1964. They are the same people who were dismissing as 'just good fun' the wanton killings in Liaquatabad and Lalookhet, committed by Ayub's power-drunk, gun-toting, blood-thirsty merry-makers. Faiz transcribed his anguish in *Kahīṅ nahīṅ hai kahīṅ bhī nahīṅ lahū kā surāgh*.

No Defence

This is really not an occasion to write a defence of either Faiz the poet or Faiz the man. He needs none and it is difficult to separate the man from the poet, something people like Dr Ayub Mirza (who may be a good children's doctor) do not understand. He has written in his book (which I haven't read) that Faiz is not really a revolutionary but just a poet and it is only some of his more committed friends to whom he can't say no, who get him into his various fracas with one government after another.

However, I would like to say that Dr Mirza's personal affection for Faiz notwithstanding, he is completely unaware of what Faiz is about. It is not possible to draw a line between Faiz's poetry and the way he has lived his life.

GENTLY

Original: *Manzar* from *Dast-e Tah-e Saṅg* (1965)
TRANSLATOR: SHOAIB HASHMI

The passersby, and the shadows, and the trees and the houses
and the bowl of the sky
And then the breast of the sky was rent by the rising moon, rising . . .
    gently
Like someone undoing the folds of a cloak, gently

And underneath the sky, the deep still blue of the shadows
A blue lagoon
And on the surface of the waters, the delicate bubble of a falling leaf
Swims and floats and bursts . . . gently

And quietly and lightly the cool hue of the wine descends into the
    cup . . . gently
The cup and the flask, and the blossom of your nearness
Like the distant image of a dream, formed, and unformed . . . gently

And the heart remembered a whispered word of love . . . gently
And you said, 'Gently'.
And overhead the moon arched, and said, 'A whit more gently'.

23

A CONVERSATION WITH FAIZ AHMED FAIZ

Muzaffar Iqbal: As one of the eminent members of the Progressive Writers' Movement, you have closely watched its ebb and flow. Like most movements, literary or political, it started off as a powerful force of its day, but, later, when its momentum broke, it left a vacuum. It developed schism, and split into so many subgroups. I understand that you had dissociated yourself from it by 1949. Would you, in retrospect, comment on the contribution of this movement to Urdu literature?

Faiz: First of all, we need to differentiate between a 'movement' and an 'organization'. It is not correct to say that the [Progressive Writers'] Movement broke into many sub-groups. What was called the Progressive Writers' Organization or the *Anjuman* of the Progressive Writers, maintained a general sort of unity as long as it remained focused on one objective at a certain given time and circumstance. The Movement and the Organization came into existence at a time when the independence movement was in full swing in our country. Therefore one objective was clear, namely, national independence, and on this point there was no difference of opinion.

The second point is that there was no difference of opinion on the social priorities of those times. It was agreed that there was a need to portray the lives and problems of the class which had always been exploited and deprived of basic rights and comforts. It included white-collar people in the cities, labourers and similarly neglected segments of society, whose lives had never before been considered a fit subject for literature. There was also the assumption that after the independence, social injustice would be brought to an end.

The third point was that instead of fabricated situations and imaginary problems, the life around us should be portrayed realistically. There was no difference of opinion on these three points and thus a movement and an organization emerged and both had unity.

However, after the independence, it became clear that we had achieved only the first objective and there were still others. The differences occurred about the course of action to attain these other objectives. These objectives—call them democracy or social justice—were not the point of dispute but the path to attain them; some wanted to take one course, the others had a different line of action in their minds; so the organization lost unity.

At this stage, differences also occurred regarding the third point, that is, the portrayal of life in a realistic way. When there is confusion and lack of direction in the society, there are two courses left to people: one inward, the other outward. Some people were so much disgusted at the prevailing situation that they said: 'Hell with it all. Let us look inward and explore our unconscious.' This led to certain purely subjective movements. Their high point was that nothing was intrinsically good or bad. The result was a kind of anarchism or nihilism or narcissism. For this, neither the Movement nor the Organization can be blamed. This [attitude] was a product of the situation. But I think that the Progressive Movement was not the invention of the progressive writers; it has always been like this in literature; some writers have always looked towards the future; others to the past; some think that our own self is the centre of the universe and there is nothing else in the world. The others believe that our own self is not the centre of the universe, but the universe and all that it contains is much more important than us and we should focus on it—so it has always been like this. But I think even now whatever is forceful and important in literature, is based on the same ideology that was adopted by the progressive writers or their predecessors, from Sheikh Saadi to Iqbal. So this is not a new situation.

Because we have not, so far, decided upon a social structure for our society, nor have we agreed upon our ultimate goal or upon how to achieve it, our literature is also being affected by this situation. But in spite of all this, I think, whatever good literature is being written today is basically realistic and progressive and instead of escapism, it strives to find solutions to the problems in a rational and realistic way.

MUZAFFAR IQBAL: Now, let us turn to your poetry. When *Dast-e Sabā* was published [in 1952], you were in prison. It was received very well and suddenly you were a popular poet. How did you take it? Did it condition your subsequent poetry? Did it create a problem of maintaining a certain standard?

FAIZ: As far as my name is concerned, when [my first collection] *Naqsh-e Faryādī* was published [in 1943], it seemed to me that I had arrived. I was, of course, somewhat surprised. After all, what had I done? Written some verses. When *Dast-e Sabā* [the second collection] was published, it was the product of a new experience—that of imprisonment. People felt that the general situation of the time was well portrayed in it and they liked it. As far as I am concerned, it did not really make any difference that people liked it so much because they have always been kind to me. And it did not affect the course of my poetry because I write what my heart feels and experiences. *Dast-e Sabā* contains the experiences of a certain period. After this, many other phases came and what I felt and what other people felt, I tried to articulate and am still doing the same—so this is not a problem, nor have I done anything exceptional; it is just this much: what happens to my heart, I try to articulate and when there is not much there, then I look outside, to other people and try to write verse about it—so I have not changed my course; nor have I made myself my own prisoner.

MUZAFFAR IQBAL: The image of 'Dawn' is a recurring image in your poetry, the purity of daybreak, its resplendent light—you use it in a variety of ways. And you belong to a generation which saw a dream: the dream of the dawn of independence. But looking back, it seems that the dream was shattered. Your generation travelled from one darkness to another; in between there is the dream of dawn but no shaft of light. There could have been two consequences of this great betrayal of the dreams of your generation: escapism and consequently a utopian literature or disgusted, angry literature. But you managed to avoid both these extremes. Though there is an underlying melancholy in your poetry, you have retained lyrical softness in your verse. In fact, with time, these two elements have deepened. How have you managed to do this?

FAIZ: First of all, I don't think that the dream has been shattered; it is merely a pause. Like Mir said, *death itself is no more than a pause/we will march on after a little rest*—and we have not even died yet—so if a great poet can call death a pause from which one moves on, we, who have not died yet, I mean our nation, our country have not vanquished, so there is no question of shattering of the dream.

Secondly, to keep a dream alive is not a choice but a compulsion; life cannot exist without it—life which is a great gift and to deny it is to deny God. I wrote a poem on this topic: *that we were compelled . . .*, I think it is in *Shām-e Shehr-e Yārāṅ*, I will remember it soon. . . . Realism also demands it; while one should not deny the presence of pain and despair when it is present, but at the same time, one should not lose one's faith and hope, for without faith and hope, one cannot survive and life cannot continue. In a recent *ghazal*, I have said: *the heavens are in motion/ you say all has already happened; it is not so.* Ghalib said it a long time ago: *the seven heavens are in motion day and night/ why should I worry, something would happen . . .* so I feel the same.

MUZAFFAR IQBAL: This seems a good way of saving oneself from disillusionment, but some writers of your generation have not managed to keep the balance and have become either extreme introverts or have started to scream. Have you never experienced this kind of situation or do you always somehow manage to avoid it consciously?

FAIZ: There is no real dichotomy between the conscious and the unconscious. Of course a kind of struggle goes on between the two to gain an upper hand. Perhaps unconsciously I too would like to scream or say to myself: 'Let's give it all up and sit at home and remember God'. But consciously, I reject it; depends on how strong one is; when one is tired and exhausted, then one gives up. But to continue, one needs a bit of faith, a bit of inner light, a bit of it from the outside and friendship with others—all this keeps one's faith alive. If you cut yourself off from people and become introvert, then you are bound to lose strength but if you move with people, with a caravan as it were, then you don't despair.

MUZAFFAR IQBAL: Your poetry is like a long struggle and, as you just said, based on faith and hope, but at times you have repeated certain old themes as well, like the couplet about asking the jurisprudent of the city about wine. Such poems seem an appendage to your other poetry which describes the struggle and is very much concerned with the modern day problems. How do you reconcile—

FAIZ: No, it is not an old theme. One advantage in the form of *ghazal* is that you can write the old themes in old vocabulary and similes and yet be describing a contemporary reality. The traditional struggle between the mystic and the sermonizing priest, between the authority and the ordinary man is also a contemporary theme.

MUZAFFAR IQBAL: Your life, I mean your poetic life, was influenced quite early by the fact that you were imprisoned. Did it in any way limit the canvas of your poetry?

FAIZ: No, on the contrary, imprisonment brought a new dimension to it. What you normally do not notice in the world because of daily preoccupations becomes much more observable; your sensitivity is enhanced; you have more time in the prison. It was in jail that I wrote my poem about Africa and other such matters which had not attracted my attention outside. So in a sense, when you are in jail, the outside world comes closer or recedes into distance; in both cases one has a sort of freedom, mentally one is more apt to think about many things.

MUZAFFAR IQBAL: In your latest book, *Mērē Dil Mērē Musāfir*, one detects a certain feeling which is absent in other books and it reads like poetry of exile—so-called exile—feeling of being away from the homeland, I mean physically being removed from the home . . . it has imparted a new dimension to your poetry. Are you now part of the international community of exiled poets like Nazim Hikmat and Mahmoud Darwish?

FAIZ: In one sense, yes; in another no. The common element is the physical separation from the homeland but the difference is that they were expelled by force while I am just wandering out of my own free will; no one has forced me to leave. I can return whenever I feel like it. The sadness of being away from one's homeland is there, just like one feels sad when separated from one's beloved, but the helplessness of those who were forced to leave is quite another thing.

MUZAFFAR IQBAL: But what about verses like: *so it has been ordained/that we be banished/calling in each street/roaming in each city.* . . .

FAIZ: Yes, that's true but not literally. I was not ordered to leave. I felt that things were not quite right, so I thought of taking a holiday. So my situation is qualitatively different from that of Mahmoud Darwish and the Palestinian people, who have not only been individually but collectively banished from their homeland; their anguish is much greater and different from mine. And Nazim Hikmat was sentenced for fourteen years; then he had to escape from his own homeland and there was no way of return. But I still feel that there are many who love me and have affection for me. However, this awareness does not lessen the anguish of separation; it is there.

MUZAFFAR IQBAL: You have been out of the country for three years by an act of volition, as it were. Has it changed your perspective?

FAIZ: Yes. From a distance one can see things more objectively, more clearly. One is not involved in what the people back home are going through. So one can understand the situation better and one's burden is lighter.

MUZAFFAR IQBAL: Your poetic diction, your similes and metaphors are purely classical. But you invest new meaning to them. Have you never felt the need or desire to use a new idiom, as some people do these days?

FAIZ: There are certain inherent limitations in every language and Urdu is no exception to this. At times I feel a strong urge to break these barriers but it requires the strength of a much greater poet; it is not a task for minor poets. But within the framework of Urdu language, there has always been innovation. Mir, Sauda, Nazir Akbarabadi, Ghalib and Iqbal—all were innovative. They changed the idiom, changed the vocabulary and imagery and structure; I have also tried within these parameters but I did not have the courage to go beyond this, because to me, prose and poetry are two different things. Poetry involves bringing things together; prose means scattering them. Poetry has certain rules to which one needs to abide; then there is the rhyme and metre—poetry is at an elevated plane whereas prose is flat. So one has to maintain this difference and still say something new. There is no simple formula. One has one's own temperament and inspiration, and I feel I have not even made full use of what our tradition has given me and there is still a lot of room. Our new generation has distanced itself from the tradition and therefore they do not try to explore it. As far as a new, a totally new kind of poetry is concerned, it requires a greater talent; I am not invested with that kind of talent and when I have the urge to do that, I use Punjabi.

MUZAFFAR IQBAL: This new poetry—so called new poetry—are these people not overly influenced by the West?

FAIZ: Obviously. This began with Maulana Hali and Maulana [Muhammad Hussain] Azad. The poetry they produced in imitation of the Western poetry, natural scenes and the call of the widow and the orphans . . . etc. All this is rubbish. It does not have native blood and force, it is only an imitation and imitation is not creative. This does not mean that one should not benefit from the poetry being written elsewhere but one has to be selective . . . one has to remain rooted within one's tradition and then try to see what is happening elsewhere and what can be used from it . . . continuity and innovation, tradition and experimentation—these should go hand in hand. . . .

Poetry is not only a matter of expressing one's emotions and ideas; it is also a craft, like that of a carpenter. A craft one must learn. It is like a musical composition. One has to see if and where a note fits. So all these things, all these demands have to be in one's view, this fashion of following the West does not make anything. The plant has to be rooted in the soil; its roots must be strong for without them, it cannot survive. Of course one has to prune it according to contemporary realities. . . .

MUZAFFAR IQBAL: There are certain poets in other countries whose poetry is similar to yours, like certain South American poets. Do you think this kind of poetry is influencing the international situation? Is it making a change?

FAIZ: The truth is that so far our poetry has had no relationship with any other poetry except English poetry, which has very little relevance to our situation. However, there are many other areas where the situation is similar to our's and there is a lot in common between their poetry and our poetry and we can learn from them. It is only in the last ten or twenty years that, instead of French, English and German poetry, we have turned to Latin American, Spanish and, more recently, to Palestinian, Arabic and African poetry. And this is very good and this has brought us closer to those poets and writers whose actual experiences are similar to our experiences.

MUZAFFAR IQBAL: Reading Marquez's *Autumn of the Patriarch,* I felt it was a story which could have taken place in our country . . . so when such writings are translated, they make an impact. But is there any real practical change through this activity?

FAIZ: Yes. For one thing, such translations are of great value because they provide an opportunity to look at our situation with other people's wisdom; this opens our eyes to our own realities. For example, translations from Turkish and Arabic have helped us in this way and they have made our literary canvas much larger.

MUZAFFAR IQBAL: Now a word about contemporary poetry. What do you think of your contemporaries and the younger poets?

FAIZ: I think that, in spite of confusion and mental chaos, a lot of good poetry is being written today. It is always difficult to make predictions about young poets, for one never knows how many will continue writing good poetry but it seems that there is no deadness in our literature. There are many good poets and writers and critics and a lot of activity, though it has not yet taken the form of a movement, like it did at the time of Progressive Writers' Movement but certainly there is no dearth of talent. There are waves but not a stream yet. But there is no need to worry about our literature. Leave Urdu aside, there is Punjabi, Balochi, Sindhi and Pashto. For the first time, people are paying attention to these languages and very powerful poetry is being written in these languages. Prose writers are also beginning to make their mark, so the caravan of literature is moving on. . . .

MUZAFFAR IQBAL: How do you write?

FAIZ: How do I write? I don't really know. Perhaps it is like this: While reading a book, a sentence, an image or a rhyme sticks in my mind and keeps on producing a kind of humming, or sometimes, while listening to music, a certain note or rhyming pattern leaves an impression. At times, an event produces a line and slowly it becomes a poem. A *ghazal* first requires the emergence of a rhyming scheme and one builds on it. For a *nazm,* one has to think and plan. First a line comes to mind and I think of the pattern of the poem and after that the carpenter's job begins. The basic image must be in a sharp focus, the music has to be right; there should not be any false notes, so the carpenter keeps working. At times, the impact of a certain event or emotion or experience is so intense that the whole poem is born immediately. At other times, it takes months to complete a poem.

Muzaffar Iqbal: Did you ever want to write a major poem which would stand-out in your poetry and couldn't write it?

Faiz: Once or twice I tried to write a long poem. I wanted to make the dedication to [the collection] *Sar-e Vādī-e Sīna* into a long poem but then I got bored and gave up. Likewise the poem in *Dast-e Sabā*, 'A Prison Morning'—I thought of making it a long poem, invested with the 'whole experience', but then I couldn't.

This conversation was held in Saskatoon, Canada, on 4 June 1981 and was translated by Muzaffar Iqbal.

GO FORTH INTO THE STREETS TODAY IN YOUR FETTERS

Original: *Āj bāzār mēṅ pā bajaulāṅ čalo* from *Dast-e Tah-e Saṅg* (1965)
TRANSLATOR: WAQAS KHWAJA

A damp eye, a distraught life, is not
enough,
the imputation of a secret passion, is
not enough.
Go forth into the streets today in
your fetters.

Your hands alight
entranced and dancing, go!
Dust in your head
bloodstains on your shirtfront, go!
The whole city of love
awaits you, go!

The city's chief
the ordinary masses
the arrow of blame
the stone of abuse
the unhappy morning
the failed day—
who else is their familiar
but us?
Who in the beloved's city
is clean anymore?
Who remains worthy
of the executioner's hand?

Pick up the goods of your heart
brokenhearted, let's go!
Ourselves, then, we may present
for execution, friends, let's go!

Sources

Articles (as they appear in the book)

Victor G. Kiernan, 'Introduction to Poems by Faiz' taken from: Kiernan, Victor G., trans., *Poems by Faiz*, New Delhi: Oxford University Press, 1971, Print.

Shamsur Rahman Faruqi, 'Faiz and the Classical Ghazal' taken from: Faruqi, Shamsur Rahman, *The Flower-Lit Road: Essays in Urdu Literary Theory and Criticism.* Allahabad: Laburnum, 2005, Print.

Ralph Russell, 'Poetry, Politics and Pakistan' taken from: Russell, Ralph, *The Pursuit of Urdu Literature—A Select History*, London: Zed, 1992, Print.

Gopi Chand Narang, 'Tradition and Innovation in Faiz Ahmed Faiz' taken from: Narang, Gopi Chand, *Urdu Language and Literature*, Vanguard, n.d., Print.

Carlo Coppola, 'Another Adolescence: The Prison Poetry of Faiz Ahmed Faiz' taken from: *Journal of South Asian Literature* 27.2 (Spring-Summer 1992): Print.

Carlo Coppola, 'Faiz in English: How Five Translators Worked their Art': This paper was presented at the seminar, 'Abiding Aspects of Faiz Ahmed Faiz', for the annual meeting of Asian Studies on the Pacific Coast, Stanford University, Stanford, California, 29 June 1990.

Safdar Mir, 'Faiz's Legacy—Love and Revolution' taken from: *An Introduction to Poetry of Faiz Ahmed Faiz*, ed. Imdad Husain, Lahore: Vanguard, 1989, Print.

Naomi Lazard, 'Translating Faiz' taken from *Columbia: The Magazine of Columbia University*, June 1985: Print.

Rimma Kazakova, 'Poet and the Modern Age' taken from: *Viewpoint* 19 February 1987: Print.

Maryam Salganik, 'Faiz and His Poetry Today' taken from: *Viewpoint* 19 February 1987: Print.

Frances Pritchett, 'The Sky, the Road, The Glass of Wine: On Translating Faiz' taken from Web. <http://http://www.urdustudies.com/pdf/15/07pritchett.pdf>.

Agha Shahid Ali, 'Introduction—The Rebel's Silhouette: Translating Faiz Ahmed Faiz', taken from: 'Ali, Agha Shahid. *The Rebel's Silhouette-Selected Poems, Faiz Ahmed Faiz*, Revised edn., University of Massachusetts/Amherst, 1995, Print.

Ludmila Vassilyeva, 'Faiz and the Soviet Union', translated from Urdu, Urdu version taken from Vassilyeva, Ludmila. *Parvarish-e Lauh-o-Qalam*, Karachi: Oxford University Press, 2007, Print.

Ayesha Jalal, 'Freedom Unbound: Faiz's Prison Call' taken from: *Two Loves-Faiz's Letters from Jail*, ed. Kyla Pasha and Salima Hashmi, Lahore: Sang-e-Meel Publications, 2011, Print.

Aamir.R.Mufti, 'Faiz Ahmed Faiz: Towards a Lyric History of India' taken from: Mufti, Aamir R., *Enlightenment in the Colony: The Jewish Question and the Crisis of Postcolonial Culture*, Princeton: Princeton University Press, 2007, Print.

Sean Pue, 'Faiz Ahmed Faiz and N.M. Rashed—A Comparative Analysis', Paper read at the
    Faiz Colloquium organized as a centennial event at the Lahore University of Management
    Sciences on 12/13 February 2011.

Ted Genoways, 'Let them Snuff out the Moon': Faiz Ahmed Faiz's Prison Lyrics in *Dast-e
    Saba*, taken from: *The Annual of Urdu Studies* 19 (2004), Print.

Karrar Husain, 'Faiz gave us the Living Word' taken from: *Viewpoint* 14 February 1985:
    Print.

M. Sadiq, 'Poets (Socialists)'—excerpt taken from: *Twentieth Century Urdu Literature*, Karachi:
    Royal Book Company, 1983, Print.

Alys Faiz, 'Faiz' taken from: *A Black Rainbow Over My Homeland: A Commemorative Volume on
    Faiz Ahmed Faiz, Mouin Beseisso, Alex La Guma*, edited by Kalpana Sahni, New Delhi: Afro
    Asian Writers' Association, n.d., Print.

Mirza Hasan Askari, 'A Life Devoted to Peace' taken from: *Viewpoint* 12 February 1987: Print.

Khalid Hasan, 'Faiz in London' taken from: *Viewpoint*: 11 June and 18 June 1981: Print.

Muzaffar Iqbal, 'A Conversation with Faiz' taken from: *Pakistani Literature* (vol. 1 no. 1)
    (1992), Print.

Tahir Mirza, 'An Interview with Faiz' taken from: *Viewpoint* February 1976: Print.

Poems (as they appear in the book)

'Poetry's Theme' translated by Victor G Kiernan, taken from: Kiernan, Victor G., trans.,
    Poems by Faiz, New Delhi: Oxford University Press, 1971, Print.

'Ghazal' translated by Agha Shahid Ali, taken from: Ali, Agha Shahid, *The Rebel's Silhouette-
    Selected Poems Faiz Ahmed Faiz*, Revised ed. University of Massachusetts/Amherst, 1995,
    and *The Rebel's Silhouette*: Faiz Ahmed Faiz Trans. from Urdu by Agha Shahid Ali, South
    Asian edition, Oxford University Press, New Delhi, 1971, Print.

'A Few Days More' translated by Daud Kamal, taken from: Kamal, Daud, trans., *The Unicorn
    and the Dancing Girl*, edited by Khalid Hasan, Lahore: Student Services, 1988, Print.

'My Heart, Fellow Traveller' translated by Waqas Khwaja, taken from: Arif, Iftikhar, ed.,
    Modern Poetry of Pakistan, edited by Waqas Khwaja, 1st edn., Champaign, University of
    Illinois: Dalkey Archive, 2010, Print.

'We' translated by C.M. Naim and Carlo Coppola, taken from: Naim, C.M., and Carlo Coppola,
    eds., 'Eleven Poems and an Introduction by Faiz Ahmed Faiz,' *Dialogue Calcutta* 19 n.d.,
    Print. [Some of these translations have appeared in *Mahfil.* Copyright 1971]

'Prison Daybreak' translated by Naomi Lazard, taken from: Lazard, Naomi, trans., *The True
    Subject: Selected Poems by Faiz Ahmed Faiz*, Vanguard, n.d., Print.

'The Meeting' translated by Yasmeen Hameed, taken from: *Pakistani Urdu Verse—An
    Anthology*, edited and translated by Yasmeen Hameed, Karachi: Oxford University Press,
    2010, Print, Poetry from Pakistan.

'If you look at the City from Here' translated by Naomi Lazard, taken from: Lazard, Naomi,
    trans., *The True Subject: Selected Poems by Faiz Ahmed Faiz*, Vanguard, n.d., Print.

'Visitors' translated by Daud Kamal, taken from: Kamal, Daud, trans., *The Unicorn and the
    Dancing Girl*, edited by Khalid Hasan, Lahore: Student Services, 1988, Print.

'Palestinians Martyred in Foreign Lands' translated by Mahmood Jamal, taken from: Jamal,
    Mahmood, trans., *Modern Urdu Poetry*, Penguin, 1995, Print.

'We who were Killed in Half-lit Streets' translated by C.M. Naim and Carlo Coppola, taken from: Naim, C.M., and Carlo Coppola, eds., 'Eleven Poems and an Introduction by Faiz Ahmed Faiz,' *Dialogue Calcutta 19* n.d. Print. [Some of these translations have appeared in *Mahfil.* Copyright 1971]

'Evening' translated by Agha Shahid Ali, taken from: Ali, Agha Shahid, *The Rebel's Silhouette— Selected Poems Faiz Ahmed Faiz*, Revised ed. University of Massachusetts/Amherst, 1995, and *The Rebel's Silhouette*: Faiz Ahmed Faiz Trans. from Urdu by Agha Shahid Ali, South Asian edition, Oxford University Press, New Delhi, 1971, Print.

'And then Spring Came' translated by Shoaib Hashmi, taken from: Hashmi, Shoaib, trans., *A Song for This Day*, Lahore: Sang-e-Meel Publications, 2009, Print.

'Dedication' translated by Riz Rahim, taken from: Rahim, Riz, trans., *In English: Faiz Ahmed Faiz*, Bloomington, IN: Xilbris, 2008, Print.

'Two Loves' translated by Victor G. Kiernan, taken from: Kiernan, Victor G., trans., *Poems by Faiz*, New Delhi: Oxford University Press, 1971, Print.

'On my Return from Dhaka' translated by Agha Shahid Ali, taken from: Ali, Agha Shahid, *The Rebel's Silhouette—Selected Poems Faiz Ahmed Faiz*, Revised edn., University of Massachusetts/Amherst, 1995, and *The Rebel's Silhouette*: Faiz Ahmed Faiz Trans. from Urdu by Agha Shahid Ali, South Asian edition, Oxford University Press, New Delhi, 1971, Print.

'Freedom's Dawn' translated by Baidar Bakht and Kathleen Grant Jaeger, taken from: Bakht, Baidar, and Kathleen Grant Jaeger, editors and translators, *An Anthology of Modern Urdu Poetry*, Vol. 1, Karachi: Al-Muslim, 1984, Print.

'In your Ocean Eyes' translated by Shiv Kumar, taken from: Kumar, Shiv K., trans., *Selected Poems of Faiz Ahmed Faiz*, New Delhi: Viking, 1995, Print.

'Last Night your Lost Memory' translated by Mahmood Jamal, taken from: Jamal, Mahmood, trans., *Modern Urdu Poetry*, Penguin, 1995, Print.

'Any Lover to Any Beloved' translated by Naomi Lazard, taken from: Lazard, Naomi, trans., *The True Subject: Selected Poems by Faiz Ahmed Faiz*, Vanguard, n.d., Print.

'To the Rival' translated by Victor G. Kiernan, taken from: Kiernan, Victor G., trans., *Poems by Faiz*, New Delhi: Oxford University Press, 1971, Print.

'Gently' translated by Shoaib Hashmi, taken from: Hashmi, Shoaib, trans., *A Song for This Day*, Lahore: Sang-e-Meel Publications, 2009, Print.

'Go forth into the Streets Today in your Fetters' translated by Waqas Khwaja, taken from: Arif, Iftikhar, ed., *Modern Poetry of Pakistan*, edited Waqas Khwaja, 1st edn., Champaign, University of Illinois: Dalkey Archive, 2010, Print.

Authors and Translators

Aamir R. Mufti is Associate Professor in the Department of Comparative Literature at UCLA. He pursued his doctoral studies in literature at Columbia University under the supervision of Edward Said. He was also trained in Anthropology at Columbia and the London School of Economics. His work reconsiders the secularization thesis in a comparative perspective, with a special interest in Islam and Modernity in India and the cultural politics of Jewish Identity in Western Europe. His most recent contribution to the study of secularism is: *Enlightenment in the Colony: the Jewish Question and the Crisis of Postcolonial Culture.*

Agha Shahid Ali (1949–2001) held a PhD in English from Pennsylvania and an MFA from the University of Arizona. He held teaching positions at nine universities and colleges in India and the United States. His original collections of poetry in English include *A Walk through the Yellow Pages, The Half-Inch Himalayas, A Nostalgist's Map of America, The Country Without a Post Office* and *Rooms Are Never Finished* (finalist for the National Book Award, 2001). His last book was *Call Me Ishmael Tonight*, a collection of English *ghazals*. His poems are featured in *American Alphabets: 25 Contemporary Poets* (2006) and many other anthologies.

Alys Faiz (1914–2003) was a British-born naturalized Pakistani, writer, journalist, human rights activist, social worker and teacher. She is best known as the wife of Pakistani poet Faiz Ahmed Faiz.

A. Sean Pue is Assistant Professor at Michigan State University. He holds a PhD in Middle East and Asian Languages and Cultures, and Comparative Literature from Columbia University. His teaching interests include Hindi-Urdu language, Literature and Culture in South Asia, and Postcolonial Theory. He has published several articles in reputable journals.

Ayesha Jalal is Mary Richardson Professor of History at Tufts University. She is among the most prominent American academics who write on the history of India and Pakistan. She has a doctorate from the University of Cambridge. She has taught at the University of Wisconsin-Madison, Columbia University, Harvard University and is a visiting Professor at the Lahore University of Management Sciences. She has several major publications; among them are *The Sole Spokesman, Democracy and Authoritarianism in South Asia* and *Partisans of Allah: Jihad in South Asia*. She has been awarded the Sitāra-e Imtiāz by the Government of Pakistan.

Baidar Bakht is Adjunct Professor of Civil Engineering at the Universities of Toronto and Manitoba, Canada. He translates modern Urdu poetry into English in collaboration with Canadian poets and scholars of English. He holds a DSc from the University of London.

Carlo Coppola holds a PhD in Comparative Literature from the University of Chicago. Co-founder and co-editor of the *Journal of South Asian Literature* from 1963 to 2002, he has written extensively on modern South Asian literature, mostly on Urdu and South Asian writers of English. His translations from various South Asian languages, often done in collaboration with the author, number in hundreds. He taught courses in Linguistics and Indian and Middle Eastern Studies at Oakland University for thirty-seven years, before retiring in 2005. He is acclaimed for his pioneering work on Faiz Ahmed Faiz.

C.M. Naim is an American scholar of Urdu language and literature. He is currently Professor Emeritus at the University of Chicago. Naim is the founding editor of both *Annual of Urdu Studies* and *Mahfil* (now *Journal of South Asian Literature*), as well as the author of the definitive textbook for Urdu pedagogy in English. He was educated at Lucknow University, Deccan College, and the University of California Berkeley. In 1961, he joined the faculty of the Department of South Asian Languages and Civilizations at the University of Chicago, from which he retired in 2001. Naim has extensively translated Urdu literary works into English. Among them are *Zikr-e Mīr*, the autobiography of eighteenth century Urdu poet, Mir Taqi Mir and a short story and novella by Qurratulain Hyder.

Daud Kamal (1935–1987) was a distinguished Professor of English, poet and translator. He was educated at Cambridge University, UK. He served as Professor of English at the University of Peshawar, until his death. Kamal's original collections of poetry in English include *Compass of Love and other Poems* and *Before the Carnations Wither*. He had translated Ghalib's and Faiz's selected verse into English. *Ghalib: Reverberations* was hailed by many as (until then) the best rendering of the master in English. His work was posthumously collected and published as *River Mist* in 1992.

Frances Pritchett is Professor of Modern Indic Languages in the Department of Middle East and Asian Languages and Cultures at Columbia University. She teaches courses on Indian civilization, Urdu literature and Islam in South Asia. Pritchett's publications include *Nets of Awareness: Urdu Poetry and Its Critics*, *The Romance Tradition in Urdu: Adventures from the Dāstān of Amīr Hamzāh*, *Urdu Meter: A Practical Handbook*, and *Urdu Literature: A Bibliography of English Language Sources*.

Gopi Chand Narang is an eminent Indian scholar and critic of the Urdu language and literature. He holds a PhD in Linguistics. He has authored and edited more than sixty books on criticism and other literary genres. Among them are *Adabī Tanqīd aur Uslūbiyāt, Taraqqī Pasandī, Jadīdiat, Mābā'd Jadīdiat* and *Amīr Khusro kā Hindavī Kalām*. He was awarded the Sahitya Akademi Award (1993) for *Sākhtiyāt Pas Sākhtiyāt aur Mashrīqī She'riyāt*. He also received the Padma Bhushan Award in 2004.

Karrar Husain (1911–1999) was a noted scholar and educationist. He had degrees in Urdu, English and Law from Agra University. He served as Vice Chancellor of the University of Balochistan and from 1977 to 1999, was Director, Islamic Culture and Research Institute, Karachi. He wrote on Islamic history and religion as well as on political, cultural and social issues. He was a founder member of the Faiz Foundation. He contributed to literature through his writings on Ghalib and Mir Anis.

Kathleen Grant Jaeger retired from the University of King's College, Halifax, Canada, where she holds the honorary rank of Inglis Professor. Earlier she taught in the Departments of English at the University of British Columbia and at Acadia University. In collaboration with Baidar Bakht she has published two volumes of modern Urdu poetry in translation.

Khalid Hasan (1935–2009) was a senior journalist, prolific writer and translator. As a journalist, he worked for prominent national and international news agencies and newspapers. He has authored and edited several books on political, literary and social issues. He translated works of Punjabi and Urdu into English. His translations of Saadat Hasan Manto and Ghulam Abbas are a significant contribution.

Ludmila Vassilyeva is a senior Research Associate in the department of Eastern Literature (Institute of Oriental Studies) Russian Academy of Science, Moscow. She did her MA Linguistics at Moscow State University and her PhD in Urdu Literature from Soviet Union's Academy of Science. She worked as a broadcaster, writer and translator for Moscow Radio's Urdu Service. Her other works include a book on Altaf Husain Hali and several essays in Urdu and Russian for distinguished journals. She has also translated Urdu literary texts into Russian and vice versa. She authored *Faiz Ahmed Faiz: Life and Works* in Russian and translated it into Urdu as *Parvarish-e Lauh-o-Qalam*. For her extraordinary contribution to the Urdu language she was awarded Sitāra-e Imtiāz in 2005 by the Government of Pakistan.

Mahmood Jamal has a degree in South Asian Studies from the School of Oriental and African Studies, University of London. He is a poet, producer and translator. As an independent producer, he has produced several documentary series, notably a series on Islam entitled Islamic conversations. Among his publications are *Coins for Charon*, *Silence Inside a Gun's Mouth*, *Song of the Flute* and the *Penguin Book of Modern Urdu Poetry* (English translations of selected Urdu verse). He was honoured with The Minority Rights Group Award for his poetry in 1984.

Maryam Salganik is a Russian translator, critic and an essayist. She is a member of the Moscow Writers' Union. She has written extensively on Asian and African Literatures. She was the chief of a Unit of the International Department of the SU Writers' Union. She also translated Faiz Ahmed Faiz's poetry into Russian.

Mirza Hasan Askari (1924–2005) was a noted columnist and writer. He started his career in the Indian army's public relations section and after the Second World War, joined the *Statesman*, Delhi, followed by the *Dawn*, Karachi as a senior reporter. He worked with Radio Pakistan's news department for several years. He also wrote for *Dawn*, Karachi after 1980. He was a founding member of the Pakistan Writers' Guild.

M. Sadiq (1898–1984) held a PhD from the Punjab University and was Professor of English as well as Urdu at the Government College (now Government College University). He also headed both the departments. His publications include *Mohammed Husain Azad: Ahvāl-o-Āsār*, *History of Urdu Literature* and *Twentieth Century Urdu Literature*.

Mohammad Safdar Mir (1921–1998) was a prominent Urdu critic, playwright, columnist, stage director, translator and a distinguished professor of English Literature. He was educated at Government College, Lahore. As a columnist he contributed to leading newspapers of Pakistan such as the *Pakistan Times, Dawn, The Frontier Post* etc. Among his published works are *Shab-e-Ākhir* (collection of historical plays) and *Karl Marx kā Tasavvur-e-Begāngī*.

Muzaffar Iqbal is a scientist, Islamic scholar and writer, residing in Canada. He is the founding president of the Centre for Islam and Science, Alberta, Canada. He is also founder-editor of the Centre's journal, *Islam and Science*. Iqbal's published works span diverse areas, such as Islam, Islam and the West, history of Islamic science and civilization, and literature. Among his publications are *Dawn in Madinah: A Pilgrim's Passage, Inkhilā and Inqitā'* (Urdu . . . first two books of a Trilogy), *Divān-al-Hallāj* (Arabic text with Urdu translation, introduction and notes)

Naomi Lazard is a noted American poet, the winner of two Fellowships from the National Endowment for the Arts, and a past-President of the 'Poetry Society of America'. She is also a children's book author and a playwright. In 1992, Lazard co-founded The Hamptons International Film Festival. Among her collections of poetry are, *Cry of the Peacocks, The Moonlit Upper Deckerina* and *Ordinances*. Her translations of Faiz Ahmed Faiz published as *The True Subject* are widely acclaimed.

Nyla Daud is a Lahore-based freelance journalist and writer. She contributes to many national and international publications and also edits organizational newsletters, translates Urdu texts, scripts and television documentaries.

Ralph Russell (1918–2008) was a noted British scholar of Urdu Literature. Educated at St. John's College Cambridge, UK, he taught Urdu literature at the School of Oriental and African Studies, University of London and also in universities in India and Pakistan. For much of his life he was a member of the Communist Party of Great Britain. Among his publications are, *Three Mughal Poets, Ghalib: Life and Letters, The Pursuit of Urdu Literature*, and *How not to Write the History of Urdu Literature*. In recognition of his services to the Urdu language and literature, he was awarded Sitāra-e Imtiāz by the Government of Pakistan.

Rimma Kazakova (1932–2008) was a Russian poet and translator. She was known as a writer of many popular songs of the Soviet era. She graduated from the History Department of Leningrad State University. She worked as lecturer in Khabarovsk. Her first verses were reminiscent of Yevtushenko, Okudzhava, Voznesensky and Rozhdestvensky. Her first collection of poetry, *Let's Meet in the East*, was published in 1958. From 1959 until her death, she was a member of the USSR Union of Writers. She also held the position of First Secretary of the Moscow Union of Writers.

Riz Rahim is a Professor of Biological Sciences, with a long affiliation with Toxicology-Cancer. He has, over the years published numerous articles in English and Urdu in newspapers and magazines in the US, India and Pakistan, on subjects concerning science, health, environment, history, politics and literature.

Shamsur Rahman Faruqi is an eminent Indian Urdu critic, theorist and fiction writer. His contribution to Urdu literary criticism is monumental. He has authored several books. Among them are *She'r-e Shor Aṅgēz* (three volumes), *Tafhīm-e Ghālib*, *Khurshīd kā Sāmān-e Safar*, *She'r Ghair She'r aur Nasr* and *Urdū kā Ibtidā'ī Zamānā*. He has also authored short stories and a novel, *Ka'ī Čāṅd t̲h̲ē Sar-e Āsmāṅ*, which is considered by some as one of the finest works of fiction in Urdu. For forty years, he was editor of the literary magazine *Shabkhūn*. In 2009, Faruqi was awarded the Padma Shri Award by the Indian government and in 2010 the Government of Pakistan awarded him the Sitāra-e Imtiāz for his contribution to literature in Urdu.

Shiv Kumar is an Indian poet, playwright, novelist and short story writer. He was educated at Forman Christian College, Lahore and Fitzwilliam College, Cambridge. He has taught English literature at various Indian, British and American Universities. In 1978, he was elected a Fellow of the Royal Society of Literature (London). He received the Sahitya Akademi Award in 1987 for his collection of poems *Trap Falls in the Sky*.

Shoaib Hashmi is a distinguished Professor of Economics (graduated from the London School of Economics) and has taught at the Government College University and the Lahore School of Economics. He is also a playwright, translator, stage director and performer. He created the popular television series, *Akkaṛ Bakkaṛ*, *Ṭāl Maṭol*, and *Suč Gup*.

Tahir Mirza (1936–2007) was a senior Pakistani journalist and editor of the daily *Dawn*. He was resident editor of the newspaper in Lahore and worked as a correspondent in Washington DC, before becoming the editor of the paper. He was a graduate of Lucknow University.

Ted Genoways is an American writer, critic and journalist. He is Editor of the *Virginia Quarterly Review*. He graduated from Nebraska Wesleyan University, Texas Tech University with an MA, and from the University of Virginia with an MFA. His work has appeared in *Double Take*, *New England Review* and *Ploughshares*. His notable works include *Graveyard of Empires: Nine Months on the Ground in Obama's Afghanistan* and *The Death of Fiction*.

Victor Kiernan (1913–2009) was a British Marxist, historian and a former member of the Communist Party Historians' Group, with a particular focus on the history of Imperialism. He studied at Trinity College, Cambridge from 1931–1938, when as a junior fellow, he went to India to teach at a Sikh school and at Aitchison College in Lahore. He was appointed Professor of Modern History at Edinburgh in 1970, a position he held until his retirement in 1977. He has authored several books on history. At the age of 80, he produced *Shakespeare: Poet and Citizen*. A second volume, *Eight Tragedies of Shakespeare*, followed in 1996. Along with Faiz's poetry, he has also translated selected verse of Allama Muhammad Iqbal.

Waqas Khwaja is Professor of English at Agnes Scott College in Atlanta and has a PhD from Emory University. He has published three collections of poetry, *No one waits for the Train*, *Mariam's Lament*, *Six Geese From a Tomb at Medum* and has edited four anthologies of Pakistani literature including *Modern Poetry of Pakistan*.

Index